LAKE DISTRICT
WINTER CLIMBS

About the Author

Brian Davison has been winter climbing for some 30 years and has notched up an impressive list of first ascents in Scotland, Wales and the Lake District. These include *Big Daddy* (VIII, 8) in Coire Sneachda, *Mort* (IX, 9) at Lochnagar and *Moss Ghyll Grooves* (VII, 6), *Harvest Crunch* (VII, 9) and *Mechanical Orange* (VIII, 8) all on Scafell. He has also made many expeditions overseas to such diverse areas as the Himalayas, Morocco, Greenland, Alaska and South Georgia. His intimate knowledge of the Lake District has further been enhanced by endurance feats such as completing an unsupported Bob Graham Round and climbing all the Lakes' routes in *Classic Rock* in a day without use of a vehicle. He lives in Lancaster with his family and is a researcher at Lancaster University.

Brian looks back with fondness to the quieter winters on the Lake District crags when this area was bypassed en route to Scotland. A series of good winters has shown what potential the Lake District has to offer the winter climber and the many new routes recorded, in excess of 200 since the last edition of this guide, should ensure that there is still plenty of choice.

LAKE DISTRICT WINTER CLIMBS

SNOW, ICE AND MIXED CLIMBS IN THE ENGLISH LAKE DISTRICT

by

Brian Davison

2 POLICE SQUARE, MILNTHORPE, CUMBRIA LA7 7PY
www.cicerone.co.uk

The Easy Way variation on Slab and Notch Climb, Pillar Rock c1900
© *Abraham Family*

The Fell and Rock Climbing Club

The formation of the Fell and Rock Climbing Club was proposed at Coniston in 1906 at the instigation of Edward Scantlebury and Alan Craig, two of a 'coterie of keen young mountaineers living on the southern confines of the English Lake District'. Before the end of the year the club had over 40 members enrolled and was officially founded in 1907 when Ashley Abraham accepted the office of President. In the same year the first Club Journal reported many new climbs. Publication has continued and today the nexus for new climbs is the database on the Club's website.

1922 saw the Club publish its first rock climbing guidebook, *Doe Crag* by George Bower and since that date has produced a continuous series of definitive guidebooks to Lake District rock climbing. These guidebooks are written and published by volunteers who update the text and check new climbs, many of which have been pioneered by Club members.

The Club now has over 1200 members and owns huts in the Lake District and Scotland. Membership has always been open to applicants who can demonstrate an ongoing interest and enthusiasm for climbing or fell walking in the Lake District. Information about the FRCC and FRCC Guides and an interactive new route database can be found on the Club's website at www.frcc.co.uk.

FRCC Guidebooks
Dow, Duddon and Slate (1994)
Scafell, Wasdale and Eskdale (1996)
Langdale (1999)
Borrowdale (2000)
Lake District Rock (2003)
Gable and Pillar (2007)
Buttermere and St Bees (2008)
Eastern Crags (2011)
Eden Valley and South Lakes Limestone (2012)

© Fell and Rock Climbing Club 2012

Second edition 2012
ISBN 13: 978 1 85284 716 6

First edition 2006
ISBN 10: 1 85284 484 1
ISBN 13: 978 1 85284 484 4

Printed in China on behalf of Latitude Press Ltd
A catalogue record for this book is available from the British Library.
Photographs edited by Tim Whiteley. Text edited by Steve Scott.

To all Lakeland winter climbers past and present.
We follow in their footsteps.

Front cover: Challenging ice, exquisite climbing – *West Waterfall Gully*, Pillar (climber: Stephen Reid; photo: Colin Wells)

CONTENTS

Acknowledgments 11
Maps and diagrams in this guide 12
Location map 13
Map key 14
Topo diagram key 14
Editor's note 15

INTRODUCTION 17
Conditions 19
Winter ethics 19
Winter climbing styles 22
Where to climb? 25
Equipment 26
Winter grades 31
Dry tooling grades 32
Using this guide 32
First ascents or first claims? 33

SOUTH LAKES 35
LANGDALE 36
   Oxendale 37
   Bowfell 48
   Langdale Pikes 75
CONISTON 87
   Dow 88
   The Old Man Of Coniston 95
   Wetherlam 100
   Tilberthwaite and the Slate Quarries 105

WEST LAKES 107
ESKDALE 108
   Little Narrow Cove 110
WASDALE 114
   Scafell Massif 122
   Scafell 124
   Scafell Pike 150
   Lingmell 158
   Mosedale 163

Western Wasdale	163
ENNERDALE	164
Mirklin Cove	166
Mirk Cove and Wind Gap Cove	169
Pillar	175
GREAT GABLE AND KIRK FELL	186
Gable South	186
Gable North	187
Kirk Fell	204
BUTTERMERE AND ENNERDALE	206
Honister Pass	206
Fleetwith Pike – North Face	208
Warnscale Bottom	215
Birkness Combe	217
Bleaberry Combe	222
Grasmoor	233
NEWLANDS	237
Coledale	239
Whinlatter	240
NORTH LAKES	243
BORROWDALE	244
Borrowdale East	245
Great End	252
Borrowdale West	263
NORTHERN FELLS	266
Skiddaw	267
Blencathra (Saddleback)	268
Carrock Fell	272
EAST LAKES	273
THIRLMERE	274
HELVELLYN MASSIF	279
Helvellyn	283
Nethermost Cove	295
Ruthwaite Cove	297
Cock Cove	304
Dollywaggon	308
PATTERDALE AND ADJACENT VALLEYS	313
Patterdale – East	313

Patterdale – West	321
Grisedale	324
Deepdale	327
Sleet Cove	335
Dovedale	345
Kirkstone Pass	353
FAR EASTERN FELLS	355
Mardale	355
Blea Water	359
Riggindale	362
Whelter Bottom	362
Swindale	363
Longsleddale	363
Kentmere	364

OUTLYING AREAS	365
THE HOWGILLS	366
NORTHERN PENNINES	367

DRY TOOLING ROUTES	369

FIRST ASCENTS	377

APPENDIX A	Winter climbing and nature conservation	433
APPENDIX B	Procedure for mountain accidents	439
APPENDIX C	Useful contacts	443
APPENDIX D	Campsites and camping barns	444
APPENDIX E	Climbing walls	448
APPENDIX F	Taking better climbing photographs	451

INDEX OF ROUTES	452

Environmental symbols used in crag and route descriptions

 crag/route is within a Site of Special Scientific Interest

 crag/route is home to rare alpine plants and only to be climbed when completely frozen, if at all

Warning

This guide is one in a continuing series written by members of the FRCC to provide a definitive record of the climbing in the Lake District. The guide is compiled from a number of sources and whilst every care and effort has been taken in its preparation the inclusion of any route does not imply that it remains in the condition described. Mountain conditions are highly variable and climbs can change unpredictably: rock erodes and fixed gear deteriorates, materially affecting the condition and seriousness of a climb.

Winter climbing is a dangerous activity carrying a risk of personal injury or death. It should be undertaken only by those with a full understanding of the risks and with the training and/or experience to evaluate them. Users of the guide must rely on their own judgement and are recommended to insure against personal injury and third party liability. Neither Cicerone, the Fell and Rock Climbing Club of the English Lake District, nor the author accept liability for damage of any nature (including damage to property, personal injury or death) arising directly or indirectly from the information in this book.

The FRCC and Cicerone endorse the BMC Participation Statement that climbing, hill walking and mountaineering are activities with a danger of personal injury or death. Participants in these activities should be aware of and accept these risks and be responsible for their own actions and involvement.

Recording Feedback and New Routes

Such is the fickle nature of Lakeland winters that it is simply not possible to check all the newly reported routes in the same way one can summer rock climbs. The author has climbed over half the new routes in this edition and canvassed as many opinions as possible to improve route descriptions and grades. If you do find any errors, or have any comments to make (comments on individual pitch gradings are particularly welcome), or wish to record a new route, then visit the FRCC New Routes Bulletin Board at www.frcc.co.uk. In the Recent Developments section of the same website you will be able to see any new routes that have been recorded since this guide was published.

ACKNOWLEDGEMENTS

The author would like to thank the FRCC guidebook production team. Particular thanks must go to Steve Scott (FRCC Guidebooks Editor) for his help and encouragement, Tim Whiteley for the long hours spent selecting photographs and Steve Ashworth, Paddy Cave and Nick Wharton for bothering to take them. Al Phizacklea drew the maps to his usual high standard. Jonathan Williams and the team at Cicerone Press have been excellent partners in this enterprise.

Thanks must also go to all those who have given their help and advice, past and present, during the preparation of this guide. First and foremost are the writers of the previous Cicerone guides on whose work this guide is based: Bob Bennett, Bill Birkett and Andy Hyslop. Contributors to the guide, other than those mentioned above, include Simon Webb of Natural England, himself a keen climber, who wrote the chapter 'Winter climbing and nature conservation', and Dr John Ellerton, an icefall fanatic, who wrote 'Procedure for mountain accidents'.

In addition there are those who have provided photographs – the names of those whose photos were selected appear in the text but many thanks also to those who submitted images which could not be included in the end. Permission to use the Abrahams photographs was most kindly given by the Abrahams family. The photographs used for the crag topos were provided by: Steve Ashworth, Adrian Clifford, Colin Downer, Al Hinkes, Al Phizacklea, Stephen Reid, Eric Shaw, Colin Wells, Nick Wharton, Dave Willis, Colin Wornham, Harry Worsnop and Phil Young. Others who have helped with information and have not already been mentioned include: David Birkett, David McGimpsey, Rich Cross, Mark Walker, Matt Griffin, Huw Davies, Mark Edwards, Ross McGibbon, Andrew Charlton, John Daly, Nick Kekus, Les Kendall, Ron Kenyon, Jim Loxham, Adrian Nelhams and Stuart Wood. The Rockfax Lake District Winter Routes Database (www.rockfax.com) and its contributors have also provided some useful information. Thanks also to Ted Rogers, Sandra Scott and Al Davies for checking the proofs.

Finally I would like to thank Fiona for her patience in putting up with my endless nocturnal visits to the attic for yet another night of guidebook writing.

Brian Davison, September 2012

Lake District Winter Climbs

MAPS AND DIAGRAMS IN THIS GUIDE

Maps

Langdale	36
Bowfell	48
Coniston	87
Eskdale	108
Wasdale	114
Scafell	120
Buttermere and Ennerdale	164
Newlands	238
Borrowdale	244
Northern Fells	266
Thirlmere	274
Helvellyn and Patterdale	280
Helvellyn	282
Far Eastern Fells	356
The Works	372

Crag diagrams

Shelter Crags	44
North Buttress and Cambridge Crag	58
North Buttress – Gimps Wall Area	66
Bowfell Buttress	69
Pavey Ark	80
Dow Crag	89
Low Water	98
Wasdale Screes	116
Scafell	125
Scafell Crag	134
Pikes Crag	151
Piers Gill	159
Mirklin Cove	167
Scoat Fell Crag	171
Black Crag	174
Pillar Rock	177
Great Gable	190
Green Gable	201
Honister Crag Icefalls – Upper Left Gantry Crag	211
Honister Crag Icefalls – Gantry Crag	212
Eagle Crag (Buttermere)	219
Chapel Crags – left-hand section	223
Chapel Crags – right-hand section	229
Dove Crag, Grasmoor	235
Hobcarton Crag	241
Great End	253
Central Gully, Great End	257
Foule Crag and Sharp Edge	270
Brown Cove Crag	284
Red Tarn Cove	288
Nethermost Cove	294
Dollywaggon North Crag	302
Cock Cove Crag	306
Tarn Crag and Falcon Crag	309
Rampsgill Head Crag	314
Scrubby Crag	332
Greenhow End	336
Hutaple Crag	339
Blea Water Crag	360

Panoramas

Helvellyn Range	292
Deepdale	328
Dovedale	346

LOCATION MAP

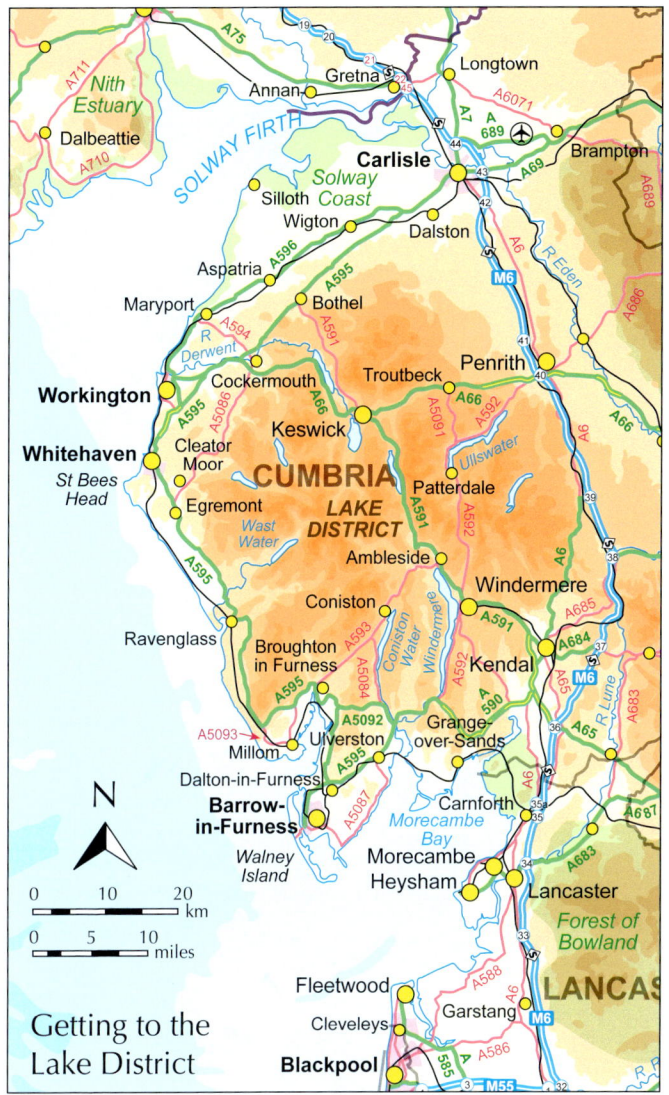

Getting to the Lake District

LAKE DISTRICT WINTER CLIMBS

Map key

- A roads
- B roads
- secondary roads
- footpath
- track
- ridge
- river/lake
- crags
- rough gound
- gill
- forest
- habitation
- parking
- peak (only on Scafell and Bowfell maps)
- 800m and above
- 600–800m
- 300–600m
- 0–300m

Topo diagram key

- route numbers (in legend)
- grades I–II
- grade III
- grades IV–V
- grade VI or over

EDITOR'S NOTE

In March 2006 'there was still plenty of "winter" around' – more than most could cope with. Some of the routes climbed as the deadline closed on the last winter guide indicated what the future might bring. There would be controversy – *The Crack Direct*. Development would be 'hard and mixed' – *The Gnomon* and *Salvation*. And there would be proper winters!

Consolidating the work of previous writers, Brian Davison did a thorough and comprehensive job and most of us thought that the 2006 guide would be the last one we would buy. Since then the Lakes has enjoyed successive hard and long winter seasons. A combination of some of the best climbable conditions for decades, increased awareness – through the internet and the popularity of the previous guide – and new, younger climbers embracing the technical challenge and aesthetic delights of winter climbing have resulted in another huge wave of exploration in the area. As a result, there are over 200 new climbs recorded in this second edition.

Once again, Brian has pulled it all together in this updated and expanded guide. Tim Whiteley had the tough job of sorting and selecting the superb photographs to inspire you. And the clear photo-diagrams and Al Phizacklea's maps should keep you from having too much of an epic! Many people have been involved collating recorded ascents so that an up-to-date 'first ascents' list could be included and we should all thank them for this research.

Controversy has continued to rage about the ethics of climbing some of these routes and a well attended but sadly inconclusive BMC Area debate took place in November 2011. Before you choose to climb think carefully about the environmental impact. Simon Webb of Natural England has carefully explained in Appendix A where the rare plants are in the Lake District and why they should be protected. In the route sections, a new icon (❦) also shows you which cliffs are home to these rare alpines. We are also indebted once again to ice-warrior John Ellerton for his guidance notes on mountain accidents (Appendix B).

This new guidebook contains all of the currently known climbs and many of the recent finds and 'last' problems are very worthwhile additions to what was already a unique and rewarding area. The past six years has been a period of significant consolidation but there is little doubt that adventurous and imaginative climbers will continue to find unclimbed icefalls and worthwhile mixed lines.

Short days, tough approaches, fickle conditions and harsh weather make any winter ascent an adventure. What you hold in your hand offers a lifetime of such adventures.

Steve Scott, September 2012

Lake District Winter Climbs

Andy Turner on Xerxes, Scafell Crag (First Winter Ascent) (photo: Steve Ashworth)

INTRODUCTION

The Lake District National Park is situated entirely within Cumbria in the north-west of England, not far from the Scottish border. It is a land of dramatic contrasts, with rugged fells rising high over lush green valleys and dramatic dark waters. Within its boundaries are the highest mountains and the deepest lakes in England. Unlike national parks in many other parts of the world, the Lake District is a populated area, full of working hill farms, villages and market towns. It bears the ancient scars of mining and quarrying and the impact of tourism and the motor car yet is still reckoned to be one of the most tranquil and beautiful areas in the British Isles.

Unsurprisingly the Lake District is popular not only with climbers, but also with hill walkers, fell runners, mountain bikers, canoeists and a host of other visitors. It has a fascinating history and is home to ancient monuments such as the splendidly named Mediobogdum – the Roman fort on Hardknott Pass – and the more recent Borrowdale wad mines. The district has long been a source of inspiration for poets and artists. Wordsworth,

Anticipating a good day from the Climbers' Traverse, Bow Fell (photo: Paddy Cave)

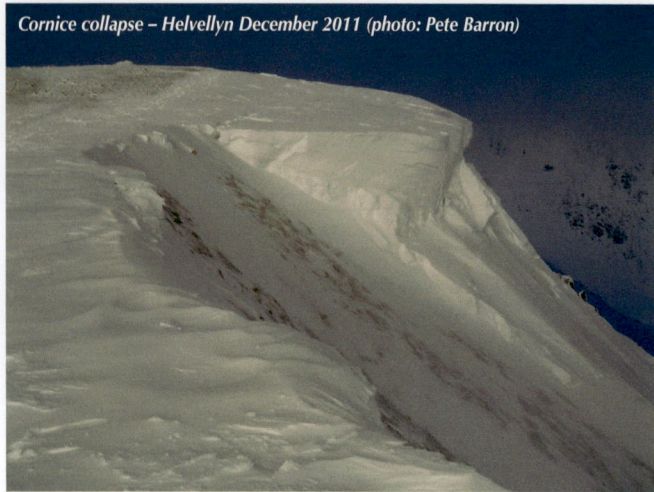
Cornice collapse – Helvellyn December 2011 (photo: Pete Barron)

Coleridge, Ruskin, Beatrix Potter and three generations of the Heaton Cooper family rank among them.

The unceasing efforts of a great number of people over many years have contributed towards keeping the Lake District as a place of great beauty to be enjoyed not only by outdoor enthusiasts, but also by myriad other visitors and the locals, although the interests of these diverse groups do not always coincide. Not least among these efforts were the long and hard campaigns for the area's special status led by those with the foresight to realise the dangers of unchecked development. Now there are several bodies, statutory and otherwise, such as the National Park Authority, the National Trust and the Friends of the Lake District and their army of wardens, rangers and others, both paid and voluntary, who fight a daily battle to maintain the fragile fabric of this much-loved landscape.

The valleys of the Central Lake District are arranged like the spokes of a wheel with the hub near Great End, the northernmost outlier of the Scafell massif. The major valleys are Langdale, the Duddon valley, Eskdale, Wasdale, Ennerdale, Buttermere, Borrowdale and Thirlmere. East of Thirlmere lies the Helvellyn massif and the parallel valley of Patterdale with its subsidiary valleys of Grisedale, Deepdale and Dovedale. Eastwards again, the Far Eastern Fells have many small and relatively unfrequented valleys. In winter cold air currents from Siberia can bring conditions that in a matter of days can transform this pastoral yet mountainous scene into an arctic wilderness: sadly for winter climbers, it can be transformed back again just as quickly.

CONDITIONS

The winter climbing season in the Lake District can lie anywhere between October and April although the coldest part of the winter usually occurs in late January. For traditional winter climbing good conditions are unlikely before the New Year, as earlier in the winter it is unusual for there to have been enough cold days to freeze the ground thoroughly and any snow which falls will soon melt. Several days of very cold temperatures prior to snowfall are the best indicator that conditions may be suitable on the fells.

If you have a particular cliff in mind, then keep an eye on the wind direction. If it has been blowing onto the cliff this aids the freezing process. While the hills may often be covered with a coating of snow, it takes a few days for fresh snow to consolidate through a freeze–thaw cycle and improve the climbing; and it takes a prolonged period of snowy wintry weather to fill gullies with the snow necessary to build up really good conditions. Successive hard frosts or a long period of sub-zero temperatures provide water ice and frozen turf creating good climbing – the important thing here is that it should have regularly been freezing at night. Some limited thawing during the day is desirable, as long as it freezes again the next night, as this builds the ice thickness up more quickly. In a mild winter buttress and mixed routes which come into condition more readily than snow gullies generally provide more reliable climbing.

Detailed weather forecasts are available by phone, apps and the web. A useful forecast for the Lake District National Park, which gives information about snow conditions on the fells, is available on the internet at www.lakedistrictweatherline.co.uk or by telephone on 0844 846 2444.

WINTER ETHICS

Practised by a skilled and occasionally insular minority, winter climbing in

Les Kendall shelters in an ice cave: North West Climb (V) Pillar Rock (photo: Ray McHaffie/Les Kendall Collection)

Britain has developed its own unique ethical code. Winter climbing was once considered to carry unreasonable risks that many were unwilling to accept but modern gear and techniques have now encouraged more climbers to climb in winter. With no apprenticeship, many find it hard to understand why some ascents are applauded and others derided. Social networking and the media strengthen the cult of the celebrity and sponsorship deals induce hunger for success on unclimbed and harder lines and glorify early repeats. Ethics get overlooked.

For the equipment and techniques available at the time, by the late 1950s the level of difficulty had peaked. In February 1960 Smith and Marshall were literally climbing at the 'cutting edge' of the possible with their ascent of *Smith's Route*. Interviewed for 'The Pinnacle', Marshall describes how Robin was at his utmost limit. During this historic week the pair had also quietly made the second ascent of *Point Five* in seven hours! *Point Five* was controversial, as the previous winter the first ascent party spent five days laying siege – drilling bolted belays and leaving ropes in place. Smith and Marshall's ascents led to a consensus among active leading climbers that the acceptance of the sieged ascent would be a mistake. A standard was set that is still maintained.

Moon over the Old Man of Coniston (photo: Nick Wharton)

Further arguments surfaced following Wielochowski and Nottidge's ascent of the *Fly Direct* on Creag Meagaidh in 1976. They climbed the line in three days spread over several weeks selecting optimum conditions. This staggered approach was then shown to be unjustified when Saunders and Fowler made the first true ascent in 1983. This ethical stance has prevailed for over fifty years and lead to British winter climbs being considered as some of the most ethically sound and admired throughout the world.

In the Lakes multi-day ascents with abseil approaches to high points have been reported on Central Buttress (1986) and the elusive ice-fall on the East Buttress of Scafell, a long-standing challenge which many had been watching and waiting to come into condition for over thirty years. Dave Birkett's two-day ascent of *Never Ever Say Never* showed that the climbing was possible. Let's hope it does re-form, can be climbed and it isn't a case of Never Ever for a true single-day ascent.

Another problem is the claiming of routes which don't go to the cliff-top. This is less clear-cut as routes which finish on easy ground with a walk or climb off are obviously fine. But when the descent is by abseil, the validity of the route needs to meet the current consensus. For example, routes which finish on The Springboard (a ledge on Black Spout Pinnacle, Lochnagar) and are descended by abseil, are accepted, whereas an attempt to climb *Crazy Sorrow* (Lochnagar) followed by an abseil off from the top of the second pitch was not.

Previous summer knowledge is also difficult. It is claimed that it prevents the 'on-sight' (a climb made without any previous inspection). Is it sensible, when conditions are so different, that someone who has climbed a summer route should then be considered to be unable to claim an on-sight ascent in winter? Abseiling a route immediately prior to its ascent in winter is clearly not acceptable unless that is the only approach, as snow covering holds and placements can be cleared. *Blood, Sweat and Frozen Tears* (Beinn Eighe) approached by abseil down the line is a good example.

As far as can be ascertained, all of the climbs described have been done in true winter condition in a single outing. Those awaiting a ground-up one-day ascent are indicated and speculative or incomplete ascents are left for future claims.

WINTER CLIMBING STYLES

Winter climbing is evolving and there are currently four separate styles. Traditional **snow and ice** climbing, **mixed climbing** of snowed up rock routes, steep **water ice** climbs and more recently **dry tooling**, originally conceived to cover areas of steep rock to reach inaccessible ice-falls.

Snow and ice is easy to understand – it needs snow and to be cold. The climatic conditions necessary to generate suitable climbing conditions for mixed climbing and dry tooling differ. The damper milder conditions found in the UK make this country suitable for mixed climbing while the colder dry conditions of the continent offer opportunities for dry tooling in order to gain steep ice stalactites.

Snow and ice

This is the most traditional style and the one most recognisable as 'winter climbing'. Snow-filled gullies have always offered simple ways up mountains. As equipment and techniques improved so did the steepness of the snow and ice that could be climbed. The great gully climbs – *Steep Gill* on Scafell, *Dove Crag Gully* on Grasmoor and *Inaccessible* on Dove Crag – epitomise this style.

Mixed climbing

The humid maritime air and variable temperature during UK winters leads to the formation of hoar frost or rime on the mountain cliffs along with a covering of consolidated snow, a phenomenon unique to such climates.

This covering of snow, ice and rime makes mixed climbing a unique challenge as climbers attempt to locate cracks for pick and protection placements. The technique of torquing axe blades in cracks to gain

WINTER CLIMBING STYLES

West Waterfall Gully, Pillar (Mark 'Ed' Edwards)

upward progress is nothing new, having been described in Winthrop-Young's seminal work on climbing techniques, *Mountaincraft* (1920). However it took until the late 1970s before the technique was refined and axe design improved enough to make progress up the steepest snow-covered buttress routes possible. Routes like *Snicker Snack*, *Harvest Crunch*, *The Gnomon* and *Evolution* indicate the possibilities.

Tension with rock climbers has naturally sparked argument as to what constitutes suitable winter conditions. While arguments will continue I have always considered a route as 'in condition' if its ascent is easier with axes and crampons than without. If you can brush a loose dusting of snow from the holds and rock climb the route then you're doing a rock route. So when you're climbing, think about the conditions and be honest with yourself (and others). Would progress be easier without your tools? If it would be, then you are doing a cold ascent of a rock route and not a true winter ascent.

Water ice

This style is about climbing pure frozen water. The challenge is in the steepness and length and is enhanced by free-standing pillars and stalactites which fail to form sufficiently to touch down or hang tantalisingly over cliff edges. There are several such climbs in the Lakes: Honister has a fair number and there are the classics at Shoulthwaite, Cautley and Blea Water.

Nick Wharton in Full Frontal Activity, Hutaple Crag, Patterdale (photo: Brian Davison)

Dry tooling

The drier, colder conditions generated by high pressure during a continental winter result in the formation of extensive icefalls. As some of these icefalls hang from steep rock and fail to reach the ground the protectionless rockwalls around them have been bolted to allow access to the ice by hooking axes on small holds. Once people realised that climbing the rock was more challenging than the ice itself the sport of dry tooling was born.

However, as the UK fails to get cold dry winters (and you could say lacks plentiful overhanging rock faces which form icefalls) the winter version of dry tooling is not available in this country. For training, and also as an end in itself, climbers have therefore started developing routes in other areas without the need for snow, ice or even cold temperatures.

The recent development of carefully-chosen dry tooling sites, usually in old quarries or areas of poor rock unsuitable for rock climbing, has proved very popular and they act as outdoor climbing walls where dry tooling can be practised all year round. Venues such as White Goods in Wales (www.whitegood.blogspot.co.uk) and Newtyle Quarry, Dunkeld in Scotland (www.scottishclimbs.com/wiki/Newtyle_Quarry) now offer year-round training without causing damage to existing crags or angering other climbers. However, it is important to stress that the existence of these venues **does not** give license to dry tool at established rock climbing crags.

WHERE TO CLIMB?

Growing environmental awareness and concern over conservation of rare species, both flora and fauna, mean that several ecologically sensitive areas are protected by law. You must safeguard these sensitive areas by climbing only when they are fully frozen and in true winter condition. Repeated hacking of unfrozen turf can cause serious damage (both to climbs and to vegetation) and should be considered completely unacceptable. This is particularly true on the crags of the Helvellyn escarpment which are home to especially rare alpine plants, but can be applied to the entire district – please read Appendix A 'Winter climbing and nature conservation' before making your choice. (A neatly placed pick in well-frozen turf causes little damage.)

As would be expected, the higher the cliff the greater your chance of finding it in condition. Consideration should also be given to the wind direction during the preceeding days. Most of the best crags face north or east and so receive limited sunshine, which allows snow to build up. Aspect, altitude at the base and whether rare plants exist is noted at the start of each crag section to help you choose.

Facing north-east, and far from the coast, Great End is one of the most reliable crags for collecting snow and tends to retain it for longer than most other areas in the Lakes. The Helvellyn coves, while slightly less reliable, can be better if the wind has recently been from the east. Both come with easy access and the price tag for that can be crowds. A prevailing easterly wind is likely to bring cold air and will help freeze turf and form water ice, but it often does not offer much chance of snowfall, so areas such as Blea Water, which readily form water ice, can be a good choice if it has been cold and dry. Blea Water is generally somewhat quieter in terms of numbers: however it is also more limited in choice of routes.

In general, if the wind has been from the east then it is often better to choose a cliff on the east side of the district with an easterly aspect. If the winds are from the west or south-west they are more likely to bring moist air, with snow or rime building on higher crags, especially in the west of the District.

Keeping an eye on the weather and the freezing levels can help give an indication as to whether conditions will be suitable. If temperatures have been below freezing for several days before snowfall the ground will probably be frozen and good for climbing. If the snow lands on unfrozen ground then it acts as a blanket insulating the ground from any subsequent freezing temperatures so frozen turf can take longer to form. Scafell is high enough that it can often rime up on a more westerly wind even if snow has not fallen and Gable Crag is another reliable venue in these sort of conditions. However, areas close to the sea are greatly affected by milder coastal winds and are seldom worth considering.

There are many icefalls and gills that freeze after a sufficient period of cold conditions. High falls like Angle Tarn and Low Water Beck come into nick reasonably quickly but even these take about a week of sub-zero night-time temperatures to form. For climbs fed by seepage, strangely enough, periods of intense cold aren't necessarily ideal as the water may freeze in the ground: better to have a slight thaw during the day and a refreeze at night allowing a build-up and thickening of the ice.

So keep an eye on what the weather has been doing for a week or so before you venture out and that should help you choose somewhere in condition and allow you to make the most of those short winter days.

EQUIPMENT

Climbing in the hills in winter requires a firm grasp of basic winter skills. You should know how to navigate using a map and compass (a GPS, although useful, is no substitute), how to use an ice axe to cut steps and arrest a slip and how to walk wearing crampons. These are the basics for getting you to a climb and back to the valley at the end of what may be a long day: they should be second nature.

The following notes on equipment may be useful as a guide for those embarking upon their first winter routes.

The author sporting all the latest gear! (photo: Stephen Venables)

Clothing

Everyone has their own personal choice of clothing. In general a multi-layer system is most versatile and allows good regulation of heat. It can get very warm walking to a crag and very cold on the route (even colder if you get benighted), so it is important to carry spare clothing to stay warm during what could be lengthy belaying sessions. Hypothermia can come on with surprising swiftness and should not be underestimated. Modern fabrics can be very quick-drying and warm and, importantly, lightweight, so use these and in addition try to get clothes that don't ride up when you stretch up during climbing.

A waterproof jacket is essential. This prevents snow sticking to fleeces and thermals and wetting them if it warms up during climbing. Waterproof trousers or salopettes, while performing the same function, can constrict movement, so whether you wear them during the climb may depend on the garment, conditions and individual preference. Modern softshell leggings can be very good and a lot more comfortable in most conditions. An alternative to a layering system is the Pertex/Pile system invented by Buffalo which certainly works well and is relatively cheap, but not perhaps as versatile.

Gloves

For technical climbing, gloves can be a real problem: they need to be warm but not clumsy. Dachstein woollen mitts, while warm, may become difficult to use and put on when wet, but they are also a lot cheaper than their modern counterpart and will do fine for easier routes. In general, mitts, although warmer, don't allow the same dexterity as fingered gloves. One solution is a thin inner glove worn inside mitts, fitted with securing wrist elastic cords, which allows removal of the mitt when necessary for tricky moves.

Harder routes often require greater dexterity than mitts allow to enable easier handling and placement of protection, not to mention the occasional use of a rock hold – and for this gloves may be essential. There are commercially available ice climbing gloves that are warm, waterproof and equipped with knuckle protection – and a hefty price tag!

The skint, or thrifty, can experiment with ski gloves or, for improved grip on axes, rubberised gardening or working gloves. Finding the right combination of gloves comes down to personal preference born out of long experience. Many years of climbing have led me to use a combination of thin gloves for technical hard pitches and mitts for general use and, perhaps most useful, to develop a tolerance to pain. Having several pairs of gloves and mitts in your sack is no bad thing, especially if your route is a long one.

Helmet

Many climb without a helmet in summer but only the foolish do so in winter – the risk of ice and rock falling spontaneously or being knocked off the crag by other climbers is just too great. Your helmet should be big enough to fit over a balaclava or hat and in winter it can be well worth putting it on below the approach slopes as they may avalanche or be prone to falling ice from the crag. The helmet should have some system to enable a headtorch to be fastened to it.

Harness

Put your harness on early as step-in leg loops can prove tricky to operate in combination with crampons, especially on steep slopes, so a harness you can put on easily without taking your feet off the ground is recommended. As you will be wearing thicker clothing plenty of adjustment is advisable.

Boots

The most important thing is that your boots should fit you well and take a crampon: B2 or B3 is essential. The lightweight boots now on the market are considered the most comfortable allowing a better feel of what your foot (and crampon) is placed on and, weighing in at just over a kilo, they are not going to slow you down on a long day. Various combinations of waterproof membrane and insulation mean they are warm and relatively dry. They do, however, still require drying out at the end of the day and are not generally as warm as a plastic boot.

Plastics are lightweight, warm, waterproof and rigid enough to take step-in or clip-on type crampons but they can be uncomfortable and it is worth loosening them for the walk-in and tightening them for the actual climbing. Unlike a leather boot they do not readily give and mould to your foot shape, so if not comfortable straight away they are never likely to become so.

If you are camping, bivvying or bothying and no heat for drying is available, you may have to, just as in the Greater Ranges, sleep with your boots to help the drying process: in which case the inners of a plastic boot are much more comfortable to snuggle up with in your sleeping bag than a full leather boot. Gaiters prevent snow entering boots and feet from getting cold. Some newer boot designs have an integral gaiter.

Crampons

Most people use step-in articulated crampons which are convenient and save cold fingers if your boots are designed to take them (B3). Strap-on crampons can be fitted to boots with slightly more bend (B2) – modern versions have the bulk of the straps replaced by an excellent enclosing plastic basket system. Monopoints are becoming more popular and are good on both ice and particularly on buttress climbs where the single front point can be inserted into a fine crack without being forced out again by the second point. Completely rigid crampons are good on hard climbs, but they are not very comfortable to walk in and, for the Lakeland fells, a semi-rigid crampon is probably the best choice.

Axes and hammers

While reverse curve (banana pick) tools are better for ice and technical routes, a traditional (alpine) curved pick is better for ice axe braking and is just as good for easier routes. Sharp axes and crampons work better than blunt ones on ice, but don't stay sharp for long on mixed routes. If you're serious about mixed climbing get a modular axe which allows replacement of picks and adze and hammer heads. While the basic concept of the reverse curve pick ice tool is unchanged, ice tool design has improved, with ergonomically designed grips and special leashless tools. However, extremely wiggly axes with bulky handrests and thin 'B'

Equipment

rated picks designed for pure water-ice climbing are not likely to be much use in the Lake District – it is better to go for simpler designs with straight or slightly bent shafts and tough 'T' rated picks. It's also worth carrying a spare set of bolts and a pick and the tools to tighten them up with as well.

Hardware

This is very route dependent. A greater selection of rock gear is needed on mixed routes than on snow and ice gullies, but watch out for camming devices which can easily slide out of icy cracks. Slings are particularly useful, both for spikes and threads and as extenders. While the placement of pegs is often frowned on, particularly on good rock routes, they may be the only source of protection if a crack is iced up. Warthogs, a type of drive-in ice screw, are good for ice and indispensible for frozen turf. Few shops stock them and on many racks they are being replaced by the versatile hook.

For pure water ice, sharp tubular ice screws, preferably with wind-in handles, are essential. A dead-man may be useful for easy gullies and long snow sections. 60m ropes dry-treated for preference and using double half ropes mean you can abseil twice as far if you need to get down quickly. It is also worth carrying several metres of tape or cord and a pocket knife so that abseil slings can be rigged quickly and although finding ice solid enough to do so may be rare in the Lakes, you should know how to construct an Abalakov thread. Every member of the party should carry a set of Prusik loops and know how to use them.

A secure peg (photo: Steve Ashworth)

Rucksack

A day out in winter requires far more kit than in summer. A 50 to 60 litre sack should allow you to get everything inside if things are to be kept dry.

Refreshments

It is important to replace lost liquids, particularly during the walk-in. A thermos means warm drinks, but may not be worth the extra weight – it's a tough choice! You need sufficient calories for the day and some spare emergency rations.

Headtorch

It's essential to carry a headtorch and pointless to do so without checking

Scafell Pinnacle (photo: Nick Wharton)

your battery and packing a spare bulb before you head for the hills.

Map and compass
Each person should have their own map and compass – and know how to use them. Incidents of parties splitting up or becoming separated in poor weather are not unknown.

Bivvy bag
If it all goes horribly wrong and you end up spending the night out, a bivouac bag can mean the difference between life and death. Each member of the party should have their own. They can range from a simple body-sized plastic bag to an expensive breathable model. From the climbing point of view, the best are semi-breathable and very light shelters that provide great protection and comfort, will not fill up your rucksack nor weigh you down too much.

First aid kit
A small selection of bandages, plasters and painkillers, together with some antiseptic cream, are well worth carrying. See Appendix B 'Procedure for mountain accidents'.

Camera
It's no use moaning about the quality of photos in guidebooks if you don't carry one and use it! If it is digital then

make sure it is set on maximum quality to make the most of your efforts. (See Appendix F for more photography tips.)

WINTER GRADES

The six years since the publication of the previous winter climbing guide have seen one of the longest winters in 30 years and one of the coldest months in 50 years. An increased interest in winter climbing and an improvement in equipment and climbing standards has seen repeats of many mixed routes, some originally climbed in the 1980s. This has helped to improve the reported grades. Where possible, descriptions and grades are from a consensus of opinion and feedback on any of the routes is always appreciated.

In this guide, the open-ended Scottish two-tier system has been used. Roman numerals are used to indicate the overall difficulty and Arabic numerals signify the technical difficulty of either the hardest moves on the route or particular pitches. In this way the system is analogous to the rock climbing grade system where routes with safe or short-lived technical sections may have a higher technical grade than overall grade – for example V (6), where a standard V would be V (5). A more serious route may be less technically demanding but still warrant V – eg V (4). However, just to confuse things, a sustained (albeit safe) route may also be given this grade. The route description should make it apparent which is the case.

THE NUMERICAL WINTER GRADING SYSTEM

I	Straightforward snow gully around 45 degrees or easy angled ridges; cornices maybe encountered.
II	Gullies with some steep snow or short ice pitches and more difficult ridges; still usually summer scrambles.
III	More sustained than a II with longer ice pitches and some technical sections on buttresses.
IV	Longer steep ice requiring fitness and arm strength or difficult rock or mixed ground which may require axe torquing techniques.
V	Sustained steep ice. Mixed routes with several technical sections.
VI	Vertical ice or serious climbs which may be sustained and technical and also highly technical but relatively well-protected mixed routes.
VII	Longer multi-pitch routes with long sections of vertical or thin ice. Mixed routes with many technical sections requiring fitness, skill and experience to link together.
VIII+	The system is open ended, with these harder grades signifying as for VII but even more tenuous, poorly protected and desperate.

DRY TOOLING GRADES

M1–3 Easy. Low angle; usually requiring minimum use of tools.
M4 Slabby to vertical with some technical dry tooling.
M5 Some sustained vertical dry tooling.
M6 Vertical to overhanging with difficult dry tooling.
M7 Overhanging; powerful and technical dry tooling; less than 10m of hard climbing.
M8 Some nearly horizontal overhangs requiring very powerful and technical dry tooling; bouldery or longer cruxes than M7.
M9 Either continuously vertical or slightly overhanging with marginal or technical holds, or a juggy roof of 2 to 3 body lengths.
M10 At least 10m of horizontal rock or 30m of overhanging dry tooling with powerful moves and no rests.
M11 A ropelength of overhanging gymnastic climbing, or up to 15m of roof.
M12 M11 with bouldery, dynamic moves and tenuous technical holds.

For each route the grade is listed after the heading. Pitch lengths are usually given where necessary, but on some of the easier sections only overall lengths are used. The familiar three-star rating has been used to indicate quality, although this is naturally dependent on conditions. Stars assigned following a first ascent are subjective. Please confirm their quality with the FRCC if you do the route and let us know of unstarred routes that deserve stars (and vice versa!).

DRY TOOLING GRADES

The dry tooling routes established in the quarries are protected by bolts and do not require snow, ice or cold conditions. These routes require considerable dry tooling technique (modern ice tools used on bare rock) and are climbed in monopoint crampons. The use of existing winter climbing grades is inappropriate for these climbs and so to differentiate these routes from the winter climbs in this guide dry tooling routes have been given M grades. A series of D grades identical to the M series is also in existence. These indicate that no ice is required to do the route. For the routes at UK dry tooling venues this is particularly appropriate with D and M grading being interchangeable.

USING THIS GUIDE

This guidebook records every known winter climb worth recording in the

English Lake District. Routes are divided into broad areas: South Lakes, West Lakes, North Lakes and East Lakes, as well as 'Outlying areas' (in Cumbria but outside the national park) and 'Dry tooling routes'.

Within each section routes are grouped by valley or area, such as Honister Pass and then by crag, like Yew Crags and sometimes by sub-crag or buttress. A brief description of the approach to a climbing area is given at the beginning of each area section, with crag approaches at the beginning of each crag section. Where not obvious, the descent from each crag is also given.

Many of the routes are shown on photo topos of the crags, depicted in contrasting colours to show four bands of grades: grades I–II (green), grade III (blue), grades IV–V (red), grade VI or over (yellow).

The crag grid reference, altitude and aspect and, where relevant, an indication of the weather conditions likely to bring the crag into climbing condition, have also been included, as well as new conservation information about which crags have rare plants and should only be climbed when completely frozen or, in some cases, not at all.

For each route length, winter grade, star rating and, in some cases, rare plant rating (✤), indication of whether an area is a Site of Special Scientific Interest (SSSI) and date of first ascent, are given as well as a route description, pitch by pitch. There is a comprehensive list of first ascents towards the back of the guide, and the appendices give information on winter climbing and nature conservation, useful contacts, campsites and camping barns, climbing walls, procedure for mountain accidents and photography.

FIRST ASCENTS OR FIRST CLAIMS?

The 1997 edition of Cicerone's *Winter Climbs in the Lake District* for the first time included a 'first ascents' list or, as was suggested at the time, a 'first claims' list.

Prior to the Great War routes were generally well recorded and where relevant these have been incorporated into the guide, along with contemporary accounts which we hope will be of interest. Early climbers were more concerned with reaching the top of the crag alive than the ethical style of the ascent. Combined tactics when a helpful shoulder was regularly used were the norm and, unremarkably, Collie cut his step in the rock. Some recorded historic ascents while climbed in full winter conditions often recount chipping and removing all traces of snow and ice from holds so that they could be used as rock holds.

Many of the early ascents that have been recorded are very likely to have been climbed in such style using combined tactics and unhampered by the ethical worries of a modern ascent. As such a post-war repeat may well be the first free winter ascent. Those wanting to learn more about the achievements of the early winter

Jack Boniface follows Engineer's Chimney, Gable Crag (photo: Paddy Cave)

climbing pioneers of the Lake District are directed to articles in recent FRCC journals describing their fascinating pioneering activities.

Between the two world wars, fewer ascents are mentioned and those undertaken during and in the years after World War II are very poorly recorded indeed. In the main this was probably because there was no winter climbing guidebook and therefore no tradition of recording routes. In addition there was the feeling common to the Lake District that everything had been done before. The memories of a number of the older climbers, to whom we are profoundly grateful (but will not name here to avoid embarrassment), have been tested in an attempt to fill in the rather large gaps in knowledge of this era, but there is no doubt that many blanks remain.

The ascents of the last three decades or so are generally more reliably documented. As the conditions and style of historic ascents can no longer be verified we have had to be cautious and only those known to have been climbed in true winter conditions have been included.

The updated 'first ascents' list has been included towards the back of this guide for your interest and amusement, but it still is, and will probably always be, really a 'first claims' list.

SOUTH LAKES

Gwynne's Chimney (climber: Dave Birkett; photo: Mark 'Ed' Edwards)

LAKE DISTRICT WINTER CLIMBS

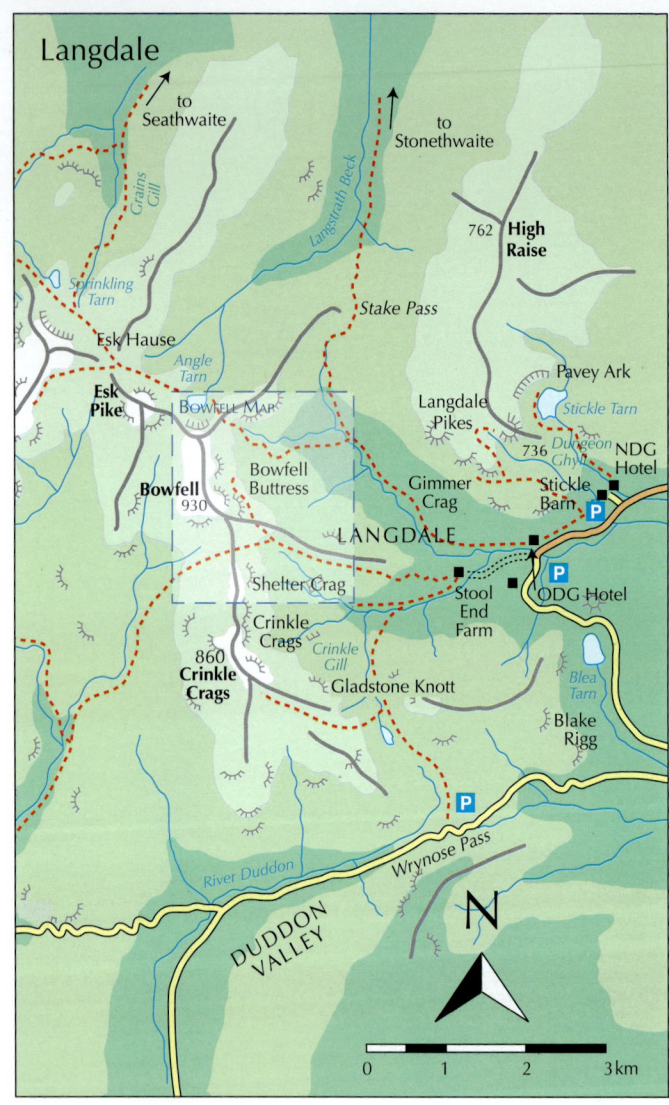

LANGDALE

Ease of access makes Langdale one of the most popular valleys in the Lake District, both in summer and winter. Bowfell in particular, one of the most accessible mountain crags in the district, has many modern mixed routes and more traditional gullies, and, after a sustained period of cold easterly winds, the seeping wall of *Crinkle Gill* can freeze to form some excellent icefalls. In such conditions, the other gills too provide good routes.

The head of Langdale is split into two branches separated by the Band, a ridge running down from Bowfell which provides an excellent path to the summit. The left (southerly) branch is known as Oxendale and heads up to Crinkle Crags, while Mickleden, the northern branch, leads to the Bowfell Crags and Angle Tarn.

The climbs are described in a clockwise direction starting in the south with Blake Rigg above Blea Tarn, then heading round into Oxendale and onto Bowfell, before returning eastwards along the northern side of the valley.

Blake Rigg

NY 287 040   *A<small>LTITUDE</small> 350<small>M</small>*   *E<small>AST FACING</small>*

This large broken crag above Blea Tarn, between Great and Little Langdale, has only one recorded route to date. Start from the car parking area on the road, if you've been able to drive up that is (it's less steep from Little Langdale side), and follow a path to the south of the tarn. Strike up the fellside, aiming for the right side of the crag.

Blake Rigg Icefall   **100m III 1996**
A watercourse falls down slabs on the right-hand side of the crag. The route steepens as you get higher. A harder variation up the corner leading out left from near the start may be possible but has yet to be caught in condition.

O<small>XENDALE</small>

The following routes are found in Oxendale, the left-hand branch at the head of the Langdale valley.

LAKE DISTRICT WINTER CLIMBS

It is best to park in the National Trust car park at the Old Dungeon Ghyll Hotel. Return to the road and take the path through Stool End Farm and along the side of the beck. If heading for *Browney Gill*, cross at the first bridge. For most other routes, continue on the north (right) bank to a second bridge over Buscoe Sike which flows into *Crinkle Gill* at this point. From here many of the climbs can be reached. At this confluence the right fork of the stream leads to the obvious fall of *Whorneyside Force*. (Although the latter is sometimes referred to as *Hell Gill*, that name is properly reserved for the deep ravine on the right, a few hundred metres further upstream from the main waterfall – this can be readily combined to provide an excellent finish to the main fall). For *Isaac Gill* cross the bridge, then traverse south across *Crinkle Gill*, before contouring round the hillside into the gill. It can also be reached by following *Browney Gill* from its confluence with *Crinkle Gill*. (When approaching from this direction, *Isaac Gill* is the first stream encountered flowing in from the right). The ice routes adorning the walls of *Crinkle Gill*, meanwhile, may be found in a ravine well upstream.

Great Knott

NY 259 043

This craggy hill on the south side of Oxendale is bound on its east by *Browney Gill*, a branch of which curves round to the south side. *Isaac Gill* is to the north of *Great Knott*.

Browney Gill ❧

NY 261 040   ALTITUDE 620M   SOUTH AND EAST FACING

This stream runs up from Oxendale to Red Tarn between Pike o'Blisco and Cold Pike. Take the path from Stool End Farm, cross the stream at the bridge and head up towards Red Tarn. Before reaching the tarn, contour rightwards across the hillside into the right-hand branch of the gill.

Browney Gill   300m II/III 2003

A 15m Grade II pitch is climbed, before a stream coming in from the left is followed; this has several short icefalls at about Grade II (2003). Continuing up the right fork, a steep rock wall on its right side drops down from Great Knott and contains several steep pitches. The right fork of the gill itself ends in a final pitch at the top of the rocks. To its right, and close into the steep rock wall, is an icy, mossy runnel (20m, III, 2003).

Three icefalls about 25m long form down the rocks themselves. Only the right-hand one has been climbed (IV, 2003). It has a steep start and finish, with easier ground in the middle.

Isaac Gill is the first gill flowing into *Browney Gill*, upstream of its confluence with *Crinkle Gill*.

Isaac Gill 250m II/III 1993 ❄
Rising to Gladstone Knott in a series of short ice pitches (I/II) the main pitch (II/III) is met halfway. A steeper pitch, with a left-hand start up a slanting groove, is also possible (IV+). A good approach to routes on *Gladstone Knott*.

Whorneyside Force 70m II/III ***
This frozen waterfall can be clearly seen on the approach up the right bank of Oxendale Beck. The fall is climbed in three steps. From above a large pool, the first icefall leads to a recess on the right and a peg belay (30m). The wide middle fall can be climbed on the left, right or centre depending on conditions, preference and crowds. The large pool at the top, which will hopefully be frozen, is furnished with a large flat rock round which a comforting belay may be taken (25m). The final shorter pitch starts from the back of the pool (15m).

Hell Gill 300m III/IV ❄❄
From the top of *Whorneyside Gill*, *Hell Gill* is found further upstream on the right. Go through the narrow, deep ravine, passing several pools and small falls, to reach the final steep fall. If formed (a rarity) climb it direct (IV). The right-hand exit, up a steep weeping mossy corner/groove, is more reliable (III, 1996).

Gladstone Knott

NY 256 046   Altitude 600m   *East facing*

Reached by following *Isaac Gill*, or the ridge between *Isaac Gill* and *Crinkle Gill*, this small vegetated outcrop is found on the left, above a level shoulder on the hillside. The right-hand (east) side of the Knott contains a compact buttress possessing five distinctive chimneys. To their left the ground is more broken, offering several

Lake District Winter Climbs

Gladstone Knott and Crinkle Crags in fine winter condition (photo: Al Phizacklea)

easy mixed routes, with *Zero Gully* being the wide easy-angled snow gully to the left of the crag – this makes a good **descent**.

Zero Gully   80m I 1996
Climb the broad gully defining the left side of the crag.

Left Corner   50m I 1996
A shallow corner-line runs up the crag about 10m right of *Zero Gully*.

Y Route One   50m I 1996
Takes the left-hand branch of the inverted Y-shaped recess just left of the main compact buttress over several ice bulges.

Y Route Two   50m I 1996
The right-hand branch of the inverted Y. Start on the left-hand side of the buttress at the bottom of the gully. The gully at the top is independent of *Y Route One*.

First Chimney   40m II 1996
The chimneys are numbered from left to right – scamper up the obvious gully on the left side of the main buttress.

Second Chimney   40m III * 1996
The first of the three gullies on the right of the main buttress has a tricky exit.

Third Chimney 30m II/III * 1996
The middle of the trio slants from left to right.

Fourth Chimney 30m IV (5) ** 1996
The deepest and hardest of the chimneys. A steep wall leads up into the chimney. Inside the chimney, face outwards and use small ledges to go directly up to a chockstone at the top of the chimney. It is possible to exit here, up easy turf on the left, or continue up the chimney for a further 15m.

Fifth Chimney 30m III ** 1996
Right of the buttress is a steep wall, then an iced corner. Climb the ice, stepping left near the top where the corner narrows.

Crinkle Gill

NY 257 049 ALTITUDE 400M *NORTH FACING*

The main gill gets more interesting with height. There are three main variations near the top. **Left-Hand Fork** (II/III) provides the longest section of ice, with several short pitches. **Central Icefall Direct** (III/IV) gives a good 40m pitch, while the steeper **Chimney Runnel** to the right is IV/V.

A few hundred metres above the confluence with *Hell Gill*, the gill begins to cut into the steep crag forming a 30m north-facing wall. Fed from the hillside above, continual seepage produces steep ice.

The Wrinkled Crinkle 25m IV/V (4) 1984
Slightly downstream from the 30m wall is a small crag. *The Wrinkled Crinkle* is the first ice streak to be reached on the left of the crag. Less reliable than the other routes.

About 12m above the bed of the gill is a large bay to the right of the crag. The next route climbs the centre of this.

Crinkle Cut 50m III 1981
Climb into the bay on a steep pitch of ice – easier options are available. Climb the back of the bay to an awkward exit up the wall forming the left corner.

Further up the gill is a long 30m vegetated wall. This can give some excellent ice pitches. *Whiteout* at the right end is recognisable by its conspicuous 'chandelle'.

Wight-Out 35m VI (6) 1986
The second ice smear left of *Whiteout*. Best done by keeping to the left edge and trending leftwards at the top. It forms less often than the other routes here.

Ray of Sunshine 30m V (6) 1986
The ice smear left of *Whiteout* is thicker in its lower section. Climb this to awkward moves at 10m, then thinner ice above, to an exit on turf. Difficult and poorly protected.

Whiteout 30m V (5) * 1986
The obvious 'chandelle' of ice at the right end of the wall. This, the most substantial of the icefalls, can be thin and poorly protected in the lower half. Take the 'chandelle' direct; protection depends on the quality of the ice.

Great Cove the most southerly cove at the head of *Crinkle Gill* contains several easy gullies, small buttresses and grooves, all of which offer short winter climbs. A few examples of the many are described. They're worth doing if you can locate them.

Long Walk 50m IV (4) 2005
When approaching up **Crinkle Gill**, a buttress (NY 251 046) with two chimney/grooves on its left side is clearly visible to the left of the prominent col which has Long Top to its north-west (right). Easy snow leads to the base of the right-hand groove.
1   25m (3). Climb the vegetated corner/groove which steepens at about 20m. Move onto a ledge on the left and then up a short groove to a ledge and large flake belay.
2   25m (4). Climb back right onto a ledge and into the base of the chimney. Struggle up this to a spike belay on the left-hand side.

The buttress to the right is a very pleasant IV.

Curving Ridge 150m III (4) 2007
The base of this north-west facing route is at approximately 650m metres (NY 252 047). Climb the obvious curving ridge line over steps and slabby corners.

At the north side of the cove is

Crinkle Picker 150m IV (5) 2007
Climb the arete of the buttress on the right-hand side of the gully to the right of Terrace Crag. Start at NY 251 049. After a saddle at the top of the first ridge

section, make a couple of steep moves through a corner before continuing up the buttress.

Shelter Crags

NY 251 055   ALTITUDE 700M   *EAST FACING*

This neglected crag is found in the most northerly of the Crinkle Crag coves, just south of the Three Tarns. The crag is split by *Central Chimney,* which cuts back into its southern section. This is the steeper part of the crag and contains several ice lines which are clearly visible when walking up the Band. *Shelter Corner* lies toward the left of the buttress, whilst *Shelter Icefall* climbs a chimney-fault filled (one hopes) by an obvious icefall. The right-hand section of the crag is a continuous vegetated wall which curves round and up the hillside. *Thirty Nine Steps* starts where the wall turns uphill into a snow gully and follows an eponymous series of pleasant steps.

Follow the Band (as for Bowfell) to where the path levels out, then strike west across the fell and descend to cross Buscoe Sike before entering the combe. Alternatively, cross the bridge over Buscoe Sike at its confluence with *Crinkle Gill* and head up the ridge on the left bank of Buscoe Sike before trending left to the same point. **Descent** is possible down snow slopes at either end of the crag, though to the left is generally quickest. The routes are described from left to right.

Sheltered Accommodation   40m II 2003
Well to the left of the corner taken by *Shelter Corner* is an easy-angled turfy buttress at the left-hand side of the crag overlooking the descent. Climb this.

Shelter Corner   70m II/III ** 1996
The fine turf corner at the left-hand end of the crag can form some easy-angled ice.
1   30m. Start right of the corner, climb over ledges of iced turf to the base of the corner.
2   40m. It is possible to climb the open corner by many subtle variations.

Shelter Stone   50m VII (8) 2010
About 5m right of *Shelter Corner* a turfy line leads from just above a large block lying out from the base of the crag to a diamond-shaped block in the steeper wall with a groove above on its left.

LAKE DISTRICT WINTER CLIMBS

Shelter Crags

1. Sheltered Accommodation — II
2. Shelter Corner — II/III
3. Shelter Stone — VII
4. Bus Shelter — IV
5. The Big Issue — IV
6. Shelter Icefall — IV
7. Gimme Shelter — V
8. Shelter Ridge — III
9. Central Chimney — III
10. 'A' Gully — III
11. 'B' Gully — II
12. Anderson — III
13. Morrison — IV
14. Air Raid Shelter — IV
15. Thirty Nine Steps — II
16. Gully Icefall — II

SHELTER CRAGS

The easy turf runnel leads to the base of the block. Traverse right under the block to a wide crack and make difficult and strenuous moves to an awkward exit leading to a cramped resting place under an overhang. A traverse left round a bulge leads to the groove and pleasant climbing to the top.

Bus Shelter   60m IV (5) * 2003
About 10m below the turfy start of *Shelter Corner* is a rectangular block lying against the crag.
1   40m (5). Start 5m left of the block and climb up a steep crack which allows a turfy runnel to be reached. Follow this up progressively steeper turf to a steep V-groove and climb this with difficulty to a ledge and block belay on the left.
2   20m (3). Climb the short ramp and mixed ground above to finish.

The Big Issue   65m IV (5) *** 2003
This climbs the next groove to the right. Start 5m down (right) from the rectangular block lying against the crag.
1   45m (5). Climb a steep crack (there is a flake to its right near the bottom) to reach a turfy ledge (this ledge may also be reached from the top of the block by a 2m traverse right). Follow grooves, then make an awkward step left into the main groove. Follow this to its top, then make delicate moves right across the top of a slab to easier ground and a block belay at a ledge 10m higher.
2   20m (3). Climb the turf ramp at the right side of the ledge.

Shelter Icefall   65m IV (4) *** 1996
A prominent icefall in the narrow chimney-fault to the right. It is steepest in its lower section.
1   50m (4). Climb the iced-choked chimney. A stubborn bulge with a step left at about 10m proves to be the crux. Above, the ice, though steep, is generally thicker and leads to a large block-covered ledge.
2   15m (4). From the back of the ledge continue up a steep iced corner, moving right near the top.

Gimme Shelter   55m V (5) 2010
The obvious right trending ramp line to the right of *Shelter Icefall*, which leads to *Shelter Ridge*.
1   45m (5). Start 3m right of the chimney-fault of *Shelter Icefall* and follow the ramp delicately rightwards to join *Shelter Ridge*. Follow this left to a thread belay after passing a couple of steps.
2   10m (3). Climb the groove above to the top.

Brian Davison edging his way to shelter, on Gimme Shelter, Shelter Crag (photo: Nick Wharton)

Shelter Ridge 55m III (4) 2003

The right-hand side of the buttress forms a ridge overlooking *Central Chimney* at a point where it narrows.
1   15m (4). Climb up small ledges to blocks at the end of a ramp-line on the left side of the ridge.
2   25m (3). Go easily along the ramp, with a couple of small steps, to belay to the right of the block-covered ledge near the top of *Shelter Icefall* pitch 1.
3   15m (4). Climb the final iced corner of *Shelter Icefall*.

Central Chimney 80m III (3) * 1996

The obvious central gully cutting back left into the crag.
1   40m (2). Easy slopes lead to where the walls of the gully/chimney close: continue to belay at the back of a cave.
2   40m (3). Make awkward moves out right onto steep ice (peg) and gain easier-angled snow and ice to finish.

Central Chimney Left-Hand Finish 80m IV (5) 2003

1   40m (2). Follow *Central Chimney* pitch 1.
2   30m (5). Climb to the peg at the overhang (where the standard route goes right up the wall). Make an awkward step left onto the left wall of the chimney,

then a long step, past two very loose blocks, to a ledge on the left wall of the chimney. Climb a wide crack at the left end of this ledge to a sloping shelf on the right. Go across this and back into the chimney, with an awkward move round a rib to gain a ledge.

3   10m (5). Climb the recess at the back of the ledge, starting up the right crack and transferring to the left crack at half-height.

Right of *Central Chimney*, the crag has a gully wall containing *A and B Gullies* and a larger front face with a well-defined ledge at its foot.

A Gully   60m III 1996
From the lower part of *Central Chimney*, where the walls start to close together, climb the left-hand of the two shallow gullies leading up the wall.

B Gully   60m II 1996
The shallower right-hand gully has a small rock step at half-height.

Anderson   70m III (4) 2003
The first feature at the left end of the front face is a left-slanting corner. Climb this to grass, then climb rightwards to dubious spikes and up to a stance. Climb easily leftwards, then take a steep little wall rightwards to the finishing corner.

Morrison   70m IV (4) 2003
In the middle of the front face is a slim left-facing groove with a good spike at 3m. Climb the groove to ledges, then traverse 2m left and climb another groove to a stance. Easier grooves and gullies lead to the top.

Air Raid Shelter   70m IV (4) 2010
About 10m right of *Morrison* and a similar distance left of *Thirty Nine Steps* is a left-facing corner part way up the crag.

1   40m (4). Start at a spike at 2m and climb up into the shallow corner and follow it to a snow bay: belay on the right.
2   30m. Follow the continuation of the line through easier rocky ground at the back of the snow bay.

Where the ledge ends and the wall curves up into a wide gully/snow slope is an easy series of icy steps on the left side of the gully – this is **Thirty Nine Steps** (II, 2003). Near the top of the snow gully is another easy snow gully with the short stepped **Gully Icefall** (II, 1996).

Lake District Winter Climbs

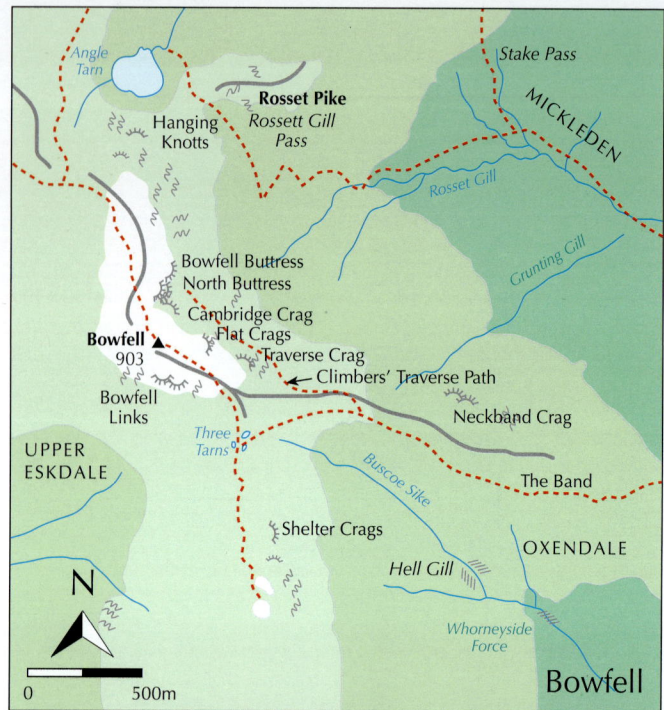

BOWFELL

NY 245 065   Altitude 902m

The jewel in the crown of Langdale winter climbing, with the highest climbs in the dale. Many fine mixed climbs can be found on the buttresses overlooking the Mickleden branch of the valley, whilst numerous short gullies cleave the remote Bowfell Links overlooking the head of Eskdale.

Bowfell Buttress and neighbouring crags are usually reached via Stool End Farm and the Band. Neckband Crag is low down on the north-east side of the Band, where the path starts to level – a vague path leading off to the right will take you there. Continuing up the Band, a narrow path, the Climbers' Traverse, leads off to the right at a point where the main ridge from Bowfell comes down to the path. The Climbers' Traverse itself leads to the main Bowfell crags, Traverse Crag, Flat Crags, Cambridge Crag, North Buttress and Bowfell Buttress. These crags can also be reached by taking the Mickleden path to part way up Rossett Gill before striking up to the base of the crags. This is a better approach in deep snow and also allows you to view the climbs en route. For Bowfell Links continue along the Band to the col and the Three Tarns. From the tarns follow the path up Bowfell for a few hundred metres before traversing west across scree and snow slopes to the Links.

The crags are described as approached along the Band, starting with Neckband Crag, followed by the isolated Bowfell Links and finally the main group of Bowfell crags facing north into Mickleden.

Neckband Crag

NY 256 062   ALTITUDE 550M   *NORTH FACING*

More correctly known as Earing Crag, this low-lying, steep and compact crag overlooking Grunting Gill is perhaps better suited to summer activity than that of winter, but has had some recent additions on its easier-angled right-hand side.

The routes are concentrated at the less steep right-hand side. The first route starts up the dirty wall right of the big mossy corner of *Virgo* and the wall to the left of the summer route *The Gizzard*.

Forked Tongue   40m VII (8) *** 2009
Originally climbed to the roof this route has now received a complete ascent. At the right-hand side of the crag climb the first turfed crack left of the corner for 6m (the summer line *The Gizzard*) to an obvious thread. Traverse left for 2m past a spike to beneath the steep wall and turfy crack (summer line of *Adam's Apple*). Strenuous climbing tackles the steep wall and turfy crack above to where it finishes beneath the main overhang. An awkward and exposed step left then leads into the top of the summer route *Tonsure* which is followed over a steep bulge and easier climbing via a right-trending ramp line to the belay.

Salvation   60m VI (8) * 2006
Start at the right-hand side of the crag at the lowest part of the buttress, right of the large corner and the arete of the summer line of *Flying Blind*, in a shallow bottomless groove (not the first corner to the left of the right-hand arete).
1   40m (8). Climb the bottomless groove on hairy hooks and tiny torques until after 5m it is possible to place a big nut runner on the left. Pull over the corner

to a semi-rest below a vegetated steep corner crack. Muscle up this with good protection and pull out to a resting spike. Move up and left to little ledges and left again to three cracks in the top wall. Climb the two that form a triangle, then follow these to the top to reach a large flake belay.

2   20m. Meander casually to the top.

The Neckband 70m IV (5) 2000

The slabby rib bounding the right-hand side of the crag is climbed with minor diversions.

1   35m. Climb the rib, passing a ledge and continue to a horizontal ledge. Traverse left to find a belay.
2   35m. Continue directly above by the easiest line.

Groove and Ramp 100m II 2000

Climb the shallow groove/gully bounding the right edge of the crag. A turfy start leads to snow and a finish up a narrow left-trending ramp on the left wall. A cornice may form at the top.

Bowfell Links

NY 246 063   *ALTITUDE 785M*   *SOUTH FACING*

This remote crag on the south side of Bowfell is split into numerous gullies and buttresses. The routes are often in condition, but a clear sunny day soon strips the crag of snow. As the routes are short it is possible to climb several in one visit. The routes are described from right to left as one approaches the crag from the Three Tarns. **Descent** is usually on the right of the crag, but is possible to the left.

No 1 Gully 50m I 1996

The **descent** gully – when there's snow in it. This is the first gully line: it bounds the right end of the crag.

Hidden Gully 50m I 1996

To the left of *No 1 Gully*, climb up easy-angled rocks until *Hidden Gully* is gained higher up the buttress. Climb the gully, passing a few short steps before the angle eases.

Chimney Crack   30m II 1996

The buttress left of *No. 1 Gully* has a prominent off-width crack splitting its left-hand side. Scramble over turf-covered rocks to its start and climb the crack, passing several helpful jammed blocks, to exit onto easier ground.

Pitch and Putt   50m II/III * 1996

The next gully to the left sometimes banks out. A large chockstone gives a 10m pitch before easy climbing gains the top. It is also possible to pass the chockstone by the easy buttress on the right before making a precarious step left, above the chockstone into the gully.

Two Under Par   70m II 1996

The next gully left again. Easy until the end, where a grassy corner on the left is taken.

Direct Finish   20m II 1996

Climb the icy corner at the top.

Tower Buttress   60m III (4) * 1996

The buttress to the left has a small col near its top. From the lowest rocks of the buttress, climb two short steep walls. Follow the crest of the buttress to the col. An easier line of turf on the left side of the crest is also possible. A short wall leads to easier ground.

Hole in One   70m III ** 1996

Left again the next gully provides a good struggle over two short chockstone pitches.

Twisting Turf   70m II * 1996

The buttress to the left. Climb an obvious turf-covered ramp up its centre. A steep wall is passed on its right near the top.

The next feature is the obvious gully with a chockstone at half-height, *Great Gully*.

Great Gully Wall   80m III 1996

A shallow groove/crack in the right wall of *Great Gully* leads to a position level with the chockstone in the gully. Continue up a shallow scoop in the buttress above.

Great Gully   100m IV (4) ** 1996

The chimney contains a large chockstone at half-height which forms a cave best climbed on its right.

Vulcan Buttress   45m II/III * 1996
The next buttress to the left has a distinctive inverted V at the top. Start up a mossy ramp slightly right of centre and follow the ramp leading onto easy turf-covered ledges. Finish up the inverted V.

The next large gully to the left (*Sunday Special*) has a cleft (*The Caddy*) running up the wall to its right and a shallow groove line (halfway up the right wall) starting just below the chockstone in the main gully.

The Caddy   70m II 1996
Climb the obvious narrow cleft on the right at the bottom of the large gully of *Sunday Special*.

Half Way Up   60m IV (4) 1996
A few metres below the chockstone in *Sunday Special* is a groove. Climb the groove to finish near *The Caddy*.

Sunday Special   70m III * 1996
Climb the chimney to the chockstone (crux at 15m). Easy climbing above leads to the top.

Green Buttress   80m II * 1996
The buttress left of *Sunday Special* has a steep start before easing off.

The remaining Bowfell crags all overlook Mickleden and can be approached from the Band via the Climbers' Traverse or from the Rossett Gill path.
 After crossing a steep scree-covered section of fellside, the Climbers' Traverse goes under some broken outcrops (Traverse Crag) to Flat Crags and the other buttresses of Bowfell.

Traverse Crag

NY 250 064   A*LTITUDE* 720*M*   E*AST-NORTH-EAST FACING*

The first outcrop passed on the Climbers' Traverse has a series of broken grooves and ramp-lines on its right-hand side and is ideal for winter climbing, although none of the routes are very long. The left side of the crag is marked by two easy gullies. **Left Gully** (70m, I, 2004) is a straightforward snow slope and a useful **descent**. To its right and close into the buttress is the more interesting *Buttress Gully*.

Buttress Gully   70m II 2004
The narrow gully tucked into the left side of the buttress. Follow this to a block and pass it via a snow runnel on the left. Above, follow easy turf to the left or, for a more challenging finish, follow the continuation of the chimney to the right.

The right side of the crag is marked by a pinnacle.

Into the Groove   65m VI (7) 2005
There are three obvious grooves towards the right side of the crag with a pinnacle to their right. This climb takes the leftmost of them and begins at a large chockstone.
1   15m (6). Climb awkwardly past the large chockstone, step left to a large block and continue up the blunt arete to a ledge below a wall at the foot of the groove.
2   50m (7). Difficult and poorly-protected moves up the wall lead to turf at the bottom of the V-groove. Exit this up and rightwards to a ledge and continue up a further series of grooves to the top.

Big Groove   65m V (6) 2005
The next and most prominently defined of the three, starts up a V-groove to the right.
1   15m (3). Climb the obvious V-groove to the right of the large chockstone-filled chimney/groove of *Into the Groove* and belay below twin grooves.
2   50m (6). Start up the left-hand of the two grooves, move into the right-hand groove and up to a ledge. Follow the groove above to another ledge and then yet another groove to a ledge. When you're bored with grooves, climb the final wall past a prominent thread runner to the top.

Band on the Run   70m IV (5) 2005
The right-hand groove is, by way of blessed contrast, almost more like a series of corners. A pinnacle marks its right side.
   Climb the corner where the pinnacle meets the broken groove on its left-hand side. From the top of the corner, cross the groove line and climb a short steep chimney. From the top of the chimney, climb the short wall on the left to a big grassy ledge. Climb the corner above and along another broad grassy ledge to join a wide gully. Climb up this and exit underneath a chockstone.

Chockstone Gully   50m II ** 1995
The gully round the corner to the right faces Flat Crags. Climb a vegetated groove followed by a chockstone to belay below another chockstone and cave. Finish through a hole at the back of the cave.

Flat Crags

NY 249 064   A<small>LTITUDE</small> *750*<small>M</small>   E<small>AST-NORTH-EAST FACING</small>

When approaching along the Climbers' Traverse, Flat Crags can be recognized by an obvious large bay in the middle of the crag and also by a leftward-sloping terrace that runs up beneath the main crag. The routes are described from right to left.

Conditionalist   50m VI (6) * 2009

At the right side of the crag the route follows the short steep corner and crack-line on the first pitch of the summer HVS *Hanging Corner*, but takes a different second pitch, more suited to winter. Immediately strenuous this route packs a lot in, with the technicalities low down.

1   30m (6). Start on top of the huge block. Climb the short steep corner to gain a crack in the slab above. Climb the rightwards-slanting crack on good hooks and exit onto a sloping ledge. Follow the faint continuation of the crack rightwards for about 3m then finish directly on turf. Trend up leftwards on easy ground towards the large terrace that splits this part of the crag. A flake belay is possible just below this.

2   20m (4). Directly across the terrace are three grooves, climb the turfy central groove. Exit this and belay on the Great Slab. Descent can be made down the Great Slab back onto the Climbers' Traverse.

Routes on the left-hand side of the crag are reached by following a ramp leftwards above the lower part of the crag.

BB Corner   40m VII (8) 2005

A winter version of the summer line which climbs a prominent mossy corner in the back of the large bay in the centre of the crag.

1   25m (7). Climb the corner right of the ramp-line start of *Crack Magic* to belay on a ledge.

2   15m (8). Continue up the corner passing an awkward bulge.

Crack Magic   60m VII 1999

A steep and technically demanding climb, following a line from the Climbers' Traverse to the sloping ramp and then up the main corner (the summer climb of *Flat Crags Corner*) in the centre of the large bay.

1   20m (5). Start 20m to the left of the junction between the ramp and the Climbers' Traverse. Climb the open corner to a gap in the rock, then move up

FLAT CRAGS

Mary Ann, Flat Crags
(climber: Chris Sterling; photo: Paddy Cave)

and right to a steep wall and bulging crack. Climb this to belay on the terrace in the centre of the bay.

2   20m (7). Step up onto a rightward-trending ramp leading into a steep corner. Climb this to an awkward step left onto a big ledge and belay.

3   20m (7). Another awkward step and a steep crack lead to a strenuous pull over some wedged blocks and the top.

Moon Shadow   55m VIII (7) 2011

At the top of the ramp past the obvious corner of *Crack Magic* a steep crack defines the point were the crag turns left.

1   25m (8). Pull up onto the right wall of the arete into the hanging crack, or alternatively start lower down and round the other side of the arete. The crack is initially thin but gets better with height. Strenuous climbing leads to a roof. Pull through this to the right and a sloping ledge. Continue up the corner then link turf ledges out left to a large ledge with a spike and flake belay (in-situ lower off).

2   30m (4). Climb the stepped corner up and left then continue up turfy grooves to easier ground.

Mary Ann   40m IV (5) 1999

The less steep left-hand side of the crag at the top of the sloping terrace has a small cave which lies to the left of a slabby bay of rock. Either follow the first pitch of *Crack Magic* to the bay, or climb more directly well to its left, or you can scramble to this point via the terrace. Start at a flake about 6m right of the cave.

The route follows the summer route in the lower half. Climb up right to a crack on the edge of a slab and follow it to below a band of overhangs. Move left under the overhangs and up into a grassy/snowy bay. From the top of this, move up to a short corner and make an awkward move up and right onto a block-covered ledge on the right. A further short corner leads to the top.

Summer Finish   IV (5) (2006)

Unsurprisingly follows the summer finish going directly leftwards rather than traversing rightwards near the top.

Cambridge Crag

NY 246 066   ALTITUDE 775M   NORTH-EAST FACING

The next crag in the group lies higher up the hillside than Flat Crags and to the north. A spring (the Waterspout) flows from the base of the crag and is a good landmark. The crag is home to many mixed routes but they do tend to catch the sun. They are described from left to right. The Great Slab runs up below the left side of the crag. Above this are a number of grooves that give enjoyable climbing around Grade III.

Professor   85m V (5) 2004
Locate the fourth obvious shallow bay to the left of, and about 50m uphill from, the Waterspout. Start on the right side
1   40m (5). A steep awkward bulge leads into a very prominent leftward-slanting, parallel-sided, shallow chimney. Follow this line to an awkward move at the top and then belay.
2   45m (3). Continue more easily up and leftwards, via an obvious V-groove and open gully. An iced-up slab and more mixed ground lead to the top.

Left-Hand Route   80m IV (5) 1986
Starting about 40m left of the Waterspout at the third groove, this climb stalks the summer route of *Borstal Buttress*.
1   35m (5). Assault the layback crack and groove to arrive, with luck, in a snow bay. Secure yourself behind a huge boulder.
2   45m (3). Batter your way up several short grooves to the top.

Rib and Groove   140m V (6) 2006
Start 10m left of the Waterspout at the foot of the crag in an open vegetated groove, *Right-Hand Route Direct Start*, just left of the ramp taken by *Right-Hand Route* and 30m right of *Professor*.
1   50m (5). Climb the groove for 5m and follow it as it trends back left and up to a recess with a steep back corner bounded on the left by a smooth wall. Climb the corner and pull out right passing through a bulge on the right with a dagger of rock in the back (good nut placement). Pass this and follow a snowy bay right to a short corner step and above to a broad snowy ledge and belay.
2   35m (6). Climb the corner on the left, mantle a turf step and balance up to hook thin moss and turf with a crack for protection, then pull over the top to snowy terraces. Traverse right for 25m passing behind a 'gendarme' to arrive at the belay of *Riboletto Groove*.

LAKE DISTRICT WINTER CLIMBS

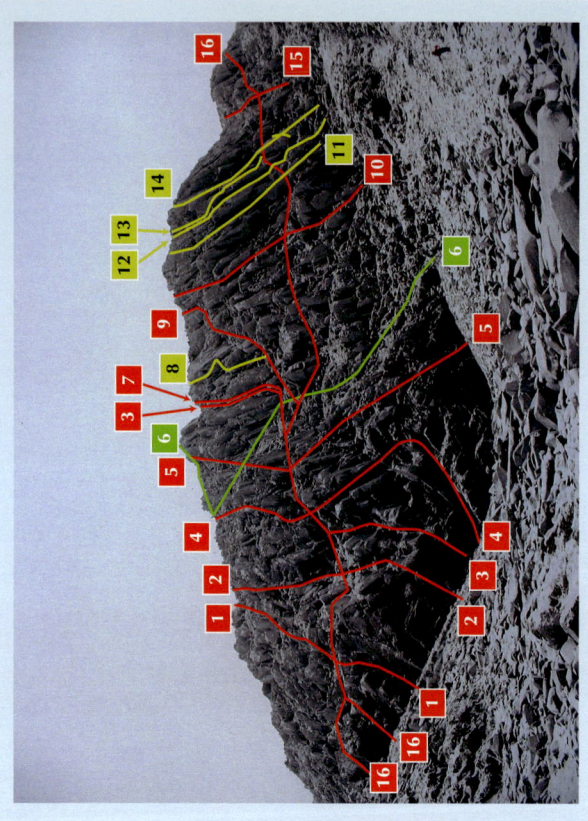

North Buttress and Cambridge Crag

1. Professor — V
2. Left-Hand Route — IV
3. Rib and Groove — V
4. Right-Hand Route — V
5. Misty Mountain Hop — IV
6. Cambridge Crag Climb II
7. Riboletto Groove
8. Fight or Flight — VI
9. No Way Out — IV
10. Siamese Chimneys — IV
11. The Gnomon — VII
12. Mindbender — VIII
13. The Gibli — VII
14. Soul Vacation — VIII
15. The Flying Gimp Trick — IV
16. Cambridge Girdle — IV

3   55m (6). Pitch 2 of *Riboletto Groove*: Climb the groove to the right of the arete, passing under the wedged block! Above this, the groove narrows to a chimney. Thrutch up this and make some hard moves to gain the turfy continuation groove. Step right and climb a short steep corner to gain easy ground.

Right-Hand Route   110m V (6) 1986

Starting at a broad slab about 10m left of the Waterspout, this climb roughly follows the line of the summer route *Cambridge Crag Climb* (CCC) (not to be confused with the winter line to the right of the crag with the same name).

1   35m (4). Climb the rightward-slanting slab to a thread. Continue diagonally right, around two aretes, to reach the foot of a stepped groove. From the top of the groove move back left to belay by another large groove.
2   20m (5). The groove above leads to a leftward-trending chimney which is followed onto a large arete. Climb this to a belay.
3   15m (6). The steep groove on the left is the crux, requiring one aid nut on the first ascent. A free ascent is unreported. This leads to easier ground.
4   40m (2). An easy gully on the left leads to the top.

Right-Hand Route – Direct Start   50m IV (5) 1991

The central groove used as the first pitch of *Rib and Groove* is followed for 35m to the bulge and a hard leftward finish. The belay at the top of pitch 2 on the ordinary route is gained by moving back right.

Misty Mountain Hop   120m IV (4) 2005

This climbs the broad buttress line to the left of the gully (*CCC*). Climb the ridge on the left side of the gully linking short corners and easier mixed steps to where *CCC* traverses left. Follow this and take any easy independent line to the summit.

Cambridge Crag Climb   75m II * 1979

This takes the shallow gully starting just right of the toe of the buttress. It should not be confused with the summer climb of the same name.

1   30m. Follow the shallow gully, keeping to the centre where it branches.
2   20m. From a block belay under the headwall, follow a leftward-sloping ramp to another large block.
3   25m. Pass the block on the right then go diagonally right across snow to finish up a short groove.

Riboletto Groove   95m V (6) 2006

Really an alternative finish to *Cambridge Crag Climb*, finishing up the steep turfy groove/chimney to the right of *Riboletto*.

1   40m (2). Follow *CCC* to belay at the headwall below a prominent arete, the summer route of *Riboletto*.
2   55m (6). Climb the groove to the right of the arete passing a large wedged block. Above this, the groove narrows to a chimney. Thrutch up this and make some hard moves to gain the turfy continuation groove. Step right and climb a short steep corner to gain easy ground.

Fight or Flight 60m VI (6) *** 2009

Yet another finish to *Cambridge Crag Climb* using the final pitch of the summer route *Swastika*, one of the highest finishing pitches in Langdale. Follow *CCC* to the big ledge below a tower. *Riboletto Groove* starts from the same ledge. Start up the big corner about 5m to the right of *Riboletto Groove*.
1   25m (6). Climb the bulging corner line moving right up a square cut niche at the top. Pull up to belay on a big ledge.
2   10m. Descend to the right down a short groove. Move around into a bay with a steep cracked wall on your left. Good spikes.
3   25m (6). Climb a crack between the cracked wall and the detached pinnacle on the left arete. Stand on the pinnacle (small wire possible above) and make a committing move rightwards to gain the crack. Teeter up the crack to better hooks and gear. Climb to the top using the crack above which eventually joins another crack coming in from the right.

No Way Out 130m IV (5) 2005

Fortunately, despite the name, there is a way using a groove in the headwall where *Cambridge Crag Climb* takes the easy leftward traverse.
1   40m (2). Start as for *CCC* and follow the shallow gully for 40m to spike and nut belays on the right side.
2   30m (3). Bear up and right and then traverse right under a prominent rock arete (summer route of *Riboletto*). Belay on a wall on the right.
3   30m (3). Continue up and right over a couple of steep walls to a belay just left of a large pinnacle.
4   30m (5). Climb a steep turfy groove to a terrace. Some trying moves reveal that there is a way out up the continuation groove.

CAMBRIDGE CRAG

Brian Davison in The Gibli (photo: Paddy Cave)

North Buttress

NY 246 066   Altitude 790m   *North-east facing*

North Buttress lies to the right of Cambridge Crag and at a slightly higher altitude. The left-hand side of the buttress has a number of short broken walls and ribs which extend down to Cambridge Crag.

To the right are three distinct groove lines: *The Gnomon*, *Mindbender* and *Soul Vacation*, the winter version of *Sword of Damocles*. The first route, *Siamese Chimneys*, starts on the north-facing wall on the left of the crag. The other routes take the right side of the buttress and more broken ground further right.

Siamese Chimneys   90m IV (5) 1986
The obvious chimney-line to the left of the prominent grooves is climbed to half-height where a second higher chimney is followed.
1   20m (4). Climb easily to the base of the chimney. Follow this to a large overhang where it is possible to move right and upwards to a ledge.
2   30m (5). Move right to the corner with a cleft on its left: use both these features to make upward progress to a ledge and move right to the bottom of the second chimney.
3   40m (3). The final chimney leads to a small headwall and the top.

The Gnomon   65m VII (8) *** 2006
To the right of *Siamese Chimneys* are three prominent groove systems: this climbs the leftmost groove. Easy scrambling leads to a spike belay at the bottom of the groove.
1   40m (8). Follow a crack in the corner up into a niche and protection. Step down and make a wild traverse left and climb a short wall to a ledge on the left rib. Make another committing swing right (old peg) to a groove and follow this to the top. Scramble up and belay below a tower.
2   25m. From the centre of the tower move up and right around to the top then follow cracks in the final wall to finish.

Mindbender   70m VIII (8) ** 2008
The central groove follows the summer E2.
1   20m (5). Climb the groove passing a large spike at half-height to a steep turfy finish on a ledge up and left at the base of the main groove of *The Gnomon*.
2   30m (8). Step round right into a groove and follow this rightwards. A ramp leads to a ledge below the main groove; follow this. The difficulties increase

with height. Have a breather on the ledge at the top then climb a crack at the back of the short corner. Above this belay in the bay above *The Gnomon*.

3   20m (4). Climb the gully above passing some loose blocks.

The Gibli   55m VII (7) 2012

From behind the large pinnacle on *Soul Vacation* this follows the short steep groove left of *Soul* then moves left across the wall to join the final gully of *Mindbender*.

1   (5). From a ledge below the pinnacle climb up and right of the pinnacle with an awkward blind crack giving one hard move to gain a block belay behind the pinnacle.
2   10m (7). Climb the left-hand V-groove to a shared belay with *Soul Vacation*. A blade peg in the shorter right-hand groove offers good protection.
3   15m (6). Move left across the cracked wall to a strenuous pull onto a ledge on the arete. Move up a groove to belay just right of the finishing chimney of *Mindbender*.
4   20m (4). Follow the chimney/gully as for *Mindbender*.

Soul Vacation   60m VIII (8) *** 2004

This, the right-hand of the three prominent grooves, follows the summer line of *Sword of Damocles*, an oft-eyed line that many failed to find in true winter condition over the past three decades. It is now safer without the hanging flake that gave the summer route its name. There is sufficient protection, although it can be strenuous to place.

1   25m. A crack leads rightwards into the base of the groove. Move up behind a pinnacle and continue up the groove to an awkward step right to gain a ledge at the edge of the buttress. Move up and traverse left across the groove to belay at the base of the main groove.
2   15m. The main pitch: climb the groove, passing a bulge on the left to a belay.
3   20m. Climb the flake-crack above. This proves strenuous but there's a rest at the end. Continue up the crack until it is possible to move right to easier ground near the top.

Fragile Existence   50m VII (8) * 2010

A winter version of the summer route *The Scabbard,* the winter variations from the summer route offer a more logical winter line. Start about 10m right of the right-hand groove line taken by *Soul Vacation*.

1   7m (5). Climb the crack up the shield as for the first pitch of *The Scabbard*. Cross the big ledge and belay.
2   15m (8). Starting 4m in from the left edge of the wall, climb up and rightwards into a corner, pull out right onto the face using a small hook. Climb directly up to a dubious looking blocky flake. Pull up and left to a positive scoop, then

Soul Vacation North Buttress Bowfell (climber: Campbell West; photo: Paddy Cave)

move up and rightwards using a very thin hook; a long move off, this gains a pinch constriction in the main diagonal fault which continues all the way up the crag. Climb leftwards up to a good belay ledge with a high thread.
3   28m (7). Climb up the fault to gain a large crack. Follow this almost to the top until a rising diagonal flake-crack runs up rightwards. Follow this with a footless swing around the arete onto the face of a slab. Climb straight up into a stepped turf groove. Easy ground leads to the top.

Scabbard   30m IV (5) 1987
To the right of the three grooves, climb steep ice and turf at the back of the bay to the right of the summer line of *The Scabbard* and left of the gully.

To the right of *Soul Vacation*, approximately 50m up the hill, the wall becomes easier angled and more broken.

The first two climbs start near the base of the same icy groove, on the left side of an easier-angled bay.

Skint and Single   40m VI (7) 2002
Start up a smaller groove immediately to the left of the more prominent corner-groove of *Die Another Day*. Climb the icy groove to a block and surmount this to a small grassy ledge. Delicately step left for a metre to a verglassed, overhanging groove (crux). Climb this and the broken groove above to the top.

Die Another Day   50m IV (6) 2003
Start in the same place as *Skint and Single*, but climb the more prominent corner-groove with an icicle at its bottom. From its top trend left up turf steps to a ledge which is about 5m below the left-hand of two overlaps. Step steeply up and right into a groove right of the left overlap and continue more easily to good belays.

Gimps to the Left of Them   50m IV (5) 2003
This line links up the two most obvious ice features on this part of the crag. A thin smear forms low down and this is gained by using turf from the right. Continue up the line of least resistance to the ice umbrella above, climb it and finish up a turfy corner.

The Flying Gimp Trick   50m IV (5) 2003
Climb the corner feature on the right-hand side of the crag, trending left up turfy cracks to finish. Alternatively move left on the obvious ledge at about 15m and follow the most distinct turf line back rightwards (at an easier grade).

Lake District Winter Climbs

North Buttress – Gimps Wall Area

1 Skint and Single   VI
2 Die Another Day   IV
3 Gimps to the Left of Them   IV
4 The Flying Gimp Trick   IV

Continuing up the hillside the wall steepens for the next 50m or so until it is split by an icy chimney with an awkwardly steep section about halfway (**Icy Chimney** 30m, III, 2004). Starting at the foot of the chimney is a ramp-line running up rightwards. This gives some excellent mixed climbing up a series of turfy holds and steep steps (**Ramp Line** 30m, II, 2004).

Cambridge Girdle   200m IV (4) 2006

A left-to-right traverse of Cambridge Crag and North Buttress. Starting at the left-hand side of Cambridge Crag an obvious rising traverse line is visible crossing both buttresses and going under the start of *Soul Vacation*. The true length is uncertain and no pitch lengths or grades are given as the route (bar the final 10m) was soloed.

A series of starts are possible: either begin up a short prominent right-facing corner-line to an easy shelf; or to the left of the corner and round an arete is a groove that leads to the same place; or from further up the Great Slab it is possible to walk easily onto the start of the traverse line. From the top of the corner go up and right and round an awkward step to easy snow. A rising traverse leads to a short descent into the gully of *Cambridge Crag Climb*. Cross this, followed by some difficult moves up to ledges at a higher level. Go round these to the bottom of *Soul Vacation*. Climb down slightly and round an arete to the base of a groove. Traverse across the base of the wall. As it was in the beginning, so it is in the end with a choice of finishes. Either walk easily right onto the hillside, or finish up the obvious corner above *The Flying Gimp Trick*, or continue traversing up a ramp-line until it is possible to climb a stepped groove about 3m before *Icy Chimney*. At last, the day is done.

Bowfell Buttress

NY 245 066   Altitude 750m   *North-east facing*

Bowfell Buttress, the large crag to the right of North Buttress, separated from the other crags by a wide scree run, is the most extensive of the buttresses in this area. It is bordered by *South* and *North Gullies* on its left and right sides respectively. This impressive buttress is tilted slightly off-vertical and is seamed by corners and grooves. It has the highest concentration of quality winter routes in the valley.

South Gully   80m I 1870

This is the broad slope to the left of the buttress and is of considerable historic interest as the first recorded winter climb in Britain. It can be used as a **descent**, but is often heavily corniced and terminates in a boulder field below: not perhaps the best place to practise glissading!

Crack and Chimney   80m IV (5) 2012

About 30m below *South Gully* is a mossy ramp-like corner bounded on its right by a short protruding buttress with a chimney on its right side. The route takes the chimney to a snow bay and any of several groove lines above.

1   40m (5). To the right of the protruding buttress 30m below *South Gully* climb an awkward off-width crack in the corner to gain a blocky chimney. Move up a groove above to the snow bay.
2   40m (3). Climb any of at least four groove lines above, the right-hand one being the easiest.

Plaque Route   100m IV (4) * 1986

This starts near a large boulder that may be seen poking out of the snow at the left side of the crag and follows the left edge of the buttress. The route lacks any real line; just progress upwards over grassy ledges trending slightly leftwards. The final section contains some loose rock so it may be advisable to move further left onto more vegetated ground.

Sinister Slabs   115m VI (6) * 1986

This follows a similar line to the summer route and holds snow well. Start by a rib 5m to the left of the bottom of the crag.

1   40m (4). Follow the rib on the right, past a block at 10m, and move left to a ledge below a slanting chimney. Follow the chimney to a corner and belay.
2   30m (6). A leftwards-slanting slab leads past blocks to a rib. Continue to a groove on the right and a tricky exit onto a belay ledge.
3   45m (3). The chimney above gives easy climbing up to continuation gullies which in turn lead to short walls and the top.

Rubicon Groove   105m VII (8) 2011

A winter version of the summer line starting up the prominent groove to the left of *Bowfell Buttress* in the lower portion of the cliff and following its continuation in the upper half.

1   40m. Start as for *Bowfell Buttress* but step up and left as soon as possible into the obvious turfy line leading to a bulge and groove. Make a few very thin moves to enter the groove directly. Easier but sustained climbing up the groove leads to the first large grass ledge and a poor belay.

Bowfell Buttress

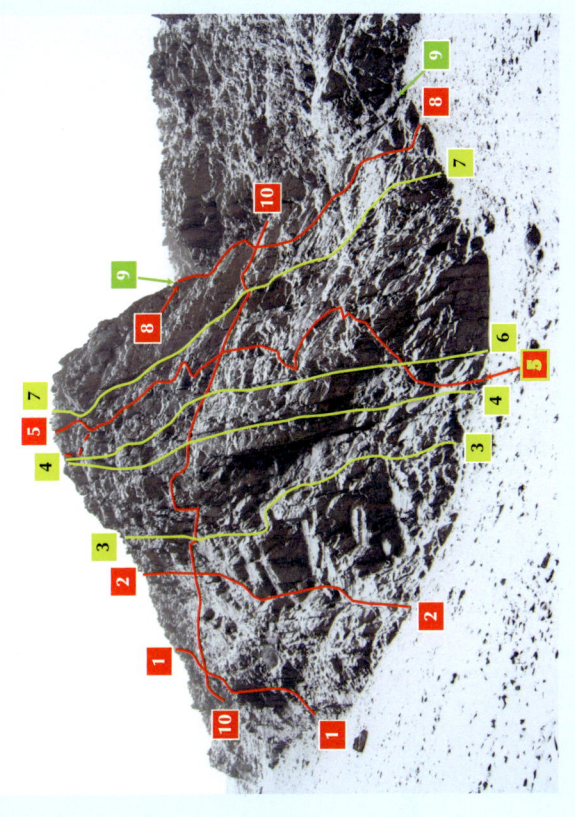

1	Crack and Chimney	IV
2	Plaque Route	IV
3	Sinister Slabs	VI
4	Rubicon Groove	VII
5	Bowfell Buttress	V
6	Central Route	VI
7	Bowstring	VI
8	Ledge and Groove	IV
9	North Gully	I/II
10	Bowfell Girdle	V

2   25m. Step right slightly and climb the wall on turf blobs to a ledge. Climb into the shallow recess directly above then make bold and awkward moves to the next grass ledge and good belay (old in-situ cam).
3   20m. Take the obvious corner/recess above, step right onto a ledge where it becomes steep and blind. Move right again to a left facing groove. Climb this awkwardly then step back left into the main line and belay on a big ledge.
4   20m. Climb the steep left facing groove above past an awkward high step. The groove is about 3m left of *Bowfell Buttress*. Finish as for *Bowfell Buttress*.

Bowfell Buttress   110m V (6) *** 1937

One of the technical test pieces of the Lakes and a futuristic achievement at the time of its first ascent which was long overlooked. Fine mixed climbing leads up the nose of the buttress. Start 3m left of the edge of the smooth wall forming the base of the crag, at a ridge in an open left-facing corner system.
1   25m (4). Follow the ridge and then a clean chimney on the right leading to a ledge on the right.
2   30m (5). Move diagonally left across slabs to a slim right-facing groove/chimney system, which leads to ledges and a large snow terrace.
3   30m (6). The 5m iced crack above on the right leads with difficulty to a ledge. Move up and leftwards, over a tricky slab (difficult if poorly iced) to a pinnacle. An exposed traverse left leads to a groove and chimney.
4   25m (5). Follow the groove/chimney to a wall. Either move left to easy ground, or, if you haven't had enough, step right and follow the icy groove to the top.

Central Route   90m VI (8) * 1991

A direct and harder line to the left of *Bowfell Buttress* which starts just to its right and crosses it after 15m.
1   15m. Start at a broken groove 5m to the right of *Bowfell Buttress* and climb the groove and the slabby walls to the top of the rib; belay as for *Bowfell Buttress* pitch 1.
2   15m. Above and left is a steep chimney, entered with difficulty and followed strenuously to a tricky exit right onto the arete near the top.
3   20m. Climb up leftwards to a large block and belay.
4   40m. Surmount the block somehow and move up a shallow groove to a rib and slab. Follow this leftwards to easier ground.

Bowstring   110m VI (6) ** 2011

A harder companion route to *Bowfell Buttress* running parallel to it on the right. It is possible to switch between the two routes at several of the belay ledges if the congestion becomes too much for you. Start about 20m right of *Bowfell Buttress* in a snow bay directly below a prominent right facing corner at one-third height.

1   45m (6). Climb directly to the prominent corner and up this to a snowy ledge. Step left into a square recess (right of the belay on pitch 2 of *Bowfell Buttress*). Climb a flake-crack up the right wall of the recess to a ledge and belay.

2   45m (6). Climb the groove on the left diagonally leftwards to join *Bowfell Buttress* at the pinnacle and then climb straight up a steep groove offering several reassuring chockstones. Belay on a ledge just below a groove; the right-hand groove exit of *Bowfell Buttress*.

3   20m (5). Follow the groove to the top.

Ledge and Groove   115m IV (5) * 1991

This attempt to follow the right edge of the buttress tends to wander and is escapable to the right at several points. Start 5m left of *North Gully*.

1   20m (3). Climb the wall to a large snowy ledge and continue to a second ledge.

2   25m (4). From the right-hand side of the ledge follow a series of steps to an overhang. This is bypassed by a traverse, left then back right, to a belay on the edge of the buttress.

3   30m (5). Follow grooves on the right to a chimney that leads to a ledge.

4   40m (5). Start up a groove on the right, then continue up short walls trending leftwards to the top.

North Gully   125m I/II * 1910

The gully bounding the right side of the crag. A steep pitch at the bottom leads to straightforward snow to the top. The steep initial pitch can be avoided by interesting climbing up broken ground on the right.

The continuation of *North Gully* cuts off the buttress from the hillside above and then drops down into **South Gully** (I). It is **not recommended as a descent** as any error in route finding will lead parties onto steep ground.

The next four routes climb the steep left wall of North Gully.

North Wall   70m VI (7) * 2010

Start at the obvious corner on the left wall, as for *Right Wall Eliminate* (winter) then traverse left from the ledge and follow a line approximately 5m right of the left-hand arete.

1   20m (4). Climb the obvious left-facing corner on the gully wall that is formed by a small subsidiary buttress. Spike belay at the top.

2   25m (7). Climb a few metres back down the first pitch until level with the bottom of an obvious spike about 4m to the left out on the wall. Traverse the wall horizontally leftwards to the base of the spike (dubious!). Climb carefully on top of the spike and the short crack above, mantle up and left onto a turfy ledge. Above the right end of the ledge climb the thin crack-line that splits the wall and enters a hanging corner (crux), continue up this to the top of the corner and pull up onto a big ledge and crack belay.

3   25m (5). Climb the crack above the belay aiming for a short wall above with a crack running up its right side. Using the crack make an awkward step left up onto a small sloping ledge, step left to reach turf above and pull up onto a big ledge. Move across this slightly to the right to a big free-standing spike. Climb onto the spike and straight up the blocky wall above. Pull up onto another big ledge and climb the short left-facing corner with a flake at its base. Haul out of this onto the summit.

Right Wall Eliminate   65m V (6) 1994

A climb based on the summer line of the same name, starting at an obvious corner on the left about 10m above the steep pitch of *North Gully*.

1   20m (4). Follow the corner to a ledge and spike belay.

2   25m (6). Move right a few metres, past a crack in the wall to where the angle eases and follow turf placements to the right-hand end of a ramp-line. Traverse left up the ramp until below an inverted bottomless V-groove. Climb this to a large ledge and spike belay.

3   20m (5). Climb a turf-filled groove to the right of the belay to a small roof at 10m. Here the groove splits into two grooves. Follow the left one.

Corner and Rib   45m IV (4) 1995

Start at a wide shallow corner near the top left side of the *North Gully*, about 40m past the steep first pitch.

1   20m. The corner is followed until it becomes an obvious V-groove after about 20m.

2   25m. Move right onto the rib and follow it more easily to the top.

The White Cross   50m III 2009

The route starts about 40m above the steep pitch of *North Gully*. The start is 5m up the gully from *Corner and Rib* and runs parallel and 2m to the right of the rib. Climb a turf ramp that leaves the gully bed up the left wall. Enter the groove and follow this feature to the top of the crag with the rib always just to the left.

Angle Tarn and Hanging Knotts

Bowfell Girdle   170m V (6) 2006
A girdle traverse of the buttress starting from the large grassy shelf on the left and finishing at *North Gully* on the right. Best preceded via the *Cambridge Girdle* – especially if you are feeling a bit crabby.

1   50m. Traverse easily to the large grassy shelf on the left of the buttress.
2   20m. (3) Downclimb about 5m to a narrow ledge and move right to belay a few metres short of a shallow corner.
3   50m (6). A wandering pitch. Traverse right to the corner, then downclimb a few metres until it is possible to go round the base of an arete into a groove. Climb the groove for 5m to a ledge on the right. Move to a wide crack at the end of the ledge and downclimb this awkwardly to a narrow ledge. Shuffle along the ledge to the start of another large ledge running across the buttress.
4   50m. (4). Cross the ledge. This can be continued with a short piece of downclimbing into *North Gully* between the two steep chockstone pitches. Or, as on the first ascent, about 10m before the gully is reached, a wide crack in the wall just right of the square recess of *Bowstring* is climbed to a higher ledge. This is then followed easily into *North Gully* above the second chockstone pitch. Either finish up the gully, or, if you have a plentiful supply of energy and provisions, keep on traversing to link in with the *Great End Girdle* in a grande enchainement.

Located about 200m above a major right-hand bend halfway up the Rossett Gill path the final route starts about 200m below *Bowfell Buttress* where an obvious drainage line spills over slabs.

Gimpsuit Fall   30m III/IV 2004
Head for the obvious ice pillar. Climb up the slab and finish direct up the short steep pillar of ice at the top.

Angle Tarn and Hanging Knotts

NY 243 075   Altitude 620m   North facing

The area around Angle Tarn contains much broken rock and short buttresses that often freeze to give short icefalls that have provided a reliable winter playground for generations of climbers. Whilst each individual pitch of ice does not warrant a separate description, many of the icefalls can be linked together to weave a route to the top. Hanging Knotts is the scrappy crag at the back of Angle Tarn. Its top buttress resembles a V of rock and is taken by *Evening Buttress*.

LAKE DISTRICT WINTER CLIMBS

Mark Scales steps into the final groove on Bowfell Buttress (photo: Paddy Cave)

The best approach is from Langdale via Rossett Gill, though it is possible, but longer, to go from Borrowdale via Esk Hause.

The routes are described in a left to right clockwise order around the tarn, starting from the Rossett Gill approach.

Evening Buttress   IV (6) 65m 1993
This route is to be found on Hanging Knotts. It climbs the iced-up right-hand end of the buttress, with the crux short and low down. Best approached via *Angle Tarn Gully* or the icefalls.

Angle Tarn Gully   100m I pre-1909
This obvious gully runs up the fellside close to the left side of the tarn and right of Hanging Knotts. Usually a straightforward snow slope.

Angle Tarn Icefalls   30m III/IV ** 1930s
In a good year there are many to choose from, but the best lie near the top of Rossett Gill. About 100m right of the gully, at the back of the tarn, a short rock buttress about 15m high provides two falls most winters. Another pitch above can be combined to give a good route to the top.

About 100m to the right of the *Tarn Icefalls* is a broad easy snow gully. The lower left wall of this gully provides several pitches up to 45m long (III). When you've finished on these, 200m further right is a frozen stream containing a 20m vertical pillar of ice in its upper reaches (III/IV). Further right again is an easier 15m ice runnel (III).

LANGDALE PIKES

NY 278 073

Having a southerly aspect, the remaining routes described in this area of the valley can soon be stripped of any snow on a cloudless sunny day. The greatest concentration of climbs is found on Pavey Ark, although the low-lying gills are fun if you find them frozen.

North-West Gully   300m I/II * 1995
The obvious gully (NY 272 072) splitting the west side of Pike o'Stickle, overlooking Mickleden, this route provides an interesting way to the summit if heading up from the valley. The gully is clearly seen from further north up Mickleden. Ramble

up easy fellside to the ill-defined lower portion of the gully. Follow a stream bed until the gully walls start to close in and a short wall bars the way to the top section of the gully. This can be passed on the left. Alternative left or right finishes are possible past a chockstone.

Optimists' Corner · 100m IV (5) 2011

This route climbs the steeper top wall to the right of *North-West Gully* starting from the prominent ledge about one-third of the way up the Pike. Start about 10m right of *North-West Gully*.

1 20m (3). Climb up grooves to a large terrace and traverse 15m right to belay below an area of icy grooves and slabs.
2 40m (5). Directly above is a large detached block; left of this is a prominent short steep iced corner. Climb up icy grooves to the corner and then follow this steeply to a ledge and belay.
3 30m (4). Just left of the belay is an icy left facing corner. Climb this and the steeper iced slab above it. From the end of the slab, move right over a slabby bulge to easier ground leading to the summit.

Gimmer Crag

NY 277 070   ALTITUDE *525M*   SOUTH-WEST FACING

Being south facing, lacking drainage and at a relatively low altitude Gimmer is not known for its winter routes though recent good winters have allowed the crag to be caught in winter garb giving several good additions. Sheltering in north-west-facing *North-West Gully*, **Hiatus** (1926) high up in the gully has seen a historical winter ascent of a sort, though little is really known about this. The FRCC Langdale guide has a full description of the climb.

The crag is defined by *North-West Gully* on its left and South-East Gully to the right. At the top of *North-West Gully*, Junipall Gully runs behind the crag to join South-East Gully isolating the crag and summit of Gimmer from the hillside. For this reason the main face receives little drainage. This and its low altitude generally make it a poor choice for winter climbing. Of the few winter routes so far recorded most are excellent rock routes and to prevent them being overly scratched or damaged by winter tools it is suggested that this main face is not used for winter climbing.

At the top of *North-West Gully* is the Pallid Buttress which forms the left north-east wall of the gully, the *Wooly Juniper*, the highest route is to be found here.

The secret's out... North Star, Honister Crag (Buttermere) (photo: Adrian Nelhams)

Wooly Juniper   85m VI 2010
This is the most shaded part of the crag and seems to hold snow and ice. Start up the diagonal line of vegetation to the left of centre of the slab.
1   35m. Start just up the gully to the left of the summer route *Pallid Slabs*. Gain and climb a line of vegetation slanting up rightwards into the centre of the crag with a bold section up a steep vegetated groove. Belay at the end of the ramp system, at the left end of a ledge ('The Haven' on *Pallid Slabs*).
2   50m. As pitch 3 *Pallid Slabs*. A better protected pitch. Climb straight up grooves from the belay to a tiny cave. Step right then up through a bilberry overhang to gain and climb a fine corner-crack then up easier ground.

The remaining routes **Gimmer Chimney** (V,5 2009), **D Route** (V,6 2010), **Asterisk** (VII,7 2010) and **Samaritan Corner** (V,5 2009) are located on the main buttress of Gimmer and **The Crack Direct** (VII,8 2006), which overlooks North-West Gully and follows the prominent corner in its entirety, all receive little drainage and rarely hold full winter climbing conditions.

Harrison Stickle

NY 281 073   Altitude 650m   East facing

The South Face of Harrison Stickle (NY 281 073) is the home of **South Face Route** (150m, II/III) which starts up a slight depression in the middle of the face before making a traverse right to the crest up which it finishes.

Generally the disjointed slabs that make up the North-East Face lack sufficient line to justify a good route, though the following has been claimed up the north-east side facing Pavey Ark.

Bryns Edge   120m IV (4) 2011

Follow the path from Stickle Tarn passing right under the craggy face and about half way up a 15m high east facing slab can be seen with an obvious groove above and right of it. The route follows these features. Start on a large terrace at the base of a steep slab which is visible when approaching from Stickle Tarn.

1   30m (4). Trend rightwards for 5m up the slab following blobs of turf before cutting back left and up a turfy crack passing a block. Continue up to reach a large ledge.
2   50m (4). Traverse up and right along the ledge passing below the undercut base of the first obvious groove. Move up and then left along rock ledges to the base of the steep groove. Climb the groove on good turf and pull out left at the top. Continue up easier ground to a belay.
3   40m (2). Continue directly up turfy slabs with occasional steps to the top.

Dungeon Ghyll   III/IV * 1985/6

Perhaps best to forget about this one unless it's a serious winter freeze; the last time it was in full condition was during the 1980s. As a further deterrent it should be noted that the gill is important as the home of rare alpine plants, especially the canyon at the top under Harrison Stickle – please climb here only in truly frozen conditions.

Starting almost from the New Dungeon Ghyll Hotel, the lower section seldom forms. When it does, the bottom fall rising from The Dungeon, beneath the great capstone that spans the gill, provides the crux. The portion above (NY 287 068, Alt 320m) has several short pitches and one longer one. Approaching Harrison Stickle the upper section gives several short pitches and one longer at 30m as the scenery becomes more impressive.

Stickle Ghyll   I/II
This open, low altitude gill (NY 292 067, Alt 180m) is actually in condition more often than one might imagine and makes an enjoyable approach to Pavey Ark if you're not rushing up for something harder.

The approach to Pavey can be delayed further at Tarn Crag (NY 290 073) to the right of Stickle Ghyll. Its low altitude (420m) means a prolonged deep freeze is required to assure conditions. One route (**Tarn Crag Gully** 70m, III 2009) has been recorded the left branch of a curving gully on the right-hand side of the crag starting above a prominent flat rock. The difficulties are found at the steep exit, or try the right branch at Grade II.

Pavey Ark

NY 286 079   ALTITUDE 570M   *SOUTH FACING*

Being south-facing, this large crag strips of snow quickly, though it can produce some very good climbs after a period of severe frost and/or build-up of snow, in which case it is worth making an early start. It is very accessible from Langdale.

From the Stickle Barn NT car park follow the path alongside *Stickle Ghyll* to Stickle Tarn. The crag is at the back of the combe at the far side of the tarn. It is split diagonally from bottom right to top left by *Jack's Rake*.

The deep-cut gully on the far left is *Little Gully*, with *Great Gully* divided from it by a large buttress. East Gully, to the right of the crag, is the best **descent**. The routes are described from left to right.

Little Gully   110m II/III ** 1930s
The first 60m has 15m of mixed climbing in it then a further 50m of easy snow leading to a choice of finishes.

Left Branch   55m III **
The most reliable route on the crag. A 25m icefall leads to a ledge and belay on the right or left (30m). Continue up 20m of steepening ice with easy snow above and a belay further back (25m). Continue up easy snow to the top.

Right Branch   50m II
The gully on the right. Climb behind the top chockstone and bridge out above it. Climb to *Jack's Rake* and finish up this.

Lake District Winter Climbs

Pavey Ark

#	Name	Grade
1	Little Gully Left Branch	II
2	Little Gully Right Branch	III
3	Middling Buttress	III
4	Great Gully	III
5	Stony Buttress	III
6	Little Corner	V
7	Roundabout Direct	V
8	Crescent Climb	III/IV
9	Deception	IV
10	Gwynne's Chimney	IV
11	Cook's Tour	IV
12	Stoat's Crack	VI
13	Jack's Rake	I
14	Bennison's Chimney	IV
15	Gibson's Chimney	III
	East Gully (descent)	- - ↑

80

Middling Buttress 150m III * 1986

The well-protected buttress between *Little Gully* and *Great Gully* is climbable under almost all frozen conditions. Take 60m ropes!

1 70m. Start just left of centre of the buttress and head straight up for the tree belay at mid-height.
2 80m. Continue straight upwards.

Great Gully 105m III * 1901

A good old-fashioned struggle but sadly not often in condition.

1 50m. Mixed climbing up the gully leads to a belay below the huge chockstone.
2 30m. Your mate's lead! Try turning the chockstone, probably best by the right iced wall. Easy snow leads to a cave.
3 25m. A choice of a through-route or outside the cave, then up steep ice to reach *Jack's Rake* and a satisfying finish via the continuation of the gully on the right which tops out on the summit.

Stony Buttress 110m III

The buttress to the right of *Great Gully*. Start as for *Great Gully* but move right onto the buttress and follow the left edge overlooking the gully. After 20m move right to a series of corners and grooves and follow these to *Jack's Rake*. The rock quality is poor – positively Alpine!

The next feature is a crescent-shaped slab and wall bounded by *Crescent Climb* on its left and the corner of *Deception* on its right side.

Crescent Climb 100m III/IV

A companion route to *Deception*. Best climbed when the slab is iced.

1 55m. Climb to an overhang at the left side of the slab taking the line of least resistance.
2 15m. Traverse right to the end of the overhang and a stance. With careful rope work this can be combined with the next pitch.
3 30m. Turfy slabs lead to *Jack's Rake*.

Deception 60m IV (4) * 1986

A well-defined corner-line at the right end of the large slab protected by a barrier of overhangs taken by the summer route *Arcturus* is hopefully distinguished by ice smears.

1 20m (3). Follow a right-slanting turfy line to a holly.
2 20m (4). Continue in the same line to belay below a steep corner.
3 30m (3). Follow the corner to *Jack's Rake*.

Now make the most of the conditions by continuing above *Jack's Rake*.

Jack's Rake   450m I/II
The prominent right-to-left diagonal line running across the face is a popular summer scramble and an interesting and substantial winter route. It is also a possible **descent** for the competent, but care should be taken when it is iced up.

Cook's Tour   100m IV * 1981
A large rowan on the left (south) side of *Jack's Rake* just after a steep section is a good landmark, just down from the top of *Deception*.
1   30m. Start at a short chimney opposite the large rowan tree and head up rightwards over easier vegetated mixed ground.
2   35m. Move left and follow an open gully then a chimney to a belay.
3   35m. Follow the easiest line up cracks and broken walls to finish.

Gwynne's Chimney   55m IV (5) * 1979
Approach by scrambling further up *Jack's Rake* to a tricky step at the left end of the first level section, the top of *Crescent Climb*. The start of a deep chimney is just right of two rowan trees.
1   25m. Follow the chimney for 15m until level with a gorse bush on the left. Move up and make delicate moves right to gain a snow ledge. Traverse the ledge for 2m and ascend blocky ground for 7m to a ledge and belay.
2   30m. Follow a groove above the belay to an exposed rib. Trend left, climb over a steep blocky step and follow the turf groove above to the top.

Direct Finish   50m IV (5) * 2006
Above the traverse the chimney narrows, continue up with a tight squeeze and some good axe placements in a crack on the right wall and turf: breathe in again at the top.

The next two climbs start a further 35m up *Jack's Rake*. High up there is a recess in the buttress: *Roundabout Direct* tackles the prominent left facing corner on the right side of the recess and *Little Corner* the long turfy corner on the left.

Roundabout Direct   75m V (6) 2008
Follow the summer route starting up a steep vegetated fault.
1   15m (4). Gain and climb a groove at the bottom of the wall in line with the top corner. The starting moves are strenuous and poorly protected. This gives access to an area of vegetation below the prominent corner. Once the angle

Brian Davison downs tools on Roundabout Direct (First Ascent) (photo: Nick Wharton)

PAVEY ARK

Langdale

eases traverse into a grassy groove and follow it to a juniper bush and belay at the base of the prominent left facing corner.
2 40m (6). Strenuous and technical climbing but thankfully with good protection leads to an easier grass recess below an overhang. Pass this on the right and continue up several short easy walls to a belay.
3 20m Continue more easily over ledges and short walls to the top.

Little Corner   75m V (5) 2008

The route starts 10m further up *Jack's Rake* at the foot of a steep slab below the corner and left of the recessed area. A prominent finger of rock lies across *Jack's Rake* a further 10m higher from the start. Follow the summer route in three pitches.
1 25m (5). Climb the wall past a prominent spike runner and enter the base of the corner. Climb the right of twin grooves for 8m to belay at the top.
2 25m (5). Climb the corner above to a good flake-crack on the left wall. Follow this to the left-hand rib and a belay ledge.
3 25m Continue up diagonally rightwards over short walls and ledges to easy ground.

At the foot of *Jack's Rake* where the crag curves round to the right into the scree of East Gully is a large buttress, the East Buttress, with a prominent overhang halfway up.

Stoat's Crack   150m VI (6) * 1976

Takes on the challenge of the East Buttress passing to the left of the prominent overhang.
1 60m (4). Climb a slanting corner trending left. Continue up corners to a spacious ledge below the overhang. A careful choice of runner placements and a 60m rope are useful, though intermediate belays are possible at several places.
2 30m (6). From the left-hand end of the ledge, climb an icy open groove to below a slabby wall.
3 30m (4). Strategically positioned turf allows progress up icy slabs to a large block belay.
4 30m (2). Continue easily to the top.

The following two chimneys start near the top of East Gully the easy **descent** gully on the right of the crag.

Bennison's Chimney   55m IV (4) 2008

High up East Gully on the right-hand side of the East Wall are two chimneys. This is the left-hand and narrower of the two.

Gibson's Chimney   55m III (4) 2008

The right-hand more open and vegetated chimney high up East Gully. The difficulties involve passing a small rock step 10m below a narrowing in the chimney and passing the narrow overhanging chimney section. This can be done on the right.

White Ghyll

NY 298 072   *ALTITUDE 400M*   *WEST FACING*

This steep crag, high up on the eastern flank of White Ghyll, normally holds little interest for the winter climber.

Approach from the Stickle Barn NT car park by either following the road east a few hundred metres to the footpath signpost on the left and then taking the obvious path up to the gill, or follow the *Stickle Ghyll* path until it crosses the gill, then continue along the path by the wall at that level to enter White Ghyll.

The corner line of **Inferno** (2006) in the lower portion of the gill is known to have received a winter ascent but no details are available and given its low altitude perhaps that's a good thing.

White Ghyll Chimney   75m IV 1982

High up the gill, near the left end of the crag, the transition from steep grooves and overhangs to a steep slab is marked by an open chimney/fault-line. Climb this to a chockstone, step left onto the slabs and continue to the top, belaying where appropriate.

Upper Scout Crag

NY 298 069   *ALTITUDE 275M*   *SOUTH FACING*

Route 1 (V, 6, 2009) was ascended during very heavy snow in the winter of 2009, but its low altitude means it won't often be in condition. Ascents may roughen the polish!

Easedale

The secluded low lying valley of Easedale just north of Grasmere offers some quiet rock climbing in summer but little in winter. The one recorded route above Blea Tarn will probably offer you a day away from the crowds.

Eagle Crag

NY 298 083   Altitude 450m   *East Facing*

Follow the minor road north out of Grasmere for 800m to the bridleway. Follow this along the valley and then take a path to the left uphill westward to Blea Tarn, 3km. A further 1km should see you reach the crag on the west, back wall, of the combe.

Henry's Rake   **200m I 2010**
An exposed but technically easy snow climb tackles the left-slanting rake high on the crag. Start in a bay to the right of the main steep buttress of rock, up and to the left of a short, deep gully which splits the lower right-hand side of the crag.

From the bay, follow a snow slope up and right over a number of slight bulges. Towards the top of this slope an appealing left-leading ramp, up slightly steeper snow, offers an interesting route to reach the right-hand end of the rake. This inescapable rake is followed as it narrows across exposed terrain. Finish by cutting back right at the rake's end and continuing to the summit.

CONISTON

With its proximity to the coast and an open south-westerly aspect, Coniston and the surrounding fells are greatly affected by milder coastal winds and so tend to be less frequently in condition than most other areas in this guide. Best conditions result from a long spell of easterly or northerly winds followed by snow. When such conditions do arise, however, a visit to Dow Crag can provide a wonderful mountain day with relatively easy access. Many of the other routes in this section are isolated icefalls, such as those in the slate quarries, or frozen gills, which are often low lying and require a prolonged period of cold weather to form.

The climbs are described starting with those on the Old Man of Coniston and the mountains around Coniston village before moving to the outlying crags.

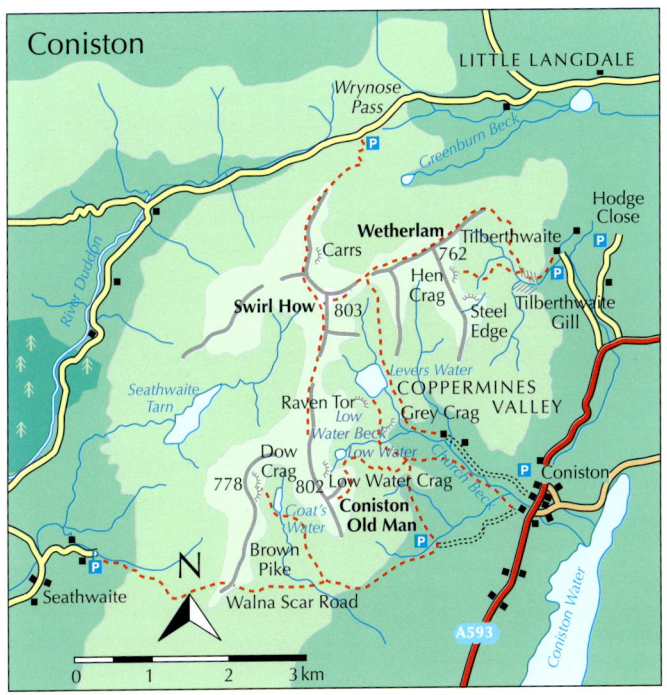

Dow

Brown Pike

SD 262 966   ALTITUDE 600M   *EAST FACING*

To the south of Dow Crag is Brown Pike with its small combe containing Blind Tarn on its east flank. Approach as for Dow Crag but continue on for another kilometre past the Dow turning to where cairns mark the start of a quarry track on the right. Follow this round the hillside into the cove.

North-East Gully   150m I
This follows the slanting gully above and to the left of Blind Tarn at the back of the combe. It takes a nice line to the summit ridge.

Dow Crag

SD 264 977   ALTITUDE 610M   *EAST FACING*

Rising over 200m, this wonderful mountain crag has a series of five impressive prominent buttresses named A to E, separated by imposing gullies.

Dow Crag is easily accessible if you can drive up the steep (and often icy) Walna Scar road out of Coniston village. However, even if you have to walk, the going up the road is easy and it's only 1.5km to a gate where the metalled road ends – park on the fell side of the gate (SD 288 971). Take the left-hand track, the Walna Scar Road, and continue to a large cairn which marks the junction with the track from Torver. Take the right-hand branch, going initially up a steep grassy slope and contour round in 1.5km to Goat's Water below the cliff (2 hrs). For routes on 'A' and 'B' Buttresses, slog up steep snow or scree to the mountain rescue box under 'B' Buttress. For Easter Gully and routes further right, cross diagonally below 'B' Buttress, or skirt around its base from the rescue post.

The routes are described from left to right.

Dow Crag

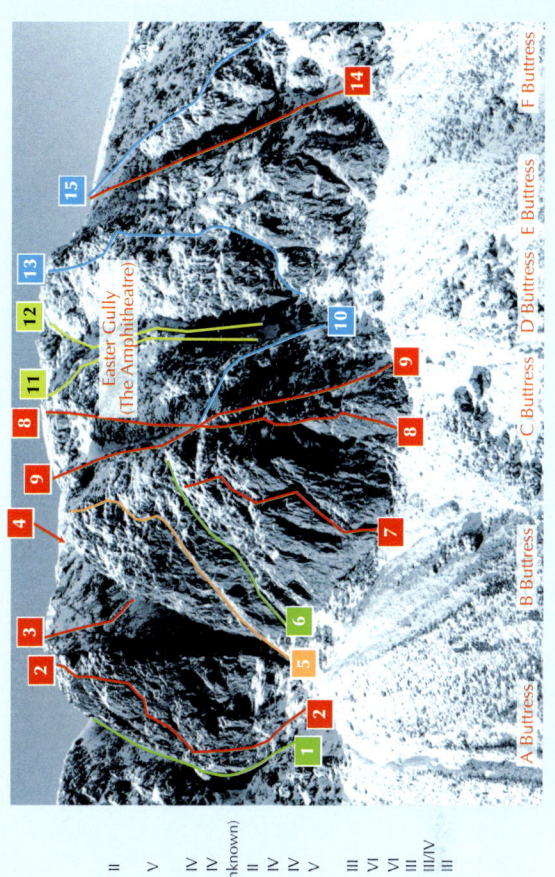

1	Easy Gully	II
2	Arete, Chimney and Crack	V
3	Traverse and Slab Variation	IV
4	Great Gully	IV
5	Giant's Crawl (grade unknown)	
6	Easy Terrace	II
7	Woodhouse's Route	IV
8	'C' Ordinary Route	IV
9	Intermediate Gully	V
10	Easter Gully – Scoop Route	III
11	Broadrick's Crack	VI
12	Hopkinson's Crack	VI
13	'E' Buttress	III
14	North Gully	III/IV
15	'F' Buttress	III

Photo: Eric Shaw

Easy Buttress

Easy Gully Left Branch 120m I
The first gully/rake at the left-hand end of the crag does not give any real difficulties and is often used as a **descent**.

Easy Gully 120m II
This deep gully marking the left side of 'A' Buttress is straightforward in its lower section with a chockstone to pass. The larger chockstone near the top can be bypassed by an exposed traverse onto the left wall or can be climbed direct.

Easy Gully Right Branch 120m * III
Start up *Easy Gully*. The right-hand branch is a smaller gully-line and leads right up the side of 'A' Buttress to its crest.

'A' Buttress

The leftmost major buttress.

Arete, Chimney and Crack 110m V (5) *** 1996
This classic route starts at the bottom left of the buttress and takes a long rightward-arching line up the face, ending directly up the centre top of the buttress.
1   20m. Start at the lowest point of the left side of the buttress and climb the 'Arete' to a ledge. Continue up the steeper wall above to gain an overhung ledge.
2   10m. Make a move left and climb a crack to blocks.
3   20m. Move diagonally right to a blocky recess and continue traversing right to belay below the 'Chimney'.
4   10m. The 'Chimney': climb it passing an awkward chockstone.
5   25m. Traverse right along the exposed ledge to beneath the chimney-crack.
6   25m. And finally the 'Crack'. This is sustained and exposed and is followed right to the top. A fitting finale.

Eliminate 'A' has been climbed although is very rarely in true condition.

Great Gully 120m IV (4) 1911
The deep gully bounding the right side of 'A' Buttress. A hard route for its day.
1   15m. A straightforward snow slope leads up to the chockstone.

2   30m (4). Generally hard unless banked out – and that doesn't happen often. Continue up for 15m to where the gully narrows to become a chimney. Climb this and surmount the capping chockstone.
3   75m. Easy snow leads to a slabby exit rightward. It is also possible to finish easily direct.

Traverse and Slab Variation   120m IV (4) 1986
1   70m (4). From the amphitheatre above the third chockstone, follow a system of ledges left across the left wall of the gully into a groove which leads to a shallow cave. From the cave, climb the obvious slab (good protection) to the corner. Layback this to an impressive block belay above 'A' Buttress. The pitch can be split at several places depending on rope drag.
2   50m. Easier scrambling leads to the top.

'B' Buttress

The next great buttress to the right – easily distinguished by the Mountain Rescue box at its foot.

Giant's Crawl, the obvious slabby gangway which cuts up across the buttress, has reputedly been climbed in winter but details are unknown.

Easy Terrace   250m II 1907
The line of the summer descent route from 'B' Buttress. Once the terrace is gained, traverse along ledges for 75m, then follow the easier continuation of *Intermediate Gully* to the summit.

Woodhouse's Route   105m IV ** 1912
The route follows a diagonal line across 'B' Buttress from the foot of the very impressive Central Chimney which bounds the right side of the buttress.
1   30m. Start below a wide groove, below the large pinnacle at the bottom left of Central Chimney. Climb the groove to the base of the pinnacle then take the wide crack on the left to the crevasse behind the pinnacle.
2   35m. Step left and enter the chimney and follow this to a ledge and possible belay after 10m. Traverse left to a deep recess. The deep rock cleft above leads to a ledge on the left in another 10m. Continue directly to a terrace and traverse right to a block beneath a steep crack.
3   40m. Depending on ice conditions climb the crack or the slab running diagonally right below the wall for 15m. A crevasse leads right to a steep wall with

a projecting block. Climb the wall to its left and up to easier ground. Trend left, or straight up, to reach *Easy Terrace*.

'C' Buttress

With the lowest base of the Dow buttresses 'C' is slabbier than the others and provides the most substantial routes.

'C' Ordinary Route   255m IV (5) *** 1919

An impressive line up the buttress. It follows the summer route throughout, but misses out the *Easy Terrace* descent by continuing directly up the buttress on easier-angled ground directly to the top of the crag. Start just left of the toe of the buttress, the lowest point of the crag.

1. 30m. Climb onto the front of the buttress to a ledge on top of a large flake. Continue to a smaller ledge and climb the scoop above. Easier-angled ground and ledges lead to a good ledge with a fallen flake.
2. 25m. From the left end of the ledge, climb an open scoop to gain a ledge up to the right. Follow easier-angled ground leftwards to a ledge on the corner of the buttress.
3. 25m. The groove on the right leads to a ledge. Move right and go up to a slab which is followed to a large ledge. Move up right again to a ledge and better belays.
4. 15m. Traverse 3m left then climb the wall above, left of the crack. Move left to beneath a small cave then climb the wide crack to the top of a large flake lying to the left of a cave. From the top of the flake, move left then back right to a small stance and belay only 3m above the flake.
5. 20m. Traverse rightwards across slabs to a good ledge. Continue rightwards along a gangway to a ledge. A short wall on the left leaves you level with *Easy Terrace* which is over to the left.
6. 140m. Take a fairly direct line up easier angled ground to the summit ridge.

Intermediate Gully   225m V (6) ** 1919

The imposing deep-cut crack between 'C' and 'D' Buttresses has seen few modern repeats and the grade is still a guesstimate. With reasonable icing it could make a good gully climb. In its normal condition as a mixed route it will be found much tougher.

1. 30m. Follow the gully easily until the walls close in.
2. 20m. Continue up the crack and chimney to a recess (possible belay). This section can also be passed by a groove on the right then a traverse back left into the gully. Continue up and over the chockstone.

3   20m. The steep crack above leads to easier ground, then steepens before reaching a recess below a large chockstone.
4   15m. Climb over the chockstone to a cave, then move right and up and left into a crack in the left wall. Follow the crack until level with *Easy Terrace* over to the left.
5   140m. As for *'C' Ordinary*: easier-angled ground leads directly to the summit ridge, or the continuation of the gully can be followed with one more awkward chockstone – best passed a few metres lower on the left wall.

Easter Gully (The Amphitheatre)

Easter Gully – Scoop Route   180m III ** 1918
The next gully right is *Easter Gully* with its preliminary short chockstone pitch leading into The Amphitheatre. This can be tricky if not banked out and is best taken on its left (15m). From here several routes may be taken, but under snow and ice the best exit at an easy grade is by a system of ledges and a scoop which starts just right of the deep chimney of South Chimney on the left wall. A crack, then ledges, lead to a block. Overcome the block and take the scoop above to *Easy Terrace* (25m). Traverse left and finish up the easy upper section of *Intermediate Gully*. A slightly harder finish, requiring better conditions, is to wind a way directly up the buttress above (140m).

The next two routes are gained by following *Easter Gully* to the Amphitheatre, whose steep back wall has cracked corner-lines at either side – *Broadrick's Crack* on the left and *Hopkinson's Crack* on the right.

The summer Diff **Blizzard Chimney** (1914), the first chimney on the left in the Amphitheatre, and **South Chimney** (1914) to its right, have both been climbed in heavy snow conditions. Grades are unknown.

Broadrick's Crack   195m VI (8) ** 1996
The long left-hand crack offers a demanding main pitch which is nevertheless escapable at a few places.
1   15m (3). Climb *Easter Gully* to the Amphitheatre.
2   30m. Easy mixed ground leads to the base of the steep crack/corner on the left side of the Amphitheatre.
3   50m (8). The meat of the route, originally climbed in one 50m pitch, though it can be split. Hard and strenuous climbing leads to where the crack widens in 20m. Pass a chockstone on its right side and belay on the right at the base of an easy snow gully.

Lake District Winter Climbs

4   50m. Climb the snow gully to a col and then downclimb into the main gully above *Hopkinson's Crack* on the right. Follow the left-hand gully where it splits.
5   50m. Follow the gully to the top.

Jones's Route (1914) follows *Broadrick's Crack* to The Bandstand and continues, crossing *Hopkinson's Crack* and traversing rightwards 5m to finish up a deceptively easy-looking scoop. It has received an ascent under heavy snow. The grade is unknown – it is Very Difficult in summer.

Hopkinson's Crack   260m VI (7) *** 1995

The big crack and corner on the right of the back wall of the Amphitheatre has been climbed in mixed conditions and also with a ribbon of ice down the main corner-line.

1   15m (3). Follow *Easter Gully* to the Amphitheatre.
2   15m (2). Move up to the base of the corner-crack at the back right of the Amphitheatre.
3   30m (7). The wide icy crack is poorly protected in its lower part. Pass several difficult steep sections and a final strenuous move (crux) to a large belay ledge on the left (The Bandstand) and move left to a block belay.
4   20m (5). Return back right into the corner-line and follow the crack more easily to belay where the crack widens to a snow gully.
5   50m (4). Follow the right-hand chimney-line where the gully splits, passing an awkward chockstone to enter it.
6   100m. Easy snow curves round to the right near its top to be barred by a small rock wall.
7   30m (3). Climb a rock rib on the right to the top.

Black Chimney (25m, 1912) a summer Diff, the dark short deep chimney on the right wall of the Amphitheatre, has received an ascent under snow; grade unknown.

'E' Buttress

Described in the rock climbing guide as a "wide sprawling rock garden between *Easter Gully* and *North Gully*. The grassy nature of the buttress gives poor discontinuous routes." With such an obviously good write up this had to offer something for the winter climber.

E Buttress 200m III ** 2010

Start a little below the chockstone in *Easter Gully* and follow a rising shelf rightwards for 30m until it finishes in a narrow gully. Climb the gully with an awkward start and then follow a rising ramp rightwards. The route trends upwards to a through route behind a chockstone. Move right to a basin overlooking *North Gully*. Take the icy groove on the left of the basin and follow this to the ridge. The summit is a short distance ahead.

North Gully 55m III/IV 1912

Climb the gully at the right side of the crag, passing the cave to the right and the top overhangs to the left.

F Buttress 180m III ** 2010

This is the short buttress to the right of *North Gully*. Start at the right-hand side of the buttress and climb broken ground until a steep nose is reached at 70m. Avoid this by turf on the left and enter a couple of chimneys leaving both on the left. The route trends left to overlook *North Gully* before the buttress narrows to the pleasant upper ridge.

THE OLD MAN OF CONISTON

SD 272 978   ALTITUDE 803M

The highest summit in this southern part of the Lake District has a few climbs around the mountain tarns of Low Water and Levers Water and several frozen gills when temperatures drop low enough. *Low Water Beck* comes into condition more often than you'd imagine and if some sections are a bit too damp, you can always wander up the side until you find an icier bit.

Low Water

SD 275 983   ALTITUDE 547M   *EAST FACING*

If you can get up the often icy Walna Scar Road from Coniston, park beyond the gate where the surfacing ends (SD 288 971). Take the right-hand track and follow it north, as per the main tourist route, taking the left fork until a further track branches right into the cove below the obvious fall. If you can't, walk up from Coniston past the Coppermines cottages.

Low Water Beck   90m III ** 1940s

This is the beck running past the left side of Cove Crag. It falls from the high mountain tarn of the same name. It freezes quickly and is easily accessible, so making it popular, and it can be combined well with the icefalls above. The lower fall is best climbed on its left side (peg) up to a chockstone. Exit left on iced slabs or more steeply up the curtain of ice to the right (Direct Finish, IV). In a good winter the beck can continue to give easier climbing up to (and occasionally even over) the tarn to the crag at the back of the combe.

Brim Fell Crag

NY 277 987   Altitude 500m   *South-east facing*

This broken heathery crag is clearly seen to the right of the upper part of *Low Water Beck* on the approach up the Copper Mines Valley. The single pitch of *Brim Fell Icefall* is visible on its left side above and right of the top of *Low Water Beck*.

Brim Fell Icefall   50m III 2010

The icefall at the left side of the crag is often in condition. Start 5m right of a short steep rock wall.

Follow the icy corner over a couple of short awkward moves to step left onto a vegetated sloping ramp which allows escape leftwards. Follow the ice up the short wall above.

Quick Draw McGraw   105m V (5) 2010

The prominent upper icefall lies just right of centre of the crag. Ice forms over slabby walls, the top one being the steepest with snow and heather climbing in between.

1   25m (3). A steep start leads to icy slabs above then a short snow slope and belay.
2   40m. Follow a snowy gangway up left then straight up to a blade peg and thread belay at the left end of a low rock wall at the base of the main icefall.
3   40m (5). Move back right and climb the main icefall direct. Block belay 8m above a sapling.

Low Water Crag

SD 272 982   A<small>LTITUDE</small> *670<small>M</small>*   E<small>AST FACING</small>

This small crag nestles at the back of the cove above *Low Water*. Climbing *Low Water Beck* makes a good approach or walk up the track. The main crag is bounded by *South Gully* on its left and *North Gully* to the right however the climbing extends across the whole fellside.

Summit Route   140m II 1962
To the left of the main crag follow snow patches and mixed ground directly to a satisfying finish at the summit cairn.

Mulled Wine   140m II 2004
The slim buttress to the left of *South Gully*. Start 30m to the left of *South Gully*. Climb initially up broken ground (slabs and steps) to the bottom of a steep 30m buttress. Turn this on either left or right at the same grade (left is better) to its top. Enter an obvious V-groove in the centre of the buttress. Go up this to more broken ground and onto the slopes above *South Gully*.

South Gully   140m III * 1962
This is the gully bounding the left side of the crag. Chockstones and boulders provide small ice pitches to be turned and these lead to the upper exit slope, which is followed to the ridge.

Spring Route   150m III 2006
A gully branches off to the left just as the main gully narrows. Follow this to where it opens out and continue up over broken ground.

Wild World   150m IV (5) * 2003
This route takes a straight line up the steep bit of buttress, just right of *South Gully*.
1   50m. Start just right of *South Gully* and trend right to the bottom of a steep corner. Climb this, then step right onto an exposed arete and spike. Bold climbing up steep turf directly above leads to a belay below a V-groove.
2   50m. Step right and take two right-angled corners. Step left from the top of the second corner and climb to a belay below an overhanging wall.
3   50m. Move round to the left then up over a chockstone and scramble to the top.

Low Water

1 Summit Route	II
2 Mulled Wine	II
3 Spring Route	IV
4 South Gully	III
5 Wild World	IV
6 Lost in the Wild/ Percy's Passage	III/IV
7 North Gully	I
8 Percy's Progress	II
9 Low Water Beck	III

Lost in the Wild   65m IV (5) 2011

This follows an obvious groove, in two pitches, in the lower buttress finishing at the large right slanting terrace at the foot of the main buttress. From the terrace it is possible to descend to the right, or continue up the right edge of the buttress to the summit at Grade II/II (150m).

Percy's Passage   150m III/IV ** 1967

This lies to the left of *North Gully*, on the right side of the buttress. The most enjoyable route links the many icefalls on the lower section of crag to a series of short steep walls and rightward-trending ramp-lines higher up. A pair of grooves with an overhanging wall at the top offers a more strenuous variation in the upper crag.

North Gully   150m I 1919

The shallow snow gully immediately right of the crag is straightforward apart from one small step.

To the right is a small hanging valley containing a discontinuous buttress offering several short pitches, some of them difficult. The most continuous, **Percy's Progress** (120m, III), is an obvious line of icefalls on the right-hand side where ice comes down the stepped buttress. This gives three or four short pitches which are open to variation or avoidance depending on the conditions. Several other discontinuous variations are possible in this area.

Levers Water

SD 279 993   Altitude 413m

To the north of Low Water lies Levers Water. The two crags here are best approached from the Copper Mines Valley, above Coniston village. The small crag of the local landmark of **Simon's Nick** (III) (SD 281 989) is easily seen from the path up to Levers Water. Ice forms rarely as it receives no drainage since the mine workings closed.

Grey Crag

SD 282 987 Altitude 330m *SOUTH-EAST FACING*

This long crag bounds the hillside above the water works in the Copper Mines Valley.

Grey Crag Icefall 30m IV (4) 1964
A good icefall usually forms at the left side of the crag. A thin sliver of ice leads to a tree belay. Climb a short 5m wall of ice and then a rocky chimney to the top.

Module 30m IV 1981
The thin smear at the far right end of the crag right of a prominent wall.

Raven Tor

SD 277 988 Altitude 550m *NORTH FACING*

This is the large broken buttress above Levers Water. Its northerly aspect means it is often in condition. Approach up the Copper Mines Valley via the Water Works track to Levers Water. Although only one route is described, the gully on the right-hand side of the crag, the buttress between the two gullies and the remaining broken buttresses present many other possibilities for good climbing all at Grade II.

Central Gully 100m II 1959
Situated to the left of centre, this is largest gully line on the crag. Rather indefinite initially, it becomes deeper nearer the top, with a steep exit providing the crux of the route – right where it should be, at the top!

WETHERLAM

NY 288 011 Altitude 762m

Sitting to the north of the Old Man of Coniston, Hen Crag and Steel Edge are worth a visit, whilst the slate quarries around the foot of the mountain contain some interesting water ice on the rare occasions that they freeze.

STEEL EDGE

Park below the spoil heaps at Tilberthwaite Cottages (NY 306 010), follow the path by Tilberthwaite Gill and head north into the combe to reach Steel Edge in just over an hour.

Steel Edge Crag, Wetherlam

NY 294 002   ALTITUDE 550M   *EAST FACING*

Steel Edge defines the southern edge of the north-east facing combe of Wetherlam. To the south of it the east facing broken crag approximately 300m south of Steel Edge contains three easy gully lines (50m). The left end of the crag is bounded by a straightforward snow gully, **Left Gully** (I, 2009) with a small cornice, the **Central Gully** (II, 2009) requires some more tricky moves up rock walls for the first 15m to enter the leftwards curving gully while the **Right-Hand Gully** (I) has a slight chockstone at one-third height.

The fellside to the south of the crag contains numerous short icy smears none of sufficient stature to warrant description. The most southerly, best and longest is just north of the small tarn (at SD 29495 99365) and ridge overlooking the Copper Mines Valley offering Grade III ice.

Cold Steel   75m II (3) 2010

High on the fellside located approximately 200m further right and just left of the ridge of Steel Edge (NY 295 004) this shallow gully above old mine workings contains a couple of ice steps. Just left is a left slanting diagonal easy snow gully. Either start up the lower continuation of the gully behind the mine workings or approach up Steel Edge to the first rocks where the ridge steepens. Traverse left for 80m then scramble diagonally up left over mixed ground for 50m to the icefall.
1   50m. Climb the steep 10m icefall and a snow scoop above to belay at the base of slabby icefalls.
2   25m. Climb the slabby icefalls or icy corner on the left.

Steel Edge

NY 294 005   ALTITUDE 500M   *NORTH-EAST FACING*

The icefalls lie above and about 50m right of the crest of the ridge of Steel Edge and are enjoyable and form quite readily. Ascend the Edge to half-height, then drop down onto its north side. In good conditions the area can be awash with ice making climbing possible almost anywhere. In leaner conditions three distinct lines are visible.

Close to the Edge 30m III (3) 2002
The leftmost and lowest of the three. If the short lower wall is iced climb it, otherwise traverse left along a ledge to the icy slab. Climb this and a grassy iced groove above.

Edge your Bets 30m III (4) 2010
Start just right of stepped overhangs at the start of the ledge traversed to *Close to the Edge*.

Tricky moves give access to a steep slabby icefall, up this to a leftward rising ramp at half-height. The icy shallow corner above is climbed to the top.

In lean conditions when the lower wall isn't iced the ramp can be used to gain the final corner, or better still climb the iced slab of *Close to the Edge* to the ramp then step down and right past a large blocky spike to the start of the final corner.

Further from the Edge 25m III (3) 2003
The right-hand line. Climb up the steep nose for 5m to an icy ledge then up an iced slab on the left to the top.

South Hen Crag

NY 293 006   Altitude 520m   *North-east facing*

Further rightwards round into the combe, this large rambling crag split by two shallow ill-defined gullies is a dispersed jumble of walls and short buttresses to the south of Hen Crag. It offers many possibilities in the lower grades which do not warrant individual description. The following routes are three of the better ones.

South South Gully 200m I * 2002
The left-hand of the two gullies just left of centre of the crag. A bit vague lower down but more obvious and better defined in its upper half.

South South Groove 200m II * 2002
Branching right from halfway up *South South Gully* is an open turfy corner leading onto easier slopes above.

Broad Gully   **200m II 2009**

Climb the broader ill-defined gully line midway between *South South Gully* and *South Gully* at the right side of the crag. There is a short crux gully headwall at half-height where the rock walls encroach on both sides.

Hen Crag

NY 290 008   *Altitude 600m*   *North-east facing*

Situated on the east side of Wetherlam, this large crag overlooks Tilberthwaite Gill. Heavy snow buries the heather to quickly produce some excellent winter climbing. The track from the car park beside Tilberthwaite Cottages leads to the foot of the climbs in about an hour. If conditions are suitable, **descent** is possible down *North Gully*.

South Gully   **200m I**

This gully bounds the left side of the crag and leads to the summit ridge of Wetherlam. To the left of *South Gully* are many other climbs of a similar grade.

Skeleton Bob   **150m II 2010**

Start 40m up *South Gully* (as for *White Spider*).

1   40m. As for *White Spider*.
2   110m. Go round the left side of the belay wall and climb directly up the snowfield to its top where it narrows and steepens into a shallow gully leading to the finishing snow slopes. Belay as required.

White Spider   **165m III 2010**

This route links the prominent snowfields and ramps up the left side of Hen Crag. The diagonal snow ramps of the start and finish are visible on the approach. Start 40m up *South Gully*.

1   40m. Climb the diagonal snow ramp up rightwards to a snowfield, continue up this to a belay beneath a small wall with three obvious rock fins.
2   50m. Right of the wall, climb a short gully headwall to gain a snowfield above. Go straight up for about 35m to spike belays just above where a snow shelf leads out right.
3   40m. Follow the shelf out right for 12m, then climb mixed ground direct to another snow shelf (belay crack up left).
4   35m. Climb the diagonal snow ramp/groove up rightwards to finish at the top centre of Hen Crag.

Hen's Teeth   200m II/III 2002

Parallel to but easier than *Hen Crag Buttress*. Start in a bay 20m left of *Hen Crag Buttress*. Follow a turfy/heather groove straight up for 90m. Climb up an easy shelf into a V-corner on the right (20m). Trend right on slabby rocks to the top.

Hen Crag Buttress   250m III/IV *** 1970

Particularly fine, when combined with the Direct Finish, this makes an excellent sustained mountaineering route under deep consolidated snow; otherwise it's a heather bash. It follows a diagonal line crossing the buttress from left to right. Start up an icy groove in the back of an open bay just to the left of the toe of the buttress and continue along a natural line of weakness. Difficult moves on the second pitch lead to a heather ledge and from there further pitches lead more easily to the top right of the crag. Belay as required.

Left-Hand Finish   250m III * 1980

Follow the original route for a couple of rope lengths until good ice leads out left. Finally a diagonal ramp leads up left to the summit.

Direct Finish   50m III 2000

From where the original route joins the heathery ledge, instead of traversing right to easy ground, go straight up stepped grooves and ledges at a similar grade to the climbing below.

Direct Start   60m VI (5) 1993

Starting right of the toe of the buttress, climb short walls and heathery ledges until it is possible to move left to the crest of the buttress. From here, follow turf to the large snowfield and join the original route.

Hen Pecked   200m II 2004

The blunt ridge at the far right side of the buttress, overlooking *North Gully*. Start at the base of *North Gully*. Climb the ridge, up a small initial steep step, then steep heather (50m). Keep right, looking steeply down into *North Gully* and continue in the same line all the way. (150m).

North Gully   200m I

The gully on the right side of the crag. This finishes at a point near the summit of Wetherlam and can serve as a useful **descent** route.

North Buttress   200m III 2002

Start immediately right of *North Gully*. Good climbing up the obvious buttress, mostly via turfy grooves, steepening near the top.

Glassy Crag

NY 292 011   Altitude 540m   *South-East facing*

This slabby lump of vegetated hillside to the right of the more prominent Hen Crag forms ice smears which have been played on by generations of climbers. One of the longest and most readily formed is described.

The Tilberthwaite Boys   100m IV (4) 1969
In a good year this is the obvious ice fall running the full length of the crag slightly left of centre.

Tilberthwaite and the Slate Quarries

When sub-zero temperatures grip the area give the slate quarries a thought if you're looking for water ice. Several steep pitches giving excellent climbing have been climbed.

Tilberthwaite Gill (NY 303 007, Alt 240m, East facing) itself can offer a few short ice steps after a good freeze and a more interesting approach to the next route.

Tilberthwaite Trundle   23m IV 1982
From the car park ascend Tilberthwaite Gill or (quicker) the path through the quarries on the left bank, cross the bridge and follow the right bank to a landslip level with a right-angle bend in the gill. An icefall forms on the left bank of the gill at this point. Follow the right side of the fall to a platform at about 10m – here the icefall steepens. Step left onto the main pillar (which drops down from a groove above) and follow this to a tree belay on the right. Easily combined with some of the nearby quarry icefalls.

Hodge Close Quarry

NY 316 017   Altitude 150m

Side Show Icefall   50m V (5) 1982
Forms if the stream is diverted. Pass through the cave to the wall of the quarry overlooking the pond.
1   20m. At the mouth of the cave climb the slab to belay in a niche on the right.

LAKE DISTRICT WINTER CLIMBS

2   30m. Move left and follow grooves and ice to the top.

Warning A major rockfall (1996) above the cave has left the area extremely unstable and makes this a dangerous undertaking. Not recommended!

At the southern end of the quarry, the summer line of **Sasquatch** (8) has been top-roped.

In adjoining Parrock Quarry (NY 317 018) a fan of slabby ice on the east side often forms about halfway down the entrance incline. Various 30m pitches can give quality entertainment at Grade II/III (1982).

Tranearth Quarry Icefall   **20m IV (6) 1982**
This quarry above Torver, at the lowly altitude of 240m (SD 277 960), can give a 20m icefall where the waterfall enters the quarry but it rarely forms.

Carrs

NY 273 012   *ALTITUDE 550M*   *EAST FACING*

To the south of Wrynose Pass, this extensive broken east-facing crag overlooks Greenburn and Little Langdale. It offers several easy gullies and buttress routes.

Little and Great Carrs are easily accessible from the Three Shires Stone on Wrynose Pass. Follow the ridge of Wet Side Edge, then drop down to the foot of Great Carrs. If Wrynose is impassable, approach from Little Langdale via Greenburn, or go somewhere else. **Descent** is best down the snow basin at the left end of the crag. In poor visibility, locating the correct route is difficult.

The gullies are obvious and do not warrant individual descriptions but are worth a visit. The two longer gullies start at the same point at the lowest point of the buttress. The slightly longer **Left Gully** (I/II, 200m) curves left, while the right-hand **Middle Gully** (I/II, 190m) is more direct. **Right Gully** (I/II) is the shorter distinct gully starting higher to the right.

Various options are also possible up the buttresses. The two outlined here give some unimaginative climbing without any real difficulties. **Left-Hand Buttress** (I, 180m, 1998) is followed from its lowest point without any real problems. **Central Buttress** (I, 180m, 1998) takes a nondescript line up the central buttress. Several other similar routes have been climbed.

WEST LAKES

West Waterfall Gully, Pillar (climber: Mark 'Ed' Edwards; photo: Dave Birkett)

ESKDALE

Situated in the south-west corner of the Lake District, Eskdale has little to interest the winter climber unless arctic conditions grip the region, in which case some water courses freeze. However, if that is the case, you probably won't be able to get to the valley!

The first two falls are found in north-facing gills on the south side of the valley. They are easily reached from the main road along the valley bottom, what's more they are both only about a kilometre from the Woolpack Inn at Boot.

Stanley Force — 60m IV (4) * Early 1970s

This lies above Dalegarth Station and at a lowly 140m is virtually salty! When approaching from the west, use a car park south of the main road (NY 171 002). Follow the track up to the waterfall (NY 174 995). A prolonged freeze produces three pitches, the first being the crux, with 15m of vertical ice. A further 35m of climbing can be had if the gill is followed a little further.

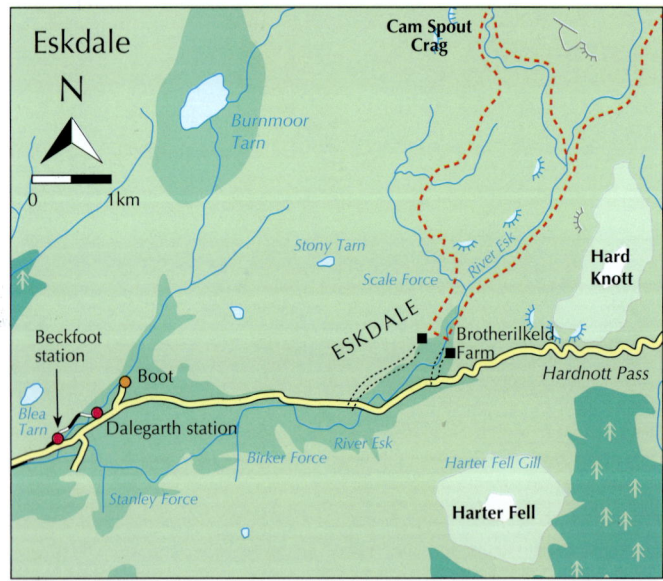

Birker Force 60m III (4) ** Early 1970s 🍂🍂
Further east along the south side of the valley from *Stanley Force* (NY 188 999, Alt 200m), this waterfall has been known to freeze in exceptional conditions.

East of *Birker Force* and due south of the cattle grid at the foot of Hardknott Pass, is a gill that is not named on the map. This is **Harter Fell Gill** (200m, II/III, early 1970s), the first gill which is encountered on the left when following the Harter Fell track from Jubilee Bridge (the bridge situated just west of the cattle grid). There is a lot of good ice bouldering on the fellside just west of this gill, don't forget your mat!

Heading north into Upper Eskdale, **Scale Force** (II/III, early 1970s) (NY 213 024, Alt 150m) can give nearly a kilometre of falls in steps with easier ice between them.

Cam Spout Crag 🍂

NY 215 055   ALTITUDE 520M   *EAST FACING*

A rambling crag overlooking the Great Moss in Upper Eskdale. It can be approached from Eskdale by following the path by the river, starting at the foot of Hardknott Pass. Alternatively a shorter, but steeper approach may be made from Wasdale, over Mickledore and down to the Great Moss. Either way is quite a trek.
   Cam Spout Crag is home to rare alpine plants – please climb here only in truly frozen conditions.

Peregrine Gully 130m I/II
The gully bounding the crag on its right. Snow for a short way leads to ice pitches up the gully bed before a final steepening. Avoid some of this by climbing onto a rib on the left leading to the summit ridge.

Slightly further north is the waterfall of:

Cam Spout 45m II/III
This fall on How Beck lies next to the Mickledore path (NY 217 058, Alt 520m) and comes into condition after a longish freeze. The main pitch can be linked with a route on Scafell if you've walked up from Eskdale and are quick (or don't mind a return in the dark!).

Esk Buttress

NY 223 065   Altitude 490m   South-East facing

The huge dominant crag at the head of Upper Eskdale, overlooking the Great Moss. Being south facing it catches the sun and is relatively low lying, so finding it in condition isn't easy and probably explains why there is only one recorded route.

Not easily accessible from anywhere, the approach will be long. From Brotherilkeld at the foot of Hardknott Pass in Eskdale follow the footpath north along the River Esk past Cam Spout Crag from where the buttress can be seen 1km to the north-east. Alternatively from Wasdale cross over Mickledore and go down to the Great Moss and take the path north-east (leftwards) to the buttress. In summer the buttress is often approached from Cockley Beck by following Mosedale northwards passing Long Crag and Gait Crag. Unless approaching from the south along the Duddon Valley reaching Cockley Beck could be the crux of the day as it involves crossing over Hardnott or Wrynose Pass!

Trespasser Groove   135m VII (7) ** 2010

This follows the prominent corner to the right of the central wall (*Central Pillar*) of the buttress.

1   50m (5). Climb the corner to the left of the slabs at the start of the summer climb *Bower's Route* to a large ledge. Move diagonally left to a higher ledge then follow a groove up to the base of the prominent corner.
2   30m (7). Move up and left into the corner. Follow the corner steeply passing two recesses to belay on a spike by a narrow grass ledge.
3   20m (5). Near the top of the corner follow snowy/turfy ledges up and right under overhangs to the large ledge of the Waiting Room.
4   35m (6). From the right end of the ledge follow a chimney out right to a ledge. Slabs above and right lead to the top. The final pitches follow the summer climb *Bower's Route*.

Little Narrow Cove

Moving clockwise round the head of the valley this secluded little cove is found at the head of Eskdale, between Ill Crag and Scafell Pike. Although it faces south-east over Eskdale, from which it can be approached, it is in fact easier to approach from Wasdale over Scafell Pike, dropping down to the head of the cove (only 200m from the summit of Scafell Pike).

Chambers Crag

NY 217 072   Altitude 850m   *North facing*

Chambers Crag is situated at the head of Little Narrow Cove towards its western (Scafell Pike) side. An easy Grade I gully leading to the left-hand side of the crag may contain good neve if you are lucky. The crag has a large sloping ledge system running about 7m above its base and slanting rightwards to a pinnacle on the right-hand side of the crag.

Halfway on Botterill's Slab (photo: Nick Wharton)

Ema Ho 100m IV (4) * 1996

Possibly the highest route in England its name meaning 'It is sacred' in Tibetan follows a prominent turfy break in the centre of the crag and a snow bay slightly to the left of its centre.

1   40m. A compact wall guards the approach to a long ledge running the length of the lower section of crag; surmount this and belay in the centre.
2   60m. The steep break is climbed to an obvious snow bay; belay where possible, then reach the top.

Chambers Pinnacle 110m IV (4) 2006

A traverse of the ledge system running along the lower portion of crag and up behind the pinnacle.

1   30m. Climb easily up through the lower wall to gain the ledge system.
2   40m (4). Follow the ramp rightwards to a steep rocky step 10m below the top of the pinnacle and belay behind it. (It is possible to escape easily by traversing off at this point.)
3   40m (4). From the belay behind the pinnacle, traverse about 10m right to below a large flake. Climb up to the flake which marks the start of a rising right-to-left traverse on ledges across the wall. Climb until right of a bottomless groove and then follow a fainter turfy groove for 15m to the top of the crag.

Chambers Ramp 80m I 2006

An obvious ramp-line rising from left to right across the base of the crag with one small step in the middle. With care this makes a useful **descent** from the right side of the crag.

Ill Crag

NY 221 072   ALTITUDE 740M   SOUTH-WEST FACING

Ill Crag is situated near the head of Little Narrow Cove on its east side, opposite to but lower than Chambers Crag.

Big Question 150m IV (4) 1996

The line is shaped like an eponymous question mark. Answer it by starting from snow at the highest point of the base of the crag, just to the right of a gully on the left side of the crag.

1   20m. Climb the steep gully on the left of the crag.

2   20m. Traverse right and climb up through a rock barrier.
3   40m. Move up to a pillar and corner on the right and make easy moves to a belay further right.
4   30m. Steep turf leads to a belay.
5   40m. The final curl of the question. Move gradually up and left to finish.

Big Answer   130m III 1999
This rather vague response starts to the right of the *Big Question*, between it and more broken ground. Follow the line of least resistance up turf and ice, avoiding the *Big Question* on its right for its entire length.

Ill Gully   130m II 2006
The prominent gully on the right-hand side of the crag. Apart from an awkward chockstone at about one-third height and a choice of finishes, there is little else to tax mind or body.

Esk Pike West Face

NY 234 077   Altitude 800m   *West facing*

Some 300m west of Esk Hause is a series of stepped buttresses, the most prominent, about 50m high has an **Obvious Gully** (I, 2010) on its left side and a **Slanting Gully** (III 4, 2010) on its right with a **Turfy Corner** (II, 2010) up the small buttress right of *Slanting Gully*.

Rib and Ridge   45m V (6) * 2010
This climbs the ridge overlooking *Slanting Gully* and is a combination of the summer routes *Broken Rib* and *Esk Ridge*.
1   10m (6). To the left of *Slanting Gully* the buttress juts forward offering a steep wall with a groove up its front leading to a large ledge. Climb the groove with tricky moves passing a steep section near the top.
2   35m (6). As for *Esk Ridge*, at the right side overlooking the gully a deep crack leads to the top of a block. An awkward step up the wall above leads to another ledge. Move left and climb a corner/groove to the top.

LAKE DISTRICT WINTER CLIMBS

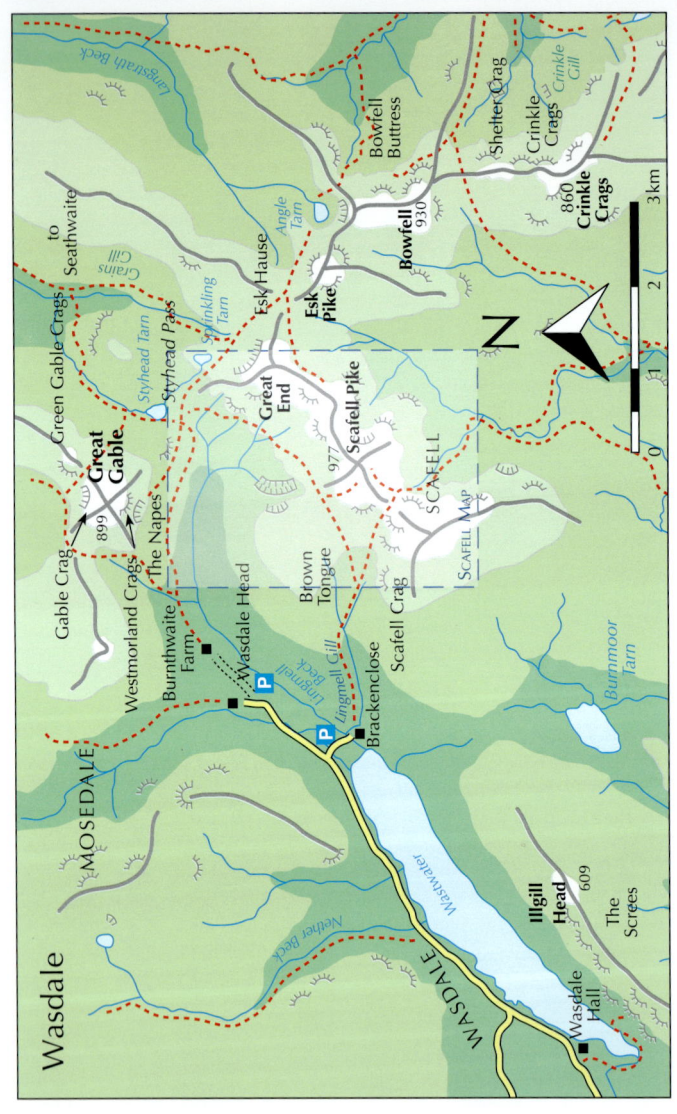

WASDALE

Wasdale provides the easiest access to Scafell and its excellent winter climbing. Scafell is described in the current FRCC rock climbing guide as 'A cold, wet crag that's miles from the road.' What more could one ask for in a winter venue? And being the highest climbing in England, the main crag on Scafell produces some of the most reliable winter conditions in the district in the form of classic gullies and modern mixed routes.

But though Scafell may be the jewel in the crown, there are other good crags accessible from the valley. The gullies of Wasdale Screes in particular can give some of the longest water-ice climbs in the region.

In summer, most people approach Wasdale over the passes of Wrynose and Hard Knott, but even in a mild winter this is not really an option, though Ulpha Pass is often drivable if the steep road out of Ulpha village is ice free. A safer but longer alternative is to take the A595 coast road, leaving it before or after Holmrook for Stanton Bridge, Nether Wasdale, then go along Wast Water to the head of the valley. If travelling from the north, leave the A595 at Gosforth.

The crags are described anti-clockwise around the valley.

Wasdale Screes

NY 155 043   ALTITUDE 260M   NORTH FACING

These large broken crags above the screes at the foot of the south-eastern end of Wast Water are seamed by a series of gullies named alphabetically from left to right. As the climbs start at a low altitude, a prolonged period of frost is required before they come into condition, but when they do, they give classic water-ice routes.

The shortest approach is by the footpath opposite Woodhow Farm (NY 140 042), at the west end of the lake. There is limited parking here or at the YHA at Wasdale Hall (NY 145 045) further along the road.

Wasdale Screes are very important for rare alpine plants – there are really rare things here, especially on the south-west end nearer Whin Rigg; generally they can be found on the most unstable and loose bits. Please only climb here in truly frozen conditions (climbing on the buttresses is discouraged at any time).

The climbs are described from right to left as approached from the west, with the pump house at the end of the lake serving as a convenient reference point. The

Wasdale Screes

1 Great (B) Gully — III
2 Right-Hand Branch — V
3 The Ramp — II
4 The Ramp Left-Hand — II/III
5 C Gully — IV
6 D Gully — II
7 E Gully — II

easiest **descent** is to gain the path running along the top of the crag and follow it south-west, over Whin Rigg summit and continue down the east side of *Greathall Gill* to the west (right, looking up) of the main crag.

Greathall Gill   Early 1970s
Situated well to the right of the main crags, this tree-filled gully occasionally freezes to give two steep ice pitches of 10 to 15m about halfway up the gill with tree belays at the top.

The iced slabs below the west end of the Screes offer a good place for beginners to practise technique.

E Gully   130m II Early 1970s
The rightmost of two shallow gullies at the west end of the crag directly above the pump house. This tends to take less drainage than the major lines so can be a bit thin.

D Gully   130m II Early 1970s
Approximately 30m left is another, slightly better defined gully.

C Gully   230m IV ** 1963
The prominent deep cleft originally named by the Victorian pioneers: approaching from the west this is the first of the major gullies.
1   50m. Short ice pitches lead to a steep corner.
2   35m. Take the corner direct, or alternatively traverse right to a ramp which leads back to the gully bed after 10m. Continue to below the big ice pitch and belay on the left.
3   20m. Climb the centre of the ice, moving left at the top.
4   20m. Amble easily up the gully bed and climb a short crack; this can be avoided on the left. Continue up to belay in the amphitheatre.
5   30m. The frozen waterslide; climb this, and easy snow, to a peg belay below the final pitch.
6   25m. The final steep ice pitch. Surmount a bulge near the top to pull into the gully above.
7   50m. Easy snow leads to a belay.

The Ramp   230m II Early 1970s
Starting just right of *Great Gully*, approximately 70m to the left of *C Gully*, a steep ramp curves up through the buttress to the right of *Great Gully*. It forms several ice

pitches interspersed with snow and old bits of aeroplane wreckage and finishes near the top of *C Gully*: the first pitch is the steepest.

The Ramp Left-Hand230m II/III Early 1970s

Follow *The Ramp* for 2 or 3 pitches until a hanging gully forming an obvious drainage line appears on the left (120m). Climb the short icefall into a narrow chimney (crux) and follow this into the deeper gully bed. Follow the gully to the top (110m).

Great (B) Gully**240m III ** 1892**

This, the biggest of the gullies, contains the huge Amphitheatre in its upper part. Most of the pitches are interspersed with scrambling.

135m. Two short icefalls and scrambling lead up to where the subsidiary gully runs up right.
220m. Steepening ice leads to a bulge and a final pull over to belay.
345m. More scrambling leads to the Waterslide Pitch and sometimes a further small pitch.
425m. Easy ground leads into the Amphitheatre.
550m. Continue up to the left branch, passing two more ice pitches, to where the gully narrows once again.
610m. Steep ice is bridged to belay below the final crack.
755m. The final steep 10m pitch leads to a snow slope which is followed to the summit.

Right-Hand Branch100m V (4) *** 1978

The magnificent icefall to the right of the Amphitheatre gives a stupendous 90m of continuous ice. After the first pitch, rock belays are available but are poor in the upper reaches where ice screws may be preferable. Once in the Amphitheatre, if formed the route is obvious.

130m. An easy gully line leads up to the start. Follow the steepening ice cone towards the overhang which is turned on the left; belay on the left.
240m. Move back right to the centre of the icefall and climb straight up over bulges. A poor rock belay can be found on the left, or use ice screws.
330m. Climb diagonally right for 15m then up to where the angle eases.

Chimney Finish65m II/III 1984/5

This lies to the right of the *Great Gully* ordinary finish, between this and the finish of the *Right-Hand Branch*. It is best approached from the foot of the *Right-Hand Branch*, passing over vegetation and an icy groove. Struggle your way up the steep chimney.

WASDALE SCREES

A Gully 160m II Early 1970s
The next gully lies 150m left of *Great Gully* and immediately left of the largest buttress. This wide gully contains just two awkward steps and may be used as a **descent** if care is taken.

Seven Pitch Gully 260m II Early 1970s
About 150m left of *A Gully*, this is the furthest left (east) of the gullies and gives several interesting short steep ice pitches in magnificent scenery. The route is obvious in its lower reaches: at the top go left for the normal finish, or take the wide gully to the right for a pleasant alternative ice pitch.

Variation Icefall III Early 1970s
At about half-height, steep ice on the right wall leads to a traverse left. An awkward descent then allows the main gully to be rejoined. Alternatively continue on up rightwards to the summit. A sheep track can also be traversed right at this point and a descent down an icy ramp leads to *A Gully*.

The small crag of Low Adam Crag (NY 158 047) lies below the Screes at an altitude of about 260m and faces north-west, opposite the point where the upper road into Wasdale reaches the lakeside. The following climb is located about 100m above it.

Juniper Ridge 130m I/II Early 1970s
The climb starts in a gully left of, and below, a big pinnacle. Under good snow conditions it provides an interesting corniced ridge route. From the gully, gain the ridge and pass the large pinnacle on its right. Continue up the meandering ridge to the summit.

LAKE DISTRICT WINTER CLIMBS

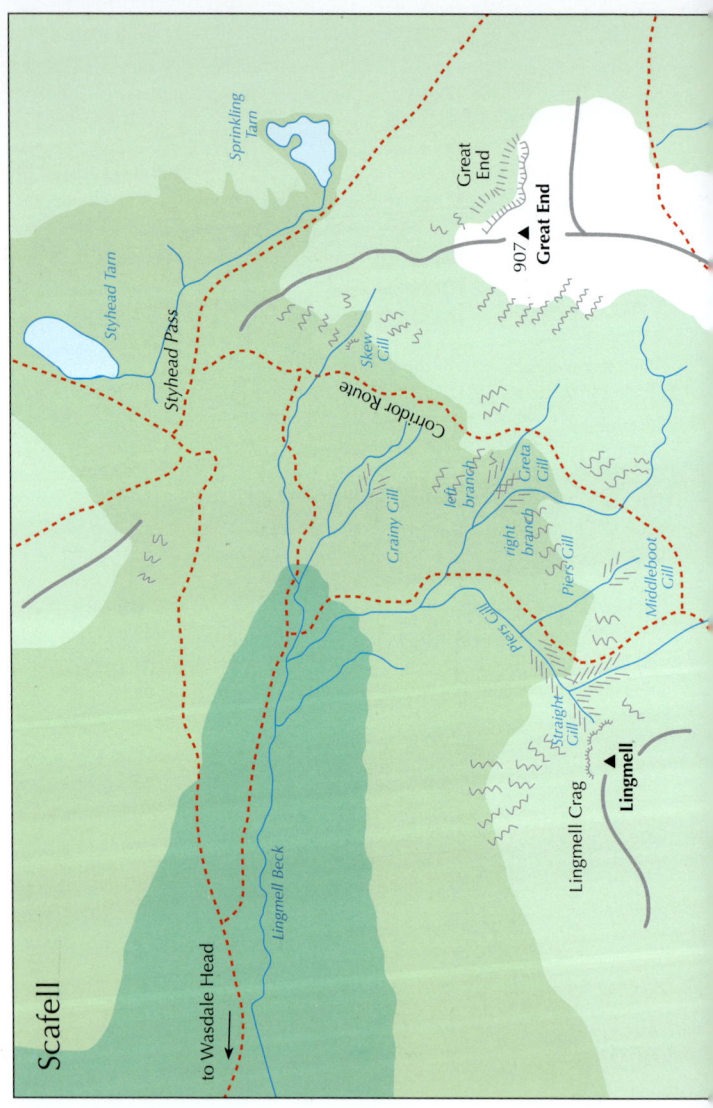

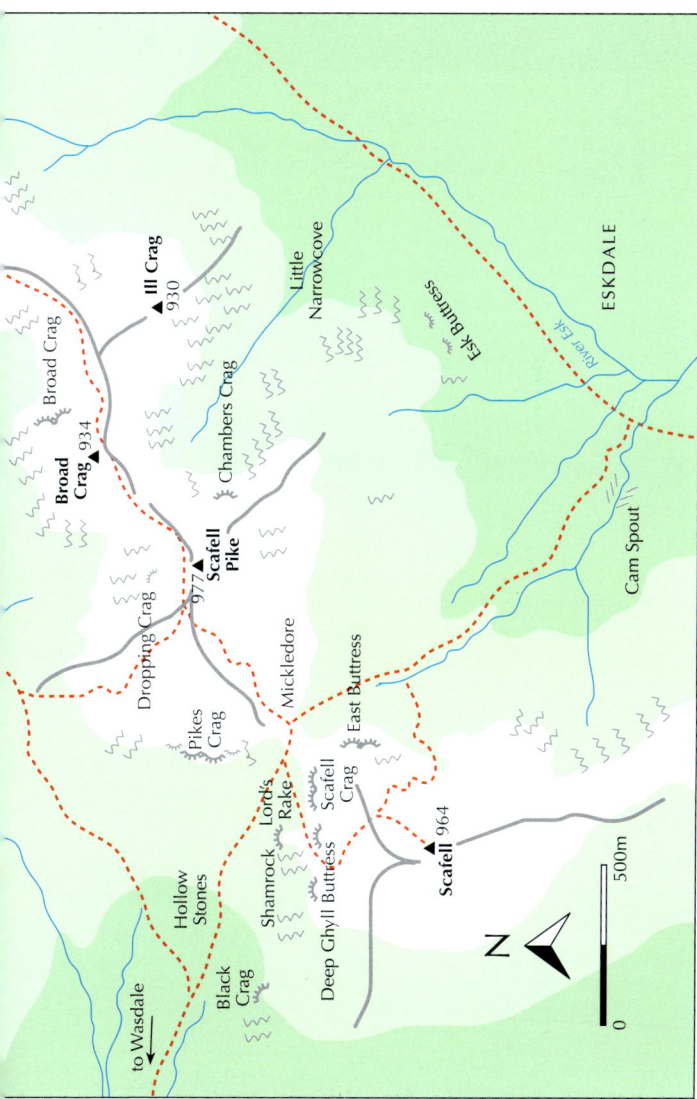

Lake District Winter Climbs

Scafell Massif

The Scafell crags are best approached from the car park at the north end of Wast Water, passing Brackenclose (FRCC hut) and ascending Brown Tongue. This route passes Black Crag before reaching the north-west facing combe of Hollow Stones. Pikes Crag stands on the left-hand (north-east) side of this combe under Scafell Pike. The main crag of Scafell is on the right-hand (south-west) side, with the distinctive Shamrock Buttress lower down to its right. The East Buttress of Scafell is hidden round to the right, over Mickledore, the col at the head of the combe.

All of these mountain crags can be gained from other valleys, but such approaches are much longer and harder. From Borrowdale take the Corridor Route via Styhead Tarn. From Eskdale, go via Cam Spout; from Langdale, go via Angle Tarn and the summit of Scafell Pike.

Black Crag

NY 201 070 Altitude 600m   *North-west facing*

Most people dash past this crag in a headlong rush for greater things on Scafell. As such it is usually quiet, while its larger neighbour can see queues forming. It is to the right of the path at the top of Brown Tongue, the steep part of the approach from Wasdale. Due to its more westerly aspect and lower altitude it is less often in condition than Scafell.

The routes are described from left to right.

Sinister Ridge   150m III (4) ** 1984

Leave something in reserve; the difficulties are at the top. Start about 15m up and right of the lowest point of the left-hand ridge.
1   25m. Climb a short wall with difficulty (if you're in luck it may be banked out) to easier ground and a belay at the foot of a groove.
2   30m. Follow the groove and continue up in the same line.
3   20m. Continue up the wall above the leaning flake (not as bad as it looks) to the foot of another wall.
4   25m. Make a traverse left, crossing a groove with some difficulty (crux).
5   50m. Climb up a shallow gully on the left to finish.

Black Crag

Black Shiver   50m III 1998
Start at a well-hidden gully/chimney tucked in on the right of *Sinister Ridge* and down and left of an obvious pinnacle high on the crag, from which an abseil descent to the foot of the route can be made.
1   25m. Climb the gully which has a steep right wall.
2   25m. Climb the ice smear on the left.

Black Crag Grooves   130m IV (4) * 1996
This route follows the line of grooves running down from the summit of the crag. As the route is mainly on vegetation it is only worth trying if fully frozen.
1   45m. Easy-angled turf leads to where the crag steepens.
2   25m. Follow a turf-lined groove to a chimney which is quit for a leftward-slanting ramp, then go up over a rock outcrop to a poor belay.
3   20m. Follow ice in the back of a steep groove and surmount the bulge to easier ground and a spike belay.
4   20m. Move left to another steep grassy groove, with the bulge at half-height this time.
5   20m. Follow easy ground to the summit.

First of Many   120m III (3) 2005
This route starts right of the central line of *Black Crag Grooves* and crosses that route. Start at a leftwards-slanting groove near the centre and about 50m left of the start of *Dexter Slab*.
1   30m. Follow the obvious groove, hard at first, to gain the leftwards-slanting turf groove which traverses to a large belay ledge. Poor anchors.
2   25m. Climb the wall behind the belay to a large stepped groove which goes first leftwards and then rightwards to a large ledge. Bomber belay.
3   25m. Climb the short awkward corner behind the belay and move easily to a left-slanting snow rake leading to a good belay in a large bay.
4   35m. Climb the weakness in the wall behind the belay to gain a groove system which is followed for 30m to a poor exposed belay.
5   35m. Step left into another groove which narrows at about 15m and which provides some thin moves before the groove fans out and is followed to the top of the crag. Good belays.

Dexter Slab   60m III 1984
Up on the right flank of the crag is a prominent gully below a buttress. This route takes a line up the centre of the slab below the gully, starting from the bottom of the gully. The difficulties can be avoided.
1   30m. Move right to some blocks after 5m, then climb the slab by the best line.

2   30m. A traverse leads up and right over a large flake to a terrace. The wall above is turned on the right.

Black Crag Gully   30m I/II 1984
Runs up diagonally left from the foot of *Hole and Corner Gully*, the short prominent gully up on the right of the crag.

Variation   IV
A vertical column of ice about 15m high can form about halfway up the gully.

Hole and Corner Gully   50m II
The obvious gully up on the right side of the crag.

Hole and Corner Gully Icefall   30m III *
The curtain of ice forming on the left wall and running up left out of *Hole and Corner Gully* gives a good pitch.

Short Cut Icefall   50m III ** 2010
Located at the far right-hand side of Black Crag. A short first pitch (10m) is followed by more ice offering the occasional vertical step.

SCAFELL

Two of the finest Lakeland mountain crags are to be found on the east and north sides of this mountain, East Buttress and Scafell Crag itself. With a steep and often overhanging base the rounded barrel shape of the East Buttress does not encourage good winter climbing conditions and little has been done in the way of complete ascents on the crag. Scafell Crag to the west of Mickledore has two contrasting sections. The main crag gives some intimidating modern mixed routes on the buttresses, with classic gullies in between. The three gills are *Deep Ghyll* (the easiest on the right), with the Scafell Pinnacle between it and *Steep Ghyll* (the central of the three), separated by the Pisgah from *Moss Ghyll* to its left.

The more broken ground of Scafell Shamrock to right of this area is separated from the main cliff by Lord's Rake which starts at the right end of the main crag and runs up diagonally right to a small col. Running off left from this first section is the impressive gap of *Deep Ghyll*. After crossing another small col, Lord's Rake emerges from a steep slope onto open fellside. **Warning** This used to provide a convenient descent route but has suffered a series of recent rockfalls so should

Scafell

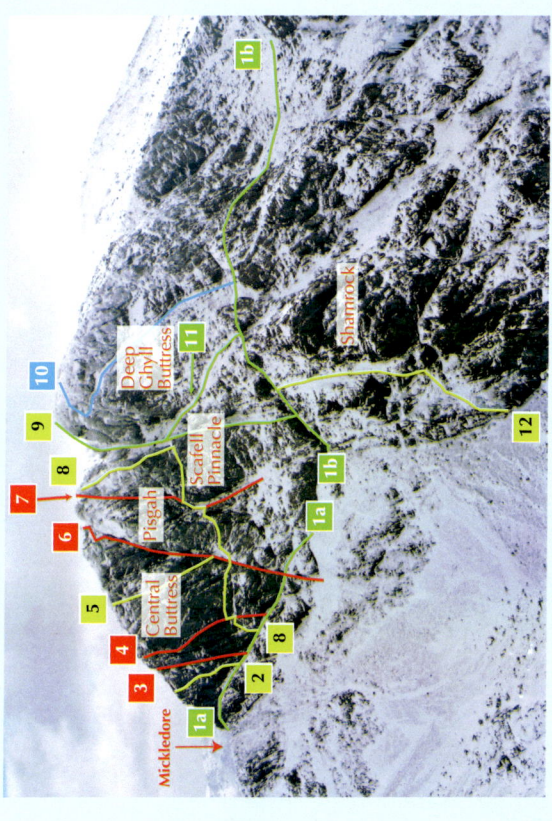

1a	Rake's Progress	I
1b	Lord's Rake	I
2	Collier's	
	Left-Hand Variant	VI
3	Collier's Groove	V
4	Botterill's Slab	V
5	Harvest Crunch	VII
6	Moss Ghyll	IV
7	Steep Ghyll	V
8	The Girdle Traverse	VII
9	Deep Ghyll	I/II
10	Deep Ghyll Integrale	III
11	West Wall Traverse	I
12	Shamrock Icefall	VII

LAKE DISTRICT WINTER CLIMBS

be treated with caution or better still avoided. The ground to the right of the Shamrock takes much drainage and can form easier climbs which complement those on the main crag. These generally consist of good ice pitches separated by easy-angled snow. The lines described can often be combined in a number of ways.

The best approach is from Wasdale, up the obvious path on the right-hand side of Brown Tongue.

Descent If descending back to the base of the climbs there are a number of choices. The safest but longest are described first. For routes finishing near Mickledore or on the East Buttress, descend via Foxes Tarn or, more carefully, via Broad Stand. This latter requires a certain amount of zigzagging past rocky steps. When just above Mickledore, move to a large boulder perched over to the left. A thread can be found at its base which allows the short abseil into Mickledore to be made. For routes finishing on the main crag, either descend as described above, or downclimb *Deep Ghyll* – the steep chockstone in the middle section generally gives the only real difficulties. Alternatively, part-way down *Deep Ghyll* below the *Great Chimney* follow the exposed *West Wall Traverse* into the lower part of Lord's Rake and descend this with care (see warning), or go over the col and carefully descend the broken ground to the right of Scafell Shamrock.

Scafell Crag

NY 209 068   ALTITUDE 790M   NORTH FACING

The routes are described from left to right. The routes start from **Rake's Progress** (I, 1908), a narrow shelf running along the base of the crag about 10m up, which can be easily gained from the foot of *Moss Ghyll*, or by a more exposed traverse from Mickledore.

North Climb   10m III 1899

A short scrappy climb starting 10m right of the highest point of *Rake's Progress*. A short wall leads to a square-cut recess; move left to abseil off, or continue up chimneys and across slabs to the summit.

Just past an awkward step in Rake's Progress a scoop and chimney marks the start of Collier's Original Start, about 10m left of Tricouni Slab.

Collier's Left-Hand Variant 45m VI (6) 2010

A series of grooves runs up and left from the point where the *Original Start* to *Collier's Route* joins the ledge at the top of pitch 1. The route takes these.

1   15m (6). The original start to *Collier's Route* up a scoop then a chimney offers a hard start to the long belay ledge. Further up the gully at the left-hand end of the ledge is an alternative belay.
2   30m (5) Climb up the groove on the left passing several helpful turf ledges. Traverse left along a large ledge, at its left end follow a second shorter groove to the top.

Collier's Groove 75m V (5) ** 2010

This follows the left side of *Tricouni Slab* before finishing up the obvious continuation chimney of *Collier's Climb* clearly visible in the crag diagrams. An early attempt (1910) on the route ended in a rescue.

1   25m (5). From the recess at the bottom of *Tricouni Slab* start up the slab past an old in-situ runner and move left immediately to the arete. Delicately balance up the arete to the ledge at the top of the slab, or more logically, climb the corner of *Tricouni Slab*. Step right into a short overhanging chimney which gives access to a large ledge and belay.
2   50m (5). Climb the gully at the left end of the ledge. Follow this passing under a large chockstone to strenuous climbing up a short V-groove to the top.

Tricouni Slab 75m IV (5) 1986

This section of the crag has a series of right-facing slabs. This is the leftmost slab, to the left of *Botterill's*. Well-protected technical climbing. Start from *Rake's Progress*.

1   20m (4). From an overhung recess, ascend the narrow slab to a ledge on the summer route of *Keswick Brothers' Climb*.
2   10m (5). Climb the short overhanging chimney to belay on the large ledge above.
3   45m (4). Continue over ledges up rightwards to a hollow and finish up the chimney/gully.

Botterill's Slab 95m V (6) *** 1984

A modern classic which is often in condition, although difficulty will depend upon the amount of ice. The obvious leftward-slanting slab starts from *Rake's Progress*. The slab is actually climbed via the corner on its right, the ascent being facilitated by icy and mossy remnants, with protection available on the right wall.

1   20m. Climb the short chimney to the base of the slab.
2   25m. Climb the right corner of the slab above, the meat of the climb.
3   30m. The short wall above leads to a deceptive wide chimney. Move up to an open gully on the left.

Rich Cross making a first ascent of Xerxes, Scafell Crag (photo: Steve Ashworth)

4   20m. Climb the open gully.

Central Buttress has one recorded ascent (1986). The climb took place over two consecutive days, the climbers returning to the valley overnight and at the Great Flake crampons were removed. A good effort by the climbers involved, but the consensus is that 'CB' awaits a true winter ascent. The route was not completed in one single push. In any event, the loss of the Flake chockstone has completely altered this section of the climb, possibly rendering it unclimbable in winter. Aspirant single-day ascentionists can find a full description in the FRCC Scafell guidebook.

Moss Ghyll Grooves   105m VII (6) * 1985
Not being a natural drainage line, heavy ice build-up is never going to be likely on this summer classic and time has shown that it doesn't come into condition often. The route starts out of *Moss Ghyll*, the obvious major gully right of the large sweep of walls that contains *Central Buttress*. It is the lowest of the major diagonal lines to the right of *Central Buttress*.
1   20m. From *Rake's Progress*, climb about 20m up *Moss Ghyll*, or easier via the wall to the right, to the first large ledge at the start of the sloping ramp/groove on the left of the gully.
2   20m. Climb the groove, passing a bulge.
3   20m. Continue up the corner above and up the narrowing slab then pull right into the next groove. Regain the corner of the groove when possible and follow this to a traverse right onto the ledge at the start of the next groove.
4   25m. Climb the second slab making the most of iced cracks.
5   20m. Move left and step up to follow the easier gully to the summit ridge.

Harvest Crunch   120m VII (9) ** 1987
One of the hardest routes in the area. The summer line was freed of aid only after the first winter ascent. It follows the second diagonal line running left out of *Moss Ghyll*, about 50m up the gill and opposite Tennis Court Wall. It takes a line up the right side of the prominent slab of the summer route *Slab and Groove*.
1   50m. Climb *Moss Ghyll* to a ledge at the start of the second diagonal line running out of the left side of the gill.
2   25m. Follow the right corner of the slab to the first roof. The climbing really starts now! Make a long reach with axes and a hard pull over the roof on ice. Climb to the second roof and step left with difficulty under the roof to thin moves on the slab leading to the belay (crux).
3   45m. If you've anything left, follow the groove, the second pitch of the summer route *Slab and Groove*. This becomes easier with height.

Moss Ghyll   135m IV (5) *** 1893

This is the large gully line dividing the Central and Pisgah Buttresses. The route follows the gully to an amphitheatre from where several alternative exits are possible, the *Collie Exit* being the classic of the district. The route is graded for well-iced conditions. It will probably feel a grade harder in lean conditions; then again you may just be climbing badly.

1. 30m. Starting from *Rake's Progress*, climb the gully to a cave pitch after 10m. This is turned on the right by a short chimney, before traversing back into the gully bed.
2. 20m. Climb up on the right of the narrow chimney/crack and continue up steep snow to belay below Tennis Court Wall.
3. 25m. The cracked wall on the right leads steeply to a ledge. A delicate traverse leads precariously back left to good neve in the gully bed and up to belay below a massive chockstone.
4. 20m. Follow the summer route under the chockstone to an exit through a 'window' on the left. Make a delicate traverse across the wall, the infamous Collie Step, and up into an amphitheatre. Belay and decide on which exit you want. In exceptional conditions the left wall below the chockstone can be climbed to the amphitheatre.

Collie Exit   40m IV 1893

The standard finish at the same grade. Climb directly up the slabs on the left for about 10m to a traverse left to a short chimney. This leads to the ridge.

Barton's Exit   40m V (4)

Follow the *Collie Exit* to where it traverses left then continue up the steep slabby corner above the overlap.

Mechanical Orange   80m VIII (8) 1987

This poorly-protected, demanding climb follows the summer line of *Clockwork Orange* from the amphitheatre of *Moss Ghyll*. On the first ascent the second unclipped from the belay and stood on the chockstone ready to jump to take up slack in the event of a leader fall. Unrepeated.

On the left of the amphitheatre, roughly parallel with the slabs of the *Collie Exit*, a thin slab runs out left from *Collier's Chimney*.

1. 40m. From 2m up *Colliers's Chimney*, follow the slabby groove left to where the wall steepens. Move left along a narrow ledge, or a flake below this, to a belay in the corner.
2. 40m. Follow the corner to the top, taking a line on the left wall to avoid the thrutch where the gully narrows.

Scafell Crag

Collier's Chimney 35m V (5) *** 1984

The true continuation to *Moss Ghyll* provides a challenging finish.

Follow the line of the deeply cut chimney on the right of the amphitheatre with some difficult chockstones. Under good conditions the wall right of the chimney gives an excellent bold pitch rejoining the chimney near the top.

Pisgah

Pisgah Buttress has *Moss Ghyll* on its left and *Steep Ghyll* to its right.

Pisgah Buttress Direct 155m V (6) *** 1937

An excellent winter route and one of the first of the mixed climbs to come into condition. Start at a chimney on the right of the buttress (the start of the summer route *Bos'n's Buttress*).

1   20m (5). Climb the chimney and step onto a ledge on the left. A more direct start up the front of the buttress is also possible.
2   30m (5). Climb the walls above, trending right to a belay on the large crevasse overlooking the lower part of *Steep Ghyll*.
3   15m (4). A difficult traverse left leads to a large ledge close to *Moss Ghyll* with an open corner above. In-situ sling.
4   30m (6). Climb the corner to a belay behind a pinnacle overlooking *Steep Ghyll*.
5   30m (4). Tackle the pinnacle above and trend left to gain a large snowfield.
6   30m (4). Take the easier buttress above.

Restless Natives 125m VI (6) 1986

This sustained route takes the line of slabs and ramp systems on the right-hand edge of the buttress, following approximately the summer line of *Bos'n's Buttress*. Start up the chimney of *Steep Ghyll Direct Start*.

1   30m. Climb the chimney to the deep crack-line on the left. Follow this with some difficult moves onto the ledge.
2   15m. Move right from the ledge and climb the steep crack to the right of the arete (hard) and the ramp above to a belay.
3   20m. Move up and right to a twisting crack and follow this and a short wall, to belay behind a pinnacle.
4   30m. Climb the wall above to a leftwards-trending gangway leading to a belay below the headwall.
5   30m. Move to easy ground on the left.

Bridge of Sighs 175m V (5) 1986

This climb follows the continuous corner system which runs up left from the easy snow at the top of pitch 1 of *Steep Ghyll*.

1   50m. Climb the first pitch of *Steep Ghyll* to the easy-angled snow. Belay in the top left corner of the large sloping ledge.
2   25m. The slabs on the left lead to a belay on thin blade pegs level with the top of the gully on the right.
3   35m. Bridge across the gully, rather wildly and continue up steeply in a direct line to the ridge.
4   65m. Easy ground leads to the top.

Steep Ghyll Grooves 115m V (6) 1986

The grooves overlooking the narrow gully of *Steep Ghyll*.

1   50m. Climb *Steep Ghyll* and belay where the gully walls close in near the start of the main pitch.
2   15m. Climb the left wall of the gully to a niche (peg). Move right 5m and, using a peg for aid, gain the ledge at the bottom of the chimney.
3   50m. The chimney and groove lead to easy slabs at the top.

Steep Ghyll 210m V (4) ** 1891

Probably the first Grade V in the British Isles, if not the World! The main pitches give fine sustained climbing with just adequate protection – if you can find it – combined with the *Direct Start* this makes a superb outing. Either start up a groove from *Rake's Progress* in line with the gully or, slightly easier, traverse right from the start of *Moss Ghyll* to reach the start of the first pitch.

1   60m. Easy climbing on snow leads to a large snowy ledge or snowfield and the narrowing gully walls of the main pitch tucked in on the top right-hand side.
2   60m. The ice pitch on the left then easy snow leads between the beetling gully walls to a stance at the foot of a 'bottleneck chimney'.
3   55m. The crux pitch and a long lonely lead. Climb the chimney for 12m into a scoop (possible poor stance for those with 50m ropes – with a buried wide crack up on left). Take courage and continue up the steep sustained groove, passing two bulging sections to the Jordan Gap (the saddle between the Pinnacle and the rest of the mountain).
4   35m. From the gap, move left to easy ground.

Direct Start 55m V (5) ** 1963

Accepts the obvious challenge of the deeply incised chimney to the left of the normal start to *Steep Ghyll*.

1   20m. An avoidable icy step leads across snow into the back of the chimney.

2   35m (5). The intimidating struggle up the constricted back wall is relieved by pulling out right at the top onto the easy snow at the start of the main groove pitch (3) of *Steep Ghyll*.

Scafell Pinnacle

This buttress to the right of *Steep Ghyll* forms the pinnacle which towers over the cleft of *Deep Ghyll* to its right. The majority of the routes here reach the top of the main buttress known as the Low Man. The fine knife-edge arete leads to High Man, the true summit of the buttress. **Descent** from here is possible by downclimbing a short wall on the left to the Jordan Gap, from where a traverse left leads one to the Scafell summit plateau.

Low Man by the Right Wall of Steep Ghyll   230m V (5) 1995
This starts high up in *Steep Ghyll* where the gully narrows and twists left. The route follows a parallel line of grooves and slabs to the right of *Steep Ghyll*.
1+2 120m. The first two pitches of *Steep Ghyll* – to the narrows.
3   35m. Follow a short wall on the right to a good ledge, then a short chimney on the right of some slabs to a belay.
4   35m. Make difficult moves right to gain the groove which is followed to easier ground and the knife-edge arete.
5   40m. Follow the arete to High Man.

Slingsby's Chimney Route   245m IV (5) ** 1995
Many of the routes up the Pinnacle meet at the base of *Slingsby's Chimney* which must be climbed to gain the summit. This route offers the quickest and easiest approach to the chimney for those eager to get to grips with it.
1+2 120m. The first two pitches of *Steep Ghyll* – to where the chimney narrows.
2   40m. Follow *Low Man by the Right Wall* to the ledge, then traverse across to the crevasse at the foot of the chimney.
3   45m. Climb a short wall then grapple up the difficult bulging chimney (crux) to easier ground – front crawl seems to offer the best approach.
4   40m. Finish up the arete to High Man.

The next feature is the shallow defined open corner of *Hopkinson's Gully* which runs up the centre of the Pinnacle.

Hopkinson's Gully   155m VI (6) ** 1986
About 10m to the right of *Steep Ghyll* is a shallow groove; start below this.

Scafell Crag

1 Tricouni Slab	IV
2 Botterill's Slab	V
3 Moss Ghyll Grooves	VII
4 Harvest Crunch	VII
5 Moss Ghyll	IV
6 Collie Exit	IV
7 Mechanical Orange	VIII
8 Collier's Chimney	V
9 Pisgah Buttress Direct	
10 Restless Natives	VI
11 Steep Ghyll Direct	V
12 Steep Ghyll	V
13 Low Man by the Right Wall	V
14 Hopkinson's Gully	VI
15 West Wall Climb	IV
16 Great Western	IV
— Girdle Traverse	VII

1   30m (6). Climb a short wall with difficulty to gain access to the groove. Sustained climbing up the groove eases with a move right just before the belay.
2   40m (4). The groove continues to a deep crack gained by an awkward step. Climb up this to belay below *Slingsby's Chimney*.
3   45m (5). Thrutch up the chimney to easier ground and follow this to the top of Low Man.
4   40m (3). The knife-edge arete to High Man with a descent to the gap.

Moonbathing   140m VI (6) *** 1986

The route follows a line up right of *Hopkinson's Gully* to a ledge overlooking *Deep Ghyll*, the site of the historic Hopkinson's Cairn.
1   30m (6). Follow the first pitch of *Hopkinson's Gully* to the belay.
2   30m (5). Start up the groove on the left for 2m (*Jones's Route Direct*). From a runner placement, traverse right nearly 15m to a ledge below a corner. Climb this to the ledge of Hopkinson's Cairn with a poor belay, best on the left.
3   40m (4). The arete above is climbed on its left-hand side to a block. Move right up a ramp, then back left, to an easier line running left across the buttress. Easier ground above leads to Low Man.
4   40m (3). The arete to High Man.

Jones's Route Direct   65m VII (7) ** 1984

Starting from a slab overlooking *Deep Ghyll*, at the bottom right-hand side of the Pinnacle, this route reaches the crevasse at the bottom of *Slingsby's Chimney*. The only known ascent to date was not completed to the top of the Pinnacle. Sadly the route is rarely in condition.
1   25m. Climb the slab on the right-hand side of the Pinnacle to gain the gangway above with difficulty. Tenuous moves lead diagonally left across the thin slab.
2   25m. The corner above leads to a traverse left to a belay in *Hopkinson's Gully*.
3   15m. As for *Hopkinson's Gully*. Follow the corner above to belay at the crevasse below *Slingsby's Chimney*.

Deep Ghyll   200m I/II 1882

This large gully, starting a few metres up Lord's Rake, cuts deeply back into the mountain. Two large chockstones must be overcome in the lower pitches, but a snowy winter can see these pitches all but obliterated. If they are impassable, an alternative start giving access to routes higher up the gill is via the **West Wall Traverse** (I, 1906/7). The start to this lies up Lord's Rake, at the col behind Shamrock Buttress and traverses into *Deep Ghyll* above the chockstones. Although a popular path in summer it can be difficult to locate under heavy snow. Great care should be taken as the traverse line passes between difficult ground both above and below, so needs to be located correctly.

To climb the gully direct, climb snow to the cave below the first chockstone. Surmounting this on the right is usually the easiest option (15m). Straightforward snow slopes lead to a smaller chockstone (65m) and easy ground above, where the *West Wall Traverse* comes in from the right.

Age Concern   110m VI (6) ** 1986

This thin and technical climb, a winter ascent of *Jones's Route Direct from Deep Ghyll*, follows the obvious curving crack on the left wall of *Deep Ghyll*, starting from just above the second chockstone and following a line to Low Man.

1   10m (2). Climb easily up to the foot of the crack.
2   30m (5). The crack is entered with difficulty and climbed to a snowy niche. Delicate moves left across slabs, and upwards, lead to a good spike runner and possible belay, or traverse left to another stance and belay on the arete.
3   20m (6). Move right and climb Gibson's Chimney, the continuation of the crack to the ridge.
4   50m (3). Climb the ridge with one awkward step to the top of High Man, then descend to the gap.

Centre Route   60m VI (6) ** 1996

High up *Deep Ghyll*, the left wall below High Man forms an impressive slab topped with some overlaps. Starting from the junction of *Deep Ghyll* and *Professor's Chimney*, this route follows the right-to-left rising diagonal summer line of *Jones's and Collier's Climb from Deep Ghyll* to a large recess, then ascends the overhung slab and the turf corner above to the summit of High Man. It catches the afternoon sun on clear days, so an early start is recommended. Start at the right corner of the slabs.

1   30m (6). From just above the right corner of the slab, make difficult and poorly-protected moves to a diagonal leftwards traverse up the slabs and belay in the snowy recess at the top left of the slabs.
2   30m (4). Low Man can be easily reached up a short corner at the back of the recess: follow the knife-edge arete to High Man. But more fun can be had by following the overhung slabs up right to a ledge. Follow the corner (*Woodhead's Climb*) to the top of High Man.

SCAFELL CRAG

There is a choice of exits from the head of *Deep Ghyll*. The main gill continues up easy snow slopes leading straight to the summit plateau. To the left are the following finishes:

New Professor's Chimney   50m II/III 1891
Start up the left-hand gully at the top of *Deep Ghyll*. Where this steepens, take the left fork, cutting steeply up behind the pinnacle to finish at Jordan Gap. Traverse left and round to the right to gain the summit.

Old Professor's Chimney   50m II * 1891
The true continuation finish to the chimney. Where the previous route takes a gully on the left, continue up to finish at a small bulge.

Slab Finish   35m II **
From below the bulge in *Old Professor's Chimney*, traverse right to an exposed finish up an iced slab.

Impunity Slabs   40m III * 1986
To the right of the *Slab Finish* to *Old Professor's* is a shallow corner: climb it.

Impunity Slab Corner   40m III 2010
At the right-hand side of *Impunity Slabs* is a prominent corner finishing to the right of the steeper rock that fringes the top of the slabs. Climb the corner with a steep start and exit.

The Girdle Traverse   275m VII (8) *** 2005
This girdle starts at *Botterill's Slab* and crosses Central Buttress, Pisgah Buttress and Scafell Pinnacle; you certainly get your money's worth! Never technically desperate, the route contains a lot of sustained climbing, with several hard pitches towards the end and – being a traverse – has to be protected for both leader and second, which can be time consuming. The only ascent to date was done with good neve on the ledges and took nine hours, with the ascentionists being rewarded with a fine sunset from the top of the pinnacle.

1   35m (6). Climb *Botterill's Slab* for 6m to a line of ledges on the right which lead diagonally to a narrow ledge. From its left end, climb a shallow corner to the left end of the Oval, the large ledge at the base of the Great Flake, which is reached by a delicate traverse right to where the ledge widens.

2   35m (5). From the right end of the Oval, downclimb and traverse right round a corner, then make a move up a slabby wall to a large turfy ledge. A short

traverse right round an arete leads to the top of pitch 1 of *Moss Ghyll Grooves*. Downclimb this to the bed of *Moss Ghyll*.

3 35m (6). Climb the turfy wall to the right of the gill, heading for a prominent corner in the middle of the buttress. The lower portion of the corner is climbed to belay on a ledge, below the steep upper corner, which contains several good chockstones.

4 15m (5). Move rightwards along a block traverse line. Follow this to the right side of the buttress and step down to a spike belay on the right of the buttress overlooking the deep chimney of the *Direct Start to Steep Ghyll*.

5 10m (3). Move up snowy slabs and traverse right to belay on easy angled snow at the top of the chimney; *Direct Start to Steep Ghyll*.

6 50m (4). Cross *Steep Ghyll* easily and climb to the start of its steep pitch. Climb the right wall of the gill to the Crevasse. Climb to the top of this and downclimb the other side to its base to belay.

7 15m (7). Go back up the Crevasse to the first large chockstone and make a delicate traverse right (Sansom's Traverse) to Hopkinson's Cairn.

8 30m (8). Climb the corner to the left of the arete and step right onto a sloping shelf leading to a corner (Bad Corner of the summer rock route *Moss Ledge Direct*). Climb the corner with difficulty to a spike belay on the arete overlooking the corner of the summer line of *Jones's Route from Deep Ghyll*.

9 20m (8). From the belay, step down and climb across the thin wall above Bad Corner to the arete. Once round the arete, follow a wide crack and easier ground to Low Man. These are the summer lines of *Gibson's Traverse* and *Low Man from Hopkinson's Cairn*.

10 30m (3). Climb the knife-edge arete and continuation ridge to the top of High Man.

Deep Ghyll Buttress

This buttress bounding the top right-hand side of *Deep Ghyll* possesses some of the highest climbs in England. It is deeply cleaved by the prominent *Great Chimney*.

Upper Deep Ghyll Route   65m II * 1986

Start at a shallow groove 50m higher than the cleft of *Great Chimney*. Gain a left-to-right diagonal line running across the crag. The first 10m are the hardest.

Upper West Wall Climb   70m VI (7) 2010

This follows the summer route starting left of *Great Chimney* and immediately left of *Into the Wild*. The route zigs left to overlook *Deep Ghyll* then once the upper ledge is reached zags back right to the top of the buttress.

1. 30m (7). Start at the base of the corner left of *Great Chimney*. Climb a recess for 3m until it is possible to move left along a right to left diagonal line which is followed to the left edge of the buttress. The moves are balancy and protection is difficult to find. Climb a short steep wall to a large ledge running up rightwards. Spike belay.
2. 40m (4). Follow the ledge easily rightwards until it levels off and it is possible to make a step up into the final snowy recess on the left. Climb the left-hand corner at the back of the recess passing a flake and ledge just below the top. A short step up this gains the top.

Into the Wild   75m VII (9) ** 2010

The route is based on the summer route *Ixodus*, starting at the shallow corner to the left of *Great Chimney*.

1. 35m (9). Climb the slabby wall towards the bottom of the obvious layback flake on the right wall. Hook the flake and make a committing pull up followed by laybacked torques to its top, landing on a broken ledge below a hanging niche and chimney straight above. Make a long move up into the hanging niche in a wild position and while you still have energy available carry on up the chimney to its top and a good belay ledge on the left.
2. 40m (3). Step up left and climb the obvious turfy groove to its top where a ledge system leads rightwards, or take any likely finish.

Great Chimney   20m IV (4) 1986

The obvious wide cleft below the upper buttress. The chockstone at half-height is passed on the right by difficult but well-protected moves to easier climbing in the gully above.

Jacob's Ladder   70m V (6) 1999

The corner-groove to the right of *Great Chimney*.

1. 35m. From just below *Great Chimney*, climb to a ledge on the right of the arete. Climb the corner at the back of the ledge to a sloping ledge overlooking *Great Chimney*.
2. 35m. Use a flake to make a balancy move right and up to below an overhang, then back left into a sentry box. Climb the wall above overlooking the chimney.

The next three routes are on the section of buttress below *Great Chimney*. A deep chimney-crack marks the start of *West Wall Climb* in its lower section and a prominent left-facing corner left of an off-width crack defines the start of *Great Western*.

West Wall Climb 70m IV (4) ** 1986

Start some 20m down to the right of *Great Chimney*, below a deep chimney on the lower section of the buttress.

1 40m. Enter the deep chimney-crack with difficulty and wriggle upwards. From the top of the crack, move diagonally rightwards over short steep steps to belay in a vague bay.
2 30m. Climb a crack/groove on the left of the thin arete situated at the back of the bay. Move right and up to a steep wall. A swing right across the blank slab leads to an arete. Follow this and the short wide crack above; then follow easier ground to finish.

Doctor Grey 90m VII (7) 2010

This climb starts about 10m left of *Great Western* in the first shallow corner to the left of the arete of the buttress. Starts up the summer route *Doctor Death* before traversing across a ledge, past a prominent spike to follow the summer route *Grey Bastion* to an in-situ sling belay. Cracks were iced up on this ascent making protection difficult to find.

1 30m (7). Start 3m up from the left edge of Deep Ghyll Buttress in a shallow corner taken by *Doctor Death*. Climb this for about 5m until level with a ledge on the arete to the right, which contains a prominent spike. Cross the wall precariously to the worrying looking prominent spike. Strenuous climbing gains the ledge above. Climb up the corner to another ledge then a second corner before moving right to an in-situ sling belay common with the 2nd belay on *Great Western*.
2 30m (4) Follow *Great Western* to the two perched blocks.
3 30m (6) Climb an off-width crack and wall a few metres right of the perched blocks to finish overlooking *Great Chimney*.

Great Western 95m IV (4) *** 1995

Start below the prominent wide crack of the summer route *Gobsite*. This route takes the prominent left-facing corner, left of the wide crack.

1 20m. Climb the corner below the prominent wide crack and belay to the left, below a large pinnacle.
2 20m. Follow another corner on the left to a ledge and belay at its left-hand end.
3 20m. The ramp above leads to a larger ledge. Follow the corner on the right to belay by a large detached flake.
4 35m. Head for two perched blocks which form an arch on a ledge up and right of the belay. From the ledge, follow a corner-line a few metres to the left of the arched blocks to finish overlooking *Great Chimney*.

The steep wall above West Wall Traverse has a steep grassy break on its right-hand side, the line of *Sod's Law*.

Xerxes   65m VIII (8) 2008

A difficult and sustained climb taking the clean crack in the left-hand side of the wall, starting up a V-groove 15m right of the start of *Great Western* and the off-width crack above. Apart from the crack, protection was hard to find.
1   15m (7). Climb the groove to the left end of a ledge.
2   25m (8). Follow the crack in the wall to the right of a rib/nose. At the top of the crack move left into a groove. Continue working leftwards to a large ledge.
3   25m (6). Follow a wide gully above on the left to a slabby finish.

Sod's Law   90m VI (6) ** 1984

This follows the grassy break.
1   25m. The shallow open groove leads to a large flake belay.
2   35m. A short steep corner on the left leads to thin slabs which are taken directly to gain the ledge of *Deep Ghyll Integrale*.
3   30m. A short overhang on the right leads to finishing chimneys.

Sodom   110m V (6) * 1990

Start at a ramp and groove to the right of the grassy break of *Sod's Law*.
1   25m. Climb the easy ramp and V-groove and belay at the flake as for *Sod's Law*.
2   45m. Move to a ramp above the belay. This leads leftwards to a ledge above the short steep corner of *Sod's Law*. A long traverse left along the ledge and some awkward climbing leads up to the ledge on *Deep Ghyll Integrale*.
3   40m. Finish as for the *Integrale*, traversing left along the ledge until overlooking *Great Chimney*, then up the arete.

Sod All   50m III (4) 1986

A long diagonal rake (*Deep Ghyll Integrale*) is situated to the right of *Sod's Law*. This runs from right to left just below the top of the cliff and is gained from between the two cols on *Lord's Rake*. Follow this rake leftwards for some distance, past a narrow chimney, to a shallow groove on the right. Climb the groove and a narrowing chimney to the top.

To the right of *Sod All*, above the start to the *Integrale* (between the two cols on Lord's Rake), are three short but interesting chimneys.

Eye Spy
40m V (4) 1997

The first of the three chimneys is steep and insecure in its lower section but has a pleasant through-route at the first chockstone.

About 20m to the right is a large sloping ledge slightly lower than the start of *Eye Spy*: the other two chimneys start from here.

Dharma Armour
45m III 1997

The middle chimney line trends leftwards.

Chimney Stack
45m IV (4) 1997

The chimney at the right-hand end of the ledge. Pass a chockstone near the start and squeeze through several narrow restrictions before moving left at the top; beware of loose blocks.

Deep Ghyll Integrale
140m III (3) * 1990**

Follow the rising diagonal line leftwards from between the two cols on Lord's Rake (this ledge system crosses the higher part of Deep Ghyll Buttress). The ramp is easy but becomes narrow and exposed as the corner of *West Wall Climb* is crossed. Continue to a belay overlooking *Great Chimney* (100m). The final pitch gives airy climbing up the exposed arete. Move up a flake then across a short slab to a final delicate exposed step right.

Castor
100m II/III 1984

This route starts 3m right (west) of the second small col of Lord´s Rake when approached from the pinnacle. The main difficulties are in the first pitch with several variations possible thereafter.
1   20m. Cross the short wall to reach the right edge of the ridge and climb this.
2   35m. The wall on the left is turned by a chimney. Continue up to a pile of blocks.
3   45m. Climb the wall behind the blocks and continue up two slabby ribs to the top.

Pollux
70m III 1987

Start left of a prominent pillar of rock projecting from the main cliff, 40m down to the right of the second col of Lord's Rake.
1   10m. Climb the corner on the left side of the pillar then head for a groove up to the left; belay just below the groove.
2   25m. Climb the groove to a niche, pull out by the left wall to gain a grass ledge.
3   35m. Follow the rib to the right to the top.

Scafell Shamrock

NY 205 070   ALTITUDE 720M   NORTH FACING

This is the area of rather broken rock below Lord's Rake. It is the first buttress to come into view when walking up from Wasdale, hence the name. The broken ground to the right of the Shamrock also has some climbing and a large rambling buttress with a prominent icefall down its centre (*Cascade*) is situated up and right of the broken ground.

The routes are described from right to left.

Cascade   215m II/III * Early 1963
This starts at the toe of the rambling buttress system and continues over three interesting ice pitches with a series of easy snowy ramps in its upper reaches.
1   40m. Follow an icy groove for 16m to easier ground.
2   40m. The ice above steepens towards the top easing to a snowfield.
3   20m. Trend right across the snow.
4   50m. Follow a shallow ice gully to a belay.
5   40m. Move up and follow a leftward-slanting ramp for 12m to gain a small col.
6   25m. Continue diagonally left, up a similar ramp system, to easy ground just west of the finish of Lord's Rake.

An ill-defined buttress marks the right end of the area of broken ground on the right of the Shamrock Buttress. Above this buttress, an open snow slope runs up into a gully, **Red Gill** (I/II), which continues up (with a small pitch in lean conditions), to cross Lord`s Rake past the second col, and continues to the top. When banked out this can make a useful **descent** from Scafell.

The Direct Route   165m II/III ** 1969
This follows the line of the stream draining down the middle of the broken ground and climbs the mass of ice that builds up in the centre of this area.
1   25m. Either climb the obvious icefall at the bottom of the shallow gully or turn it on the left.
2   30m. Easy-angled ice leads to steeper ice out of a gully on the right.
3   30m. Climb the icefall to belay on easier ground.
4   35m. Above, easy snow leads to a leftward-slanting rake below icy cascades.
5   45m. Climb the ice cascade from the bottom of the rake for 25m, then snow, to finish at the second col of Lord's Rake.

Pillar Variation 45m IV Early 1970s
A vertical pillar of ice sometimes forms at the left end of the icy cascade near the top of *The Direct Route*. Climb the pillar direct and its continuation ice bulge.

The Lost Arrow Traverse 75m II 1972
From the left-slanting rake below the final ice cascade of *The Direct Route*, traverse a system of ledges and grooves across the buttress above *Easy Gully* to emerge onto Lord's Rake, opposite *Deep Ghyll*.

Easy Gully **170m I/II**
This broad leftward-slanting gully/rake cuts into the top of the Shamrock. Take the easiest line into the gully and exit right from its top onto Lord's Rake. A more exacting start can be made immediately right of *Tower Buttress*. Combined with a finish up *Deep Ghyll*, this provides 300m of easy climbing to the summit of Scafell.

Drainage from the rock nose below the Shamrock often forms some exciting looking icicles to 'boulder': sadly they seldom extend to ground level.

Twisting Gully **150m IV (4) 1996**
On the right side of the *Shamrock*, between the summer lines of *Rampart* and *Silk Cut Slab*, is an obvious S-shaped gully. The lower pitches involve climbing steep icy chimneys, before finishing up the last 50m of *Easy Gully* to the top of the Shamrock.

The Tower Buttress, Winter Variation **200m VI (6) 2010**
This technical and strenuous route follows the summer route *Tower Buttress* to the base of the second tower in two pitches, then takes easy ground to the left of the towers to gain Lord's Rake. Start at the first prominent chimney lower down the slope from the icefall.
1 50m (6). Climb turf and ledges to the base of a narrow chimney; quite technical. Then squirm up the narrow chimney to a ledge.
2 50m (6). Climb the chimney-corner to a chockstone and make brutal moves to a small ledge. Somehow insert yourself into the narrow slot above and wriggle upwards to easier ground.
3 100m. Follow easy ground leftwards to Lord's Rake.

Shamrock Icefall
150m VII (6) 2010

An impressive stalactite forms down the steepest overhanging section of the Shamrock Buttress. Often eyed, as it forms to some extent most years, it rarely (if ever) touches down and in such a state is inherently weak meriting the seventh grade.

1   45m (6). Psyche up and climb the groove behind the icefall until it is possible to step gingerly onto the ice. Work your way up the ice to the snowfield above and find a large block at its top.
2   50m (4). A second shorter and easier icefall forms at the top of the snowfield, climb this with a helpful groove on its left. Follow the snowfield above to belay on the left.
3   55m. Easy climbing leads to a descent into Lord's Rake or to the top of the Shamrock.

Intermittent Chimneys
100m IV 1985

On the left side of the Shamrock, this series of three stepped chimney pitches starts some 60m down from the bottom of Lord's Rake.

Scafell East Buttress

NY 210 067   ALTITUDE *800M*   EAST TO SOUTH-EAST FACING

This spectacular barrel-shaped buttress east of the col of Mickledore rarely forms ice to its base; the few winter climbs here are generally very steep and until recently complete ascents have proved elusive. In the 1980s the upper sections of several routes were climbed using an abseil approach. This certainly makes for an exciting day out in an impressive setting. Some of these climbs now provide satisfying finishes to the lower approach pitches, although they still await complete ascents.

Mickledore Chimney
115m III * 1891

This distinctive deep rift starts some 50m down from Mickledore. Steep snow between vertical rock walls leads to a prominent chockstone (65m). This can be bypassed by escaping out right. If you accept the challenge, then climb the double chockstone pitch (15m) and continue up steep snow to finish up a short chimney on the right (35m).

Icefall Start
30m III/IV 1960

Just right of the start of *Mickledore Chimney*, a groove gives a short ice pitch with a hard start.

Icefall Finish
15m IV * 1960

The ice pitch which forms on the left side of the upper gully.

Tia Maria
50m V (6) 1996

This route follows the first crack system up the left wall of *Mickledore Chimney*, where the wall steepens.
1   30m. Start up the lowest of the parallel cracks. Difficult and poorly-protected climbing leads to a recess and block belay.
2   20m. From the left side of the recess, climb the continuation of the crack.

Overhanging Wall and *SOS* are the only routes to have had complete ground-up ascents on this section of the crag; where they connect these two routes provide starts to the routes above previously approached by abseil. Now described as variation finishes, these create a number of very challenging ways up. While the slabs higher up the cliff may become iced this doesn't tend to extend to the ground so any climbing will probably involve steep mixed climbing linking isolated hanging icicles.

In locating the starts, a low stone wall bivouac site found several metres downhill from *Mickledore Chimney* makes a useful reference point.

SOS
65m IX (10) 2007

A very hard first pitch following the mossy groove leads to a finish up *May Day Climb*. Start at the mossy groove adjacent to the walled shelter
1   15m (10). The mossy groove is followed to the first belay on *May Day Climb*.
2   12m (6). Traverse leftwards round the tricky arete and up turf ledges to below an off-width corner formed by a semi-detached pinnacle.
3   25m (7). Climb the off-width using a chockstone. From the top of the pinnacle step up to a higher ledge and climb a V-groove. Turf ledges are crossed to the bottom of a slab where a faint groove leads straight up. Bold moves left where the groove fades will get you to a turf boss and in a few metres more onto a long grassy ledge.
4   15m (3) The corner on the right leads more easily to the top.

A variation finish is

May Day Direct
50m VI (6) 1984

From the top of pitch 1 of *SOS* this takes take the prominent right-facing corner. The crack above the belay leads into the steep corner which if well iced can be followed to a ledge. The continuation corner-crack leads to the top.

Paddy Cave attempts Moondance in superb condition – Scafell East Buttress (Steve Ashworth)

Overhanging Wall 25m V (6) 1985

Start at an overhung ledge containing a large boulder, about 10m left of, and several metres lower than, the bivvy wall.

Climb up a corner to the left of the ledge: this leads to a small ledge. A traverse up and right leads to a rib and the crack to its right, reached with some aid. Follow this to a ledge. Move to a mossy crack on the right and surmount a bulge with aid. Continue up and right to another ledge. A traverse leads to a corner on the left: climb this to a belay.

Three finishes are possible from here depending on the conditions. These top pitches come into condition more regularly than the lower pitch and have been approached by abseil.

Minotaur 50m VI (5) *** 1984/85

Used on the first ascent *White Slab* is followed until a move right is possible onto an iced ramp-line which is followed to its top. It can be climbed in one 50m pitch.
1   25m. Follow *White Slab* to belay just below the iced ramp-line.
2   25m. Climb the corner to a slab on the left, this is followed to easier ground.

White Slab 40m III (3) 1984

In summer this is a distinctive white-coloured slab: with luck, you'll find it so in winter as well. Often thinly iced, this obvious white slab on the left of the belay contains a large block in its centre. Climb the ice.

Overhanging Wall – Original Finish 45m IV (5) 1994

From the belay, climb the right-facing corner, right of the prow overlooking *White Slab*. Step right and climb the iced corner running up to a chimney. The chimney is climbed by a series of awkward bridging moves leading to easier ground.

Moondance 85m VII (8) 2011

A winter line based on the summer route of *Moonday*. Start down and left of the ledge of *Overhanging Wall* at a slab containing a damp mossy streak which ices up in winter.
1   20m (8). Climb the iced slab and bulging wall above passing a block to belay on a grassy ledge below an overhanging groove.
2   15m (7). Pull over a block and bulge on the left leading to a ramp. Follow this to the foot of the *White Slab*.
3   50m (5). Follow *White Slab* for a few metres to a slab leading off rightwards. Follow this passing a steep crack on the left wall (possible belay) and continue up the ramp to finish up a chimney, the original finish of *Overhanging Wall*.

SCAFELL EAST BUTTRESS

Great Eastern Route   125m V (6) 1960
A winter ascent of one of the easier East Buttress routes. One exposed move on the crux pitch is far harder than anything else on the climb. Start at an opening 5m to the right of the lowest part of the crag.
1   5m (3). Easy rocks are followed by a walk to the left.
2   25m (6). Ascend the cracked slab/ramp-line slanting up to the left. At the top of the ramp an exposed move leads to a ledge and good spike.
3   35m (4). Continue up the corner to a slab below a large overhang. Go diagonally right across the slab and up a short step to a peg belay.
3   40m (4). Continue right to another awkward step up, then continue along the ledge to a deep cleft. Step up onto a grassy ledge and use the off-width corner-crack and wall to gain the ledge above.
4   20m (3). Climb up and round from the left end of the ledge and move up to easier ground.

Direct Start   V (6) 1999
A direct start up the icy first pitch of *Gold Rush*, about 12m left of *Great Eastern Route*.
1   30m. Climb the icefall that forms at the start of *Gold Rush*: if it is thick enough, follow it to the ramp-line of *Great Eastern*; otherwise follow an overhung ledge, trending right to join the ramp-line at a lower point.

Never Ever Say Never   VIII (8) 2010
The exceptional winter of 2010 saw the elusive East Buttress icefall form completely. This almost mythical icefall has seen several generations of climbers patiently waiting for its upper section to be fully formed. The starting ice, coming out of the summer line *Gold Rush*, readily forms and offers an alternative start to *Great Eastern* which can be followed to the base of the Yellow Slab where the second and steeper icefall forms down the headwall of *Overhanging Grooves*. Dave Birkett was the man on the ground when it finally formed and his ascent took him and two partners (Mary Jenner on the first day to the Yellow Slab, then Andy Mitchell) two days with an approach by abseil on the second day. Due to its aspect a complete ground-up ascent in a single push will be a notable achievement. Hopefully it will form again soon.

The wide crack at the extreme left-hand side of the main crag is *Slime Chimney*.

Slime Chimney   131m IV (4) 1984
Identified by a huge perched block that forms a cave above a short wall at its foot. The winter route roughly follows the summer line.

1   65m. Climb easily up mixed rock and snow steps to beneath the three parallel chimney cracks on the extreme left side of the buttress: belay.
2   15m. Move left onto the blocks, traverse left, then delicately diagonally left to belay in a bay.
3   35m. Climb the narrow chimney-crack at the back of the bay, then the easier ramp system.
4   16m. Move to easy ground on the left, then finish up an easy gully on the left.

Scafell Pike

The highest point in the country doesn't offer as much climbing as its neighbour, but there are some interesting coves and gullies tucked away on both sides of the mountain. For those crags on the southern (Eskdale) side of the mountain, see the Eskdale section.

Pikes Crag

NY 210 071   Altitude 750m   *West facing*

Pikes Crag overlooks Brown Tongue and is visible from the road in Wasdale. The crag is south of the col to Lingmell. Looking left from Mickledore, the crag is seen as a series of short slabby buttresses which catch the sun. Further round, the most extensive buttress is known as Pulpit Rock. This is separated from the rest of the mountain by a deep cleft. Left of the Pulpit are several gullies (lettered for convenience), while the final long gully marking the left end of the crag is imaginatively named *Long Gully*. The crag generally gets more sun than its larger neighbours, so an early start or a cloudy day can help find the best conditions. Sticking to the alphabet, the routes are described from left to right.

Long Gully   250m I
The long gully to the left of the crag. There are no real difficulties but it makes a pleasant route to a small col and then to Scafell Pike's summit.

Buttress Route   100m II
The buttress between *Long Gully* and *A Gully*. A left-sloping ramp leads to a few short pitches before the top.

Pikes Crag

1 Long Gully	I
2 'A' Gully	II/III
3 'B' Gully	III
4 'C' Gully	II
5 'D' Gully	II
6 Jumper Buttress	V
7 Left of Centre	IV
8 Right of Centre	IV
9 Grooved Arete	V
10 Slanting Groove	IV
11 Crenation Ridge	II
12 Descent Gully	I

A Gully 150m II/III

The first of the three gullies lying close together in the centre of the crag.
1   45m. A short chimney leads to steep snow then a belay below a small chockstone.
2   20m. Bridge up past the chockstone to further steep snow and a belay below a large capstone.
3   50m. Struggle past the capstone on the right wall for 10m and belay at a small chimney.
4   35m. Follow easy snow to the top.

The buttress between the two gullies (**AB Buttress**, 1908) has been ascended in heavy snow and ice conditions but its grade is not known.

B Gully 175m III

The most difficult letter in the alphabet – in fact, a bit of a B! A steep chimney/gully with a through-route for the thin.
1   35m. Follow ever-steepening snow slopes to a buttress splitting the gully: belay on the left.
2   40m. Follow the right branch past several ice bulges to a vertical chimney. Climb the chimney with difficulty and either belay below the chockstone or climb another 10m via the 'through' route on the right or, for the more substantial climber, go outside to easier snow above.
3   100m. Continue in the gully line to the top.

C Gully 180m II

Next in the alphabet!
1   30m. Follow the steepening concave snow slope to a belay in a cave below a large chockstone.
2   20m. Pass the chockstone by a traverse onto the left wall. Climb awkwardly back right to gain snow slopes above the chockstone.
3   130m. Easy snow leads to the top.

Horse and Man Rock 165m III ** 1983

A varied climb with an awkward finish; take care with the rock on the Horse and Man. Start at a groove 15m down and left from the huge chockstone in *D Gully*.
1   50m. Trot up the groove.
2   20m. From the groove, hurdle left round two corners.
3   50m. Canter up a series of chimney pitches to a belay in a cave.
4   45m. Hurdle over easier ground to the right to gallop up *Steeplechase Groove* and dismount.

Steeplechase Groove   115m II/III 1983
A good climb; the grade varies with conditions. Start at the groove of *Horse and Man Rock*.
1   50m. Take a direct line up to the right of the cracked wall to a peg belay.
2   35m. Head for the cave above.
3   30m. Easier ground leads to the top.

D Gully   140m II
The gully behind Pulpit Rock, on its left side. The imposing chockstone at the bottom of the gully can be passed by a short groove on the left. Move up to a small slab on the right, before traversing back into the gully. A choice of finishes: the subsidiary gully on the left poses few difficulties, or, more interestingly, continue up to the ridge between Pulpit Rock and the Pike.

Pulpit Rock

Some of the best climbing on the crag is to be found on Pulpit Rock. The buttress immediately right of *D Gully* is known as Mare's Nest Buttress. To its right, and separating it from Pulpit Rock, is a grassy or snowy gully, *Mare's Nest Gully*. All the routes here require a short abseil descent to reach the top of *D Gully* and *Descent Gully*: this runs down the Scafell (south) side, with *D Gully* dropping down from the col on the north side.

Mare's Nest Gully   40m I/II 1905
A steep wall bars entry to easier snow at the start of the depression. Above the gully narrows giving more interesting climbing. Finish on snow at the summit of Pulpit Rock.

The next distinctive feature is a depression in the centre of the Rock. This is taken by *Urchin's Groove*. To its left, the corner-line running the height of the crag is *Central Line,* which has left and right starts. The buttress left of the corner is *Juniper Buttress*.

Juniper Buttress   100m V (6) 2011
A line up the buttress between the prominent corner line of *Left of Centre* and the left edge of the Pulpit Rock. Start by a large detached block as for the summer route *Juniper Buttress*.
1   25m. From the block trend right across a wall into a right facing corner come wide crack. Climb this to a small bulge, step right and pull over at an obvious layback flake and turf blobs to a short crack leading to a large ledge.

2   20m. Step left and climb a chimney past some stacked blocks to another large ledge.
3   30m. Above and right is a large alcove with a hand sized crack rising from its apex. Climb slabby grooves to gain a small pedestal then make a tricky step right to gain the hand crack above the alcove. Follow it past a projecting block to another large ledge and huge block belay.
4   25m. Follow a short right facing groove to a small ledge then the off-width crack which has some handy chockstones at the back.
5   Easy ground leads to the summit of Pulpit Rock.

Left of Centre   95m IV (4) ** 1987

The prominent corner line running the height of the crag. The clean buttress left of the depression is split by the crack of *The Citadel*, a summer VS. Start to its left.
1   30m (4). Climb the groove on the left of the buttress to belay on the right at a large ledge.
2   35m (3). Follow the large slabby corner on the right to a belay.
3   30m (4). The chimney above is undercut and awkward to enter; follow it to the top.

Right of Centre   90m IV (5) * 1989

Start up the corner to the right of the clean buttress.
1   25m (5). Climb the corner leading to the right end of the large ledge at the top of the first pitch of *Left of Centre*. The steep off-width crack near the top of the corner proves the crux of the route.
2 and 3 65m (4). Follow *Left of Centre* to the top.

The Snow Patrol Finish   30m V (6) 2007

From below the final undercut chimney finish step left from the belay and climb the stepped turfy corner between *The Sentinel* and the normal *The Citadel* finish.

Urchin's Groove   100m V (4) ** 1984

This follows a series of disconnected grooves up the wide shallow depression in the centre of the buttress. The first pitch benefits from a good build-up of snow. It is possible to climb the depression by a number of lines: the one described offers good climbing and is most often in condition.
1   35m. Start near the centre of the depression. Back and foot to a peg belay above a traverse line.
2   35m. Climb the slab above, then a short icy wall to a stance; peg protection useful.
3   35m. A difficult traverse left leads to a finish up a well-iced wall.

Coldplay 145m IV (6) 2008

This roughly follows the arete falling from the highest point of the crag starting and finishing up the summer route *The Nave* and following *Grooved Arete* in its central portion. Start 5m down from *Grooved Arete* at the crags lowest point.

1   55m (6). Start left of *The Nave* and follow a line up the buttress above. A difficult pull onto a turfy ledge just left of the *The Nave* at about 15m, then turf climbing, leads to a steep crack filled with little pebble chocks. Climb this for 10m to the big belay ledge as for *Grooved Arete*.
2   30m. Pitch 3 of *Grooved Arete*.
3   45m (5). Follow *Grooved Arete* pitch 4, but move right after the crack in the corner, then progressively left, heading directly up underneath a big square roof. Turn this on the right. Belay on the ledge.
4   15m (5). Go up to the chockstone in the chimney, pull onto the ledge to its left and directly up using a thin short crack (steep) to the top of the crag.

Grooved Arete 130m V (5) 1970

An entertaining climb starting from a V-groove below a large overhang to the right of the prominent arete at the right-hand side of the crag. There are some loose blocks.

1   10m. Climb up a left-sloping grassy groove to a steep crack below the overhang.
2   25m. Climb a crack on the left then make a step left to the arete. Follow this to belay at a grass ledge.
3   30m. Climb the chimney above to grassy/snowy ledges and a belay at a rectangular corner.
4   50m. Follow the corner until it is possible to move right onto the arete. This is followed past a large block on the right.
5   15m. Slabs lead to the summit of the Pulpit.

Slanting Groove 130m IV (5) * 1987

The obvious corner on the right of the crag. Start as for *Grooved Arete*.

1   45m. Follow the grassy groove as for *Grooved Arete* to the steep crack. Move right to a small overhang which is passed with difficulty. The crack above leads into the corner-line.
2   45m. Follow the corner-line passing an overhang: several belay options.
3   40m. Continue up the corner to the large block on *Grooved Arete*. This is followed to the top.

Southern Cross   145m IV (5) * 2006

Essentially a direct line on *Southern Corner*. The climbing is more in keeping with the first pitch of that route and provides a direct line up this part of the buttress, taking in the groove immediately right of *Slanting Groove* on pitch 2.

1   40m (4). Start as for *Southern Corner* and climb the initial groove. Where *Southern Corner* moves rightwards, continue up and slightly left to a good ledge beneath a steep wall.
2   30m (5). Climb the wall for 3m until it is possible to move left around the edge. Trend leftwards into an open groove and climb this to where it steepens beneath another rock wall.
3   25m (5). Climb the wall above for a few metres, then move rightwards using a series of cracks to gain a precariously perched block, just below the right arete. Follow the arete to a good ledge and belay where *Southern Corner* comes up from the right.
4   50m (3). Follow *Southern Corner* to the top of Pulpit Rock.

Southern Corner   155m IV (4) 1979

The corner and groove system right of the clean wall to the right of *Slanting Groove*.
1   50m. Start at a shallow groove 10m right of *Grooved Arete*. Follow this to easier ground. Move into a corner on the right and follow a grassy ramp to the belay.
2   45m. A groove above leads to cracks. Follow these leftwards to a pedestal and so into the base of a chimney.
3   45m. From the top of the chimney move left to broken ground.
4   15m. Continue more easily to the top.

Crenation Ridge   110m II 1983

Good climbing up the left arete of *Descent Gully*. Start from *Descent Gully*, where its walls are only a few metres apart. A good build-up of snow is required to get past the difficulties on the first pitch. Keep to the arete where possible, belaying as required.

Descent Gully   120m I

The obvious gully on the right-hand side of Pulpit Rock dividing it from the mountain. The gully curves up and left behind Pulpit Rock: take what difficulties you can find direct. A straighter right-hand finish leads up through some narrow gully walls to the path above Mickledore.

Vestry Wall   **20m III 1998/1999**

This name has been given to the broken wall overlooking *Descent Gully* at the rear of Pulpit Rock. Start approximately in the mid-section of the wall (a broken chimney-line lies further down to the right). Ascend via short icy corners and ledges passing a block/flake on the left.

Dropping Crag

NY 215 074   A*LTITUDE 880M*   N*ORTH FACING*

Found to the east of Pikes Crag, and lying just north of the summit of Scafell Pike, this is probably the highest crag in England. It has several short groove lines on its left side.

Drop Out   **50m III 2005**

Start below the left-hand groove and climb the left side of a block to a stance. Swing left to easier ground which leads to a short headwall. Finish directly up a shallow groove.

Broad Crag

NY 220 077   A*LTITUDE 850M*   N*ORTH FACING*

Broad Crag, the mountain to the north-east of Scafell Pike, contains this broken crag of the same name on its north side. This steep but small buttress has a snow slope running up towards its right-hand end and the buttress is split by a gully.

Left Ramp   **50m I/II**

Follow the aforementioned snow slope on the right-hand side of the buttress to below steep ice. A leftward traverse below the buttress leads to an icy ramp. Follow it to the top.

Broad Crag Gully   **50m II/III ****

The gully splitting the buttress is short but perfectly formed and gives a good ice pitch – and all above 850m! Start up the snow slope as for *Left Ramp* to a peg belay.
1   25m. Steep ice leads to a stance on the right.
2   25m. Easier climbing leads to a finish on the mountain summit.

Broad Crag Gully Left Wall   45m IV (4) 1991
From the peg belay of the gully, start up steep ice in the gully, then move onto the icefall on the slabby left wall. This is followed steeply to the top with a belay well back.

LINGMELL

NY 209 082   ALTITUDE 802M   NORTH-WEST AND NORTH-EAST FACING

The isolated summit of Lingmell, situated to the north of Scafell, has some exciting gills to climb on its north-east flank. Despite the height of the peak, many of the climbs start at a lowly 300m.

One route has been recorded on the north-west flank.

Lost World Gully   200m II/III Early 1970s
The obvious gully high up at 500m and cutting up into the face that looks over to the Napes (NY 207 086).

Moving round to the east side of Lingmell, the main line is the distinctive deep gorge of *Piers Gill* with its right-angled bend, but there are many other gills. Previously there has been some confusion over the names of these becks and gills which has led to them being claimed more than once. Grid references are given below to avoid confusion, as long as you can read your map! Lingmell Beck, to the north of the mountain, is formed from Spouthead Gill, which flows east to west, and *Piers Gill* which cuts deeply in a roughly north to south direction.

Facing upstream the gills are, from left to right:
- *Skew Gill* flowing into Spouthead Gill and described in the Borrowdale section.
- The two branches of *Grainy Gill*, separated by a narrow ridge: these flow into Spouthead Gill further downstream.
- Two hundred metres to the right are the two branches of *Greta Gill* that flow into *Piers Gill*; *Middleboot Gill* and *Pier Review* flow into *Piers Gill*; and *Straight Gill* which flows into *Piers Gill* from the west side.

Follow Lingmell Beck round the north side of the mountain towards Styhead Tarn, but, once round the spur of the hill, turn south and follow *Piers Gill* which flows into Lingmell Beck at (NY 212 092). *Piers Gill* and the routes directly connected to

Piers Gill

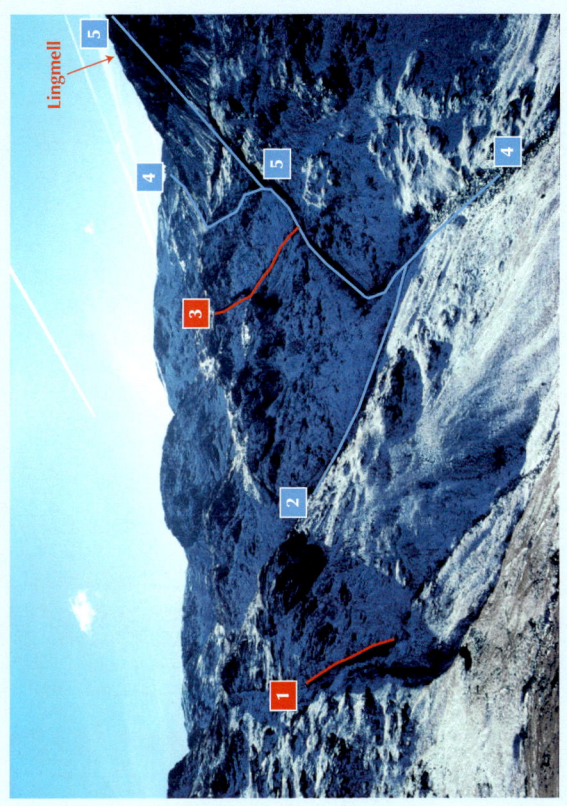

1 Grainy Gill — II/IV
2 Greta Gill — III
3 Middleboot Gill — IV
4 Piers Gill — II/III
5 Straight Gill — II/III

Lake District Winter Climbs

it are described first from right to left. These routes generally start at a low altitude and need consolidated snow for the best conditions.

Lingmell Crags and all these gills are home to rare alpine plants – please only climb here in truly frozen conditions.

Piers Gill II/III 1936/7

This deep ravine forms three ice pitches which can be buried after heavy snow. More an outing than a climb, it finishes just below the path of the Corridor Route. Keep to the gill.

Straight Gill 265m II/III

Starting out of the right side of *Piers Gill*, this route climbs the side of Lingmell to end at the summit. For the full experience follow *Piers Gill* to Bridge Rock above the second waterfall. Alternatively traverse the slopes of Lingmell on the right bank of the gill until *Straight Gill* is reached, coming down from Lingmell on the right.

At the convergence of the two gills, climb a steep ice pitch out of *Piers Gill* for 15m. Continue for another 200m up fairly steeply angled snow, passing several small pitches and a cave formed by a chockstone, passed on its left. Another 50m leads to the summit cairn; possible cornice.

Antarctic Monkeys 220m II/III 2006

This route takes the gully-line north of *Straight Gill* and south of the ridge of *Straight Gill Right-Hand Arete,* with its prominent pinnacle at one-third height.

Climb easily up the widening gully to a small amphitheatre with a corner on its right. The corner can be climbed (III) or avoided by climbing turf on the left, then traversing back right into the main gully. Climb easily until the gully forks. Take the left fork up steepening turf, then steepening ice until the gully widens near the top. Follow broken ground to the plateau. Belays as you find them.

Straight Gill Right-Hand Arete 200m III (4) 1984

Mixed climbing up the right side of *Straight Gill* leads to a gap. Either continue up the ridge and drop with difficulty into another gap or reach this point by a detour into *Straight Gill*. Various finishes are possible. Either keep to the ridge passing over a rock tower or avoid the difficulties of the ridge by an awkward step up to easy snow, heading back to the final section of the ridge; or climb an icy groove on the left of the tower to a col below the final section of the ridge.

The area to the right of *Straight Gill Right-Hand Arete* contains several short gullies (II/III). The large snowfield on the left-hand bank of *Straight Gill* leads to **Curving Gully** (I/II) and the summit.

Scafell and Chambers Crag from Eskdale (photo: Steve Ashworth)

The next route downstream leaves the left side of *Piers Gill*.

Pier Review   300m V (4) 1996

Approach *Piers Gill* from Lingmell Beck and bear right into the impressive deep gorge of the main gill. At the point where further progress up *Piers Gill* becomes difficult due to deep water and steep rock at each side, look up left and you will see the way up into the gill of *Pier Review*. The route keeps on the right of the main drainage line then follows the general line of this branch gill. After some 70m the main gill takes a right turn and here you have the option of taking the slightly steeper line straight ahead, with a short but interesting icefall, joining the original gill a little higher; or, alternatively, following the gill rightwards then back left. Just a little higher, following the general drainage line, an icefall forms on a slab that ramps up on the left: climb this and easier ground to meet the corridor route close to Piers Gill Crag.

Midway between *Greta Gill* and the upper portions of *Piers Gill* is an impressive icefall formed by a small beck falling over Middleboot Knotts (NY 214 082) at an altitude of about 600m.

Middleboot Gill   25m IV ** 2005

Middleboot Gill drains into *Piers Gill* downstream of the narrow gorge. The lower part of the gill gives three short Grade III pitches to the icy top pitch. This is an icy slab leading into a cave on the left (peg) where the top 10m is almost vertical: a good pitch.

From the Corridor Route, *Greta Gill* drains down to the west (right) of the small Stand Crag (NY 219 088) and into *Piers Gill*. Below Stand Crag, the right branch forms an impressive icefall clearly seen from the approach.

Greta Gill (NY 217 085) starts with two short icefalls, 5m and 10m pitches above pools, before splitting into a right and left branch.

Right Branch of Greta Gill   50m III

From the top of the second short icefall, the right branch gives a series of short ice steps leading to an impressive top pitch and, above that, the Corridor Route.

Left Branch of Greta Gill   65m III 1991

From the top of the second short icefall, the left branch follows the easy gill bed past two steeper sections to the final headwall. A steep wall to the right of the final headwall offers two variation finishes on steep ice.

At the top of the gill, just before the final steep exit pitches of the standard *Left Branch* route, an impressive icefall forms down the right wall, *Greta Garbo*. A less steep fall forms lower down to its right, *Silver Screen*. These offer two variation exits from the left branch.

Silver Screen   40m III 1996

Start from the bed of the gill, just upstream from a small ice cave and a few metres right of *Greta Garbo*. Climb the thinly iced wall and slab above before moving right into a narrow gully exit. (The lower wall can bank out.)

Greta Garbo   40m V 1997

The impressive icefall just upstream on the right. Follow ice to a natural break midway (peg in place and very large nut or Friend placement under the roof). Move out onto the icicle and ascend in a fine position, steep at first but then easier, to finish in a small amphitheatre (the Dressing Room). Continue up a couple of short icy walls. Nut and tree belay up and round on the left of the Dressing Room.

About 200m left of Greta Gill, past Stand Crag, are the distinctive parallel streams of *Grainy Gill*.

WESTERN WASDALE

Grainy Gill **II to IV 1890** 🌿🌿

To the left of Stand Crag, the twin branches of this gill are separated by a narrow ridge (NY 218 089). The left branch is II, with the right branch a more interesting IV with two pleasant icefalls. During the snowier winters of Victorian times the gill was considered a useful approach to Great End.

Due to their proximity to Great End, Skew Gill (NY 219 092) and Spout Head (NY 223 092) are described in the Borrowdale section.

MOSEDALE

This valley, the left-hand branch of the valley at the head of Wasdale, runs north by north-west from the Wasdale Head Inn towards Steeple and Pillar. On the west flank, the crags below Red Pike (NY 165 104) are split, right of centre, by the wide **Mosedale Gully** 120m (II/IV, 1985). It has *Left* and *Right-Hand Starts* and numerous mixed variations, including the steep **chimney pitch** (III/IV) halfway up the gully.

WESTERN WASDALE

Returning to western Wasdale, on the opposite side of the lake from the Wasdale Screes is Overbeck (NY 169 077, Alt 320m, marked as Dropping Crag), a low-lying and south-west-facing crag that is seldom in winter condition. Access is from Overbeck Bridge on the north of the lake, from where an obvious path heads up to the crag. In the centre of the crag are the three obvious **Overbeck Chimneys** (30m, III/IV, 1913) – from left to right, **B**, **Central** and **Ash Tree**.

Lake District Winter Climbs

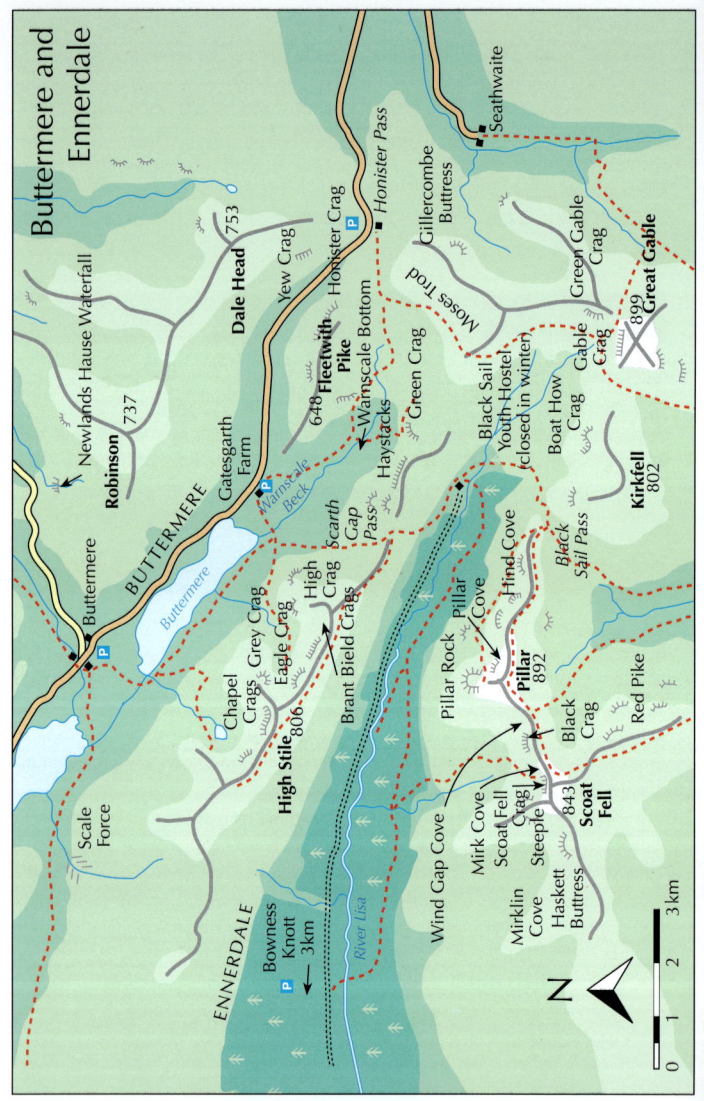

ENNERDALE

This secluded valley, running east to west, has no recorded winter climbing on its north side, nor much likelihood of any. The south side, however, is a different matter, playing host to a series of high north-facing venues including Steeple, Scoat Fell, Pillar, Kirk Fell and, at the head of the valley, Great and Green Gables. The last two crags, and to a lesser extent Kirk Fell, have become increasingly popular in recent years due to their reliable conditions and ease of access from Honister Pass. Since this approach is less suitable for the other crags in Ennerdale, these Upper Ennerdale crags are described in the following chapter – Great Gable and Kirk Fell.

Vehicles are not allowed past the Forestry Commission car park at Bowness Knott (NY 109 154). For the crags lower down the Valley, either approach from Bowness Knott car park in Ennerdale (a mountain bike is useful) or from Wasdale or Buttermere. All of these approaches make for a long day in winter.

Providing some of the most remote and secluded venues in the district, the summit of Steeple has a cove to either side, Mirklin to the west and Mirk to the east.

From Bowness Knott in Ennerdale the best approach is to cross the concrete ford on the River Liza before Gillerthwaite and take the path up onto Lingmell; follow this path eastwards to Low Beck and cross it to continue up onto the crest of the spur running north from Steeple. It is possible to contour into either combe from Long Crag (2hrs 30mins – 3hrs; using a mountain bike cuts this to 1hr 30mins).

The crags can also be reached in about 2hrs 30mins from Wasdale Head. Follow Mosedale Beck to Wind Gap between Pillar and Black Crag on Scoat Fell. From here Black Crag is easily reached. For the other crags, continue along the ridge westwards to Scoat Fell, from where various descents can be made into either combe.

From Gatesgarth Farm in Buttermere take the path to Scarth Gap and on the Ennerdale side follow the path west through the clear-felled forest to cross the valley opposite the memorial footbridge. Cross the bridge and turn right (west) and take the upper track, eventually crossing a bridge, until a path leads through the trees and up the west bank of High Beck into lower Mirk Cove. By contouring round under Long Crag, Mirklin Cove can also be reached (3hrs).

MIRKLIN COVE

NY 154 115   ALTITUDE 700M   *WEST FACING*

The cove contains a number of easy snow gullies (I) mainly on its west (right) flank. While the gullies have been climbed they have not been described or recorded; they are left for you to explore. From a distance the two steeper buttresses, Steeple West Buttress and the more impressive and central Haskett Buttress, are the main features.

Haskett Buttress

NY 155 114   ALTITUDE 700M   *NORTH-WEST FACING*

An obvious feature situated at the back of the cove. The main buttress is bounded on its left by the vegetated *Haskett Gully* and on its right by *Western Gully*. To the left of *Haskett Gully* is a tiered vegetated buttress with an easy 100m snow gully to its left (**Left Gully**, I , 1970s) which can be a useful **descent**.

Haskett Gully   90m IV (5) 2004
The deep cleft defining the left side of the buttress. Follow the gully to within a few metres of the steep jammed blocks where it narrows. Climb turfy ledges on the left wall for about 5m until it is possible to move right into the back of the gully. A few more metres of steep climbing lead to easy ground.

Western Gully   90m I/II 1970s
The gully immediately right of Haskett Buttress is followed to a choice of finishes. The right-hand and easiest one leaves the main gully bed and continues up on turf and rock, where it steepens at about two-thirds height. The central finish continues up the gully, where it steepens at a small ice step. The left-hand finish climbs a slightly steeper ice step from this point.

Mirklin Cove
showing Haskett Buttress and Steeple West Buttress

1 North Gully — IV
2 West Buttress — II/III
3 West Chimney Route — II/III
4 Left Gully — I
5 Haskett Gully — IV
6 Western Gully — I/II

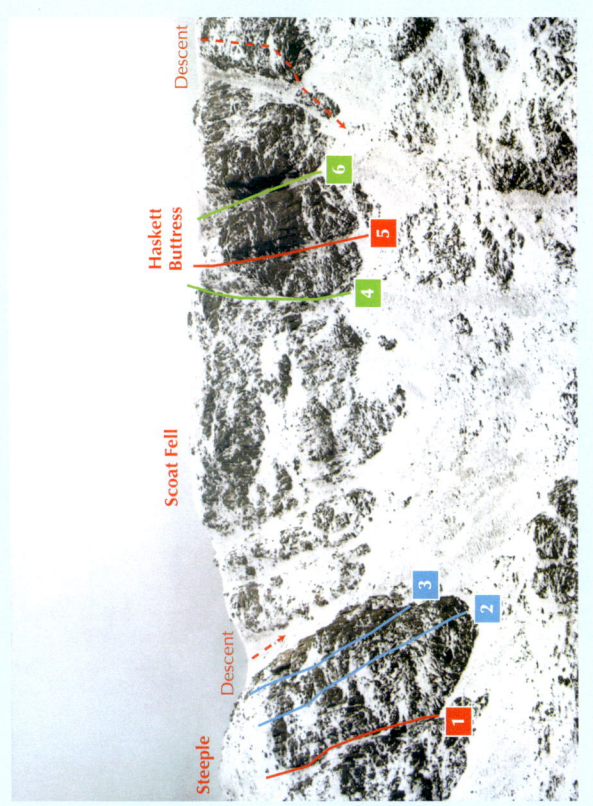

Steeple West Buttress

NY 156 117   ALTITUDE 700M   *WEST FACING*

Directly below the summit of Steeple, this buttress faces west into Mirklin Cove. It is bounded on its right (south) side by a wide easy-angled scree gully (a useful **descent**) and on its left (north) by a gully with a cave at about one-third height.

About 20m to the left of the crag some pleasant 10m pitches of steep ice form. The easier turfy buttress above can be followed to the top.

North Gully   100m II/IV (5) 2004

The gully is a straightforward snow-plod except for a steep cave pitch about a third of the way up – best climbed on its right where ice tends to form; the more there is, the easier the climbing! An easier alternative is to bypass the cave altogether by traversing right onto the buttress about 5m below it, then climbing easy steps up the buttress until past the cave before traversing back into the gully above at a grade more in keeping with the rest of the climb (II).

Insufficient information is available about the following two routes to be sure that they do not cover similar ground (or indeed are not one and the same). The lines on the diagram therefore should only be regarded as providing an approximate indication.

West Buttress   100m II/III 1986

A line to the left of the band of continuous rock running up the centre of the buttress. Aim for a snow patch in the middle of the buttress and continue on up.

West Chimney Route   100m II/III 2004

The right side of the buttress contains a continuous rib of rock. To its left is what, from below, looks like a shallow chimney curving left at its base. From the lowest point of the crag, climb a turfy corner on the left to reach the base of this shallow curving chimney-line. (When viewed from close-up this is not obvious and then appears more like a wide turf-covered depression running up the crag.) Follow this to the top.

SCOAT FELL CRAG

MIRK COVE AND WIND GAP COVE

NY 160 116 AND NY 164 118 ALTITUDE 700M   *EAST FACING*

The coves on the east side of Steeple are really one large cove divided by a vague rocky spur that lies to the west (right) of Black Crag. Wind Gap Cove lies east of this; Mirk Cove to the west. **High Beck** (15m, II/III, 1997) flows out of Wind Gap Cove and can make a good alternative approach to the crags. The crags are described from right to left.

Steeple East Buttress

NY 158 117 ALTITUDE 700M   *EAST FACING*

At the right-hand side of the cove near the top, and leading to the summit of Steeple, is the *East Buttress*.

Steeple East Buttress   150m III ** 1986
Follow a shallow gully line to the left of a rock rib. Climb the rib, taking belays where required, to finish on the summit.

Scoat Fell Crag

NY 159 115 ALTITUDE 750M   *NORTH-EAST FACING*

While Scoat Fell Crag can sometimes be a miserable summer venue being high up, north facing, turfy and slow to dry, these qualities make it an excellent winter climbing ground that comes readily into condition. The crag nestles high on the west side of Mirk Cove under the summit of Scoat Fell. Without a mountain bike, an approach from Wasdale Head up Mosedale or following the path along Nether Beck to Scoat Fell is shortest. From the summit drop down into the descent gully found between the crag and the ridge leading North to Steeple.

The crag is divided just left of centre by a huge square-cut gully (*East Gully*) flanked by fine rock towers.

Turf Wars   55m IV (4) * 2005
Based on the summer line of *Travesty Cracks*. Start 4m left of *East Gully* at a short wide chimney, the left-hand of two.

1   15m (3). Climb the chimney and easy ground above to belay at a crack in a block down and left of an impressive vertical corner.
2   20m (4). Starting several metres down and right of the corner, traverse horizontally rightwards on turf ledges and then follow a leftwards-slanting groove line (crux) to a large ledge.
3   20m (4). Climb a short way up the groove above then traverse left to gain a small ledge on the arete on the left. Drop down off this into a hanging gully on the left of the arete and battle with rope drag up this to the top.

East Gully   80m IV (5) * 1995
The major square-cut central gully is harder (and better) than it looks from below. Start under the right-hand rib defining the gully, just left of a short chimney.
1   25m (4). Climb up turfy steps and then step right over the top of the chimney before climbing back left under the rib and into the gully (can be climbed direct but is rather bold). Continue up the gully with interest to a belay on the right below a short wall.
2   20m (5). Overcome the wall with difficulty and move up to a bigger square wall that completely blocks the gully. Surmount this via a narrow cleft on the right (crucial ice-hook runner) and belay in the bay above. This pitch may bank out under good snow cover.
3   15m (3). Climb diagonally leftwards (almost to the crest); spike belay.
4   20m (3). Step down, traverse right and pull up a short corner to gain a rising snow traverse line. Follow this up rightwards to the top. A harder finish looks possible up the obvious crack system leading directly out of the bay.

To the right of *East Gully* is a clean grooved tower and on the right of this a rightward-rising chimney fault-line separates the tower from more broken vegetated ground to its right.

Twin Ribs Climb Direct   70m VI (7) 2009
This climbs the grooves in the arete to the right of East Gully. Start below the prominent groove.
1   40m (7). Climb directly up and into the groove. Follow this until the short wall on the left allows access to another groove. Follow this to a niche below a large roof. Pull round the roof on the left and climb easier ground for a few metres to belay.
2   30m (4). Step back right onto the ridge; follow this joining *Scoathanger* near the top.

Scoat Fell Crag

1 Turf Wars — IV
2 East Gully — IV
3 Twin Ribs Climb Direct — VI
4 Scoathanger — IV
5 Sod this for a Lark — IV
6 Scoating for Boys — II
7 Serendipity Ridge — III

Scoathanger   80m IV (4) * 2005
Start directly under the chimney fault-line.
1   50m (4). Climb easily up to the right wall of the tower. Move up right to the first chimney and climb this. The second chimney proves more awkward and is entered from the right. A difficult exit leads to a large platform.
2   30m (4). Climb steep and not too well-protected turf up the wall above, with a hard move left to gain easier ground and move up to the ridge. Avoid a steep slab by striding left into a hanging chimney and climb this awkwardly to easier ground (the climb originally finished via *Scoating for Boys*).

Sod this for a Lark   70m IV (4) * 2005
Twenty metres to the right of *East Gully* is a bay, at the back of which easy-angled ground leads up to a prominent steep dark chimney. Start from this bay.
1   30m (2). Follow a vague chimney-line up the centre of the bay to below the steep chimney.
2   20m (4). The chimney is technically sustained but well protected.
3   20m (2). Follow a turfy groove just left of the rock rib above (and just right of a smooth wall), moving out left at the top.

Scoating for Boys   75m II (3) 2004
Start 30m to the right of *East Gully*.
1   25m (2). Climb easy leftward-sloping ground to gain a ledge system and follow this leftwards, passing underneath the deep square-cut chimney of *Sod this for a Lark*.
2   20m (3). The chimney is avoided by a rising groove/ramp-line on the left which leads to a platform and a junction with *Scoathanger*.
3   30m (2). Follow the fault-line up rightwards onto an easy-angled slope, then move right round a rib into an easy gully and so to the top.

Serendipity Ridge   115m III (4) * 2004
A very enjoyable climb. Many variations can be made to the first pitch: the one giving the most exciting climbing is described. Start at the lowest point of the crag, a few metres left of the descent gully.
1   40m (3). Trend rightwards to gain a short chimney overlooking the descent gully. Go up the chimney to a ledge and then follow the obvious horizontal traverse line leftwards round the buttress to a block belay under a roof.
2   35m (3). Just left is a short open groove; climb it to a platform. The steep wall ahead is avoided by traversing left and ascending an exposed rib. Follow the rib above and then easier ground to belay on a block under a steep wall barring access to the final rib.

3   25m (4). A slim groove just left of the block leads to a narrow ledge. Traverse rightwards along this and make an awkward and exposed step down and around the rib on the right to gain easier ground. Straightforward climbing up the broad ridge leads to block belays below a short step.
4   15m. Surmount the step and continue easily to the top.

In the centre of the two coves, slightly lower than Black Crag, and 250m to its west, the low rocky dividing spur which curves up to join the main Scoat Fell ridge makes a pleasant winter outing.

Black Crag

NY 165 117   Altitude 650m   *North-north-west facing*

Black Crag is situated high in the middle of the cove. It is lower than and well to the left of Scoat Fell Crag and just to the left of the top of the vague ridge that separates Wind Gap Cove from Mirk Cove.

Easy Gully   120m I 2003
Follow the wide gully between Black Crag main buttress and the smaller one to its left. The left side is a little steeper and various interesting exits can be followed at the top.

The Main Ridge Climb by the
Lower Slabs Ordinary Route   115m IV (5) 1997
Generally follows the summer line with the same variations. Start from a snow basin above and right of the start of *Easy Gully* (this may be reached by following *Easy Gully* to the chimney then traversing right at its start, or by traversing right under the crag for about 50m then back left until about 10m from the start of the chimney).
1   35m (3). Follow the turf ramp leftwards for 5m to a ledge before climbing a shallow groove up and leftwards to a short arete and a rock platform.
2   15m (5). Gain the steep cracked buttress on the right and climb straight up to thin and committing moves to gain a small footledge on the left and the top of the buttress.
3   50m (3). Climb the easy-angled turfy ridge to a short awkward wall and a ledge below a chimney.
4   15m (4). Follow the chimney strenuously to a sloping rock platform. Escape left on easy turf ledges.

Black Crag

1 Easy Gully — I
2 The Main Ridge Climb by the Lower Slabs Ordinary Route — IV
3 West Gully Cave Route — IV
4 West Gully Tunnel Route — IV

Gully Finish 60m III 2003

4   60m. Avoid the final strenuous chimney at the top of the route by continuing up towards a short buttress and up the ridge beyond this to the huge rock glacis. Walk across this and go left around the base of the upper buttress and briefly into *Easy Gully* before following the shallow gully which curves right along the edge of the buttress to the summit.

West Gully Cave Route 60m IV 2003

Start at the right-hand side of the crag by the deep gully.
1   25m. From the foot of the gully go up into the lowest cave. Exit via the left wall, aiming for the small chockstone and grassy ledge. Pass the large block on the left then go up to the next cave and belay in the back of this.
2   15m. Traverse out on the left wall, then go straight up to the next cave, but belay at its mouth.
3   20m. Go straight up the gully, keeping left of a small block, to the top.

West Gully Tunnel Route 45m IV 2003

Start as for *West Gully Cave Route*. Go up towards the lowest cave but take the ramp to the right from just below it, then go left to the ledge below the slab which leads to the chimney of the summer climb *Crack, Chimney and Slab Route*. Climb the slab corner-crack to the right of this up to the chimney. Bridge up this for about a metre then cross over to the groove on the buttress to the right. Go up the wide crack for 2m then step right to the flake-crack, which is climbed to a big ledge on the left. Go into the cave at the end of this and exit from a gap at the top of the cave. Easier ground leads to the top.

PILLAR

There are several possible approaches to Pillar, all of them long.

From Ennerdale take the right fork in the forest track about 2.5km beyond Gillerthwaite (YHA) which leads directly to a concrete bridge across the River Liza. Cross the bridge, turn left and after 50m some small wooden steps mark the start of a good path which ascends diagonally through the forest, crossing an upper forestry road and continuing again in a diagonal direction before emerging, with fine views, at the base of the combe below the Rock. If on a bike, the upper track can be reached by cycling on up the valley, past the first path to a junction where you turn back sharp right for 600m (1hr 30mins with a mountain bike, otherwise 2hrs).

The traditional approach from Wasdale Head takes the path to Black Sail Pass. Head north-west past Looking Stead to pick up the well-marked track known as The High Level Route, which contours the northern slopes of Pillar. Follow this route to Robinson's Cairn, where Pillar Rock's magnificent eastern profile can be seen. Continue the traverse to the base of the Rock (about 2hrs 30mins).

From Gatesgarth Farm in Buttermere, follow the path to Scarth Gap. Do not descend to Black Sail Youth Hostel, but follow a path which starts a short distance down on the Ennerdale side and heads diagonally down in a westerly direction to reach the valley bottom opposite the memorial footbridge. Cross the bridge and turn right (west), take the upper track and, after 600m, follow a diagonal path back leftwards and then ascend steeply to the combe beneath the Rock (about 2hrs 30mins).

West Cove

NY 172 125   ALTITUDE 750M   *NORTH FACING*

West Cove Gullies   100m I
There are two very obvious gullies that start above the steeply sloping ground immediately west (right) of Pillar Rock. Both run up to the summit of Pillar.

High up in the cove, immediately right of the most westerly (rightmost) gully is the following buttress.

West Cove Buttress   90m IV (5) ** 2010
This route climbs straight up the middle of the buttress above West Cove. Looking up at the buttress an obvious wide crack with wedged blocks at its top can be seen. About 5m to its right is a square-cut niche with a small tree below it; the start of the fault-line that the route follows. Start at the toe of the buttress at about its lowest point.
1   50m (2). Climb a twisting runnel of snow to its top, then follow a short step up a corner and exit rightwards. Cross a ledge to belay at a small tree below a square-cut niche.
2   40m (5). Move up the niche. As it steepens climb the corner-crack at the back then pull out rightwards onto a turf ledge. Climb the chimney above with a variety of techniques to its top, pulling up into a snow bay. Move to the top of this and climb up the gully still following the same fault-line. Belay on a big ledge on the left. Above easier (II) scrambling leads up a stepped ridge to finish on the summit of Pillar.

Pillar Rock

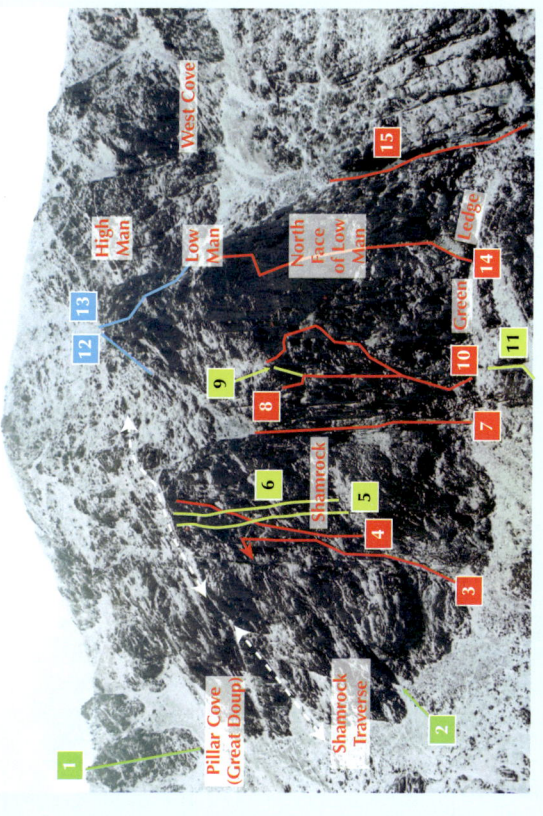

1. Great Doup Buttress — II
2. Shamrock Gully — II
3. Photon Corner — IV
4. Shamrock Chimneys — IV
5. Electron Positron — VII
6. Tower Postern — VI
7. Walker's Gully — V
8. Savage Gully — V
9. Savage Gully Direct Finish — VI
10. North Climb — IV
11. Green Ledge Icefall — II
12. Slab and Notch Climb — III
13. The Old West Route — III
14. North-West Climb — V
15. West Waterfall Gully — IV

Pillar Rock

NY 172 123 ALTITUDE 600M EAST, NORTH AND WEST FACING

Once a centre for classic rock climbing, the long approach seems to deter all but the keenest and so this is a good choice of venue for those seeking solitude. While many of the classic gullies received very early winter ascents, recent winters have seen a renewed interest in the mountain and there is still scope for further development.

Pillar is a complex crag comprising of two cones stuck together, one higher than the other, termed High Man and Low Man respectively. In plan it juts out to the north at right angles to Pillar.

Pisgah and East Face of High Man

The East Face of High Man is the short face of Pillar, well seen from the top of the Shamrock Traverse and overlooking the scree funnel at the top of *Walker's Gully*. Pisgah is the small summit immediately south of High Man and separated from it by the Jordan Gap.

Pisgah from Jordan Gap (6m, IV, 1933) follows the summer line up a short wall on the north side of Pisgah. On High Man itself, **Central Jordan** (15m, III, 1913) has been climbed under heavy snow conditions. It follows the corner to the right of the highest point of the Jordan Gap which leads to a large sloping ledge. A crack on the left takes you to the top of High Man. **West Jordan** was also descended the same day.

Slab and Notch Climb   50m III (4) 1890

On the east side of the High Man this route provides the easiest way to the top, as well as being the best **descent**. There are numerous belays and pitches can be split. Start near the foot of *East Jordan Gully*.

1   20m. Climb up right and onto the big slab, descend slightly and continue right along the base of the slab to a step. Climb the step to a corner and gain the Notch above.
2   30m. Move 4m right then go up an arete to a ledge. Step right and climb the stepped slab to a chimney above and right. Follow this to a deep notch and up to the top of the High Man.

The Easy Way

The variation humorously known as *The Easy Way* is considerably harder, unless you are clad in tweed and sporting nails. Beyond the Slab, instead of climbing up to the Notch, make an exposed traverse rightwards along the Ledge to round the Curtain and descend slightly to the s*teep grass* in *Great Chimney*. Go up this and struggle up a short chimney to rejoin the standard route.

The Curtain and the Arete (1899) has been climbed in winter. It is the ridge that *Slab and Notch* crosses.

Shamrock

The large area of rock containing many grooves and aretes left (east) and separated from the main rock by *Walker's Gully*. The usual track up Pillar via the Shamrock Traverse goes up snow/scree on its left-hand side and then traverses across just above the Shamrock summit. It is divided into an Upper Tier and a Lower Tier by the Great Heather Shelf which runs diagonally up rightwards across its centre and is reached by easy scrambling from the left. Up on the left side of the Great Heather Shelf is a fine groove and corner-line, which gives *Photon Corner*. The routes are described from left to right.

Shamrock Gully   160m II/III 1890

The obvious gully bounding the far left side of the Shamrock, to the right of the path and to the left of a long low overhang. In summer it is a loose and vegetated gully: wait for it to freeze and fill with snow and it becomes more interesting. The grade depends on the amount of snow.

Harlequin Chimneys   225m V (5) ** 2009

A superb winter route, following the summer line. The crux section is mercifully short. Start just left of the Great Heather Shelf below a deep chimney at the right end of the rock band.

1   25m (3). Climb directly up steep turfy ground to belay just left of the chimney.
2   35m (6). Grovel up into the depths of the chimney, then traverse back out of it using a narrow foot ledge on the left wall. When you reach the edge of the chimney turn round and climb its right rib (in-situ ice hook in crack). Carry on up easier ground and then step left to regain the line near a Christmas tree. Move up a few metres to a rock belay.
3   20m (5). Climb the first short rock wall above the belay, overcome the next one directly with interest and belay below a third one.
4   25m (5). Another short wall reaches a hollow under a chimney. Climb the chimney with more interest to a second Christmas tree belay on the right.

5   20m (2/3). Climb the turfy wall just left of a wide crack or take a harder alternative climbing up rightwards to the highest Christmas tree (under the Diamond Wall), then moving up to traverse leftwards round the rib to the same point. Drop down into *Shamrock Gully* (Christmas tree belay).
6   50m (5). On the far side of *Shamrock Gully* is a very obvious chimney. Enter this with difficulty and climb it to an awkward through route behind a huge chockstone. Belay on the left.
7   50m (5). Traverse up and right into a corner on the right. Climb this and traverse back left over a bracket and exit into the easier upper gully which is followed to the Shamrock Traverse.

Photon Corner   135m IV (4) 1983

This follows the summer line of *Photon* to the top of pitch 4 then descends into *Shamrock Gully*. Start by scrambling 60m up the Great Heather Shelf to the foot of a clean groove on the left.
1   65m. Climb directly up the groove to below the main corner/groove on the right.
2   25m. A ribbon of ice forms in the corner – follow this to a poor belay.
3   25m. Move left and continue on steep mixed ground up the corner above.
4   20m. Traverse left for 15m to a belay overlooking *Shamrock Gully* which is used to escape.

Shamrock Chimneys   160m IV (4) * 1985

1   30m. About 5m right of the groove of *Photon Corner*, start up the narrow chimney on the left, breaking out left at 15m. Follow the slab then the chimney on the right.
2   20m. Continue up the chimney passing chockstones and a cave.
3   25m. Easier ground leads to a V-chimney then further easy ground.
4   85m. Follow the easiest line up the shallow gully to the top.

Electron-Positron   100m VII (7) ** 2010

A logical link up of these two rock routes on the first bit of Pillar Rock to get white. Start about 80m up the Great Heather Shelf, some 15m past *Shamrock Chimneys* at a right-angled corner.
1   25m (7). Take the corner passing a chockstone after 6m then a bulge to a grassy belay ledge. Technical but well-protected climbing.
2   25m. Continue up a groove for 12m to a small ledge and climb the wall to a block belay below and left of a prominent crack.

3   50m. Climb across the grassy gully to a corner and climb this for a few metres before stepping right to climb the edge to a crack and corner above leading to a finish at a large block: the Tea Table.

Tower Postern   92m VI (6) ** 2011
A turfy mixed route, based on the summer line, following corners and cracks up the front face of the Shamrock. Large hexes and cams protect the first pitch. Start on the Great Heather Shelf at a turfy groove just right of the corner of *Electron-Positron*.
1   25m (6). Follow the corner with escalating interest to reach a thread belay below a vertical cracked wall.
2   15m (5). Climb the cracked wall (strenuous and exposed) to belay below the obvious steep corner above.
3   25m (6). Ascend the steepening corner.
4   27m (3). The corner on the right is followed more easily to the summit of the Shamrock.

Walker's Gully   140m V (4) ** 1914
First climbed by Siegfried Herford in a Golden Age of snowier winters, this classic Lakeland gully divides the Shamrock from the North Face of Low Man. Unfortunately seldom in condition, particularly the steep top pitch which is the crux of the climb.

North Face of Low Man

Right of *Walker's Gully* is Green Ledge, a long grassy terrace which traverses under the main crag, separating it from easier ground below.

Green Ledge Icefall   60m II * 2004
This takes the buttress under Green Ledge on its left-hand side. Climb a short steep groove to exit onto snow. Follow very easy-angled ice up rightwards to a steeper left-slanting ice runnel which exits onto Green Ledge at the start of *North Climb*.

North-East Climb   117m V (6) ** 2010
A winter ascent of the summer line. Varied climbing with good positions throughout. Start from the very left end of Green Ledge where a short wall leads to a square platform, as for *North Climb*.
1   54m (5). Climb to the foot of a broken gully/groove, up this for 10m to a ledge. Move up, then left across a rib and up a short chimney. Moves left round the next rib lead onto a slab; traverse this to a snow ledge (possible belay). Climb

the chimney and slab above to the base of a long V-groove on the wall overlooking *Walker's Gully*. The pitch can be split at various places.
2   30m (4) Climb the groove to its end, drop down 1m into *Grooved Wall* to belay.
3   18m (6) Regain the groove, the wall ahead leads to a ledge besides a large pinnacle, take the steep chimney behind this leads to a corner.
4   15m (4) The groove line above is followed to its end.

Savage Gully   104m V (6) *** 1997

This sustained test follows the obvious gully/groove line from the left end of Green Ledge. Start from the very left end of Green Ledge where a short wall leads to a square platform. The first two pitches are as for *North Climb*.
1   10m (3). Climb onto the square platform and traverse left to the foot of the main groove.
2   25m (4). Climb the groove into the gully line proper and continue past a chockstone to a spike belay below a steep groove with a thin crack in its right wall, on the left, and the deep Twisting Chimney of *North Climb* on the right.
3   25m (6). Climb the groove on the left to a grassy ledge and large thread.
4   20m (6). Continue up the groove then move left to the continuation of a shallow chimney. Follow this to a steep bay and dubious block belay just below the final overhanging headwall.
5   24m (6). On the first ascent, a steep corner/groove/chimney just to the left of the belay was taken reaching a belay in a small rock outcrop well back.

Direct Finish   VI (7) ** 2004
5   24m (7). Tackle the undercut square chimney above the dubious block belay. Escape by returning to the gully bed, then a rising traverse left over steep heather gains the snow above *Walker's Gully*.

North Climb   101m IV (5) ** 1907

Start from the very left end of *Green Ledge* where a short wall leads to a square platform.
1   10m (3). Climb onto the square platform and traverse left to the foot of the main groove.
2   25m (4). Climb the groove into the gully line proper and continue past a chockstone to a spike belay below a steep groove on the left and the deep Twisting Chimney on the right.
3   34m (3). Climb Twisting Chimney and then trend leftwards up an open groove. Scramble up to a belay on a small ledge at the meeting of two narrow chimneys.

4   9m (4). The Stomach Traverse. Climb the right-hand chimney which curves to its right in the upper half.
5   18m (3). The chockstone-filled corner above is climbed via a capstone, followed by a walk of 6m to the Split Blocks. These are climbed by the obvious chimney. Traverse to the left, crossing the Strid, to a ledge below and right of the Nose.
6   5m (5). The Nose. From the corner, work out left to stand on the tip of the projecting flake. Hard moves up and left gain better holds and a ledge just above. Move up without further difficulty to belay 5m higher on the right wall of Stony Gully, which leads to Low Man.

North-West Climb   130m V (6) *** 1960
Climbed under exceptional conditions. A tour de force – probably harder than graded!

For a full description the FRCC Pillar guide will need to be consulted. The route was started by following the slabs of *Nor'-Nor'-West Climb* which were banked out with snow. The short tricky groove at the start of pitch 3 of that route led to the top of the Bounding Buttress. From that point, *North-West Climb* was followed (via Lamb's Chimney) with only Oppenheimer's Chimney being free of ice.

West Waterfall Gully   200m IV (5) ** 1969
A magnificent pitch (but it has been known to bank out). This is the deep cleft that bounds Low Man on its west side and is home to rare alpine plants and should only be climbed in truly frozen conditions.

Start on the right of the broken crag under Green Ledge at a well-defined gully. Short pitches lead up to the final main 30m pitch. This very steep often chandeliered ice is usually much harder than graded. Climb it to finish on the Western Scree under the West Face of Low Man.

If the final pitch is not formed there are several possibilities: you can quit the gully on the right some 30m below it by ice that forms where the summer scramble from Green Ledge crosses it (III 4); or quit it on the left at the same point and follow **Waterfall Climb** (50m, III 4), up a groove system in the rocks which bound the gully on its left side to gain the Western Scree – or traverse leftwards and then descend slightly at this point to gain Green Ledge and walk off.

West Face

The Old West Route   165m III ** 1913

A route following a line of weakness running up diagonally left across the West Face of Pillar Rock, effectively dividing Low Man from High Man. From the top of Low Man, it runs up the front (north) of the rock to its summit via the well-worn summer scramble. With a good banking of snow the lower section is not without interest, whilst the upper part can be awkward in icy conditions. **Descent** is either by abseil into Jordan Gap or, more traditionally, by downclimbing *Slab and Notch Route*.

High Man's imposing West Face contains a prominent groove line on its left-hand side.

Gomorrah   85m VII (7) ** 1986

A fine hard route that has yet to see a second ascent. On the only ascent to date a peg was used for aid at mid-height. Start directly below a huge triangular roof.
1 45m. Climb a corner to the roof, then traverse left to the foot of a crack. Climb this steeply and the ledges above to a loose block belay.
2 40m. Traverse right to a crack-line and climb cracks, a chimney and a groove direct to the top.

New West Climb   87m IV (4) ** 1903

A fantastic lead for its time but sadly rarely in condition. Start just above a big embedded block, 25m or so down the snow/scree from *West Jordan Gully*.
1 *20m.* Follow easy rocks in a shallow chimney, trending slightly to the left, to a rib which leads to a small corner. Follow a steep staircase to belay on a good ledge.
2 10m. Climb a wide shallow chimney leading to a small platform and traverse horizontally left for 4m to step down to a good belay.
3 17m. Climb the obvious groove to ledges and make an awkward traverse left to the foot of a chimney (chockstone belay).
4 20m. The imposing chimney above is followed to a chockstone at 9m. Avoid the chimney beyond by a difficult traverse horizontally right and around a rib. Continue rightwards, then up, to surmount a pile of blocks which form a magnificent belay.
5 20m. Climb the crack up the slab above to a small ledge. Finish via a block-filled grassy groove on the right or, better (if iced), the slab on the left.

West Jordan Gully, which bounds the West Face of High Man on the right, separating it from Pisgah, has been climbed under snow but does not appear to come into proper winter conditions.

Pillar Cove

NY 173 121   ALTITUDE 750M   NORTH FACING

First recorded in 1887 the cove immediately east of Pillar Rock, sometimes called Great Doup, sports two or three short Grade I gullies which finish steeply on the mountain ridge.

Great Doup Buttress   200m III 1972

The ridge forming the left side of the cove generally offers easy-angled climbing with the odd steeper section near the top.

The buttress is the lowest and most prominent central buttress of the outcrops in this isolated cove. Follow the crest of the buttress, overcoming the steepest section via a leftward-slanting chimney/groove before moving back rightwards onto the crest. The final summit tower where it is joined to the main ridge is accessed along a knife edge arete.

Hind Cove ♦♦

NY 178 122   ALTITUDE 600M   NORTH-EAST FACING

Further east is Hind Cove, which is crossed by the High Level Route just before it ascends to Robinson's Cairn.

Hind Cove is potentially one of the most sensitive areas to climb in the Lakes in marginal conditions, for here is the healthiest Cumbrian population of scrubby cinquefoil, a plant whose only British locations are in the Lake District and Teesdale. Cinquefoil is really vulnerable to turf climbing or climbing in poor conditions as it favours the wetter areas (where the ice will be).

Hind Cove Gully   100m II 1999

From the path below the cove just east of Robinson's Cairn, the dark cleft of the gully can be seen about 100m above the path. A through-route passes the jammed blocks and one further step poses the only other obstacle to the easy top section.

Rib and Gully Climb   120m I/II 1999

The rib on the left side of the cove (with a gully on its right) offers a pleasant route to the top with avoidable difficulties.

Lake District Winter Climbs

GREAT GABLE AND KIRK FELL

The crags of Great Gable, Green Gable and Kirk Fell are easily approached from Honister Pass, Borrowdale or Wasdale. Napes Needle, situated on the south side of Great Gable, is traditionally considered to be the birthplace of British rock climbing. The Napes, being south facing, cannot be recommended as a winter climbing venue. By contrast north-facing Gable Crag on the other side of the mountain is home to some of the best mixed routes produced in the Lakes over the last 30 years. These are often in condition and relatively accessible. See the map 'Buttermere and Ennerdale'.

GABLE SOUTH

The first routes described on Great Gable are located on the south side of the mountain and best approached from either Borrowdale via Styhead Tarn or from Wasdale.

South-west-facing Kern Knotts (NY 215 096, Alt 520m) is hardly worth considering as a winter climbing venue. However, a party attending the popular FRCC Easter meet of 1913 ascended **Kern Knotts Chimney** in wintery conditions – so you never know.

On the south-west-facing Napes (NY 210 101, Alt 700m), the historically resonant rock climbs of *Napes Needle* and its popular extension, *Needle Ridge*, have both seen ascents under heavy snow conditions (1891 and 1896 respectively), as has *Arrowhead Ridge Direct* (1911). None of these hold snow or ice well in winter. *Needle Gully* behind the *Needle* was likewise the scene of early activity (1899), as was *Eagle's Nest Gully* to its left (1890). **Tophet Bastion** (II, 1960), the left-to-right diagonal line up the left arete on *Tophet Wall*, has also been climbed.

Westmorland Crags

NY 211 102 ALTITUDE 800M   *SOUTH FACING*

As with the other climbs described on this side of Great Gable, an early start or a cloudy day are advantageous for these routes. Although it is south-facing, the crag is high, being situated just below the summit, and as such can offer some good (if fleeting) winter climbing, with the best being on the buttresses (the gully lines are turfy and can hold neve, but not normally ice). Only two routes have been recorded here in winter and the descriptions are a little vague.

The crag lies directly above the Napes and below the summit of Great Gable. From Wasdale it is best approached from Beck Head between Great Gable and Kirk Fell; from Borrowdale take the climbers' path under Kern Knotts and cut up Hell's Gate Screes past *Tophet Wall* to the crag; from Honister Pass, it is best to approach by descent from the summit of Great Gable to Westmorland's Cairn at the top of the crag.

Butterfingers   70m III (4) 2005

A line up the central buttress, starting just to the left of the small pinnacle, some 15m right of *Sparrowfart Rib* and some 20m right of the lowest part of the crag below a steep wall. This route is basically the broken lower part of *Flake Gully Buttress* (and this climb appears to be mainly via *Chockstone Chimney*) finishing around the Cairnbrian. It is climbed in three pitches of decreasing difficulty, with the trickiest stuff on the first pitch. Some caution should be exercised due to the presence of large loose blocks.

Follow Your Nose   90m V (4) 2005

The steep gully to the right of the buttress containing *Butterfingers*.
1   50m. Start at a steep groove/gully line 5m left of a small pinnacle at the lowest point of the crag. This is followed at around Grade III through a couple of steep narrow sections to a block belay. Traverse left to right and climb a further steepening to a large ledge.
2   40m (4). The crux pitch involving delicate hooking.

GABLE NORTH

Easily approached from Honister Pass, which, if not ice bound, offers convenient access. (Beware of heavy snowfall during the day which can quickly close the pass.) It is also possible to approach from Seathwaite in Borrowdale or from Wasdale via Styhead Tarn and over the col of Windy Gap, whence Green Gable Crag is only a few minutes away on the right (north-east), with Gable Crag to the left (west).

Gable Crag

NY 213 105 *ALTITUDE 800M* NORTH FACING

Located on the north side of the mountain, this remote high crag is really a collection of buttresses with the weaknesses between them giving reliable winter lines. The buttresses provide classic high standard mixed routes in the modern idiom.

When approaching from Windy Gap the first route to be encountered is *Windy Ridge*, which has a wide gully on its left and a narrower gully to its right separating it from the main crag. A path traverses under a series of isolated buttresses, with the Bottle-Shaped Pinnacle up on the right and then, high up, the distinctive wall of *Engineer's Slabs*, with *Engineer's Chimney* on its left-hand side. Approximately up the middle of the crag, and serving as a good reference point, is *Central Gully*. *Moses's Back Door* starts up the obvious wide gully on the right side of the crag. **Descent** is possible at either end of the crag. The routes are described from left to right in the order in which they are most likely to be approached.

Windy Ridge   40m III 2002

This buttress at the left of the crag stands on its own, isolated by a wide gully on its left and a narrower gully to its right separating it from the rest of the crag. Start up a turfy corner at its lowest point.

1   40m. From the lowest point of the buttress climb a turfy corner to a large snowy bay. This can also be easily entered from the left. Choose a groove above (the left-hand one is probably the easiest) and follow this onto the easier-angled ridge.

Either ascend or descend the wide gully easily reached from the top of the ridge, or:

Variation Finish   80m III 2003

2   30m. Move right across the top of the gully to the ridge above the right-hand side and take the prominent slab above.
3   50m. Follow the crest of the ridge to pop out just by the tourist path.

Late Season Flurry   200m II 2006

Start in the narrow gully immediately right of *Windy Ridge*. An interesting easier route enhanced by impressive surroundings.

1   80m. Start up the gully but move right and climb the left edge of a buttress until almost level with the top of *Windy Ridge*. Follow a ramp up to the right, then traverse right to gain a gully line.
2   25m. A short ice pitch and mixed ground leads to the foot of Aaron's Slab.
3   25m. Go left into the icy gully and follow it past another short ice pitch to an upper amphitheatre.

4   70m. The ramp on the right leads to the summit slopes.

Pinnacle Crack   70m V (6) 2000
This turf and snowed-up rock route lies up the wall immediately to the right of the narrow gully.
1   40m. Climb a rib to the base of the Upper Buttress (left of the summer routes of *The Slant* and *Mallory's Left-Hand Route*).
2   30m. Climb the crack up the slabby wall and exit behind the pinnacle.

Torquers Are No Good Doers   50m VII (7) 2002
This route, whose name arguably holds the trophy for the most awkwardly contrived pun in the book (and there's quite some competition), follows the crack-line of the summer route *The Serpent*. High up on the left end of the crag is an obvious slab with a crack running through it (*Mallory's Left-Hand Route*). To its right is a prominent corner/groove (*Mallory's Right-Hand Route*) and, between, some very steep crack-lines. This route takes the second crack-line left of the slanting ramp-line of the summer route *The Slant*. Scramble up and right to the start.
1   30m. Move right off the belay onto a slab and steeply into a hanging niche on good hooks. Pull right out of the niche round a blunt arete and climb a shallow groove above to a belay. (The first pitch of the summer route *The Serpent*).
2   20m. Follow the continuation crack above to the left side of a detached block pinnacle. Climb the left side of this to easy ground.

Access to the next few routes can be gained by a variety of enjoyable pitches on the broken lower tier. A bay with a big slab forming its left side acts as a good reference point. The right-hand side of the bay is marked by the mixed line of *Pinnacle Ridge*. The slab can be climbed via a right-to-left weakness at V (6), 20m, or direct at VI (6), 20m (thin). The chimney at the back of the bay can be climbed over the chockstone V (7), 20m. Above, an easy ridge or turfy grooves lead to the foot of Mallory's Buttress which is bounded on its left by the slabby wall of *Pinnacle Crack* and to its right by the corner of *Bottleneck Blues*.

Mallory's Corner   75m IV (6) 1997
The route follows part of the summer climb of *Mallory's Right-Hand Route* which takes the next groove system to the right and the large grassy corner above. Start at a crack right of a glacis.
1   25m. Climb the crack on excellent placements and follow the continuation flake rightwards into the main line of the corner. Two steep steps lead to a corner with belays at the foot of a chimney.
2   50m. Take the fine corner on the right to the summit.

Lake District Winter Climbs

Great Gable

1. Bottleneck Blues — IV
2. Pinnacle Ridge — III
3. Bottlescrue — IV
4. Oblique Chimney — IV
5. Summer Time Blues — V
6. Mid-winter Madness — VI
7. Hooch — IV
8. Seasonal Affected Disorder — V
9. Clark Gable — II/III
10. Sledgate Ridge — IV
11. Engineer's Chimney — V
12. Troll — VII
13. The Angel of Mercy — VIII
14. Snicker Snack — VII
15. Engineer's Slabs — VI
16. The Jabberwock — VII
17. Gable End — II
18. Trundle Ridge — VII
19. The Smart Exit — IV
20. The Contrived Eliminate — IV
21. Central Gully — III
22. Bootlegger's Groove — III
23. Back Off — VI

Gable Crag

Direct Start
IV 1999

1   30m. Ascend ledges diagonally rightwards to the undercut crack of the summer line. Climb this and the groove above to a big ledge and belay. (This is the summer line of *Mallory's Right-Hand Route*).

Bottleneck Blues
45m IV (4) * 1997

Superb well-protected mixed climbing up the huge corner to the left of *Pinnacle Ridge*. Start at the base of the open corner.

1   25m. Move up to a flake and step right into the right-angled corner. Follow this direct past a hollow flake (crux), then traverse right to an obvious block belay on the ridge overlooking the bottle-shaped pinnacle.
2   20m. Follow the continuation grooves to the top (various options depending on conditions).

Pinnacle Ridge
200m III ** 1947

The ridge to the right of the huge corner of *Bottleneck Blues* has a reputation for coming into condition very rapidly. Follow the obvious curving ridge from the left to the top of a pillar. Make an awkward step up and left on the wall behind the pillar (crux), then follow easy ground to the top.

The wide gully between *Pinnacle Ridge* and *Sledgate Ridge* to the right is the base of the summer descent route from climbs on *Engineer's Slabs* and the next climb roughly takes this line.

Clark Gable
130m II/III 1960

Start up the corner-line right of the ridge and follow the gully to the amphitheatre below the headwall. Move diagonally right round the rib to gain the top of *Engineer's Chimney*.

The next routes are all reached by following *Clark Gable* to the amphitheatre; the well-defined *Oblique Chimney* is on the left. For *Hooch* and *SAD* continue up *Clark Gable* to a large block belay above *Clark Gable*.

Oblique Reference
120m IV (4) * 1995

A direct start to *Pinnacle Ridge*. Start at a pillar 10m down from the foot of *Oblique Chimney*.

1   30m. Follow a groove on the left of the pillar to its top.
2+3 90m. As for *Pinnacle Ridge*: make an awkward step up and left to reach easy ground.

Oblique Chimney   55m IV (5) * 1996

The prominent leftward-slanting chimney-line on the left, above the amphitheatre. Cave belay at half-height.

Bottlescrue   75m IV (5) 1995

A right-to-left diagonal line starting 10m up right from the toe of the buttress and finishing in *Oblique Chimney* above the difficulties.
1   20m. Follow *Summer Time Blues* to the belay.
2   30m. Ascend leftwards over ledges and ice smears to belay at a snow ledge.
3   25m. A crack at the left end of the ledge leads up to a large ledge and continues left to a flake. A traverse left under the flake leads into *Oblique Chimney*.

Summer Time Blues   70m V (6) ** 1995

Climbed on the first day of British Summer Time, this route takes a shallow chimney-line in the left side of the headwall immediately above the amphitheatre and to the right of *Oblique Chimney*.
1   20m (5). The chimney is guarded by a small steep buttress. From the amphitheatre, move up 10m over steeper ground to a ledge below slabs, just left of the chimney proper. Belay in the corner just left of the shallow chimney.
2   50m (6). Follow the steep chimney with improving protection as it becomes more defined. A through-route finish is available for the slim.

The next three routes are on the headwall to the right of *Oblique Chimney* and *Summer Time Blues*.

Mid-winter Madness   70m VI (6) 2007

The corner-line approximately 10m to the right of *Summer Time Blues*.
1   50m (6). Start at a point below and in line with the corner. Climb easy ground to a tricky step to gain the base of the corner, level with the belay on *Summer Time Blues*. Continue up the corner to belay on a ledge on the right. Beware of loose blocks.
2   20m (5). Move up and right from the belay and climb the wall immediately right of a shallow corner to climb through a small overlap near the top.

Hooch   40m IV (6) 2000

At the right-hand side of the headwall are three corner come groove lines; the left-hand one starting high on the wall is *Hooch*. A mixed climb with reasonable protection, taking the wall just right of the summer route of *Moonshiner*. Start at a large block.

Follow the corner behind the block then step left to a spike on the arete. Take the prominent bulging rib on the left to a good ledge below the smooth top wall which has a groove on its right-hand side. Climb the wall using cracks to grasp a block in the groove then continue straight up. Pinnacle and chockstone belays are available up to the left (but beware of loose boulders).

Seasonal Affected Disorder (SAD)   40m V (5) ** 2007

The next prominent groove with a protruding block near the crag top is *SAD*. This offers excellent well-protected technical climbing in its upper half.

Climb the wall behind a large flake at the base of the wall, as for *Hooch*, but continue up into the middle corner. Step left and climb the groove to the protruding block at the top of the corner. Pass this to finish.

A buttress extends below the line of *Engineer's Chimney*; this is *Sledgate Ridge*.

Sledgate Ridge   80m IV (5) 1985

A useful approach to the routes higher up on *Engineer's Slabs* as well as a route in its own right. The start of the ridge is just above the path at the base of the crag, below and left of the prominent buttress containing *Engineer's Slabs*.

1. 20m. Either start up a hard crack or, if you're going for bigger things higher up the crag, use the easier chimney on the right and continue up the iced grooves to a ledge.
2. 20m. Ascend a wall at the left end of the ledge, moving diagonally rightwards over slabs to a large grassy platform.
3. 40m. Climb the chimney, or (if your arms are up to it) any of the other routes around this area.

The prominent buttress with *Engineer's Slabs* up its centre and *Engineer's Chimney* on its left side is found up and left of the start of *Central Gully*. The best approach is leftwards over broken ground from a snow bay just left of the start of *Central Gully*.

Engineer's Chimney   50m V (4) ** 1910

Bounding the left side of the big wall containing *Engineer's Slabs* is an obvious chimney. The chimney does not hold a lot of snow and the crux may be on verglassed rock. The original ascent, in very icy conditions, was a futuristic achievement.

1. 15m. Start up snow to a fork in the chimney.
2. 25m. Follow the left branch, the difficulties easing where the chimney widens. Pass a chockstone to finish up an iced crack.
3. 10m. Easier ground leads to the top and a belay.

Troll   60m VII (8) ** 2003

To the right of *Engineer's Chimney*, a block overhang can be seen about halfway up the crag. The route climbs this feature.

1   30m (8). Start right of *Engineer's Chimney* and climb the wall to the overhang. Surmount this using a crack on the right and belay on a ledge.
2   30m (5). The summer line moves right and climbs a steep slab to a break, then traverses right to the flake on *Snicker Snack*, which is followed for a few metres before moving into a groove on the right to finish. On the first ascent the groove wasn't viable, so the team went straight up on stepped ledges following the obvious snowiest line.

The Angel of Mercy   60m VIII (9) 2012

Another hard technical route starting up *Troll*.

1   25m (8). Climb as for *Troll* up to the niche below the overhanging block and belay.
2   25m (9). Climb up to below the block, pull out right to gain the hanging slab. Make technical moves rightwards using the crack below the overlap. Pull around to gain the crack. Climb the crack to belay below the overhanging crack (level with *Snicker Snack* belay).
3   10m. Move left to finish up an easier snow ramp.

Snicker Snack   60m VII (9) *** 2003

The classic steep crack-line in the wall left of *Engineer's Slabs*.

1   45m (9). Start up the wall as for *Engineer's Slabs* but continue up thin cracks to belay at a huge flake.
2   15m (7). Climb the flake and traverse right to a small overhang. Gain a thin crack above and follow this to the top.

Winterceptor   70m VII (8) *** 2008

A mixed route, literally, mixing the start of *Engineer's Slabs* with the middle crack of the summer line *Interceptor* before finishing up the exposed prow of the summer route *Mome Rath*.

1   25m (7). As for *Engineer's Slabs*, follow cracks, then a chimney to the sentry box.
2   45m (8). Follow the crack above the sentry box to the overhanging headwall and step right at two large loose blocks to climb the overhanging prow of *Mome Rath* to the spike on the arete above and finish as for *Engineer's Slabs Arete Finish*.

GABLE CRAG

Steve Ashworth treads carefully on Snicker Snack (First Ascent) (photo: Stuart Wood)

Engineer's Slabs   65m VI (7) *** 1985
An established modern test piece this gives excellent mixed climbing. It starts up cracks in the middle of the big face: the belays are somewhat cramped.
1   25m (7). Follow cracks, then a chimney leading to a sentry box.
2   25m (7). A difficult traverse right (crux) for 10m on iced cracks leads into a vertical crack, which is followed to some strenuous moves onto a belay ledge.
3   15m (6). Follow the steep groove above.

Arete Finish   20m VI (7) ** 1997
3   20m (7). From the belay below the final groove, follow the stepped crack to a spike on the arete and make delicate moves up this to easier ground and the top.

The Jabberwock   75m VII (7) *** 2003
This follows the crack system on the right-hand side of the prominent steep headwall, approached by scrambling from the right.
1   20m (5). Climb the cracked wall to a ledge on the right of a large flake.
2   30m (7). Climb a crack to a large ledge at 20m and continue to a ledge and shattered block belay.
3   25m (6). Follow the exposed groove above to the top. It is also possible to finish further left.

Gable End
150m II ** 1960

Start up easy slopes to the left of *Central Gully* and head to a gully and corner-line running directly up the crag immediately right of the main rock buttress of *Engineer's Slabs*.

Trundle Ridge
140m VII (7) ** 2003

A climb following the left ridge overlooking *Central Gully*; if you stray too far left you'll end up on *Gable End*.

1. 40m (7). From the lowest rocks of the ridge, climb a grassy corner to a saddle in the ridge. Climb a short wall and steep off-width crack to the top of a pinnacle.
2. 10m (4). Step down from the pinnacle and cross a chimney using a jammed block to gain a ledge.
3. 30m (7). Climb the steep crack directly out of the gap to gain a shallow corner. Follow this, and the short wall when it runs out, to a large stance.
4. 60m (3). Easier climbing leads to the top via *Gable End* or one of the *Central Gully* finishes.

Brilliant by Design – Engineer's Slabs (photo: Paddy Cave)

Gable Crag

Central Gully   225m III ** 1891
An interesting outing with avoidable lower steep pitches and several alternative exits. The traditional route is described first. All of the variations start up this and go to the headwall after the second pitch.
1   35m. Climb the chimney direct (if iced), or the arete on the left.
2   20m. Climb the second chimney direct, or a smaller easier chimney on the left over a chockstone. Traverse back to the gully bed.
3   50m. Continue up easier snow to a small stance at the gully headwall.
4   20m. On the right is a small steep corner-chimney leading onto a large terrace.
5   30m. Head easily up to the right to steeper rock at the right end of the terrace. Climb a small pitch above, the Smuggler's Retreat, then follow the easy gully which runs out into a rake.
6   100m. The rake leads easily to the summit.

The Contrived Eliminate   50m IV (5) 1960
5   (20m). From the headwall in the main gully, climb directly up an iced crack for 5m to a large snow slope. Cross this to a belay below a slabby stepped headwall.
6   (30m). Take the line of least resistance through the wall to summit snow slopes.

The Smart Exit   73m IV (4) ** 1937
5   (18m). From the stance at the headwall, follow the left-slanting groove to the left end of a large snow slope.
6   (16m). Ascend the snowfield easily up left to the gully-chimney at the top left.
7   (45m). Climb 10m of steep ice and exit onto snow leading to the summit plateau.

Less than Smart Exit   60m III * 1996
5   (20m). Follow *The Smart Exit* to the snow slope but traverse left for about 15m to a lower gully with a small chockstone. Belay.
6   (40m). This leads to the exit slopes above the ice pitch of *The Smart Exit*. The gully steepens at a detached pinnacle on the left. Pass this to easier ground and a corner at the top of *Gable End*.

Bootlegger's Groove   150m III * 1999
Excellent mixed climbing up the big corner right of *Central Gully*. Start at the base of *Central Gully*.
1   40m. Climb up rightwards to an overhanging block at 12m. Pull over (first crux), then straight up the corner to a belay below a left-leaning corner-crack.

2   40m. Climb the crack (second crux) to easy ground, then continue straight up a prominent groove. Pull out to easy snow and follow this for 15m to a large block and thread belay.
3   40m. Move right and finish up the ridge, or traverse right into the easy top part of *Smuggler's Chimney* or *Central Gully*.
4   30m. Easy snow to the top.

The next obvious feature is a steep crack/chimney, the summer route *Smuggler's Chimney*. The next two routes take a fairly similar line up the groove system midway between this and *Moses's Back Door*.

Back Off   65m VI (7) 2003

This follows a natural winter line based around the summer route of *Smaug*. Start in the first snow bay to the right of *Central Gully*.
1   40m. Start up an iced corner to belay below an obvious rib.
2   25m. Move right to a thin crack to the right of the rib and follow this to a steep crack. Avoid the overhanging crack and go right. Follow *Moses's Back Door* to the top (a further 125m).

Gone with the Wind   60m IV 1997

A climb which takes the buttress and groove system located between *Smuggler's Chimney* and the start of *Moses's Back Door*. This and the previous route possibly share the 'steep ice groove' variation (described as part of *Moses's Back Door*) to give a more direct line. To the right of *Smuggler's Chimney* is a small buttress. Start at the foot of the buttress below a wide open gully. From the start a vertical crack and block are visible high up on the left edge of the buttress.
1   25m. Ascend the buttress to a large ledge. From the left-hand end of the ledge, move up to the edge, ascend the crack and surmount the block (crux), pulling up onto a ledge. Move up into a large bay directly below a groove (the same point can be reached by going directly up from the right-hand end of the large ledge).
2   20m. Ascend the groove system to emerge near the top of *Smuggler's Chimney*.
3   15m. The short corner direct to the large terrace below the headwall. Easier ground leads up and left to the summit.

Moses's Back Door   190m II 1960

From the wide open gully on the right of the crag, gain a ramp which leads left to a snow bay. Cross the snow bay and traverse left again to a groove which leads to the *Smuggler's Retreat*. Finish as for *Central Gully*. A steep ice groove also leads from the snow bay to the same place.

In Her Mouth
90m V (6) 2003

Below *Doctor's Chimney* and above the grassy gully of *Moses's Back Door* is an obvious rock ramp running from right to left with a chimney/groove at its base. Start at the chimney/groove, which is the start of the summer route *Sundowner*.

1. 30m. From a spike on the left, traverse right into a chimney/groove and climb directly to a belay on a large ledge above.
2. 60m. Climb the corner to the right of the belay until a traverse left is possible along a narrow ledge. Follow this to its end and swing round an arete. Climb direct to the top of crag.

Doctor's Chimney
130m III * 1962/3

Start up the wide gully at the right side of the crag and after 50m ascend the obvious chimney on the left. Follow this (30m) then continue easily to the top.

Great Gable Traverse
600m II 1960

Also known as the **Traverse of the Gods**. The traverse follows a great bow-shaped natural weakness starting from the foot of the easy gully near Windy Gap. From the foot of *Oblique Chimney*, the line runs along the base of *Engineer's Slabs* to cross *Central Gully,* beyond which it dips to reach easy slopes below *Doctor's Chimney*. It is not without interest in its own right and is a useful approach to many of the routes on the face.

Green Gable Crag

NY 214 106   ALTITUDE 750M   WEST FACING

This crag sits on the West Face of Green Gable at the head of Ennerdale and faces across to the more imposing Gable Crag. Reached in about an hour from Honister Pass, access is also straightforward from Borrowdale via Styhead Tarn and up Aaron Slack to Windy Gap: the crag can be seen immediately on the right. If travelling from Wasdale, follow the path to Beck Head to the west of Great Gable, then skirt along the path under Gable Crag to the head of the valley and contour round to Green Gable Crag. Although short by traditional winter standards, several routes may be climbed in a visit, making it a worthwhile venue. **Descend** on the left-hand (north) side.

The climbs are described from right to left.

Turfed Out
70m II (3) 2006

Start on the right side of the first buttress about 10m up from its lowest point and up and right of *Calculator*.

1 30m (3). Follow a wide crack to gain a ledge. Move right and up a short awkward wall to reach iced slabs. Follow these up left to the top of the buttress.
2 40m. Pleasant mixed ground leads to the top.

Calculator   72m V (5) * 1995

From the lowest point of the buttress climb easily to the large ledge at 10m which can also be accessed by walking in from the right side of the buttress. From the centre of the buttress move up steep rock to a diagonal left-sloping ledge system which is followed to the base of a shallow V-groove, just left of centre of the buttress. Follow the V-groove to the top with an exposed move where the groove ends. The V-groove can also be reached by climbing up the centre of the buttress to a second ledge then stepping left into the groove. It is also possible to escape right along the higher ledge to the awkward wall of *Turfed Out*. A further 30m of easy climbing leads to the summit.

Sod-U-Like   75m II 1995

Starting at the lowest point of the buttress, next to *Calculator*, climb up and left of *Calculator* to pass to the left of a shattered overhang which is on the left side of the buttress. Climb an open turfy groove close into the left of the buttress to its top then follow *Calculator* to the top.

Parallel G   80m II/III 1995

The parallel-sided gully to the left of the buttress. Follow the gully to the point where it widens above and finish to the right of the next buttress.

Beta Hammer Belter   75m III 1995

The lowest point of the crag is characterised by a deeply cut chimney. Start in a recess, to the left of the chimney, at a turf-filled gully. Climb the gully to more open ground then steeper iced rock above, turning an overhang on its left.

Mutley's Icy Wait   90m II 2002

Start up ice on the right side of the gully wall just below the short rock step at the start of *Gully of the Plods*. Frozen turf leads to a short cleft at 10m. Continue up easier ground and at 60m climb a short icy chimney with a large chockstone in it. Follow easy ground to the top.

Gully of the Plods   120m I/II 1978

An obvious gully which effectively separates the crag into two sections. It is climbed via the right-hand branch. The left-hand branch gives some steep moves on turf at a similar grade.

Green Gable

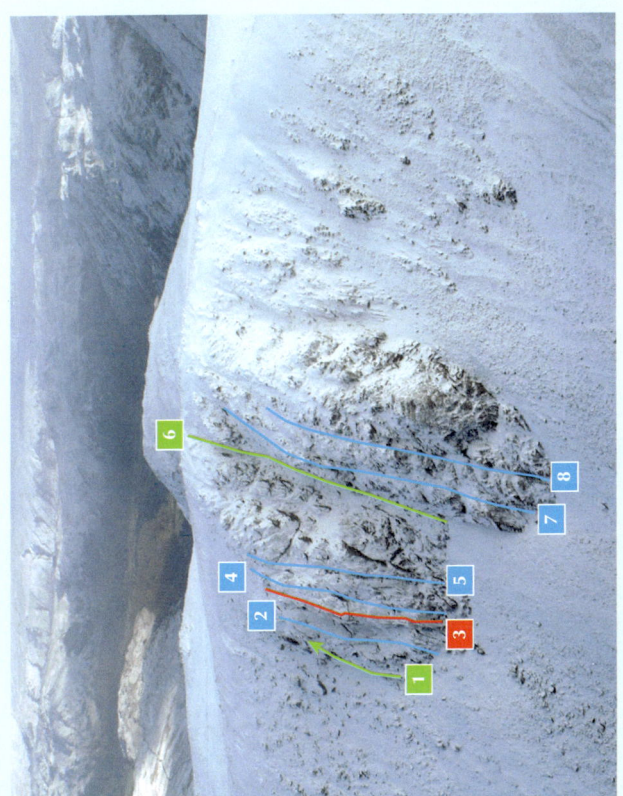

1	North Gully	I/II
2	Garden of Eden	III
3	East of Eden	IV
4	Ride the Wild Turf	III
5	Epsilon Chimney	III
6	Gully of the Plods	I/II
7	Beta Hammer Belter	III
8	Parallel G	II/III

Stuart Allinson on belting mixed ground on Green Gable's Beta Hammer Belter (photo: Harry Worsnop)

Epsilon Chimney 57m III ** 1995
To the left of *Gully of the Plods* are some slabs with a chimney on their left. Climb the chimney.

Ride the Wild Turf 45m III (4) 1995
About 10m to the left of *Epsilon Chimney* is a small detached buttress. Start on its left and continue up a grassy corner right of some rocky ribs to finish up grooves.

East of Eden 60m IV (5) * 1995
This route follows the wall just left of and below the broken ribs of the previous route.
1 10m. Climb the wall and go up leftwards at its top to a recess on the right.
2 30m. Turn the slab and short steep wall to the left to a ledge below the overhang (crux). Move right under the overhang and enter the chimney above. Belay at the back of the chimney.
3 20m. Climb the corner above and finish up and right.

Garden of Eden 80m III *** 1995
Follow easy ground to the grass-covered recess of *East of Eden*. Continue up the icy corner to the top.

Green Gable End 80m IV (4) * 1995
Start up the easy ground as for *Garden of Eden* but belay at the left-hand side of the recess to the left of the largest slab, below a grassy corner groove. Continue up the corner and move right into the continuation groove at the top.

Arjuna 43m III (5) 1995
Start a few metres up the descent gully at the left-hand side of the crag. Follow a corner-line filled with turf to an overhang and chockstone. Pass this (crux) and follow a groove above to the top.

North Gully 30m I/II 1995
The wide shallow gully between the left edge of the buttress and the smaller buttress to its left.

North Face 20m I 1995
Easy climbing up the buttress left of *North Gully*.

LAKE DISTRICT WINTER CLIMBS

KIRK FELL

NY 195 105   ALTITUDE 802M

Kirk Fell is the shapely hill immediately west of Great Gable. It can be most easily approached from Honister, or from Wasdale via Blacksail Pass or Gavel Neese.

On the south (Wasdale) side of Kirk Fell is *Ill Gill*.

Ill Gill 265m II/III 1963

A prominent long gash seen on the Wasdale side of the mountain close to the path up to Styhead. After a period of hard frost, the gill gives an excellent mixed route which, in a good season, can be followed to the summit of the mountain.

All of the remaining climbing on Kirk Fell is on the north (Ennerdale) side.

The path leading under Boat Howe from Great Gable via Beckhead Tarn crosses **Boat Howe Gill** (150m, II) at (NY 204 109, Alt 580m) just before Boat Howe is reached: it can give 150m of water ice in a sharp freeze.

Boat Howe

NY 199 110   ALTITUDE 700M   *NORTH FACING*

This crag is situated high on the Ennerdale side of Kirk Fell and is best approached from Wasdale by Beck Head or, slightly longer, via Black Sail Pass. It is also possible to approach from Honister Pass following the approach to Gable Crag. The crag has a number of obvious gullies at Grade I/II. The climbs are described from left to right.

When approaching from Beck Head the first prominent ridge on the right-hand skyline is **Longshoreman's Arete** (180m II/III, 2007). To its right the broken easterly buttress contains **Esplanade Climb** (II/III) up the centre – follow your nose. Further right is a steep pillar of rock, The Boat, with the obvious cleft of *Starboard Chimney* to its right.

Starboard Chimney 40m IV (5) ** 1990

To the right of the main buttress is a short cleft. Climb it if you like that sort of thing: strenuous.

To the right of The Boat across a gully is the West Buttress.

Horizon Climb
100m IV (4) 1989

A good mixed route that is often in condition. Start up a corner to the right of a series of slabs.

1. 40m. Climb up the corner right of slabs and move right to broken rock and a series of ledges.
2. 20m. Follow the corner-line on the left to a ledge.
3. 40m. Follow a series of ledges trending right to finish up a ridge.

Black Sail Buttress

NY 194 111   *ALTITUDE 620M*   *NORTH FACING*

This crag is found high up on the north-west side of the mountain, above Black Sail Pass and is best approached from the Wasdale side. It is marked on the map as Kirkfell Crags.

Kirk Fell Gill
165m II/III * 1963

Marked as Sail Beck on the map, *Kirk Fell Gill* (NY 194 113) is approached from the Black Sail path via upper Ennerdale or Wasdale. The northerly aspect and high altitude produce some good and relatively long-lasting ice.

The climbing in the gill actually starts where it enters a cleft a hundred metres or so below the buttress itself. The stream crosses the old smugglers' track between Black Sail and Beck Head at the lowest point of the path. From this point, several minor pitches lead to a large ice pitch, all of which are escapable.

The remaining climbs lie on the crag itself. The first two may in fact be one and the same.

Central Groove
100m II/III 1984

Start at a steep vegetated groove leading to a terrace. Move up the mixed ground above via the easiest line. From the terrace it is possible to go right and descend into the easy gully or traverse left to easy ground.

Ignition Buttress (100m, III, 1963), the buttress just right of *Kirk Fell Gill* offers some steep mixed ground leading to a snow terrace. Above, a large icefall can be followed to the top.

Black Sail Gully
180m II (3)

This pleasant gully marks the right side of the crag and finishes almost on the summit of Kirk Fell.

BUTTERMERE AND NEWLANDS

Tucked away in the north-west corner of the Lake District is the remote valley of Buttermere, a noticeably quieter area than many other parts of the National Park. Access to the valley from the north and east is usually via Honister or Newlands passes and from West Cumbria via Lorton Vale to the north-west (the latter is often passable when other roads are closed due to ice).

Buttermere runs in a south-east to north-west direction and contains the lakes of Buttermere and Crummock Water. The head of the valley is dominated by Fleetwith Pike, which has Honister Pass to its east and Warnscale Bottom to its west. There is climbing on both sides of the valley. The south side contains the low-lying crag of Haystacks and its various gullies. To its west, between the summits of High Crag and High Stile, is Birkness Combe, with a number of classic winter climbs such as *Birkness Chimney* and *Birkness Gully*. West again lies Bleaberry Combe and Chapel Crags. The gills on the north side of the valley can hold good ice in prolonged cold spells, with additional, more reliable climbing being found on the mountains of Hopegill Head and Grasmoor. The north face of Fleetwith Pike contains arguably the best pure icefall climbing in the Lakes, only a short walk above Honister Pass.

The Newlands Valley, Coledale and Whinlatter Pass, which lie to the north-east of Buttermere, are also described in this section.

HONISTER PASS

NY 225 135

From Honister Pass a number of winter climbs are easily accessible, the greatest concentration being the icefalls which form on Honister Crag. This north and north-east facing crag lies immediately above the road on its south side. Fed by drainage from the old mine workings, great curtains and chandeliers of ice form to create a superb collection of routes up to 150m in length within 20 minutes walk of the car.

The road on the west (Buttermere) side of Honister Pass has a gentler incline than the east (Borrowdale) side, from which most people usually approach. Unfortunately this is readily prone to icing. If the pass is rendered inaccessible by car, an approach by foot on the Buttermere side, is not too arduous.

The first two routes described are found on the north side of the road below the summit of the pass.

Yew Crags

NY 219 147   ALTITUDE 350M   *SOUTH-WEST FACING*

Yew Crag Gully is the only major gully in the broken crag on the northern slopes of the upper Buttermere Valley. Being south facing, it is seldom in condition – an early start is worthwhile when it is.

Yew Crag Gully   140m IV (4) *
The gully is approached in twenty minutes directly from the road.
1   30m. Follow easy snow to the first chockstone which is passed on the right.
2   20m. A small chockstone pitch leads to the foot of a big icefall.
3   30m. The bulging icefall leads to easier snow above from which it is possible to escape to the right or...
4   60m. For a fuller mountaineering experience, continue up the gully for several short pitches emerging onto the summit ridge.

Buckstone How

NY 223 143   ALTITUDE 400M   *SOUTH-WEST FACING*

Situated just to the north-west side of the summit of Honister Pass, Buckstone How is easily reached by taking an old quarry track that contours northwards opposite the car park by the Youth Hostel and slate mine works. (NB This is not to be confused with 'Buckstone Hows', which is marked on the 1:25,000 OS map much further north.) Descend diagonally across slate spoil to the crag. It is rumoured that the summer VS *Sinister Grooves* has been climbed in winter, though no further details are known. Following the base of the crag round to the left about 50m up the hillside is a higher section with a steep broken wall. The route takes prominent ice oozing from the depression right of centre with an amphitheatre in its upper portion.

One Armed Bandit   80m V (5) 2010
A stream flows down the central amphitheatre and depression forming a steep icefall.

1 50m (4). Easy ice leads to steep ice guarding entry into the amphitheatre. Easier angled slopes lead to a belay at the back left-hand corner of the amphitheatre.
2 30m (5). Climb the icy left-hand slabby walls into a left-facing flake come corner and follow this with ice thinning near the top. The natural continuation of the depression heads up and rightwards from the belay offering a poorer alternative finish.

The remaining climbs are located on the south side of the pass.

Quarry Fall   25m IV (5)

This free-standing icefall is located just behind the quarry and Youth Hostel car park in a small stream basin to the right of the fence, about five minutes' walk from the road. The steep bit is short and the route ends abruptly in the stream bed.

FLEETWITH PIKE – NORTH FACE

This face sports the greatest concentration of icefall climbing in the Lake District.

Honister Crag Icefalls 🌿

NY 217 140   Altitude 350m   *North-east facing*

A long period of cold northerly or easterly winds are required to bring this fine collection of icefalls into condition. Many of these routes, which are draped over the old slate workings of Honister Crag, were climbed in the last quarter of the 20th century when conditions were on occasion quite fantastic. Unfortunately the recent resumption of working at the quarry seems to have reduced drainage down the crag; consequently these icefalls form less frequently and less densely than they used to.

The line of the icefalls, the old mine workings and the crag itself are home to rare alpine plants – please climb here only in truly frozen conditions.

The next routes are reached by taking the lower of two inclines from the Honister Mine car park at the top of Honister Pass, marked as the 'Monkey Shelf' on a slate inlaid on the track. Follow it to the fourth bridge, about 5 minutes from the car park. The stream has been climbed by two routes, one below and one above the bridge.

HONISTER CRAG ICEFALLS

Lower Incline Fall 50m III * 🌳 2010
Beneath the fourth bridge on the lower incline, descend (to the right as you're looking down) to a fallen tree in the gully some 50 to 60m below. Climb easy-angled iced steps to a more challenging finish.

Incline Fall 25m III 🌳 2004
A nice short pitch narrowing steadily all the way to an awkward finish. Limited rock protection can be arranged on the left. There is a tree belay set back at the top.

The remaining icefalls are all reached from an incline running off the Honister to Great Gable track. From the top of the Honister Pass take the main track towards Gable, but after a short distance branch off on the quarry incline to the right and where this divides take the lower fork. This exposed renovated railway incline, which follows occasional tunnels, strikes a rightward-rising diagonal line across the Honister Face of Fleetwith Pike. The incline is a useful general reference point for the three main climbing areas.

After a few hundred metres the incline enters a tunnel, access to which is barred by large gates. Traverse on the downhill side for a few hundred metres before scrambling back up to the incline over snow/slate scree on the other side of the tunnel. Alternatively, a rising ramp containing spikes also to the right of the tunnel entrance leads around a rock bluff to emerge at a gully adjacent to Upper Left Gantry Crag, gained by scrambling across the gully. This aptly named crag usually holds three steep icefalls. The other end of the tunnel emerges beyond Upper Left Gantry Crag. To the right the incline now continues above a slate buttress topped by an old iron gantry standing on the incline. This gantry, obvious from the road, serves as a useful landmark amidst the complex slate-strewn surrounds. Gantry Crag, which lies below it, is bounded on the left by *Cable Gully* and on the right by Quarryman's Gully, a wide gully filled with slate scree aka Bull Gill.

Tunnel Vision 30m III/IV 🌳 1997
The icefall to the left of the first tunnel entrance. Climb a groove to a bay, passing an overhang and an iron spike (if the icefall has failed to form down to the incline this bay can be gained by a traverse in from the left). From the bay, climb the ice to a small overhang which is taken on the right, then move back left above it. At the top, either follow the steeper centre of the icefall (IV) or a groove on the left (III).

Upper Left Gantry Crag

This crag lies to the left of the gantry above the tunnel portal and usually holds three distinct icefalls, with a crooked lesser fall issuing from below the top to their right. The crag is gained by following steep ground above the tunnel portal. **Descent** is down an easy rake to the left of the crag or by abseil.

Slate Cap   40m IV ** 1987
The left fall containing an obvious wedged slate chockstone.

Turf at the Top   40m V (5) *** 1995
The central fall is the steepest and may form a free-standing cigar.

Captain Patience   40m III/IV ** 1995
The easiest of the trio, though harder if the top section is not fully formed.

Lesser Fall   45m III 1997
The fall furthest to the right comprises easier ice with a steeper lower section.

Gantry Crag

This, the most significant buttress on Honister, presents four major lines and numerous variations. When in condition a large curtain of ice forms right of *Cable Gully* and further right, on the front face of the crag, a striking and independent icefall forms which sometimes has two parallel lines.

Directly below the crag, extensive slate scree drops to the valley floor. The shortest approach is directly up this from the road in about 20 minutes. This is straightforward if snow covered, but purgatorial otherwise. A longer alternative (which, admittedly, is not much better) is to take the quarryman's ramp from the pass, bypass the tunnel and rejoin the incline at the other side of the tunnel. Descend a scree/snow slope before traversing to the base of the crag – this is also the usual **descent** route from the crag.

The climbs are described from left to right.

Cable Gully   100m III/IV * 1970s
Follow the gully; a heavy rusty cable provides convenient belays. The right side of the dry stone headwall usually contains a good ice finish onto the gantry ledge.

Honister Crag Icefalls – Upper Left Gantry Crag

1 Slate Cap	IV
2 Turf at the Top	V
3 Captain Patience	III/IV
4 Lesser Fall	III

Honister Crag Icefalls – Gantry Crag

1. Lesser Fall — III
2. Cable Gully — III/IV
3. Left-Hand Gantry Curtain — IV
4. Right-Hand Gantry Curtain — IV/V
5. Right Gantry Icefall Left-Hand — IV/V
6. Right Gantry Icefall Right-Hand — IV/V
7. Quarryman's Falls — IV

HONISTER CRAG ICEFALLS

Left-Hand Gantry Curtain   100m IV (4) *** 1970s
A direct line can be taken starting just to the right of the base of *Cable Gully*. Two pitches lead to the ledge which runs across the left side of the crag at two-thirds height; belay on the break (70m). Follow the top icefall above the ledge direct (30m).

Right-Hand Gantry Curtain   100m IV/V (4) *** 1970s
The right-hand icefall is generally steeper.
1. 35m. Follow steep ice to bare rock and a peg belay.
2. 35m. Move left and up to the ledge. A traverse right leads to a belay below the right-hand top icefall.
3. 30m. Climb the icefall, or the smaller though steeper icefall to the left, to finish direct onto the gantry ledge.

Right Gantry Icefall (Left and Right-Hand)   120m IV/V (5) 1970s
The distinctive ice smear on the right front face of the crag. The main pitch may form as two independent icefalls, with the right-hand usually the harder and thinner of the two.
1. 30m. Climb easy-angled ice to where it steepens beneath the main fall.
2. 30m. Follow the nearly vertical ice direct, before the angle thankfully eases.
3. 30m. Scrambling and easier-angled ice leads to the base of a great corner.
4. 30m. The ice corner leads to the gantry ledge – a great pitch.

Quarryman's Gully Falls

Follow the incline further right until it crosses Quarryman's Gully. Beneath the incline, a 30m curtain of ice can form. Access is by abseil from the small gantry on the incline above.

Quarryman's Falls   30 to 45m IV (4) ** 1996
The falls comprise three obvious icefalls, all of a similar nature.

Long Bendy Straight Thing   135m VI (5) 2010
This icefall is found by following the gantry right until right of Quarryman's Gully. Traverse right past a series of roofs to the start.
1. 40m (3). Traverse leftwards above the roofs to the base of an iced up corner and belay.
2. 30m (5). Climb the thinly iced corner onto a ramp (crux) then move right to belay below an icicle.

3   50m (4). Climb the icicle to easier ground above.
4   15m (3). Continue up easy ground to the top.

Honister Crag Gully   350m IV (4) 🌿 1969

To the right of the large buttress right of Gantry Crag, a long distinctive gully splits the Honister face. Rising from the screes not far above the road it soars serenely to the top of Fleetwith Pike, finishing at the top of the Via Ferrata; – this is *Honister Crag Gully* (NY 214 142) aka Ash Gill.

Avoid an impressive overhanging block at the foot of the gully on the right by a traverse before returning to the gully and climbing it direct. Several short but steep ice pitches lead to the top.

Honister Crag

NY 214 143   Altitude 550m   North-East facing

The crag right of Honister Crag Gully. Either approach as for the existing climbs, probably the best option unless you know the terrain, or follow the Fleetwith Pike path until at the small tarn at the col between its two summits. Descend steeply to the west of the crag until a terrace runs back under the crag. The two routes to date are at the left side of the crag.

Aurora   75m VI (6) ** 🌿 2010

The left side of the crag contains three corner lines. This follows the left-hand one (the rock route *Seraph*).
1   10m. Follow a left facing groove to a ledge at the foot of the corner.
2   30m. Move rightwards into the corner and keep going.
3   35m. Continue up the corner.

North Star   70m VII (7) ** 🌿 2010

The central corner line (the rock route *Intimidator*) starting about 10m right of *Aurora*.
1   15m. Start up the short corner and move rightwards at its top to belay at the base of the main corner system.
2   30m. Battle up the prominent corner on ice runnels to where it steepens.
3   20m. Climb the steepening corner to an easier finish.

Warnscale Bottom

This low-lying valley at the head of Buttermere, between Fleetwith Pike and Haystacks, contains a number of gullies and streams making for good water-ice climbing following a prolonged frost and cold northerly or easterly winds. Warnscale Bottom and the adjacent gills are home to rare plants and climbing should be done only in truly frozen conditions. Approached along the bridlepath from Gatesgarth Cottage (NY 196 149) Fleetwith Pike lies to the left (east), with Haystacks across the valley to the right (south-west).

On the west side of Fleetwith Pike overlooking Warnscale Bottom is:

Fleetwith Gully 60m II 1928
The gully, which is situated to the right of Striddle Crag (NY 204 139) – the crag high up on the Fleetwith Pike, is best approached by following the Warnscale Bottom bridlepath which runs below it, then ploughing straight up to it. The gully contains one 25m pitch.

A number of the water courses draining into Warnscale Bottom can give pleasant ice pitches of II/III after a prolonged freeze. The following two, tucked away in the south corner between Haystacks and Green Crag to its left, are worthy of description. Both are tributaries of Black Beck, which feeds **Warnscale Beck** (I, 🛡️ 🌿🌿 1963).

Green Crag Gully 60m II
This deeply cut gully is home to a stream tumbling down from Blackbeck Tarn. It contains a waterfall which gives the main pitch.

Toreador Gully 100m III
This steep gully is found on the left side of Haystacks (NY 199 132). Start at a chimney.
1   20m. Climb the chimney to icy slabs at its top.
2   30m. After easier-angled climbing, the gully steepens to another chimney which leads to a small amphitheatre.
3   50m. Continue steeply up the gully, over mixed snow and ice, past two large chockstones.

Haystacks

NY 197 131   Altitude 400m   *North facing*

A large rambling and broken crag, situated on the fell of the same name. An easy rake, useful in **descent**, can be seen rising from bottom right to top left across the left half of the crag. The rock is very poor and the gullies only form in exceptional conditions. The routes are described from right to left, in the order that they would normally be approached. The first route, *Long Gully*, lies between two large buttresses to the right of the rake. The steep chimneys of *Stack Gill*, *Warn Gill* and *Y Gully* (located beneath the rake) lie on the far left.

Approach as for Warnscale Bottom, along the bridleway from Gatesgarth Cottage (NY 196 149). Cross the beck and climb directly up steep snow/scree to the crag.

Long Gully   300m III *

A water-ice gully taking a direct line between the buttresses which make up the right side of the face. A series of easy short pitches with poor belays lead to a steeper 50m pitch and a peg belay. A further steep section (15m) leads to easy ground and the summit.

The next three gullies can be found at the bottom of the far left end of the face.

Stack Gill   150m III   1963

The rightmost of the three gullies. The first cave pitch, climbed from right to left, proves the crux. Further climbing up chimneys and over chockstones leads to a final ice pitch. Said to have given superb water-ice climbing on the first ascent.

Warn Gill   200m IV (4)   2001

The middle of the three obvious gills. The steep initial entry to the gill bed can be avoided (if unfrozen) by climbing a heathery groove to the right for about 20m, before making a delicate traverse left across two rock ribs to gain the bed of the gill (40m). Continue up the gill bed passing some jammed blocks then a steep wall (60m) and more heathery climbing lead to the top.

Y Gully   100m IV (5)   1963

The leftmost gully and possibly the best of the trio. Climbed in the 'big freeze' of 1963, this gully was said to be a fine climb under such conditions – certainly finer than it is in summer, when it has been described as having 'areas that make Lego look solid'.

High Crag

NY 182 145   ALTITUDE 450M   *NORTH-EAST FACING*

This low lying crag can be clearly seen on High Crag Fell to the south of the entrance to Birkness Combe. Take the bridleway from Gatesgarth Farm around the south end of Buttermere and follow it up steeply turning left above the plantation for Scarth Gap. Leave the path in about 200m at a recent land slip (2010) and follow a faint track on the right of a wall to the crag in about 1hr.

Gatesgarth Chimney   55m IV (5) * 2010
This is the deep chimney bounding the right side of the crag.
1   40m (5). Climb directly to the base of the chimney proper, move left into it at a small spike and ascend to belay a few metres below the chockstone.
2   15m (5) Thrutch victoriously over the chockstone and belay well back.

BIRKNESS COMBE

NY 175 145

Marked on OS maps as Burtness Combe, this north-east-facing combe lies between the summits of High Crag and High Stile. As well as constituting the rock climbing centre of the Buttermere valley, it has some good winter climbing in its gullies and on its cliffs.

From Gatesgarth Farm, cross the valley at the head of the lake. Follow the main Scarth Gap track up the hillside, but branch off right on a much smaller track after 50m or so. Cross the fellside, passing under a steep dank outcrop. Pass this on its right and go straight up, crossing some boggy ground and a stile into the combe (1hr). The buttresses are described in a clockwise direction.

Descent is possible down either side of the buttresses described.

Brant Bield Crags

NY 175 145   ALTITUDE 520M   *NORTH FACING*

Named on OS maps as Comb Crags, this is an area of rocky outcrops at the back of the combe to the left of Eagle Crag. There are four distinctive gullies visible from the lip of the combe: all give about 100m of straightforward climbing and a good way to the top of High Crag. In many cases the difficulties can be outflanked using heathery buttresses either side of the gullies. The buttresses do not fulfil the potential they promise from below, being somewhat scrappy with loose rock.

The leftmost gully (II/III) is easy apart from a capping stone approximately one-third of the way up, which is best climbed on the right. About 100m to its right is an easy shallow snow gully (I) with no real difficulty, other than finding it frozen. Further right are twin gullies with a common start past a short chockstone. The easier left branch (II) runs up to the left of a steep buttress, while the more interesting right branch (III) runs diagonally rightwards across the steep buttress and has a few short icy steps, many of which can be outflanked on the buttresses to either side.

The next buttress is split by two parallel gullies and is separated from Brant Bield Crag by a grassy gully. The gullies (**Parallel Gully Left** and **Right** (II, 70m, 2001)) both contain short steps. The gully to the right of the buttress, **Right-Hand Gully** (II, 100m, 2001), contains several pleasant short ice steps.

Eagle Crag

NY 172 145   *Altitude 600m*   *West and north facing*

This large centrally situated crag dominates the back of the upper combe. From the base of the combe the following features can be recognised. The easy *West Gully* lies right of the striking main buttress. This buttress is split by the cleft of *Central Chimney*, obvious in its upper portion. Left of this, and hidden by the bulk of the buttress, is *Birkness Chimney,* with the slanting *Birkness Gully* further to its left. *Border Buttress* bounds the far left side of the crag.

The routes are described from left to right.

Border Buttress bounds the left side of the crag and lies high up in the combe. It is situated about 50m along a grassy/snowy terrace running left from *Birkness Gully*, at the point where the gully steepens and its walls close together. On the left is the short **Easy Gully** (I).

Border Buttress Gully   50m III/IV 1986

The first gully to the left of *Birkness Gully* and bounding *Border Buttress*. It starts just right of *Easy Gully* and is hidden from sight until you are underneath it. A steep and strenuous ice pitch leads to a narrow bay with poor potential for rock runners or belays. Above is a short but very steep (sometimes undercut) column of ice which eases off onto easier ground after about 5m.

Eagle Crag

1 Border Buttress Gully — III/IV
2 Border Buttress — III/IV
3 Birkness Gully — IV
4 Birkness Gully Wall — V
5 The Eagle's Claw — V
6 Birkness Chimney — IV
7 Central Chimney — V
8 Eagle Front — VI
9 West Gully — I

Border Buttress 50m III/IV 1986
In a good year presents an obvious ice sheet between *Birkness Gully* and *Border Buttress Gully*. Two similar pitches of moderately steep ice can be climbed with a belay at the base of a corner half way up.

Birkness Gully 50m IV (4) ***
The left-slanting diagonal gully tucked away coyly on the left side of the main crag; a hidden gem. Short but interesting. Follow easy snow up the gully until it steepens dramatically.
1. 25m. Climb to a large jammed boulder and behind it to a peg belay.
2. 25m. The meat of the route. Move onto the boulder and traverse the right wall to gain ice which can be climbed to a peg belay in a rock outcrop.

Birkness Gully Wall 50m V (4) ** 1984
This pearl forms more readily than the gully. Start 10m below the steep pitch in *Birkness Gully*.
1. 20m. Climb diagonally rightwards over mixed ground to a spike belay.
2. 30m. Climb up the icy groove and icefall on the left to the top.

The Eagle's Claw 70m V (5) * 1985
Between *Birkness Chimney* and *Birkness Gully* an impressive hanging icefall forms high up on the headwall.
1. 25m. From the foot of *Birkness Gully*, traverse rightwards and then climb up to a large snow ledge at the foot of the narrow section of *Birkness Chimney*.
2. 45m. Climb the large icefall on the left wall. Finish to the left or right depending how the ice has formed.

If the ice doesn't reach the snowy ledge carry on up from the lower left side and zig-zag left then back right to reach the ice after 20m.

Birkness Chimney 65m IV (5) * 1941
The chimney-line which divides the steeper Easter Buttress from the slabbier Far East Buttress to its left. It is not an obvious route to spot from below during the approach.
1. 15m. The initial chimney pitch can be fun, though is not often iced. It is usually avoided by traversing in from *Birkness Gully*.
2. 20m. Follow the next chimney pitch to a ledge (a large icefall, *The Eagle's Claw*, often forms above here on the left). Above is the crux where the chimney narrows. Belay below the wider terminal chimney above.
3. 30m. Easier climbing up the final chimney leads to the top.

Central Chimney   150m V (5) 1963

The astute will instantly discern that this is the chimney in the middle of the crag. Start at the lowest point of the crag.

1. 50m. Follow the chimney, which is not well defined initially and is escapable by traversing to the left at a number of points.
2. 40m. The chimney steepens and the climbing starts in earnest. Although it follows the line of the chimney, the climbing is exposed and requires well-frozen turf. Saved till last the crux comprises difficult and precarious moves over chockstones to gain the deeper sanctuary of the chimney proper.
3. 60m. Conspicuous on the approach, the deep upper cleft does not often contain much ice and is climbed in traditional style. The enclosing walls take away any feeling of exposure on the hard moves.

Eagle Front   140m VI 1963

This classic VS was climbed during the exceptionally long hard winter in 1963 when neve and ice built up on the crag: essential for the ascent, particularly for crossing slabby sections. The route follows the summer line winding its way up the more vegetated lower section of the cliff to a prominent left-facing corner high at the top of the crag. As far as is known the climb is unrepeated.

Pigott's Route   100m IV 1963

A slightly more direct line than the summer route. *Pigott's* lies on the west face of the crag and starts 5m above the snow at the corner of the buttress.
1. 30m. Climb a hanging chimney and bulging rock above (crux).
2. 70m. Follow various snow banks and small icefalls steeply rightwards to the top.

West Gully (150m, I) on the right of the buttress is an easy snow climb and makes a useful **descent**.

Above right of Eagle Crag in an area of broken buttresses and scree gullies is a conspicuous narrow ridge to the left of the second gully, **The Barn Door** (45m, II, 1935), an interesting route.

Grey Crag

NY 172 147   ALTITUDE 670M   *EAST FACING*

This crag comprises a collection of buttresses on the right-hand side of the combe. Facing south, they tend to catch the sun and snow strips readily. The climbs

Lake District Winter Climbs

described can be combined to produce a good outing – but only if you can catch the fleeting winter conditions.

Mitre Ridge (1925) is recorded as having been climbed under snow (1925). The assumption is that this was an ascent of *Mitre Buttress Ordinary*, which lies on the left-hand of the two lower buttresses. The grade is unknown but it is M in summer and the description can be found in the FRCC Buttermere guidebook.

Harrow Buttress   45m III 1960

This is the right-hand and smaller of the two lowest buttresses. A sunny route which can get quite hot.

1   10m. Start up a corner, just left of the toe, to a ledge.
2   35m. Follow the chimney above then move 3m left and up a groove.

Oxford and Cambridge Ordinary Route   42m IV (4) 1986

The uppermost buttress is the Oxford and Cambridge Buttress. Start up an arete separating the left and right faces of the buttress. Climb the arete for 15m to a ledge then move leftwards across the face to a right-facing corner. Near the top of the corner step onto an arete on the left.

BLEABERRY COMBE

The next combe to the north, between the summits of Red Pike to the north and High Stile to the south, contains Bleaberry Tarn and above it the buttresses that make up Chapel Crags.

Sourmilk Gill   350m I/II

This gill, situated at the north-west end of Buttermere and overlooking the village, tumbles down from Bleaberry Tarn. It can provide a lengthy outing during an ice age but its low starting altitude means it is rarely in complete condition (NY 172 163).

Chapel Crags

NY 167 149   ALTITUDE 670M   *NORTH-EAST FACING*

A series of damp vegetated crags ring the back of the combe. The highest and leftmost is Number One Buttress, which stands below the summit of High Stile and is

Chapel Crags – left-hand section

1 Turf Wars — II
2 Deep Cut Chimney — III
3 Little Sod — II
4 Grass Corner — IV
5 Bear Left — IV
6 Right Frog — IV
7 Black Chimney — III
8 Gully Arete — I/II

split by a gully (*Little Sod*) on its right-hand side. To the right, across a wide scree chute, is Number Two Buttress. The right side of this vegetated buttress is split by a wide gully containing two large chockstones (*Black Chimney*). Down and right of these upper buttresses is the largest buttress, *Central Buttress* (also known as *Number Three Buttress*), which is bounded on its left by the obvious *Curving Gully* and split by the prominent faults of *Bleaberry Chimney,* just right of centre and *Chapel Crag Gully* towards its right-hand side. It is bounded on the right by the easy *Wide Gully,* which makes a good **descent**. Right of *Wide Gully* lies Number Four Buttress, which is split by two lesser faults, the right one being *Sunday Chimney*. Right of this final buttress is the easy *Narrow Gully*. Many of these features are discernible from the valley.

Although many people appear to have climbed here over the years, nothing was recorded in the early days. However, we do know that Don Greenop climbed *Chapel Crag Gully* and *Curving Gully* after being told about them by 1940s and 50s Buttermere pioneer Bill Peascod.

From the village of Buttermere, take the path past the Fish Hotel to the foot of *Sourmilk Gill*. Follow the steep but well-made path up leftwards through the woods, then back right across the hillside into the combe. The main track continues onto Red Pike; however, once in the combe, leave it, passing to the south-east of Bleaberry Tarn and head up to the buttresses above (1hr 30mins).

Descent is down one of the easy gullies bounding the individual buttresses.

Number One Buttress

The highest buttress in the combe. It lies high on the far left side, below the summit of High Stile. The middle of the buttress has a prominent corner starting about halfway up the crag and a deep chimney (*Deep Cut Chimney*) cutting through the right-hand wall. The right-hand side of the buttress is bounded by the gully of *Little Sod* and right of this is a pinnacle.

Turf Wars   45m II * 2003

At the left-hand side of the crag are several lines of turf running to the top of the crag. Climb the left-hand one, stepping right into the right-hand line at about half-height.

To the right, a prominent bay lies about halfway up the crag, with a striking corner above it (as yet unclimbed).

Turf's Up
70m IV (4) ** 2003

Start at a turfy ramp below the prominent bay.
1. 30m. Climb up turf into a bay below the prominent corner.
2. 20m. Follow the first line of turf to the right of the corner with an awkward finishing move onto a large ledge.
3. 20m. Trend leftwards up easy ground to the top.

New Turf
70m IV (4) 2003

A line between *Turf's Up* and the deep cleft of *Deep Cut Chimney*. Start as for *Turf's Up*.
1. 30m. Reach the bay below the corner.
2. 20m. Climb the turf runnel immediately left of the deep chimney to the large ledge above. An awkward move at the top provides the crux but is escapable by stepping right into the chimney.
3. 20m. Trend leftwards up easy ground to the top.

Deep Cut Chimney
70m III 2003

To the right of the turf ramp used by the previous two routes is a short icy and turfy corner.
1. 30m. Use the short corner to reach a bay at the base of the prominent chimney.
2. 20m. Enter the deep chimney and squirm up between chockstones to pop out just below the large belay ledge used by *New Turf*.
3. 20m. Easy climbing trending leftwards leads to the top.

Turf Walls
70m IV (5) * 2003

1. 30m. Follow *Deep Cut Chimney* to the base of the chimney.
2. 20m. Move right with a tricky step to get established on some large sods which allow progress to be made up the wall right of the chimney to reach the large belay ledge above.
3. 20m. Trend leftwards up easy climbing to the top.

Little Sod
65m II 2001

Bounding the right side of this short buttress is a gully. Climb it passing a phallic pinnacle. The gully is likely to bank out into a Grade I snow slope given a good build-up.

The pinnacle which forms the right wall of *Little Sod* has two grooves on its right side.

Pinnacle Groove 30m II 2003
Climb the right-hand of the two grooves in the right-hand side of the pinnacle. At the top of the groove, either walk off right or spiral round the top of the pinnacle to the summit.

Number Two Buttress

The next buttress lies to the right of a wide gully and has a prominent slab at its top. The left side of the buttress contains a large grassy corner. The first route climbs this feature. On its right-hand side the buttress is split by the deep cleft of *Black Chimney*.

Grass Corner 60m II 2002
At the left side of the buttress, before it runs round into the wide gully, is a grassy corner/recess with a capstone at its start: this is about 20m left of a pinnacle. Passing the capstone on its left gives access to a large meadow and a choice of lines for the upper half. On the first ascent a turfy line on the left leading into a wide open corner was taken.

The next route climbs a turfy recess below and left of the prominent slab. Two further routes take the slab direct.

Turf Time 90m III 2003
1   40m Climb easy turf to the left of the deep gully a few metres left of *Bear Left*.
2   25m. Below the prominent overhanging slab move left into a turfy recess and make steep moves to break through the overhang and come up to the left of the slab.
3   25m. Climb corners above to the top.

Bear Left 90m IV (6) * 2002
The right side of the crag is split by the deep gully of *Black Chimney*. To its left, high on the crag, is a prominent slab. This climb starts at a turfy depression, or at the rib to its right overlooking the chimney and follows either to the overhang.
1   50m. Climb the turf to an overhang overlooking the gully to the right.
2   40m. Climb through the overhang at a corner by stepping off a small pedestal. Move up the corner for 5m before a delicate move left allows a left-trending groove/corner to be gained and followed to the top.

Right Frog 90m IV (5) ** 2002
1 50m. Start as for the previous route up the turfed recess to the overhang.
2 40m. Break through the small overhang as before, but follow the corner upwards until it peters out at an overhang. Step right onto the front of the buttress and follow turf to the top.

Black Chimney 100m III (4) * 2003
This deep gully is a fun route. Easy snow leads to the first of two steep chockstones which is turned on the right wall. The second provides useful hooks and foot-ledges on the outside, or sometimes a squirmy through-route. The remainder of the gully is straightforward.

Between the two chockstones, the gully can be entered or exited at either side. The access point to the right leads to an easy ramp-line up to the ridge. That to the left leads to a ledge and the small pinnacle and the belay of *Right Frog/Bear Left* below the prominent slab. The buttress can be traversed (II, 2003) at this level using these sections to pass the gully and turf to move along below the prominent slab.

Right of *Black Chimney* is a pleasant mixed ridge **Gully Arete** (I/II, 2002).

Central (or Number Three) Buttress

The largest, lowest and most prominent of the 'buttresses' actually consists of several discrete individual buttresses.
   Descent is down the easy *Wide Gully* on the right.

Straight Gully I 130m 1999
This route is situated more or less in the centre of Chapel Crags. It starts further up the hillside than the lowest rocks, up and left of the start of *Curving Gully* and is joined by the *Left-Hand Branch* after about 50m.

Straight Buttress 150m I/II 1999
Climbs the buttress between *Straight Gully* and *Curving Gully*. Several lines are possible and it has been climbed on its left and right sides. All routes culminate at a miniature rocky subsidiary summit from which a short section of down-climbing is required before following one of several easy options to the top.

Curving Gully 60m II 1960

The gully bounds the left side of *Central Buttress*. As was their wont it was christened *Central Chimney* by the Victorian pioneers who scrambled up it; this rather misleading name has been changed to something more meaningful to modern climbers. A small chockstone bars the way after the first 20m, after which the left-hand branch of the gully leads to a bay. From here it is straightforward to climb to a col, where a junction is made with *Straight Gully* which is followed easily to the top.

Variation Finish 20m III 1999

Follow *Curving Gully* to the junction in the bay. From the bay, follow steep snow and turf rightwards to arrive at the top of the steep ice pitch of the *Direct* and climb more easily to the top.

Curving Gully Direct 160m * III (4) 2001

Follow the gully, but take the right branch to a cul-de-sac, avoid the impasse by an iced left wall. Easy ground leads to the top.

Central Buttress 170m III (4) *** 2010

This climbs the buttress right of *Curving Gully* and overlooks that climb for much of its length. The steeper upper portion of the route was originally climbed starting from *Curving Gully*.

1   110m (2). Starting right of *Curving Gully* climb the easy angled turfy buttress from its lowest point to a large block on a crest overlooking *Curving Gully* where the angle of the buttress suddenly steepens.

2   30m (4). From the crest, follow the steep buttress above, via turf grooves and a short wall, moving slightly right to a pinnacle belay.

3   40m (2). Easier ground leads to the top.

Curving Gully Start 100m III (2) 2005

Originally the upper buttress was climbed via this start. Follow *Curving Gully* to where that route steepens and narrows.

1   100m (2). A short steep gully up the right wall gives access to the ridge and block belay at the point where the upper buttress steepens.

Number Three Buttress 160m V (5) *** 2010

A weaving line up the steep centre of the buttress traversing across a ledge about 10m above where the upper buttress steepens.

Chapel Crags – right-hand section

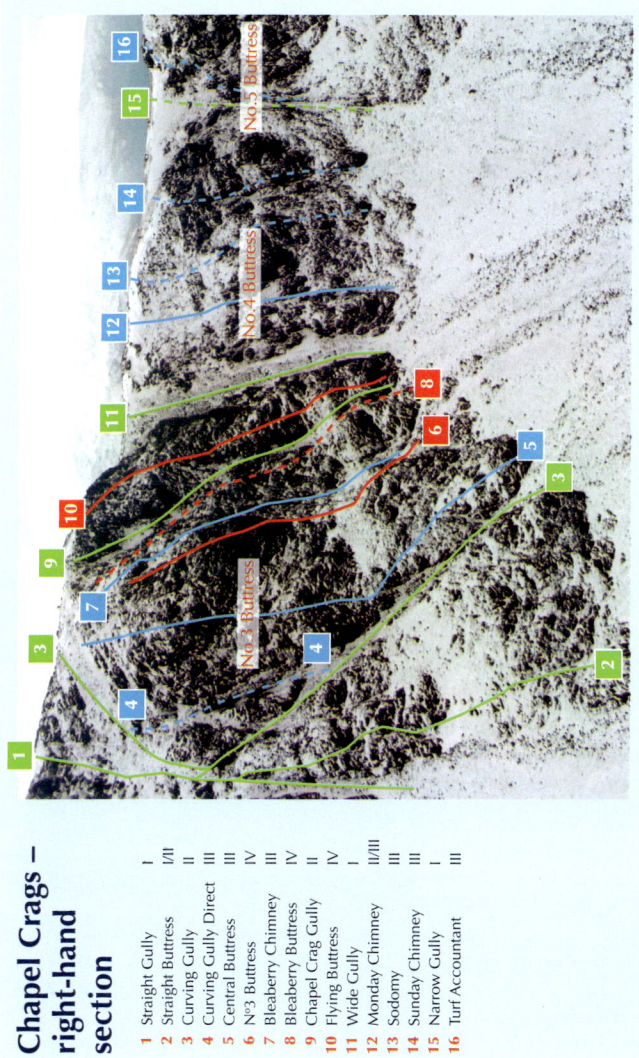

1 Straight Gully — I
2 Straight Buttress — I/II
3 Curving Gully — II
4 Curving Gully Direct — III
5 Central Buttress — III
6 Nº3 Buttress — IV
7 Bleaberry Chimney — III
8 Bleaberry Buttress — IV
9 Chapel Crag Gully — II
10 Flying Buttress — IV
11 Wide Gully — I
12 Monday Chimney — II/III
13 Sodomy — III
14 Sunday Chimney — III
15 Narrow Gully — I
16 Turf Accountant — III

1   120m (2). From the start of *Bleaberry Chimney* trend left up the lower easier angled part of *Central Buttress* to belay at a pinnacle where the angle steepens just below the left end of a ledge.
2   50m (5). Gain the ledge above and traverse it 5m rightwards to below a rightward facing corner with a wide crack in the back. Climb this to easier ground.

Bleaberry Chimney   170m III (4) *** 1960

The obvious shallow chimney in the grassy buttress to the left of the prominent *Chapel Crag Gully*. An entertaining route on turf and ice smears.
1   30m. Scramble up the gully bed to the foot of the chimney.
2   40m (4). A sustained pitch. Gain the narrow chimney via steep ice and climb it to a belay at an open break and division in the chimney.
3   50m (4). A short, hard, but well-protected section up the left-hand branch soon leads to much easier climbing.
4   50m (2). Follow the easy gully to the top.

Bleaberry Buttress   170m IV (4) * 2010

Start at the lowest point of the buttress between *Bleaberry Chimney* and *Chapel Crag Gully*. Climb the buttress first on the right then in the centre for the steeper top section to reach easier ground. This route needs well-frozen turf.

Chapel Crag Gully   160m II (3) ** 1960

This gully splits the right side of the buttress 10m left of *Wide Gully*. A fine atmospheric route.
1   50m. Bypass the first chockstone by heading up the shallow gully at the start of *Bleaberry Chimney* to the left, then traverse back right above the point of the first chockstone. Alternatively use turf to climb the buttress just to the left of the gully, or climb a turfy groove just right of the gully to a narrow ledge and traverse back left into the gully. All these ways lead to a spike belay on the left.
2   50m (3). Move up to where the gully narrows. 20m below the second chockstone an icy chimney sometimes forms an icefall on the left; climb this to a small pinnacle belay.
3   60m. From the pinnacle, traverse right back into the gully above the second chockstone and follow it to the top.

Direct Start   70m V (6) * 2003

The direct route tackling both the chockstones requires a reasonable build-up of ice – and it may get banked out in heavy snow.

Chapel Crags

1. 20m (6). Climb a short pitch to the icy chimney. Back and foot to a rest in a small cave below the chockstone before launching out over it to the gully above.
2. 50m (4). Follow the gully bed to the second chockstone which is taken direct.

Right-Hand Variation   80m III 1998

2. 50m. To the right of the second chockstone is a narrow subsidiary gully. Follow this and either move left back into the gully above the chockstone or move onto the buttress on the right.

Flying Buttress   180m IV (5) 1999

The ridge between *Chapel Crag Gully* and *Wide Gully*. Start at the foot of an obvious chimney/groove in the centre of the buttress.

1. 45m (5). From the foot of the chimney, follow a line of turf diagonally right to a ledge on the right crest of the ridge (crux), then move up and back left to a turfy corner and go up to a large ledge.
2. 135m. Another steepening leads to a second ledge and belay. Follow the turf close to the crest for a further three pitches.

Right-Hand Start   III 1999

An easier start is possible from the gully on the right from which the ledges can be reached.

Wide Gully   130m I

The easy wide gully on the right of the buttress. A good **descent**.

Number Four Buttress

To the right of *Wide Gully* is a buttress containing two merging fault-lines (*Sunday Chimney*) towards its right-hand side.

Monday Chimney   90m II/III 1999

The first gully right of *Wide Gully*. Take the first two chockstones direct, with the larger third stone passed by climbing onto the buttress on the right and back into the gully just above it.

Sodomy   95m III 95m 2001

Immediately left of *Sunday Chimney* is a chimney which merges with that route after its first pitch. Just left of this is a shallow depression. Climb the depression directly, then the continuation cleft and finish easily leftwards.

Sunday Chimney 95m III (4) *** 1999
The chimney splitting the buttress slightly right of its centre. The lower half contains two faults that merge after about 50m and has a large chockstone near the top.
1   20m. Climb the right-hand of the two initial chimneys to a ledge and a flake belay on the right.
2   45m. Continue up the steep narrow chimney until it widens and the angle eases. Follow this to just below the large chockstone: a pedestal belay is possible on a ledge on the left.
3   30m. (4) From the top of the pedestal, move up onto ledges, which lead back right into the gully and climb easily to the top.

Narrow Gully 90m I 1999
The narrow snow gully on the right of *Sunday Chimney*.

Number Five Buttress

The buttress to the right of *Narrow Gully* has the following climb on its left side.

Turf Accountant 75m III 2001
Go up easy ground to a shallow bay at the foot of the buttress proper. (This point is 10m left of a pinnacle a short way up the crest.)

Climb the left-hand of two faults (the right one looks similar) to a gain a broad depression. Climb this and its narrower continuation. Trend left, then back right, over ledges to the top.

Scale Beck

NY 151 172   ALTITUDE 250M

From the village of Buttermere, take the path to Crummock Water, then follow the right-hand branch north along the side of the lake for about 500m until the path moves round into the next gill line. The beck descends down the left flank.

Scale Force 40m V (4) ** 1962
The longest free-falling waterfall in the Lake District lies at low altitude. In its solid state, after a prolonged intense freeze it offers a magnificent and sustained icefall.

GRASMOOR

NY 175 203 ALTITUDE *852M*

This bulky mountain, standing on the eastern shore of Crummock Water, has the amenable *Lorton* and *Buttermere Gullies* on its western flank and the rather more impressive Dove Crag hidden away on its north side.

Dove Crag

NY 177 205 ALTITUDE *700M* NORTH-EAST FACING

Dove Crag runs along the right flank of a large combe which lies secreted on the northern flanks of Grasmoor. On its right is *Spiral Gully* and it is bounded on the left by the deep cleft of *Dove Crag Gully*. Left again, a broad easy descent gully takes the central area of the combe. The left side of the combe holds three shorter, easier-angled buttresses steepening towards the top.

The shortest approach is from Lanthwaite Green. A path contours the north slope of Grasmoor above Gasgale Gill. A small ruined building is passed before a steep arduous ascent leads directly to the base of Dove Crag. The path may also be followed until a second ruined stone building is reached on the north bank of the stream, where a natural corridor leads up until easier ground may be traversed rightwards to the base of Dove Crag. **Descent** is down the easy gully to the east of the crag, or by descending to Coledale Hause and down Gasgale Gill.

The climbs are described from right to left.

Spiral Gully   135m III/IV 1970
The obvious twisting break about 60m from the right end of the crag.
1   15m. Climb a small wall to gain a rightward-sloping ramp with a peg belay on the right.
2   20m. Follow the gully ahead by a short bulging ice pitch then snow to a peg belay in a cave.
3   30m. Vertical ice is climbed to where the angle eases after 15m, then continue up easy snow.
4   70m. Continue up easier snow slopes with the odd short ice step. Snow belays and deadmen may be useful due to the poor nature of the rock.

Robinson's Gully   190m V (5) *** 1978

A superb steep and technically demanding climb. The ice build-up is usually slight and protection is sparse: it is graded accordingly! Located to the right of *Dove Crag Gully*, this undercut line starts high up the cliff with entrance gained from a rightward-sloping ramp.

1   30m. Follow icy slabs to gain the ramp and follow it with increasing difficulty rightwards to move round to a sloping stance but no belay at the foot of the gully proper: do not despair, a further 5m above, below a bulge, is a good peg crack on the left.

2   20m. A poorly-protected pitch. Climb the gully to an awkward stance and poor anchors below a bulge.

3   50m. Step right, up and round the bulge with difficulty and continue to a small cave. A narrow overhanging chimney above provides the crux (Friend) and respite in a small bay and possible poor belay. Better to continue, passing a bulge above then a chockstone, to pull out left to a ledge and belay.

4   90m. Move back right and follow the easier-angled gully above, with one further steep section, leading to a snow finish.

Dove Crag Gully   165m IV (4) *** 1966

An excellent climb with two fine contrasting steep ice pitches. The first pitch is slow to form but the buttress to its left provides a worthy alternative start.

1   15m. Climb up ice debris into the cave at the back of the gully where it narrows.

2   50m. (4) An unusual pitch. The gully narrows above to a chimney and down the left wall an intimidating ice curtain forms falling vertically from a capping chockstone: climb the ice then back and foot, reaching an awkward exit on the left to steep snow. A belay can be taken under the rock wall on the left. Alternatively, if the ice hasn't formed climb the buttress on the left to reach the belay.

3   50m (4). Another good pitch finding the easiest way up the steep icefall directly above to an easy snow slope: look for a peg belay up to the right. If this hasn't formed – or is too scary! – an easier alternative is afforded by *The Chicken Variation*.

4   50m. Finish direct or by variations to the right or left.

The Chicken Variation   165m III (3) **

An atmospheric traverse through impressive ice formations (often climbed due to the main icefall pitch of *Dove Crag Gully* not being formed).

1   15m (3). Climb the buttress well left of the initial chimney of *Dove Crag Gully*.

2   50m (2). Make a diagonal traverse rightwards round into the gully, under its main icefall and up a wide easy-angled snow ramp on the right to belay where the snow steepens beneath an extensive shield of icicles.

Dove Crag, Grasmoor

1 The Chicken Variation III
2 Dove Crag Gully IV/V
3 Edge On Variation VI
4 Chicken Out V
5 Robinson's Gully V
6 Spiral Gully III/IV

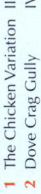

Garth Bradshaw surveys Dove Crag, Grasmoor, on the day in 1978 that he and Colin Wornham made the first winter ascent of Robinson's Gully (V)

3   50m (3). Up a short steepening, then follow a series of exposed ice ramps back left across the top of the steep lower section of *Chicken Out*.
4   50m. Either continue into the easier upper part of *Dove Crag Gully* or take an alternative snow ramp out to the right.

Chicken Out Variation   115m V (5) ** 1990s

A worthy companion route to *Dove Crag Gully* and more likely to be in condition. Start from the top of pitch 2 of *The Chicken Variation*.
3   20m (4/5). Pick a line up the steep icicled wall to a large belay ledge.
4   30m (5). Continue up the steep icicled wall above – it gradually eases.
5   65m. Easy ground leads to the top of the crag.

Cluck It Variation   30m VI (6) ** 2010

A stunning ice pillar left of *Chicken Out* forms in exceptional winters. From a belay behind the pillar a serious and delicate start leads out onto the front, followed by very steep climbing up the pillar front.

Edge On Variation   30m VI (6) ** 2010

Yet another variation of *Dove Crag Gully* linking a series of icicles on the wall left of *Chicken Out*.

Start about 8m to the left of *Chicken Out*. Climb some steep ice bulges on the wall behind and slightly left of the hanging icicle of *Cluck It*. Climb up the wall behind the icicle for 5m. Traverse the hanging ice fringe on the left for 5m to pull up onto a ledge. Exit through the steep fringe above and right with some steep moves. Climb the easy angled ice ramp and snow above to various possible belays, a rock belay is possible on the big terrace above and right. Follow one of the *Dove Crag Gully* exits to the top.

Dove Crag Left-Hand (II/III) consists of three short buttresses to the left of the combe: all have been climbed. The gullies in between are easier (I), but may be corniced and can be prone to avalanche.

West Face

NY 164 204   A*LTITUDE 350M*   W*EST FACING*

Returning to Buttermere, the West Face of Grasmoor has two easier gullies (NY 164 204) described below. It is sometimes possible to park on the road nearer the routes but more parking is available a short distance to the north at Lanthwaite Green.

Lorton Gully   275m II 🧗 ❄❄ 1963
This large forked gully consists of straightforward snow interspersed by steeper ice. The exit may be awkward and should be treated with care after heavy snow.

Buttermere Gully   250m II 🧗 ❄ 1963
Situated to the south (right) of the Y-shaped *Lorton Gully*. It involves mainly easy scrambling in its lower section, with one 10m steeper ice pitch before easy ground leads to the steeper upper section.

Goat Crag

NY 190 163   ALTITUDE 300M   *SOUTH-WEST FACING*

Further up Buttermere, east of the village, the broken south-west facing Goat Crag is obvious on the hillside above Hassness, the large white house near the lake shore.

Goat Gill   150m IV ** 🧗 ❄ 1954
The bed of the gill is followed pleasantly to a steep vertical pitch near the top. This can be avoided, reducing the route to a Grade III.

NEWLANDS

The Newlands Valley lies between Buttermere and Borrowdale and is accessible from the village of Braithwaite in the north (4km to the west of Keswick on the A66) or from Buttermere village via Newlands Hause.

Newlands Hause Waterfall   110m III *
Situated only five minutes from the road at the top of Newlands Hause (NY 193 175, Alt 330m) the frozen waterfall, more correctly known as Moss Force, gives an excellent and accessible introduction to water-ice climbing. If it's 'in', follow the queue of climbers up the path from the car park.
1   15m. The shortest and easiest pitch up ice.
2   25m. More of the same water ice but slightly longer.
3   50m. The longest and steepest pitch, the crux is passing a protruding block just below halfway up. Either side of the block may be climbed.
4   20m. Easier ice to easy ground.

Lake District Winter Climbs

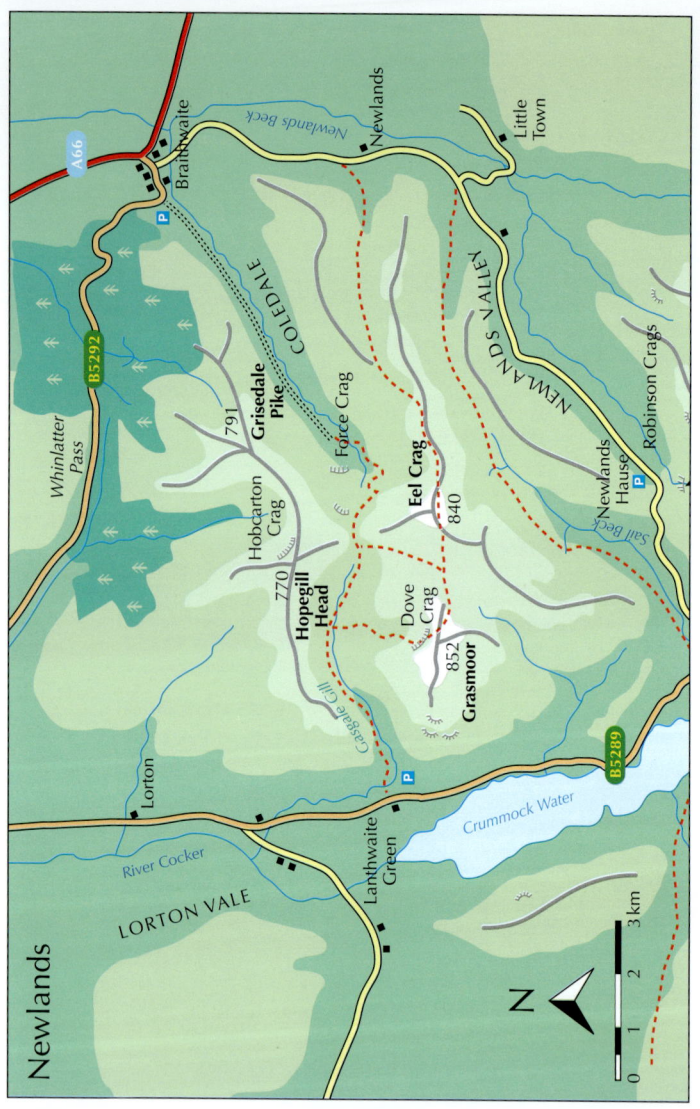

COLEDALE

This small valley contains the remnants of old mine workings at its head. It lies parallel to, but north-west of, the Newlands Valley and runs in a north-east to south-west direction. From Braithwaite, head west on the B5292 towards Whinlatter Pass. Just after leaving the village, the road zigzags at the start of the climb up to the pass. There is limited parking on the left at the start of a private track which leads to mine workings at the head of the valley. All the climbs are accessible from here and are clearly visible.

Force Crag

NY 197 215   Altitude 300m   *North-east facing*

Force Crag lies at the head of the Coledale Valley and can hold an excellent ice climb on the waterfall which gives the crag its name.

Force Crag Waterfall   250m IV (4) *** 1966
A prolonged freeze and/or strong north-easterly is necessary for this magnificent climb to be complete. A series of short pitches lead to an interesting 25m pitch. Above, the stream widens and leads to a vertical curtain of ice offering some tremendous climbing with harder direct variations possible (IV/V). Beyond, the ice eases slightly and is then followed by a further 30m of ice.

The Enforcer   70m V (5) c1991
A mixed route which can rescue the day if the main fall is incomplete. Start at the foot of the main fall.
1   35m. Traverse up a gully on the left to a tree belay.
2   35m (5). Climb up to the right and traverse right above the overhangs on ice smears and torquing to a shallow gully leading to the top.

Pudding Beck   150m III 1982
This is essentially a continuation of *Force Crag Waterfall* and provides a good way onto the tops.

Eel Crag

NY 192 209 *Altitude 600m* *NORTH FACING*

The crag overlooking Force Crag. Continue past the mine workings; the path passes under the crag which is on the left.

Eel Crag Gully **I 1994**
The easy gully at the left end of the crag (NY 192 207), often full of snow.

Eel Crag Main Ridge **I 1994**
The ridge to the right of the *Eel Crag Gully* gives a pleasant winter scramble to the minor summit above the crag (NY 195 208 to NY 191 206).

Scott Crag

NY 195 204 *Altitude 630m* *NORTH-EAST FACING*

Scott Crag stands prominently on the north-east face of Crag Hill. The impressive central icefall is *Arctic Spring*, with *Scott Gully* to its left.

Scott Gully **70m III 1994**
Follow the left-hand gully. This steepens and narrows into a chimney before exiting onto a faint ridge and steep vegetation.

Arctic Spring **70m III (4) 1996**
The prominent central icefall.
1   30m. (4) Climb the right side of the central fall.
2   40m. Further ice trends rightwards into a wide gully. Vegetation and broken rocks lead to the top.

WHINLATTER

Hobcarton Crag 🌿🌿

NY 187 221 *Altitude 600m* *NORTH FACING*

This is a large crag on Hopegill Head which forms the head of Hobcarton Combe. It sees few visitors, although the approach from the Whinlatter Pass road requires little altitude gain. A forestry track leaves the main road at (NY 192 246) – either branch

Hobcarton Crag

1. Cave Route — II/III
2. Slab and Groove — II
3. Left-Hand Gully — II
4. Middle Gully — II/III
5. Sheep Buttress — I/II
6. Right-Hand Gully — I/II

will get you there but the right-hand one is the shortest and runs up into the valley below the crag. The crag is a reasonable middle-grade venue when well frozen. Please note that Hobcarton Crag is the only English site for an exceedingly rare plant, the alpine catchfly and that the gullies on this crag are very prone to erosion – please climb here only in truly frozen conditions or, better still, climb somewhere else!

Two easy-to-recognise routes are located at the back of the combe: *Thompson's Chimney* is an obvious right-to-left diagonal line, while *Cave Route* is a gully about 20m to its right. On the right-hand side of the combe is another buttress containing three gullies. The routes are described from left to right.

A Carton of Hobnobs   100m III ❦ 2001

The route takes a shallow depression in the buttress left of *Thompson's Chimney*.

From the foot of *Thompson's Chimney*, walk up leftwards on an easy terrace to a ridge in the ground at the crag's foot, below a tiny rock tower. Climb diagonally right to gain the depression and climb it, passing to the right of a bigger tower, to the top.

Thompson's Chimney   100m II/III ❦

The clearly defined right-to-left chimney contains a 15m ice pitch halfway up.

Cave Route   100m II/III ❦ 1983

To the right of *Thompson's Chimney* is an easy runnel.
1 60m. Follow the runnel and the steep continuation chimney to a gully which leads to a cave.
2 40m. Exit from the cave, using ice on the right and climb to the top.

Slab and Groove   130m II ❦ 1998

About 50m right of *Cave Route* is an obvious shallow corner starting about 50m up and running to the top of the crag. Start up an ice runnel and climb over slabby rock to reach the corner, then follow this to the top.

The right-hand side of the combe has three obvious gully lines all climbed in 1998. **Left-Hand Gully** (170m, II) is the most continuous, but nowhere as steep as the ice pitch of the **Middle Gully** (II/III), which gives a 15m ice pitch before easing off to a pleasant ice line passing through some impressive pinnacles. **Sheep Buttress** (200m, I/II, 2001) starts between *Middle* and *Right-Hand Gullies* and climbs the buttress between them, close to the crest. The only problem encountered by the first ascentionists was crampons balling up with frozen sheep turds! **Right-Hand Gully** (I/II) is an easy ramble up rock and turf. All provide a satisfying climb to the summit of Hopegill Head.

NORTH LAKES

Sarah Kekus enjoying harsh conditions on Sharp Edge (photo: Nick Kekus)

Lake District Winter Climbs

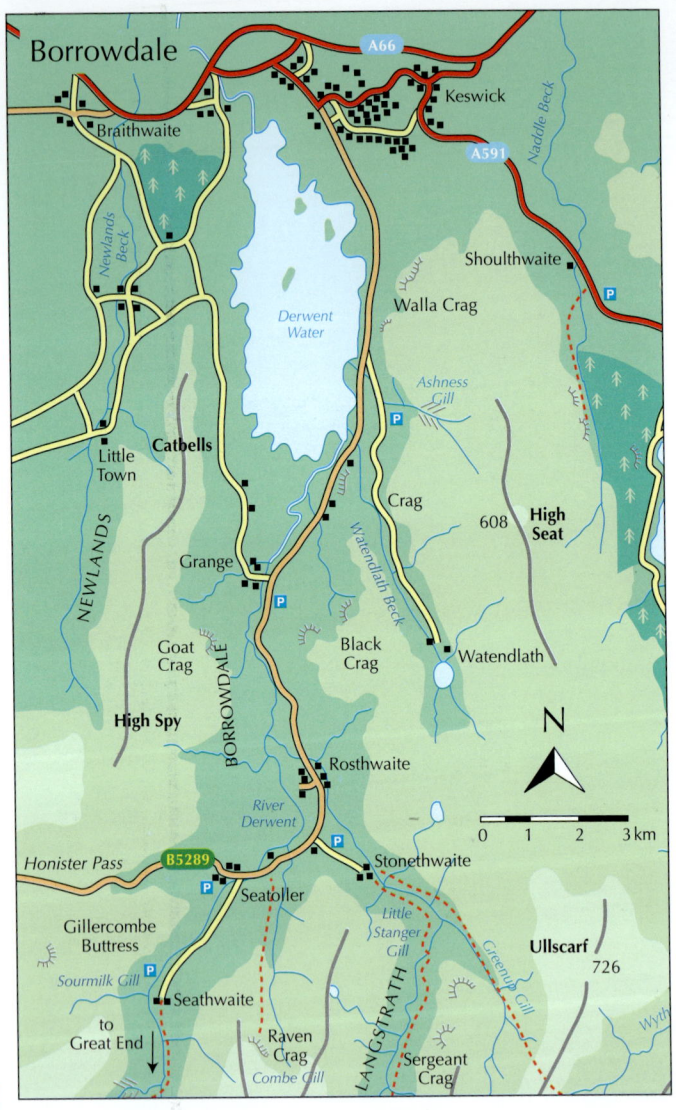

BORROWDALE

This popular valley to the south of Keswick, famed for its rock climbing, has many low-level gills that require extremely cold spells to form, but also boasts several more reliable venues. In fact Great End, at the head of the valley, gives some of the most consistent winter climbing in the Lake District, thanks to its northerly aspect and high altitude.

The crags and climbs are described from left to right clockwise around the valley, starting on the east side and heading south from Keswick before returning back northwards along the west side.

BORROWDALE EAST

This section describes all the climbs on the east of the valley as far as Great End.

Walla Crag Gully 50m III 1978

Located on the east side of the valley, Walla Crag (NY 274 212) is the first cliff on the left of the road going south from Keswick. *Walla Crag Gully* is in the centre of the crag. Situated at an altitude of only about 250m, an exceptional winter is required to find reasonable conditions in this gully. Fifty metres of climbing concludes at a tree which marks the end of the major difficulties and from which an abseil may be made. Alternatively, the less well-defined continuation gully can be followed to the summit.

Ashness Gill II/III

From Ashness Bridge on the Watendlath road, go upstream until this waterfall (NY 283 193) is reached at about 500m after about 20 minutes. The left fork in the gully is best: a 12m vertical ice pitch (III). The right fork is easier (II).

Ashness Bridge

NY 271 201   ALTITUDE 230M *WEST FACING*

From Ashness Bridge follow the path north to a kissing gate stile in the wall. From here either take a rising path north-east to reach the south end of the crag or remain

LAKE DISTRICT WINTER CLIMBS

on the more prominent lower path for a further 300m. The icefalls, if they have formed, will become apparent above you before the first stream is crossed. A fence well back from the top of the crag can offer a suitable belay, 10 minutes.

The four main icefalls are all about 20m long, offering stepped or easy gradient ice. Being low-lying they only form in exceptionally cold conditions.

Line 1   30m II 2010
Follow the stepped ice to the left of the main section.

Line 2   35m II 2010
Start from the lowest point, following a thin line of ice initially until much thicker ice can be followed to the top.

Line 3   33m II 2010
Follow the thickest ice up and slightly right of centre at a friendly angle until a steep section near the top. Finish up the highest section of ice to the right.

Line 4   30m III 2010
To the right is a thinner smear of ice. Follow this to a difficult finish.

The popular summer rock climb **Little Chamonix** (1961) on Shepherd's Crag (NY 263 185) received a number of ascents under thick snow and ice during the 1960s. Recent milder winters have not provided the conditions to climb on low-lying valley crags without causing severe damage and scarring to the rock. In the event of climatic miracles the route description can be found in the FRCC Borrowdale guide.

Black Crag

NY 263 172   ALTITUDE *300M*   WEST FACING

Troutdale Pinnacle had several winter ascents during the 1960s which closely followed the summer route throughout. It would be hard to imagine it having been less than Grade V (and even harder to imagine it with sufficient snow on it nowadays). The route description can, again, be found in the FRCC Borrowdale guide.

Troutdale Gully   60m III
This partially hidden gully is found to the right of the crag, just right of the descent path where it crosses the stile. **Descend** down grassy/snowy slopes to the start.

The gully gives two reasonable ice pitches of 15m and 25m with a belay in between.

Moving south up the valley, the next climbs are accessible from the village of Stonethwaite.

Stanger Gills   150m 1980
Directly above the campsite in the valley of Stonethwaite, Big and Little Stanger Gill can be seen among the trees, accessible through a stile gate. A footpath runs up the left side of **Big Stanger Gill** (IV, 4) which generally offers four pitches, while further right **Little Stanger Gill** (III) offers a shorter pitch.

Sergeant Crag Gully   170m II/III * 1960
Situated high up on the east side of Langstrath at an altitude of 450m, this gully forms a dark cleft splitting Sergeant Crag (NY 274 116). The gully does not take a great deal of drainage and, combined with a relatively low altitude, may not often be found in condition. From Stonethwaite, take the Langstrath valley path, crossing the stream via a footbridge and then go straight up the fellside.
1   50m. Ledges lead into the gully. Two short steps lead to a belay below a chockstone.
2   50m. Climb the left wall to the snow slope above. Follow this past another small step.
3   70m. Continue upwards to the top of the gully passing two further steps and a belay on easy slopes.

Combe Gill, the small but picturesque valley to the west of Langstrath, is home to the classic *Raven Crag Gully*. Where the Rosthwaite to Seatoller road crosses the humpback bridge over the River Derwent, a side lane runs off left opposite some houses (NY 251 137). There is limited parking about 200m up this road on the right next to the river. Return a short way back down the lane and over a stile to follow a footpath that curves up through trees and into the combe.

Raven Crag

NY 248 115   ALTITUDE 460M   *NORTH-EAST FACING*

Raven Crag, on the west (right) of the combe, is reached in about 45 minutes. The routes are described from right to left (as approached).

Crowdless Raven   180m V (6) 1995

This winter version of *Summit Route* may help avoid the crowds in the gully. The summer route was followed throughout; three pitches up broken walls and corners lead to a steep corner with a tricky exit. The crux is the final crack over an overlap, overlooking *Raven Crag Gully*.

1–3   135m. Follow the line of least resistance up short steep walls and corners on the right-hand side of *Raven Crag Gully*.

4   20m. (6) From the bay, climb the steep corner/scoop (crux) to an awkward exit onto a sloping ledge on the left and go round the corner leftwards to the foot of a steep crack.

5   25m. Climb the steep tricky crack to the top.

Raven Crag Gully   145m III/IV (4) ***

The obvious deep gully towards the right side of the crag. A popular and classic route, with unusually varied climbing and an atmospheric finale, although its low position makes it less than reliable as a winter climb and it is much harder in anything less than perfect conditions. The ice climbing, though technically interesting, is not too serious in banked out conditions, with large stances between pitches. In a prolonged freeze with little snow (the condition it has been found in most often in recent years), it may form an exciting challenge on steep chandeliered water ice and is then technically around Grade 5, with potentially poor protection between stances.

1   15m. A small preliminary pitch on the left leads to a good stance and belay.

2   15m. Bulging ice on the right leads to another good stance beneath a chimney. In lean conditions, this pitch may be transformed into a much longer and more serious pitch which constitutes the crux of the climb. Steep and strenuous climbing up brittle 'organ pipe' chandelier ice and umbrellas may be necessary. An alternative up a verglassed ramp on the right is less steep but can be precarious with scant protection.

3   20m. Scale the wide crack on the right then the chimney. Step left across the chimney and up to yet another large stance. If the chimney is insufficiently iced, a good mixed alternative can be taken up the rib on the left.

4   20m. Wander easily up the gully to the waterfall pitch. Climb to the chockstone; this is usually easier on the right wall.

5   50m. A steepening snow slope leads to the foot of the final pitch.

6   25m. The magnificent broad ice flow above is regarded by many as the most beautiful pitch in the Lakes. Climb bulging ice into a corner on the left (rock protection possible) and continue right and up to an often tricky and exposed finish over a lip, followed by easy snow to a tree belay.

RAVEN CRAG

Tyro's Gully   110m I/II
The left of two shallow gullies to the left of *Raven Crag Gully*. This gully normally presents an easy snow slope from top to bottom.

Corvus   150m IV (6) * 1960s
This classic and very popular summer route has been climbed under good winter conditions. Start as for *Tyro's Gully*.
1. 30m. Avoid the well-marked slabs of the summer route by climbing up *Tyro's Gully* to a V-shaped cleft in the left wall.
2. 30m. Climb the cleft, then move left along ledges to an ice-filled corner.
3. 30m. Climb the corner and an ice-filled chimney above to a large belay ledge below a rib on the right.
4. 30m. Climb the rib to belay below the Hand Traverse pitch of the summer route.
5. 30m. Take the icefall that forms on the right of the Hand Traverse, then another rib to follow. Continue to top of crag. The Hand Traverse can be followed at the same grade if the icefall hasn't formed.

Raven Crag Grooves   130m VI (6) 1995
With a low crux this starts up cracked slabs in a recess to the left of *Corvus*.
1. 20m. Follow the right-hand crack in the centre of the slab moving left and then back right (crux) to belay at a large ledge below a groove.
2. 20m. Follow the grooves to a belay ledge below a chimney-crack.
3. 45m. Climb the chimney-crack and the groove above to a belay.
4. 45m. Trend up left over broken ground to the top.

Raven Crag Buttress   115m III (4) 2001
This route starts up the chimney at the left end of the ledge 5m left of *Raven Crag Grooves*.
1. 35m. Climb the open chimney then ledges above to a good belay ledge.
2. 25m. Move left and up to a ledge overlooking the gully on the left. Move up past a spike to a belay ledge.
3. 30m. Climb a groove above then a short corner to a large ledge.
4. 25m. Easier climbing leads to the top.

Nexus   90m IV (4) * 1980
This follows the iced wall at the left side of the crag, 30m left of *Corvus*, in the area of the summer line of *Slab Route* – the exact line taken can depend on the ice build-up.
1. 50m. Climb the iced slab to a tree belay.
2. 40m. Move left and climb steep mixed ground to a belay near a dry stone wall.

On the open hillside to the left of the crag a series of icy steps form. Linking them up gives three or four pitches of good ice (III) and can be a useful way of salvaging a visit if *Raven Crag Gully* is full of people or too thin to climb.

Combe Head

NY 249 110 Altitude 640m   *North facing*

This vegetated and dank crag lies at the head Combe Gill. When frozen it is possible to climb almost anywhere at Grade III, with the harder sections generally near the top and bottom of the crag, but they can often be out-manoeuvred. A line has been climbed up the centre starting from the lowest point of the crag (80m, III, 1996). It is a worthwhile alternative to an unfrozen *Raven Crag Gully*. Other routes have been claimed, but are not worth recording: follow your nose!

The upper ravine of **Combe Gill** (III *, 1963) is also entertaining.

Doves' Nest

NY 253 117 Altitude 400m   *West facing*

On the left of the valley directly across from Raven Crag and clearly seen on the approach from the point where the valley levels out. The Doves' Nest is formed from a massive rock slip which has left some interesting if unstable caves and passages that disappear into the depths of the crag. An ascent of **South Chimney** (45m III, 2010) the rightmost of the wide chimneys with an escape rightward along the passages has been made.

The broken crag to the north (left) of Doves' Nest is split by the well defined but short *Columba's Gully*.

Columba's Gully   30m IV (5) 1960

Rarely in condition. If you do find it in nick, climb into the back of the gully, then up the iced wall to the chockstone. Climb out around the chockstone to easy snow above.

In Seathwaite, on the north-west side of Glaramara, **Hind Gill** (II ❦ 1963, NY 240 116) has some interesting icy steps when frozen.

Arctic conditions

Great End

The area to the south of Styhead Tarn is dominated by Great End, the large crag that forms the north-eastern end of the Scafell group.

Being centrally located, Great End is very accessible from a number of points. The approach from Seathwaite in Borrowdale, passing through the farmyard at the end of the valley road and following the path alongside **Grains Gill** (II, 1963), is probably the best and shortest (1hr). Grains Gill itself and **Ruddy Gill** (II, 1963) which flows down from Great End into *Grains Gill* (NY 234 098), can be climbed as an alternative to walking if conditions are good. **Note** Ruddy Gill 🌱 is important for its **rare flora** – please do not climb here unless it is fully frozen.

Alternative approaches can be made from Wasdale Head via Styhead Pass and Sprinkling Tarn and from Langdale – by struggling up Rossett Gill and over Esk Hause. The routes are described from right to left.

Skew Gill   180m I 🔺 🌱🌱 1887

Actually situated in Wasdale, but included here because of its proximity to the crag, the gill forms an interesting but easy chasm in the upper reaches of the Wasdale Valley. It makes a good approach to Great End.

Starting just above the old packhorse route from Wasdale Head to Styhead (NY 219 092), at an altitude of about 420m, it is crossed at the bottom by the path of the Corridor Route. Scramble up the bed of the ravine for 150m to the exit wall which is best climbed starting on the left. Finish up a small gully on the left onto easy snow.

Skew Gill Left-Hand Branch   200m II/III 🔺 🌱 1996

Approximately 150m up *Skew Gill*, the left-hand walls recede and the gill opens out. A rock tower stands at the foot of the left-hand branch. To the right of this, a short icefall runs into the bed of the main gill. Starting here, climb the little icefall and easy snow to a large table block resting on the left-hand wall. The steeper gully above is defined by rock walls on its left and a large rib on the right overlooking *Skew Gill*. Climb either on the left to an icicle in a corner before stepping right to finish up steep ground (II, 1996) or the harder off-width crack on the right to the same point (III, 1997).

Skew Gill Direct Finish   20m III 🔺 🌱 1987

This is right of the normal finish to the gill.

Great End

1	Left-Hand Groove	IV	5	South-East Gully	III
2	Right-Hand Groove	III	6	South-East Buttress	III
3	Buttress Right of Right-Hand Groove	III	7	Central Gully	II
4	Aspirant	IV	8	Window Gully	II/III
			9	Cust's Gully (hidden to left of Branch Gully)	I
			10	Branch Gully	I

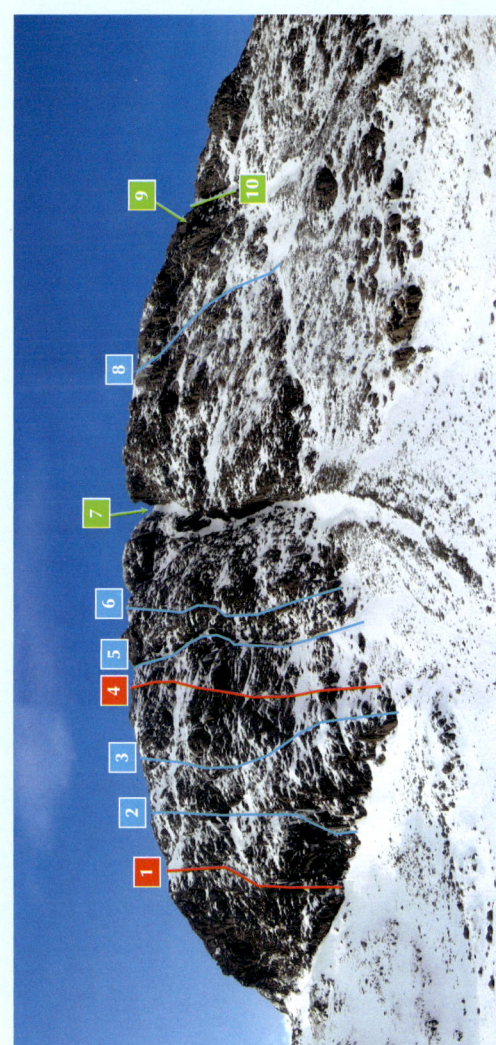

Borrowdale

Spout Head (NY 223 092) is the west-facing outcrop (Alt 530m) just to the left of *Skew Gill*. **Central Icefall** (90m, III/IV, 1985) is, as might be expected, the icefall down the centre of the crag, just right of a snow gully. Follow a narrow snow gully to gain the icefall.

From *Spout Head*, a walk up the snow slope to a small col on the ridge brings one to the right end of *Great End*. Immediately to the left is *Cust's Gully*, which is easily recognised by its large bridged chockstone halfway up.

Great End

NY 228 086   Altitude 720m   North-east facing

This large crag forms the north-eastern end of the Scafell group. Its northerly aspect and high altitude mean it is in winter climbing condition more often than any other crag in the Lake District apart from the Helvellyn coves. Needless to say, such reliable conditions make it a popular climbing ground in winter and queues are to be expected; if it is too busy, it is worth considering some of the other venues close by such as Great Gable and Green Gable Crags. Although the crag itself is not steep, its gullies cut deeply into it, giving some great pitches.

The buttresses of Great End, particularly on the ground between *Central* and *Cust's Gully*, offer many possibilities for mixed climbs at about grade II/III – only the most compelling lines have been recorded.

Branch Gully   200m I * 1886

The open gully branching out rightwards from the start of *Cust's Gully*.

Zitternd   65m III (3) 2009

The route takes a gangway and groove to the right of *Cust's Gully* starting about 70m up the gully.

1   35m. About 20m below the chockstone climb rightwards out of *Cust's Gully* to a snowy gangway up to a turf ledge beneath an open groove nearly level with the chockstone in *Cust's Gully*. It is also possible to reach the gangway by leaving *Cust's Gully* at a lower point about level with the fault-line of *The First Cut is the Deepest*. Either way its a scrappy pitch.

2   30m (3). Climb the pleasant open groove above past a couple of short rock steps to belay. It is possible to move left from the groove and cross the top of the chockstone if you need more excitement.

GREAT END

A good day on ice: just about to tackle the Left Branch of Central Gully, Great End (photo: Justin Shiels)

Cust's Gully   310m I (2) * 1880
Commonly confused with *Window Gully* because of its large chockstone arch which appears to form a big 'window', this gully is generally a straightforward snow slope, but early in the season it can offer two or three short steps (2). Often used as a means of **descent**. Combined with *Skew Gill* it gives a classic winter mountaineering excursion to the summit of Great End.

The First Cut is the Deepest   40m V (7) ** 2004
Start 30m up *Cust's Gully*. The most obvious fault-line in the left wall of the gully is climbed on hoared-up rock and turf.

Evolution   70m VIII (8) ** 2005
Starting higher up *Cust's Gully*, this very hard route climbs the left wall of the gully up underneath the big chockstone before heading up and over it. The nature of *Cust's Gully* means that you can have a reasonable look at the crux section from below before embarking!

On the first ascent an axe was dropped and after its retrieval the highpoint regained by climbing straight to the end of the traverse on pitch two. This is a safer option for a second but misses out some of the best climbing.

1 30m (6). From the first step in *Cust's Gully*, climb big flakes leaning against the left wall to a belay.
2 40m (8). From the belay, step up to place gear under the roof, then step back down. Traverse right across the wall level with the belay; on the first ascent ice was needed to make a crucial move pulling off the traverse, where there is groundfall potential! From the end of the traverse, the next objective is the chockstone. Move up to place a crucial Friend 5. The pull into the overhanging niche above proves to be the crux. Having done this a couple of committing moves on poor hooks allow the relative security of the gap between the chockstone and the gully wall to be reached; now head for turf over the top. Move up and right for 10m to a good belay.

Cry Wolf   80m VI (6) * 2009
This takes the obvious corner ramp up the right side of *One Pitch Gully*. Start a short way up *One Pitch Gully*.
1 30m (6). Climb the ramp with continuing interest keeping to a crack in its centre passing several turf ledges to a steep finish.
2 50m (3). Continue direct up the easier ground above.

One Pitch Gully   120m II
This runs left of the left-bounding buttress of *Cust's Gully*. Easy snow steepens with height to where the gully splits into two small chimneys. Climb the right one which offers a short pitch on the left wall to the top.

Duncan's Groove   30m IV (5) 1986
Takes a prominent groove through the steep rocky band high on the buttress right of *Window Gully*.

Window Gully   110m II/III **
An interesting climb made better by taking the *Icefall* to finish. The climb takes its name from a peculiar rock formation on the left below the final pitch. The climb forms quite quickly, is at its best early in the season as a runnel of water ice and is often one of the only routes in condition on the crag. Start above a shallow snow bay midway between *Central* and *Cust's Gully*, where an ill-defined gully leads to a line of weakness through the upper buttress.
1 35m. A variety of lines can be taken up snow to belay at the foot of a chimney.
2 30m. Follow steepening ice for about 10m onto further snow. Step left and climb up an ice bulge and out onto an easy snow slope.
3 30m. Cross the snow slope to another ice pitch below a defined gully section. Climb this and the slope above to belay below the final pitch.
4 15m. The final pitch to the top.

GREAT END

Central Gully, Great End

1	South-East Gully	III	
2	The O.G.J. Way	III	
3	Far Left Branch	III	
4	Left Branch	III	
5	Left Branch Middle Way	III/V	
6	Central Gully Arete and Grande Finale	VI	
7	Chimney Finish	IV	
8	Central Gully Right Branch	II	
9	Central Gully Right Arete	II	
10	Window Gully	II/III	
11	Upper Icefall Finish	II/III	
12	Window Gully Icefall	III	

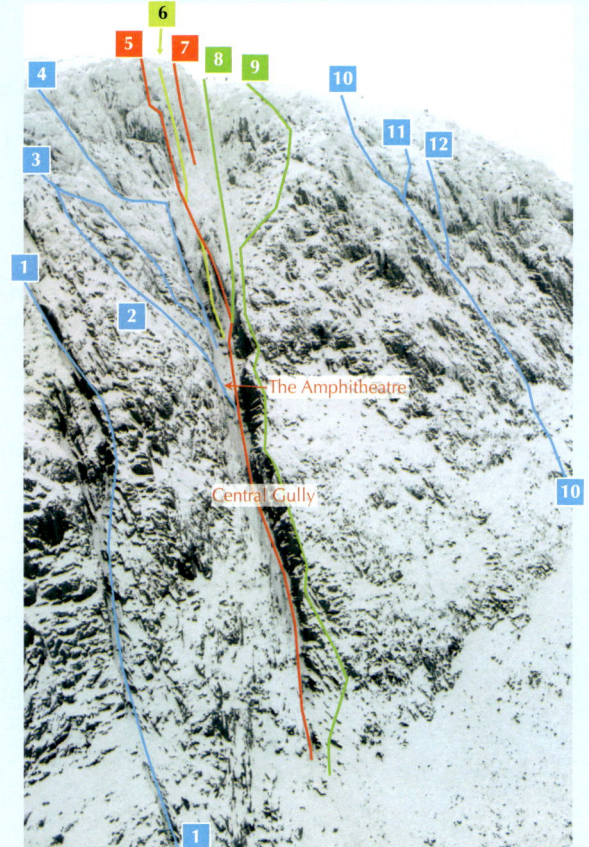

Lake District Winter Climbs

Window Gully Icefall　　　　　　　　　　　　　　　　　　　30m III ** 1974

Also known as the 'Wall and Groove Finish': an interesting icefall is frequently present to the right of the gully just above ice leading to the upper defined section on pitch 3. From the gully bed step up and right onto the ice bulge. Continue up into a leftward-slanting groove and follow this to the summit. Several other variations of this climb are possible depending on conditions.

Upper Icefall Finish　　　　　　　　　　　　　　　　　　　　　　　　II/III

Continuing up *Window Gully* above the start of the *Icefall* a good alternative ice pitch usually forms on the right of the snow bay, just below the final pitch and opposite the Window.

The buttress between *Window* and *Central Gullies* can be climbed almost anywhere (II/III).

Central Gully Right Arete　　　　　　　　　　　　　　　　　　　**170m II**

A useful alternative to *Central Gully* when it is knee-deep in powder snow and/or climbers.

From the base of *Central Gully*, it takes the right-hand arete. Follow easy-angled snow for 60m, then a series of small grooves through a stepped rocky section. For the final 30m trend right or join the final slopes of the *Right Branch* to finish. This arete can also be gained via a ramp from further up the gully if the queues become too much.

Central Gully　　　　　　　　　　　　　　　　　　　　　　　　　　1887

This, the best-known winter climb in the district, is invariably busy. It follows the long rightward-slanting gully which starts to the right of the centre of the crag and passes through some fine rock scenery to the Amphitheatre, where there is a choice of numerous variation finishes if the press of flesh becomes too much.

Warning The broad upper slope of the *Right Branch* collects blown snow from the plateau above and is very **avalanche prone** during fresh snow conditions – any avalanche will (and frequently does) sweep down the lower gully. There have been fatalities here and this is definitely a gully to avoid after heavy snowfall. Also, there has been considerable rockfall in the gully over the last few years – so also a place to avoid if it is not fully frozen.

The variations are described from right to left.

Central Gully Right Branch　　　　　　　　　　　　　　　**200m II (2) ** 1890**

The classic route and frequently done but very variable in condition. An ascent in lean conditions can give a difficult crux (3) on the pitch above the Amphitheatre, whilst a snowy year may only offer a banked out snow plod (1) and leave you wondering what the fuss is all about!

1   35m. Start at a small chockstone pitch followed by easy snow or ice pitches.
2   45m. The cave which follows can be turned on the left and leads to the small *Amphitheatre,* where the gully branches.
3   30m. A short stretch of steeper snow leads to a short pitch of vertical ice on the right (if it is not banked out). This may be turned on the left by some rock moves or via the chimney-groove formed between the rock and ice on the right, stepping left at the top, or climb the ice direct; normally harder. Continue past a chockstone to the upper snow slopes.

4+5 90m. Continue up a straightforward snow slope to the top.

Chimney Finish   30m IV (5) 1972

This takes the prominent corner high up on the left from the final snow slope of the *Right Branch.* It was first climbed with ice but goes as a mixed pitch and is usually in condition if *Central Gully* is climbable.

Climb the corner to where it steepens. Traverse out right then up a line formed by a crack and a flake to further iced cracks and the top.

Left Branch Middle Way   90m VI (6) ** 2006

The obvious continuation up the cleft in the headwall directly above the line of the V-corner makes an excellent finish.

1   45m (3). Just to the right of the main ice pitch in the *Left Branch* is a small pitch up a V-corner leading to the final snow slopes of the *Left Branch*. You can exit via the *Left Branch* at Grade III or continue up the cleft in the headwall.
2   45m (6). Climb into the cleft, the continuation line directly above the previous pitch and about 5m left of the *Grande Finale* finish. It is steep at first until a large turfy niche is reached. Continue up easier snow slopes to another recess then hard poorly-protected moves lead to the top.

Central Gully Arete and Grande Finale   60m VI (7) * 2001/6

From the Amphitheatre the narrow arete splitting the *Left* and *Right Branches* gives delicate climbing in an exposed position and is a bit thin on gear. The parallel cracks in the headwall above provide a more muscular finish.

1   20m (3). Climb up to belay below a prominent parallel crack system on the crest of the buttress in the headwall above the *Amphitheatre*.
2   40m (7). Climb the easy groove to a ledge below the cracked wall. Climb the wall using both cracks to an overhung niche, swing left and follow the groove above, stepping right to finish up easy steps.

Lake District Winter Climbs

Left Branch
110m III (3) ** 1887

Keep to the left of the buttress dividing the amphitheatre. A good climb which benefits from an early start before the good ice pitch is hacked to pieces
1   20m (3). A good pitch on ice.
2   90m. Ascend the pleasantly open snowfield with a further small ice pitch sometimes present near the top.

Far Left Branch
90m III

Left of and opposite the start of the dividing buttress in the gully amphitheatre, a further branch runs out left.
1   60m. Climb out of the main gully on ice and follow snow to the headwall of a small couloir.
2   30m. Climb a chockstone pitch on the right to a final snow slope. The chockstone can be awkward in lean conditions with a poor landing above.

The OGJ Way
130m III *

This next variation follows a well-defined chimney line to the left of the amphitheatre of *Central Gully*, but invisible from that route. Start just above the big chockstone at the bottom of the amphitheatre. An ill-defined groove goes up the left wall opposite a pinnacle belay.
1   20m. Climb the groove on ice for 10m and then easier snow above to belay at the wall.
2   15m. Climb up into the chimney and belay before the steep section.
3   20m. Continue up the steepening chimney moving right at the top. An awkward move left leads into a short steep groove and easier ground.
4   25m. Traverse easy snow above the couloir to the base of a steep corner.
5   30m. The final pitch of *Far Left Branch*. Turn the chockstone on the right to an awkward landing and go up snow above to belay on the right.
6   20m. Continue to the summit.

South-East Buttress
180m III 1891

No detailed description of this route is available, but it climbs the buttress between the two major gullies of *Central* and *South-East*.

South-East Gully
190m II (3) *** 1890

If *Central Gully* is crowded, here is another classic to the left, starting just right of the lowest point of the crag. *South-East Gully* is the only Cumbrian location for a plant called dwarf cornel – **please climb here only in truly frozen conditions**.

Great End

1   60m (2). An often icy snow slope leads to a chockstone, which is turned on the right.
2   40m (3). Follow the right fork up steep snow to an icy chimney. Climb this direct or turn it on the right wall.
3   90m (3). The gully curves gently to the right with one or two small pitches leading to the summit.

Left Fork
On pitch 2 follow the left fork to an open snow slope. Not as good as the original.

South-East Gully Left-Hand Buttress   200m III 1996
Quite a worthwhile variation when there is a traffic jam in the gully or if you have done the others.

Follow *South-East Gully* to just below the first step (the chockstone). Exit the bed of the gully by a shallow V-groove which leads onto the buttress on the left. Ascend the buttress direct, breaking through steeper sections at their weakest points to gain easier slopes above.

Aspirant   210m IV (4) * 1987
To the left of *South-East Gully*, before the lowest point of the crag, a leftward-facing corner starts at mid-height up the cliff: the highlight of this route. This is part of a fault-line running up the full height of the crag. Follow the fault. Easy climbing leads to the corner. This gives a good full-length pitch (45m (4)) before further easier ground leads to the top.

To the left, 20m past the lowest point of the crag, are two prominent groove systems separated by a steep grooved wall. Both, particularly the left one, require heavy snow and ice conditions for an ascent. The buttresses to either side also give interesting climbing with much scope for variation.

Buttress Right of Right-Hand Groove   200m III (3) 1995
Follow the obvious way up the buttress. The best finish is by a direct line but an easier finish is possible to the right.

Right-Hand Groove   150m III * 1978
The right-hand groove system, 20m left of the toe of the buttress. A good build-up of snow is needed.
1   35m. Climb the groove for 15m, then move to a second groove above on the right. This leads in 20m to a snowfield.

2   50m. Cross the snow slope up rightwards towards a recess in the upper rock band. Climb ice to the recess with a crack in the back.
3   20m. Follow a small iced groove on the right then traverse right and climb the wall at a weakness. Continue up leftwards then rightwards to easier ground.
4   45m. Continue up easier snow and ice bearing leftwards to the top.

Left-Hand Groove   150m IV (4) ** 1978
This large left-facing corner-groove lies further to the left, about 10m from *Right-Hand Groove*. It has four excellent pitches and in lean conditions can prove quite a battle!
1   20m (4). Climb bulging ice onto snow, followed by a short but overhanging ice section. Zigzag up leftwards over easier ground, then back right to belay in a small bay at the bottom of a groove. Sometimes it is possible to climb the initial groove direct.
2   30m (4). A steep pitch. Ascend the groove to an icicle and bear left over steep mixed ground, with a final 5m ice groove to pull out right onto easier snow.
3   45m. Ascend the snowfield directly to a stance below a steep icy crack.
4   15m (3). Climb the crack or, if it is not in good condition, a left-facing shallow turfy corner just to the left to a small snow ledge.
5   40m (3). Continue up a turfy groove to a steep snow slope and bear leftwards to the top.

Original Finish
The climb originally moved diagonally right on easy ground from the top of pitch 2 and finished as for *Right-Hand Groove*.

A winter ascent of the summer line of **Born Free** (IV, 1983) has been recorded. It reputedly gave two big ice pitches, but unfortunately has not been possible to locate, either in summer or winter!

Buttress Left of Left-Hand Groove   110m III (4) 1995
Follow the easiest turfy line 20–30m left of *Left-Hand Groove*. A slanting ramp near the top provides the crux.

Towards its left end the crag becomes distinctly more rocky and towards the right-hand side of this area is a large open corner, the most prominent feature in this area.

Arlecdon Aquarian   65m V (5) 1991
A good line but seldom in good winter condition. Start under the corner.
1   20m. Easy scrambling leads to a large block at the base of the corner.

2   45m (5). Climb the corner and at its top follow a short groove which is set slightly back from the steep left wall.

Further left, the crag turns another corner and just round this is a huge cave (the summer line of *Briggs's Climb*). Roughly halfway between the far left end of the now broken crag and *Briggs's Climb*, a 25m icefall (II) sometimes forms in a break to the left of a roughly triangular area of rock.

Girdle Traverse   340m IV * 1978

A left-to-right traverse starting up either the *Left* or *Right-Hand Groove*, crossing the two main gullies and finishing up *Window Gully*. The start up *Left-Hand Groove* and the descent into *Central Gully* across slabs provide the cruxes. Originally climbed in very good snow/ice conditions, the crux sections would prove much harder if lean.

1   50m. Climb *Left-* or *Right-Hand Groove*.
2   45m. Traverse the large snowfield right and slightly upwards.
3   60m. Continue the traverse right, then follow a line slightly downwards, descending into *South-East Gully* at the fork.
4   30m. Go up rightwards to below a steep chimney then up the small ramp to a ledge above.
5   60m. Descend diagonally rightwards for 10m then continue traversing, taking the easiest line over snow and slabs to descend slabs into *Central Gully*.
6   50m. Follow *Central Gully* for about 20m, to where a small right-sloping ramp leaves the gully bed. Follow this then continue the traverse under a rock band and some icefalls to below the second main pitch of *Window Gully*.
7   45m. Finish up *Window Gully*.

Grossbuttock   270m III 1973

Another shorter left-to-right girdle starting up *Right-Hand Groove* and finishing up *South-East Gully*.

BORROWDALE WEST

On the west side, towards the head of the valley, the first three routes are approached from Seathwaite. Park in the lane approaching the farm.

Taylor Gill Force   50m III * 🗡 1962

Draining from Styhead Tarn, Taylor Gill leaves the hanging valley (NY 229 109) just above Stockley Bridge, where it results in a spectacular waterfall. At an altitude of only 300m, like most Borrowdale winter climbs it seldom freezes fully but when it does it gives a fine 30m ice pitch.

Base Brown   250m II 1995

On the south side of Base Brown at the top of *Taylor Gill Force* (NY 229 112) is a crag which is split by three clefts. The central one makes a good **descent**, being the broadest and easiest. The left gully gives several short steps and one longer 10m pitch, taken on turf on the left or mixed ground on the right. At the top the gully splits to give a left and right finish. The right finish has a short ice pitch to exit.

Sourmilk Gill   245m II/III ***

On the west side of the upper Borrowdale valley, this gill cascades from the hanging valley of Gillercombe (NY 233 122). At an altitude of only 120m, a long period of frost is required for complete formation, though the higher reaches may be in condition more often. Take the path due west from the farm at Seathwaite and follow the path towards the hanging valley of Gillercombe. This follows the left bank of the stream and gives a convenient way of joining or leaving the climb at any point. The bed of the stream is followed in its entirety. Halfway up, a long pitch gives some interest, but the top icefall is the crux and may contain 15m of steep ice.

Gillercombe Crag

NY 222 124   *Altitude 460m*   *South-east facing*

Marked on the OS map as Raven Crag. Although not noted for its winter climbing, in exceptional conditions this south-east-facing crag can provide a continuation to *Sourmilk Gill*.

Approach via the path on the left of *Sourmilk Gill* or climb the gill (if frozen). The crag is directly opposite the top of the gill. It can also be quickly approached from the summit of Honister Pass.

Gillercombe Gully   70m II

The obvious gully to the left of the main section of buttress and just left of *Gillercombe Buttress*. This provides a worthwhile way up the crag and is a much better winter climb than a summer one. The main pitch is near the top. The difficulties can vary quite considerably with conditions.

GILLERCOMBE CRAG

Gillercombe Buttress   110m IV (5) ** 1960

This classic summer climb starts at the foot of the buttress right of *Gillercombe Gully* and just left of a rocky ramp in the path. Take a line diagonally left towards the gully then back right and up the centre of the buttress – a copy of the summer description would probably be useful (see the FRCC Borrowdale guide). The climb can be very good, but the snow conditions necessary for an ascent are rare.

Against All Odds   150m III (4) ** 2010

A winter route based on the summer line of *Grey Knotts Face*, which follows a line just right of the centre of the buttress.
1 35m (2). Start where the fence line meets the crag as for *Grey Knotts Face*. About 20m to the right is a snowy and icy ramp. Climb this over a few steps to reach a terrace after 30m. Follow the terrace left to below an icy chimney.
2 25m (3). Climb the icy chimney to another terrace.
3 35m (2). The rocky chimney above was bare, so easier mixed ground on the left was taken to below the final chimney-fault.
4 55m (4). Take the fine chimney-fault to the top of the crag, passing several steep sections.

On the north side of the Honister Pass road are the east-facing gills of **Scaleclose Gill** (II, 1963. 🚶) (NY 244 146) and **High Scawdell Gill** (II, 1963. 🚶) (NY 244 150) on High Scawdell Fell. When frozen these low-lying gills give some enjoyable pitches.

On the west side of Borrowdale, 2km south of Grange, is Tongue Gill. A track runs up the south side of the gill and leads to the York Mountaineering Club Hut and also on to north-east-facing Rigghead Quarry, 400m, the highest of the old slate quarries (NY 238 153). Seepage from the upper cave may produce a thick continuous wall of ice. However four distinct 25m ice lines **Rigghead Quarry Icefalls** (Grade III–IV) leading to the cave are more likely; all were climbed in 1991.

During hard winters an icefall forms in Goat Crag Gill above and right (just north) of Goat Crag (NY 245 165). This is **Goat Crag Icefall** (IV, 1963).

Heading north on the minor road from Grange, a signpost marked 'Place Howe' is reached before the hamlet of Manesty. The broken, heathery Blea Crag (NY 238 172) on the east flank of the High Spy/Maiden Moor hillside contains three gullies. The left one is **Mouse Gill** (II, 40m); **Bridge Gully** (II, 45m) is the central one; and the short gully on the right is nameless.

LAKE DISTRICT WINTER CLIMBS

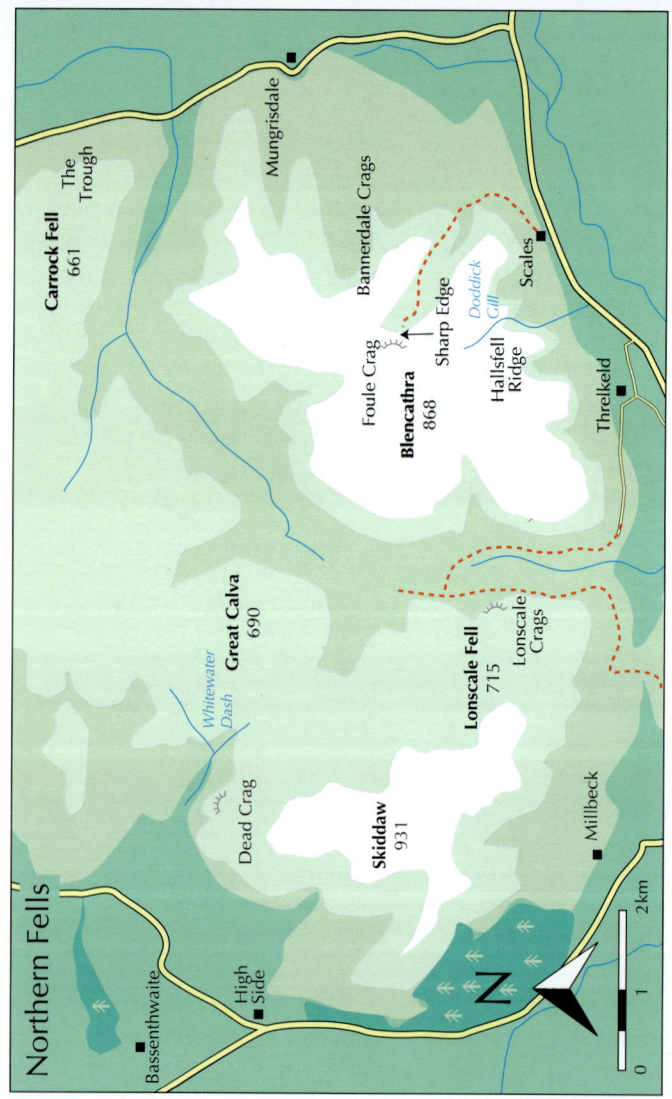

NORTHERN FELLS

The mountain crags of Blencathra, Skiddaw and Carrock Fell are all included within this area. Generally at low altitudes a prolonged freeze is required to bring them into condition.

Skiddaw

The great bulk of Skiddaw dominates the view north from Keswick, but although one of the highest of the Lakeland Fells it provides little winter climbing. On the north side of Skiddaw can be found the impressive *Whitewater Dash* and to its west Dead Crag. Lonscale Fell to the south of Skiddaw has one route. All of these climbs start at a low altitude and do not come into condition often.

Whitewater Dash Waterfall 50m II *
The waterfall of Dash Beck (NY 273 313) gives a pleasant outing on ice which looks steeper than it actually is, but its elevation at 400m ensures that sustained cold temperatures are required. Approach easily from Bassenthwaite on the north side of Skiddaw.

Dead Crag

NY 267 311   Altitude 550m   *North-east facing*

Dead Crag lies to the right of the path when approaching *Whitewater Dash Waterfall* from the north.

Central Icefall 160m IV 1991
The obvious central icefall.
1   50m. Climb the steep ice in the centre of the crag, then follow ice bulges trending left to a small tree belay.
2   40m. Traverse the snow bay on the right and round into a narrow gully with a peg belay.
3   50m. Follow the gully past several small steps to just below the top and another peg belay.
4   20m. From the top of the gully exit right to the summit.

Diagonal Gully   150m II 1991
This aptly named gully is not visible from the path. It splits the crag from left to right.
1   60m. Follow steepening ice to the start of the diagonal gully.
2   40m. Continue up the gully passing icicles on the left into a snowy amphitheatre.
3   50m. From the top of the gully move left up the amphitheatre headwall to the summit.

Lonscale Crags

NY 293 270   ALTITUDE 500M   EAST FACING

These crags are to be found on the east flank of Lonscale Fell, the hill that lies to the south-east of its larger neighbour Skiddaw.

Kirkby's Folly   230m II 1991
Follow the mine track to the east of Lonscale Fell. Climb an obvious gully to the left of an arete (possible large cornice).

BLENCATHRA (SADDLEBACK)

NY 323 277

This bulky and distinctive mountain is immediately recognisable by its saddle shape as one drives west along the A66 from Penrith; it lies just north of that road. Its numerous truncated spurs offer some fine ridge climbs and scrambles which make enjoyable winter outings.

Hallsfell Ridge   300m I *
While only really worth the grade in icy conditions, this ridge still provides an interesting and scenic route with which to ascend or descend the mountain. From Threlkeld village, follow the footpath that contours round the foot of the spurs to the east. **Doddick Gill** (II) to the east of the ridge may be followed for a while before joining the ridge.

North of the A66, a minor road leads east from the White Horse Inn (NY 343 269) to a small parking area whence a path leads up Mousethwaite Comb and then north-west to Scales Tarn (NY 328 281), at which point the ridge of *Sharp Edge* is most easily gained. If this road is blocked by snow or ice, or the car park full, an alternative approach can be taken starting by the A66 at NY 340 268 (300m west of the pub). This gives an easy walk which contours around the east end of Scales Fell to join the track to Scales Tarn.

Several 200m shallow snow gullies run up from Scales Tarn to the summit of Atkinson Pike. They are mainly Grade I, but the one immediately left of *Sharp Edge* gives more worthwhile climbing with quite an alpine feel (**Sharp Edge Gully** I/II).

Sharp Edge   215m II ** 1873

This fine ridge (NY 328 284) lies just to the right (north) of Scales Tarn. Initially fairly level, the ridge steepens where it abuts the mountain and becomes steep and slabby. **Warning** This point has been the scene of numerous accidents. For the full experience and exposure follow it directly. An easier alternative is to follow the snowy trough on the right.

A good **descent** from this ridge is to continue left across the saddle to the summit and then follow *Hallsfell Ridge* down to Gate Gill.

On the east end of *Sharp Edge*, at the foot of the main ridge, may be found **Brunt Knott** (II) a 50m turf climb which can make an interesting alternative start to *Sharp Edge*. Well to its right is the prominent chimney of *Blunt Gully*.

Blunt Gully Buttress   60m II/III 2009

The turfy buttress immediately left of *Blunt Gully*. A good route when everything else is buried under powder. The initial overhanging wall can be avoided on the left or right, or could be taken direct at an increased grade.

Blunt Gully   60m II/III * 1995

This gully/chimney starts almost at the point where the base of *Sharp Edge* meets the base of Foule Crag, just left of *Foule Crag Gully*. The steep start soon eases and leads to the crest of *Sharp Edge*.

Foule Crag

NY 324 284   A<small>LTITUDE</small> *750M*   N<small>ORTH FACING</small>

To the north of *Sharp Edge* lies the long blocky face of Foule Crag. It is generally easy angled and it is possible to wander almost anywhere here in good winter conditions, making the recorded lines rather difficult to identify. The rock, being Skiddaw Slate, is poor and there is little reliable rock protection to be found. Being

Foule Crag and Sharp Edge

1. Sharp Edge — I
2. Brunt Knott — II
3. Blunt Gully — II/III
4. Foule Crag Gully — I
5. Traverse of the Sods — II/III
6. Pulse Direct — III/IV
7. Pulse — II/III
8. Wowzers — II/III
9. Vegiburger — II/III
10. Smoken — II/III
11. Secondhand — II/III

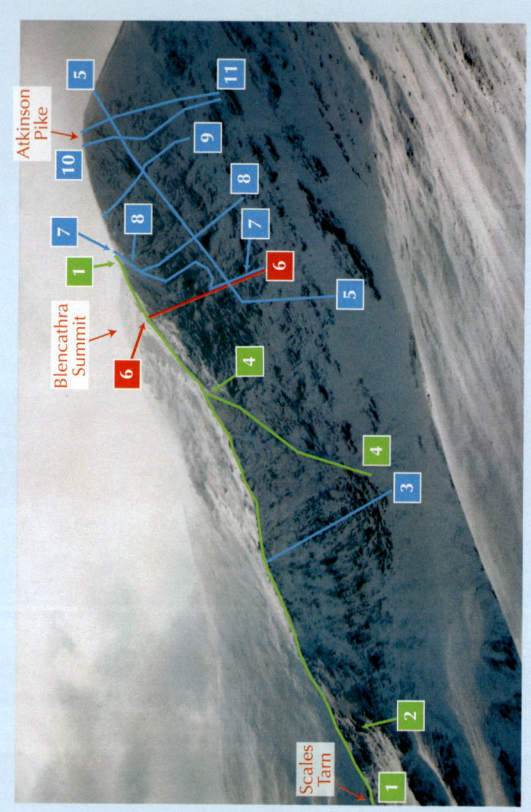

on the side of a ridge water drains quickly and so there is little ice build-up and the climbing is mainly on frozen turf or snow.

Follow the path as for *Sharp Edge,* but where this ascends to Scales Tarn continue traversing beneath Brunt Knott and ascend beneath the northern flank of *Sharp Edge* before traversing left and up to the crag.

Foule Crag Gully   80m I/II

The obvious easy right-slanting gully formed by the junction of *Sharp Edge* and Foule Crag ends on *Sharp Edge* at the point where it steepens. It is only easy in good snow cover – in lean conditions it is mostly bare rock. There are two branches; the right-hand one can sometimes give a 5m icefall (II).

Seen from *Sharp Edge,* or from below, a faint diagonal rises across the crag from bottom left to top right. This starts about 50m right of *Foule Crag Gully*.

Traverse of the Sods   180m II/III 1995

Follow the diagonal traverse line rightwards, starting up a bay located roughly one-third of the way in from the left side of the crag.

Pulse   60m II/III 1995

Start right of the bay where *Traverse of the Sods* starts. Climb a corner to cross this route, then follow a wide crack until the angle eases and a steep wall is reached. Avoid the chimney-crack directly above and traverse down and right, avoiding the impending steps, until a crack leads up rightwards to a platform in a corner. Continue directly up the steep wall and ledges above to the top.

Pulse Direct   III/IV 1996

Continue directly up the chimney-crack on frozen turf.

Wowzers   60m II/III 1995

In the centre of the crag a hanging triangular rock corner forms a distinct feature. This route starts up a rib immediately to its right and follows a fairly direct line until near the top, where it pulls out rightwards onto easier ground.

Vegiburger   60m II/III 1995

A blank-looking wall can be seen at mid-height. This route climbs a line left of this. Move up and follow a ramp rightwards to the bottom left corner of the blank wall before moving left and following the line of least resistance to the top.

Smoken
60m II/III 1996

Below and to the right of the blank wall there is a corner below which some ice can usually be found. Climb the ice and pass ledges to gain a corner. Climb this, exiting left to easy ground. When this steepens, trend right to easier ground.

Secondhand
30m II/III 1995

The line of least resistance up the far right side of the crag.

CARROCK FELL

NY 348 336 ALTITUDE 450M *EAST FACING*

This Lakeland outlier stands north of Blencathra. From the A66, a minor road is signposted to the north leading to Mungrisdale. Follow this through the village and past a phone box to park just north of Stone Ends. From here the crag is visible about 150m above the road. The eastern side of the fell contains a number of small outcrops; the most northerly is separated from the others by a stream and contains a deep gully.

Trough Gully
70m III ** 1950s

Known locally as The Trough, the short gully splitting the buttress gives a very worthwhile two-pitch route that forms quite readily in a freeze and has a tricky section in the middle.

Icicle Start
15m IV 1986

To the left of the start of the gully, an impressive icicle can form. Climb it if you dare.

Common Courtesy Icicle
20m IV 2010

Start up *Trough Gully* and just before the first major steepening after about 20m an icicle forms from the steep left wall. Climb this with care to a dead tree belay well back.

Carrock Fell Icefall
25m II/III 1950s

Slightly lower and about 300m south of *Trough Gully*, a short slab forms an icefall. Several other short icefalls on this hillside make good practice routes.

EAST LAKES

Paddy Cave on Rape and Pillage, Viking Buttress West, Helvellyn (photo: Jack Boniface)

Lake District Winter Climbs

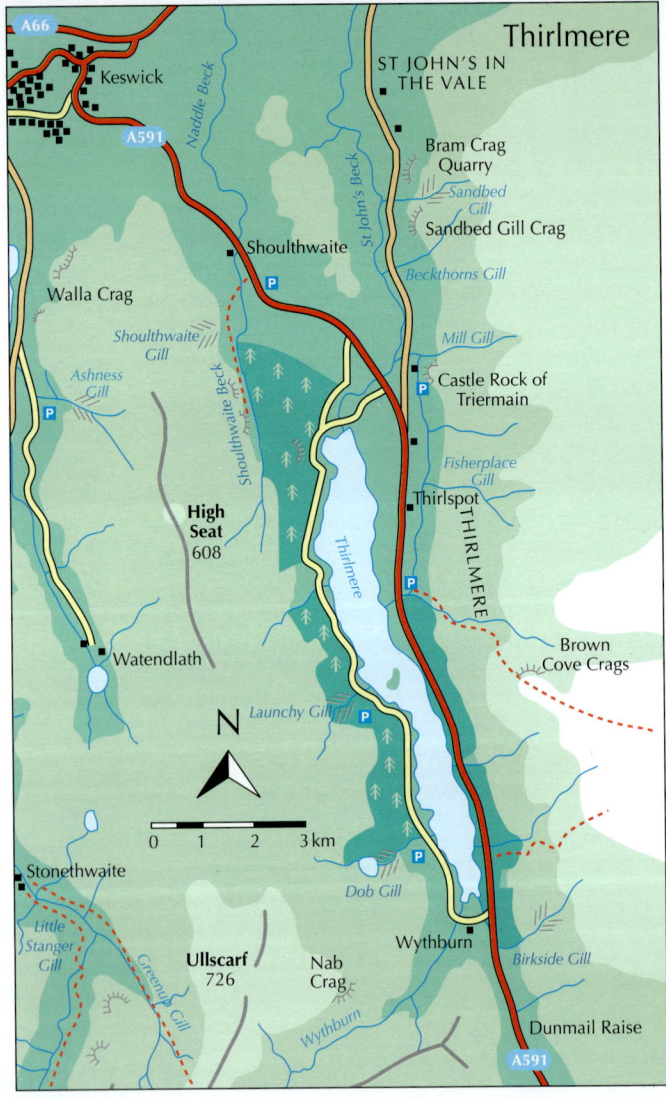

THIRLMERE

The Thirlmere valley runs in a north–south direction and is bisected by the A591 Ambleside to Keswick road. Most of its climbs follow watercourses and, as many of theses routes start at low altitude, a sustained period of cold temperatures is required before they come into condition.

The climbs are described clockwise around the valley starting from the north-eastern corner.

The east side of the valley contains a number of water courses which can offer some good ice pitches during a prolonged cold spell. Bolted belays have been placed in some of the gills by 'canyoners'. This practice is discouraged. The first climbs are in the subsidiary valley of St John's in the Vale.

Bramcrag Quarry Fall   III/IV * 1976

A two-tier icefall sometimes forms in the right-hand lower quarry (NY 319 219).
1   20m (4). The obvious iced corner to a huge ledge. Walk 15m left to an iced slab.
2   20m (3). The slab.

Sandbed Gill   180m II/III

Situated above the east side of St John's in the Vale (NY 320 218). A deep atmospheric rift cuts through the crags. The difficulties may be short but quite exciting when thin ice build-up may force a turf expedition onto the left wall. The *Right-Hand Finish* is Grade III.

Descent is possible down Fisher's Wife's Rake to the north (left looking up); don't try descending *Beckthorns Gill* to the south as it contains a number of troublesome hidden steps.

Sandbed Gill Crag   40m VI (5) 1985

The crag to the right of the main gill (NY 322 215) can give a steep technical problem. A thin ice smear runs down from the main overhang. Climb this and move left onto the rib to gain the top groove.

Beckthorns Gill   200m II/III 1996

The next gill to the south at (NY 321 210). Follow the gill; the right-hand branch gives the best continuation.

Mill Gill   150m III 🌲 1995
The gill just north of Castle Rock of Triemain (NY 324 198). Follow the gill bed passing two 15m icefalls. Rock and tree belays.

The remaining climbs are within the main Thirlmere valley.

Fisherplace Gill   200m III/IV ** 1991
The gill located at (NY 321 183) about midway between the King's Head Hotel at Thirlspot and the junction of the A591 and the St John's in the Vale road contains many interesting small ice pitches and a steep 20m pitch with three bolts at its top. It is best approached by the bridleway from the hotel.

Comb Crag

NY 335 135   ALTITUDE 600M   *WEST FACING*

Easily approached from the United Utilities car park (NY 325 135) at the small church on the east side of Thirlmere. This well-constructed path offers the shortest approach to Helvellyn summit and Nethermost Pike. Follow the path into the combe. Leave the path at the point where it heads west to bypass the crag and head for an obvious short chimney in the rocks at the back of the combe.

Comb Crag Gully and Corner   30m III 2010
This 15m gully is split in its lower section, either side offering enjoyable climbing with more ice on the right. From the top head up diagonally right to a 15m stepped iced corner offering further climbing to rejoin the path.

Birkside Gill   I/II ⚠ 🌲🌲 1986
Easily accessible from Dunmail Raise, this gill runs down from Dollywaggon Pike to the south of a plantation (NY 326 125) and gives several hundred metres of easy and pleasant climbing and an interesting way to the summit.

The west side of the valley contains fewer routes.

Nab Crag

NY 312 123   ALTITUDE 330M   *SOUTH-EAST FACING*

This crag on the north side of Wythburn Valley can be clearly seen in profile from Steel End Farm at the south end of Thirlmere. Parking is available in the car park across the road from the farm. From here a path heads up the valley until a rising traverse leads to the crag.

Crypt and Fingers Climb   **80m IV (5) 2010**
This disjointed route follows the left-hand buttress.
1   20m. The first two summer pitches were combined starting at a steep cracked groove and following the slab to the Crypt. A traverse left from here leads round the buttress to a ledge.
2   30m. Regain the ridge and follow it to the top.
3   20m (5). The Finger is on a lower buttress 10m to the left. Move across to this and climb The Finger.
4   10m. Easy mixed ground to the top.

Pointing the Finger   **80m IV (4) 2010**
Across the wide gully on the left-hand side of *Crypt and Fingers Climb* is another buttress. Start on its bottom right-hand side by the remnants of a tree. Climb a slight diagonal fault-line in two pitches. A series of steep walls above ledges gives continuing interest.

In good conditions **Dob Gill** (170m, II, 1991/2) (NY 315 138), the stream leading up to Harrop Tarn, gives 170m of climbing with the most difficult part in the lower section. The conspicuous **Central Tarn Crag Gully** (1915) in the crag above the tarn has also been climbed, but the grade is not known.

Standing Crag

NY 297 135   ALTITUDE 560M   *NORTH FACING*

Follow the path as for Harrop Tarn and continue along the path on the north side of the tarn heading for Blea Tarn. Near the top take the bridleway to the left and where the ground starts to level out before Blea Tarn the crag is found approximately 300m to the south of the bridleway.

The one recorded winter route shares a similar line to that of the summer route *Freddie Flintoff*.

Stand Out   50m IV (2010)

From below the prominent slab at the start of *Standing Slab* move rightwards over turfy ledges to a groove system near or right of the rock route *Freddie Flintoff*. Follow this up the turfy corners, cracks and grooves to the top.

Launchy Gill   180m III ***

Situated on the west side of Thirlmere. Approach straight from the car park at Fisher Gill (NY 306 171). The climb starts at an altitude of around 250m (NY 308 158) and needs a decent freeze, if nothing else but to avoid falling into one of the deep pools! Climb a number of small pitches to an impressive 20m main fall. Continue above, either direct or via the more interesting right fork. **It is home to rare plants.**

There are several short icefalls, both on Iron Crag and in its environs. **Mere Gill** (1982) (NY 295 187) to the south of Iron Crag produces a series of icy steps. A full day can be had climbing the following three good quality icefalls.

Shoulthwaite Gill   50m IV (4) ** 1976

Situated on the hillside between Iron Crag and Goat Crag at an altitude of around 300m (NY 297 196), this quickly forms to produce an impressive single-drop icefall. It is very obvious from the road and gives an exciting pitch. Protection is mainly from ice screws and halfway, rock gear in the buttress on the right. Generally considered a serious lead as the narrow top section can be thin and becomes detached from the rock. Good and 'fat' it will be found low in the grade.

Diclofenac   20m IV (5) 2009

The icefall at the north end of Goat Crag about 300m to the right of *Shoulthwaite Gill*, in a line directly above the bridge where the path leaves the forest. The first 10m are steep.

Zipsor   30m III (4) 2010

If you prefer an alternative anti-inflammatory try this one. This two-tiered icefall right of *Diclofenac* is above the bridge just out of the forest. From the bridge follow the wall and then break left up steep grass to its foot.
1   20m (2). Climb the apron to a bay.
2   10m (4). Follow the pillar from its lowest point from right to left.

For both routes **descend** by steep grass to the north.

HELVELLYN MASSIF

Being the highest mountain outside of the Scafell massif, Helvellyn and its close neighbours hold snow well in their east-facing coves and are often in condition. The climbing areas extend from Brown Cove Crags in the north to Dollywaggon Pike in the south. There are five major coves all told, as well as Tarn and Falcon Crags at the southern extreme, all containing a variety of climbs including many easy gullies at Grade I/II. Whilst all of these have been climbed numerous times, only the more obvious have been described. These coves offer an excellent place for beginners, but **beware**; the cove headwalls tend to form steep snow slopes, usually with a cornice along the top, and **avalanches** can occur. More recent mixed routes provide plenty to go at for the more experienced. In contrast to the rugged crags and coves of the eastern flank, the easy-angled western slopes of Helvellyn offer climbing only on frozen gills; these are covered in the Thirlmere section of the guide.

Without question the Helvellyn and Fairfield range is the most important and vulnerable area of the Lake District with regard to rare plants. This north–south ridge possesses a geological structure, altitude and aspect that is conducive to the growth of rich upland vegetation. All these east-facing coves, their backwalls and their gullies contain the most important English populations of many alpine plants. There are extensive stands of tall herb ledge vegetation together with locations for the rare arctic-alpines and mountain willows. The real rarities grow here – alpine saxifrage, scrubby cinquefoil, holly fern and downy willow.

Climbing should only take place in these areas in true fully frozen winter conditions to minimise any potential damage to the flora and in order to obviate the very real risk of restrictions being imposed on mountaineering.

Jim Fotheringham hammering up Right Buttress Crack, Brown Cove Crags (photo: Nick Kekus)

Lake District Winter Climbs

LAKE DISTRICT WINTER CLIMBS

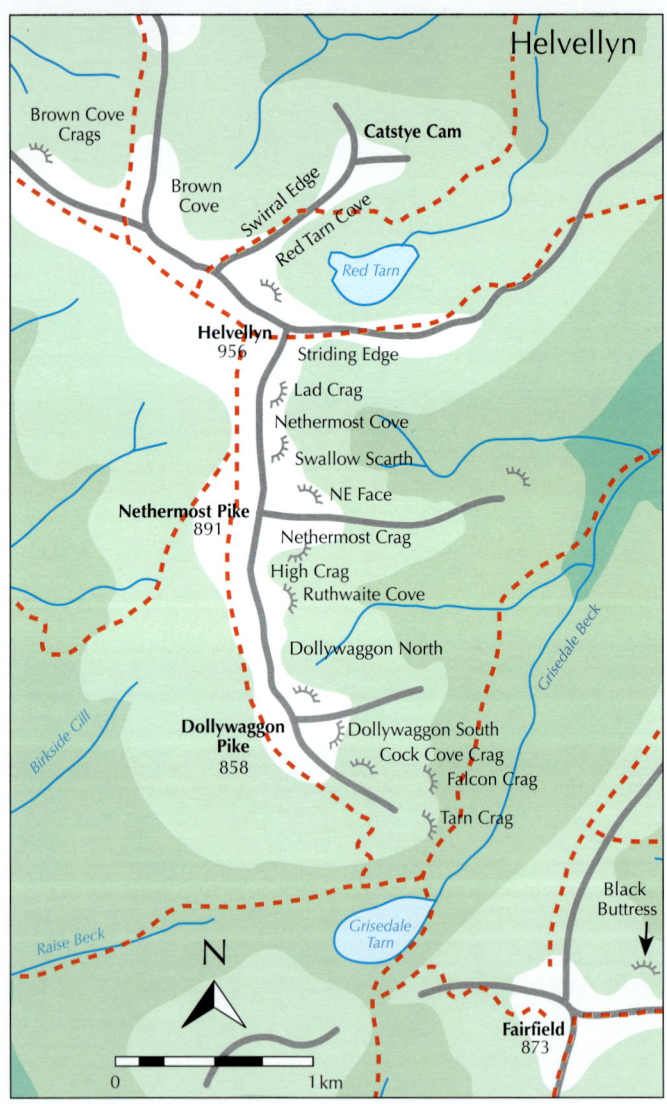

Helvellyn

Brown Cove Crags

NY 330 158   Altitude 800m   *North-east facing*

The most northerly climbing in the area and easily accessible, Brown Cove Crags (which confusingly are not in Brown Cove) are best approached from The Swirls car park on the A591 on the Thirlmere side of the mountain (NY 316 169). From the car park, follow the well-made Helvellyn path north-east up the ridge, but traverse left into Brown Cove Crags after about 1km. The crag, which is visible for most of the approach, consists of two main buttresses bounded by easy gullies and separated by *Central Gully*.

Two Grooves   80m IV (6) ** 2006

The first route is found on a two-tiered buttress to the right of the main concentration of climbs. A short steep buttress at the top of the combe is split by a prominent V-groove (the top pitch) which can be clearly seen on the approach.

1   40m (3). Below and left of the higher prominent V-groove is a less steep, more vegetated groove. This leads to a sloping ledge below the top groove.
2   40m (6). The prominent V-groove is gained via an easy introductory wall. Go up the groove, tricky in the middle, to an awkward exit up an excellent crack on the right.

Variation Finish   45m IV (6) * 2010

From two-thirds height on the final pitch stay in the main groove and climb it on the left, as for the original summer line.

Grace and Favour   100m III 2010

Start to the left of the wall containing the lower groove of *Two Grooves*. The route takes as direct a line as possible up the left side of the buttress containing *Two Grooves*.

Start up a left-slanting groove and step right at the top. Climb the slabby wall directly above, first by a turfy recess and then by a delicate and shallow right slanting groove. Continue above to belay from a selection of big blocks. Continue directly above by a series of steps and one steep move to the top.

Brown Cove Crags

1 Left Buttress — II
2 Stepped Ridge — III
3 Left Branch — II
4 Central Gully — I
5 Right Buttress Crack — III
6 Chimney and Crack — IV
7 Summer Step — II
8 Two Grooves — IV
9 Groove Girdle — II

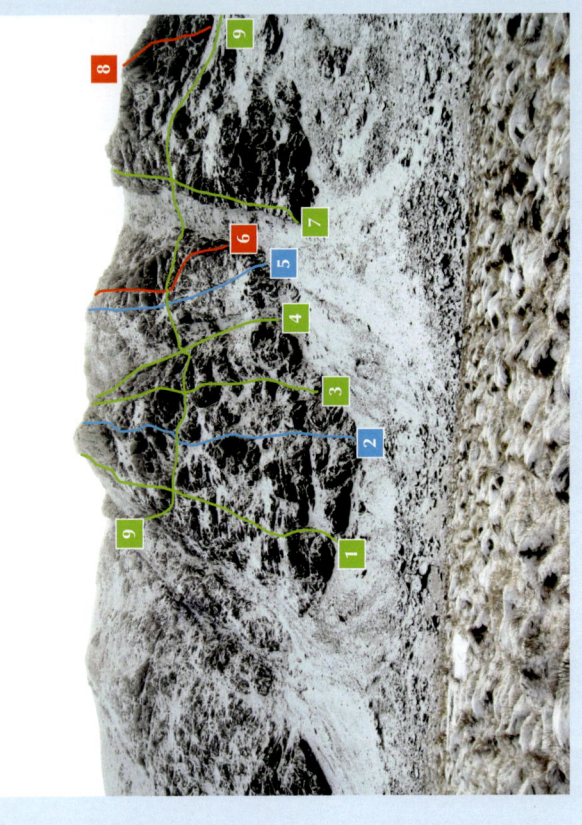

Summer Step   100m II

A winter version of the summer scramble, far inferior to its winter cousin across the gully. Follow the left edge of the buttress overlooking the wide descent gully. Deviations to the right are possible but keep close to the edge to gain the full grade.

Chimney and Crack   90m IV (4) 2011

Start 50 metres up the descent gully to the right of *Right Buttress Crack* beneath the short chimney. A worthwhile route.
1   45m (4). Climb the left wall of the gully up a steep grassy ramp to the base of a chimney. Ascend the awkward chimney to easier ground and a good belay.
2   45m (3). The large slab above is split by three obvious diagonal cracks. Take the more prominent left one leading to a ledge and a short buttress above. The middle crag slants left ending just short of the original finish which can be gained with an awkward step left before the ledge. The right-hand crack offers an independent finish.

Right Buttress Crack   100m III * 1994

The slabby right-hand buttress is split down its centre by a wide crack.
1   10m. From the toe of the buttress, follow a groove to a ledge.
2   60m. From the ledge, move right to the wide crack and follow this past several chockstones.
3   30m. A variety of lines are possible at a similar grade through the broken upper portion of the buttress.

Central Gully   100m I

The broad open gully dividing the two distinct buttresses. Initial steepening snow leads to a small pitch (in lean conditions) at the bottom of the gully. Above, snow is followed to a cornice finish.

Left Branch   120m II

This gully runs up diagonally left of the indistinct buttress immediately left of *Central Gully* and finishes behind the main buttress. It can present a small pitch at the start.

The next routes are on the larger, more distinct buttress left of *Central Gully* with a steep rock wall at two-thirds height. The buttress below the wall is quite broken and it is possible to climb almost anywhere at II. The steep wall is bypassed at either side by the routes described with a few variations through the rock wall being possible.

Stepped Ridge   140m III *

The right-hand side of the final right-hand buttress offers an excellent winter route on short walls and grooves in its upper half, about 20m left of *Central Gully*. Follow a rock rib halfway up the buttress and from its top trend right to the foot of a steep wall. Climb under a chockstone forming a window to gain a ledge overlooking *Central Gully* (a groove to the right also leads to the same ledge). Continue up to the centre of the final steep section of the buttress and, following a vague depression from just right of centre, make a rising traverse to the right arete. Continue easily to the top.

Corner Finish   40m III

An easier exit through the headwall. Midway between the central corner *Féler Putain Finish* and the flat step in *Stepped Ridge* on the right edge of the buttress is a left-facing turfy corner which offers the easiest access through the steep wall.

Fêler Putain Finish   40m IV

From the largest central snowfield below the steep wall, the centre of the wall is breached by a stepped left-facing corner. The exit from the top onto a sloping ledge can be awkward.

Left Buttress   160m II

The left side of the larger of the two buttresses. A shallow gully towards the left of the buttress may be gained by several alternative starts. Follow the gully past several steepenings. In about 100m this leads to the steeper upper buttress which is turned by short walls and chimneys on the left to finish on the summit ridge.

Variation Finish   30m III

A line of cracks up a right-facing groove are taken directly through the upper tower of the buttress.

Groove Girdle   500m II 2008

A right-to-left traverse mainly following the prominent ledge system at around two-thirds height. Starting on the right-hand side of the crag and crossing all the gullies to the top of the crag, more of a walk than a climb. Descend down a shallow small gully into the wide *Central Gully*. Traverse turf onto the central buttress and cross *Central Gully*. At this point it is possible to go diagonally up above the steep wall on the left buttress or if you want some climbing you can descend and downclimb the window of *Stepped Ridge* to continue traversing the buttress below the steep wall.

Red Tarn Cove

The twin parallel gullies left of *Left Buttress* are both Grade I and the stepped ridge in between them is a pleasant Grade II, as is the buttress to the left of the gullies.

Brown Cove

NY 338 154   Altitude 890m   East facing

Brown Cove is the cove on the north side of Swirral Edge. It contains many short possibilities but nothing worth an individual description.

Red Tarn Cove 🌿

NY 343 152   Altitude 830m   North-east facing

This north-east facing cove provides some of the most accessible mountain routes in the Lake District and is often in condition early in the season. The cove is bounded on the left by Striding Edge and on the right by Swirral Edge, the complete traverse of which gives a popular winter day out. **Warning** A large cornice forms along the summit ridge between Striding and Swirral. Keep well back!

There are two main approaches. From Thirlmere, leave The Swirls car park (NY 316 169) on the A591 and follow the obvious Helvellyn path north-east up the summit ridge path of the mountain. A descent of *Swirral* or *Striding Edge* allows access to the climbs around Red Tarn. From Glenridding, vehicular access to the old Greenside Mine is permitted from October to Easter. Follow the path on the left side of the beck. About 1km above the mine follow the right branch of the stream – a path leads up into the cove.

Red Tarn Cove (especially the low crags around the base of *Viking Buttress* and a couple of lines to the left) is home to **rare alpine plants** – please climb here only in truly frozen conditions.

In the cove itself, the open snow bowl to the right of the summit sees the occasional ski descent and numerous sliding descents (not all voluntary!). The broken buttress right of the snow bowl contains several easy lines, while *Viking Buttress* on the left of the snow bowl is home to numerous mixed routes, including the original classic of that name. Left again, two obvious and prosaically named gullies, 1 and 2, separated by a narrow buttress, lead almost to the summit. The more broken ground between the gullies and *Striding Edge* has a few interesting pitches which may be linked together to provide some entertaining climbing to the summit plateau. The rim of the cove often contains a large cornice and avalanches, especially of the snow bowl, are not infrequent.

Lake District Winter Climbs

Red Tarn Cove

1	Gully 3	III
2	Wall and Ramp	III
3	Arete between V-Corner and Wall and Ramp	III
4	V-Corner	III
5	V-Corner Extended Finish	III
6	Gully 2	I
7	Gully 1 Buttress	II/III
8	Blade Runner	IV
9	Gully 1	II
10	Rape and Pillage	IV
11	Viking Buttress	IV
12	Thor's Corner	IV

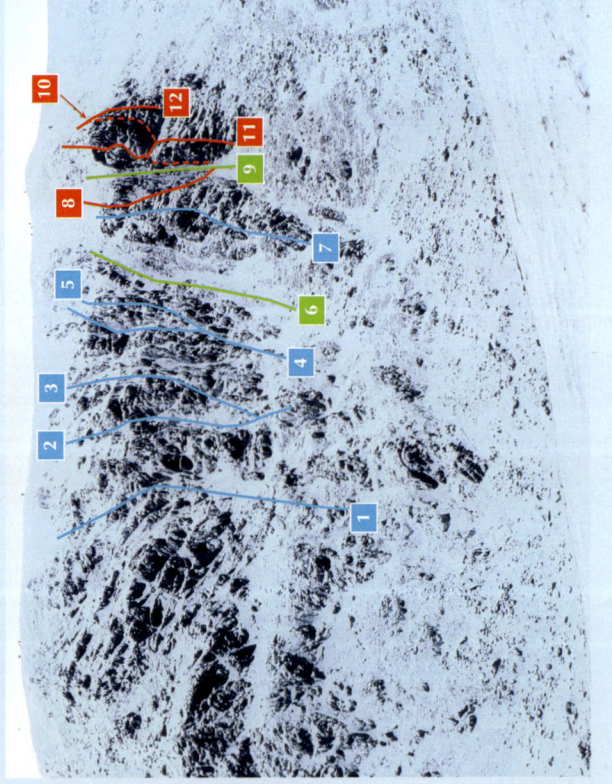

A team carefully descending Swirral from the plateau (photo: Simon Reynolds)

The hill at the east end of Swirral Edge is Catstycam. Its north flank contains the pleasant **Catstycam Gully** (I/II) which makes a fine way to the summit. To the right is a large block with a corner and then an open gully above, **Ambroise's Amble** (II, 2012) offers another approach to the summit.

Striding Edge and Swirral Edge　　　　　　　　　　　1500m I ** 1894

These are the ridges bordering Red Tarn Cove. Their passage, up *Striding*, taking in the summit of Helvellyn and carefully down by the 'easier' *Swirral*, is one of the most popular winter excursions in the Lake District (and one of the most frequently fallen from by those not equipped with ice axe and crampons). From the entrance to the cove, continue along a good path which leads up the slopes on the left to where the ridge becomes more defined and the arete proper starts.

Either follow the arete, keeping to its highest point with the occasional rock step, or take the line of the path which runs 15–20m below the arete summit on the Red Tarn side. Where the ridge abuts the mountain, a small 6m chimney may be awkward to descend in icy conditions. The snow slope leads up to the summit of Helvellyn and the crossed walls shelter. Continue 300m north along the ridge to another snow slope (NY 34118 15255), which is descended to *Swirral Edge*; take care on this as it can be icy. *Swirral* is shorter and less well defined than *Striding* and soon leads onto a broader ridge. Continue over the summit of Catstycam or follow the path down to Red Tarn Beck and back to Greenside Mine.

In bad weather locating either ridge from the summit area can prove difficult. If ascending *Striding Edge* and the weather deteriorates, rather than chance finding *Swirral Edge* in a whiteout, it is better to continue north along the main ridge to the summit of White Side. This can then be descended on easy slopes.

Pear Buttress

This is the small buttress right of the snow bowl. It gives several short pitches (III).

Viking Buttress

This is the largest buttress in the cove. It is bounded on the left by *Gully 1*.

Mjölnir 30m IV (4) 1980s
The short corner-groove at the extreme right side of *Viking Buttress*, right of *Thor's Corner* gives pleasant climbing, best when it's heavily iced.

Viking Buttress 190m IV (5) * ♣ 1986
This ridge forms the right-hand side of the obvious gully just right of the centre of the crag.
1   60m (4). From the lowest rocks climb directly to arrive at the base of a small high-angled slab.
2   35m (4). Go diagonally rightwards to a recessed belay.
3   15m (5). Move left and up to an obvious groove which, if iced, is followed to the top. Otherwise continue by the *Left-Hand Finish* onto a ledge and make difficult moves back right into the groove to the ice.
4   80m. Continue up the easy snow ridge to the top.

Thor's Corner 20m IV (4) 2002
2   20m (4). From the belay at the top of pitch 1, move right to climb a turfy groove forming the right-hand side of the upper buttress.

Left-hand Finish 25m IV (5)
3   25m (5). A better alternative under lean conditions. From the base of the groove on pitch 3, step round left to a large flat platform and climb the wall

RED TARN COVE

via a thin crack/block (crux) before traversing rightwards back into the groove and continuing as for the standard route.

Arete Finish   25m IV (6) 2007

3   25m (6). From the base of the groove on pitch 3, step round left to a large flat platform (possible belay). Climb the crack in the corner with the small jammed block (as for the left-hand finish) for about 2m then pull out left to a thin crack in the middle of the wall with an excellent hook. Move up and left again (crux) towards a small scoop at the top of the left arete, mantle over the top finishing on the top left of the crag overlooking Gully 1.

The next two routes start up *Gully 1*, the gully which bounds *Viking Buttress* on its left.

Rape and Pillage   80m V (7) 2001

Starting 10m up *Gully 1*, this route starts up the gully wall of *Viking Buttress*.

1   40m (7). Climb the obvious corner on the right wall to the roof. Pull through the roof and step right to easier ground and a belay.
2   20m (5). Climb the steep groove to the right of *Viking Buttress*, negotiating a small roof at half-height. Continue up the groove left of *Thor's Corner* to a good ledge.
3   20m (4). Continue up the groove above until it is possible to step right around the arete. Follow turf to the summit ridge.

Variation Finish   IV (6) 2002

3   25m (6). Step left where the groove finishes and continue straight up cracks to the left of the arete.

Loki   80m IV (5) 2004

A series of variations on *Viking Buttress*. Start 15m up *Gully 1*.

1   40m (3). A few metres up from the capped corner of *Rape and Pillage* is an open groove in the right wall of the gully. Climb this to the *Viking Buttress* belay.
2   40m (5). Climb a few metres of *Viking Buttress*, pitch 2, but where *Viking Buttress* moves right, continue up the obvious corner to join *Viking Buttress* at the top groove and finish up *Viking Buttress*.

Gully 1   90m II ❄

The narrow gully to the left of *Viking Buttress* gives about 50m of climbing to a snow slope which leads to the summit. Harder in water-ice conditions. The ramp on the right running parallel with the gully and tucked in below the right wall can offer a method of bypassing traffic jams during busy periods.

Helvellyn

Helvellyn Range

The Nethermost/Dollywaggon escarpment to the south of Helvellyn's Red Tarn Cove showing the location of the coves, major crags and features

Red Tarn Cove

Blade Runner   100m IV (4) 2002
Start about 10m up *Gully 1*, opposite the obvious short corner of *Rape and Pillage*.
1   50m (4). Climb the turfy chimney-groove then continue in the same line to a short wide steep turfy groove. Pull up left out of this to a belay.
2   50m. Easier ground, trending left at first, leads to the top.

Gully 1 Buttress   100m II/III
Start to the right of the toe of the buttress and climb out left onto the buttress. Continue to easier ground, cross a snow basin and finish up another steepening buttress.

Gully 2   90m I
The broad gully to the left of the narrow buttress gives straightforward climbing to the summit either straight up or via the left branch: the higher slab can offer more entertainment if iced (III).

V-Corner   80m III ** 1987
A distinct V-corner lies about 70m left of *Gully 2*. It can be banked out or give plenty of ice.
1   10m. A stepped icefall leads to a good ledge and block belay.
2   10m. Climb the short slabby groove to the final V-corner.
3   20m. The V-corner.
4   40m. Easier snow leads to the plateau.

Extended Finish   20m III (4) Pre-1995
3   From the base of the V-corner pitch, traverse easily right and cross the rib bounding the corner, to the bottom of a large turfy slab with an overhanging left wall. Belay at the base of the slab. Climb the slab (peg) and exit directly up the corner (crux). The final tricky corner can be escaped on the right. Follow easy broken ground to the top.

The arete between *V-Corner* and *Wall and Ramp* has been climbed (III).

Wall and Ramp   70m III
About 30m up and left of *V-Corner* is a distinctive wall with a left-facing groove to its right.
1   30m. Climb the groove, then a leftward-trending ramp over blocks, to a continuation groove.
2   40m. Easier snow leads to the plateau.

LAKE DISTRICT WINTER CLIMBS

Nethermost Cove

1 Striding Edge — I
2 Nethermost Gully — I/II
3 Crazy Torque (Lad Crag) — V
4 Swallow's Rake — II
5 Swallow Gully — I

Photo: Nick Wharton

Gully 3   165m III

This gully starts about 20m left of *Wall and Ramp*. Follow the gully on snow with some steep ice near the top and rock belays where required (65m). A further 100m of snow leads to the summit.

Nethermost Cove

NY 347 145   Altitude 650m   *East to south facing*

This high cove is bounded by *Striding Edge* to the north and broken buttresses and outcrops below Nethermost Pike to the south.

Nethermost Cove is most easily accessible from Patterdale, via the road into Grisedale.

Nethermost Cove, and in particular Nethermost Gully, is home to **rare alpine plants** – please climb here only in truly frozen conditions.

The back of the cove contains two crags, Lad Crag (containing the classic *Nethermost Gully*) on the right and Swallow Scarth Crag on the left.

Lad Crag

NY 345 147   Altitude 700m   *East facing*

Nethermost Gully is the only one of the four gullies on this crag that really warrants a description.

Nethermost Gully   200m I/II *

An excellent climb of its sort, this popular gully can be found running up just left from where *Striding Edge* joins the main mountain ridge. There is often a large cornice.

From the floor of the cove, ascend a long snow slope to where the gully divides after about 100m. The right branch may have a small pitch leading out onto steeper snow (70m). This is followed through to the summit ridge (130m). The left branch contains a small pitch in early season or lean conditions.

Chimney Variation   65m II

The buttress between the two branches of *Nethermost Gully* is split by a chimney which gives an interesting variation finish to the gully.

Crazy Torque   200m V (6) 2009
At the top of crag about 50m left of *Nethermost Gully* is a steep right-facing double corner line. Ramble up the easy lower section of crag to below the corner.
1   40m (6). Climb the corner to below a small roof. Pass this using good cracks and continue up the corner to a ledge.
2   30m (4). Climb the second corner to the top of the crag.

Variation Finish   50m II 2010
Climbing at a grade more in keeping with the rest of the climb. From the start of the second corner at the top of the crag move left passing several short rock steps to finish near the top of the corner.

To the left, the rest of the crag contains three more distinct gullies about 200m long. All are Grade II. The first two are continuous from the bottom of the crag but the farthest left starts only about halfway up the crag.

Swallow Scarth

NY 345 143   ALTITUDE 700M   *EAST FACING*

This small east-facing crag in the back of Nethermost Cove, between Lad Crag and Nethermost Pike, contains some interesting lines and short icefalls that can be linked to provide worthwhile climbing. These have been climbed for many years, yet remained unrecorded; the two routes described here give a feel of what's on offer.

Swallow's Rake   150m II ❦ 2003
The highest of the obvious diagonal rakes running from left to right from a snow basin at the base of the crag.
1   45m. Climb the easy gully between the buttress on the left and the slope on the right. Belay in a corner on the left.
2   45m. Follow the wide rightwards-sloping ledge to its top left-hand corner. Traverse right 5m around a block on a narrow ledge, follow easier ground for 5m to a wide sloping ledge and belay at a small rock spike.
3   50m. Climb the narrow rightwards-slanting groove, bounded on its left by steep rock (in lean conditions this can be bypassed via a steep turf rake 5m to the right). Follow the gully above to belay on the right side of a large block as the gully ends.

4   10m. Follow easy ground over a possible corniced finish.

Swallow Gully   150m I ♣ 2003
The shallow gully to the left, at the back of the snow basin. For added interest, the lower section may be climbed via easy lines through rocks below and to the left of the gully, before traversing right over easy ground to the open snow gully. Follow the narrowest groove up the centre of gully: this may contain water ice. Turf and snow lead to the top.

Nethermost Pike North-East Face

NY 346 142   Altitude 760m   *North-east facing*

The north-east face of Nethermost Pike is made up of numerous small buttresses and ridges interspersed with many gully lines, making it possible to ascend the face almost anywhere at about Grade III. Below are two suggested lines.

Pike Gully   120m I/II ♣
The following route goes up through the centre of this face.
1   30m. Climb up steepening snow between two small buttresses.
2   40m. A steeper section mainly on snow ice follows.
3   50m. The snow slope to the cornice which may be quite large and has been known to require tunnelling.

Huckleberry Grooves   100m III/IV ♣ 1986
Start about 15m right of *Pike Gully*, below the highest point in the crag and traverse left along a shelf. Climb grooves just left of the steepest part of the crag. Exit rightwards along ramps to finish near the highest point of the crag.

Ruthwaite Cove ♣

NY 346 136   Altitude 700m   *South-east facing*

This large cove sits between Nethermost and Dollywaggon Pikes. Prominent at the back of the cove is the buttress of High Crag. A small subsidiary cove containing

Hard Tarn sits between High Crag and Nethermost Pike and contains the classic and relatively reliable *Jogebar Gully*.

For Tarn and Falcon Crags and climbing at the southern end of the mountain, park at Dunmail Raise on the A591 and take the path up Raise Beck to Grisedale Tarn. For Tarn and Falcon Crags and Cock Cove, contour round beneath these crags. Ruthwaite Cove is best approached by following the path from the tarn over Dollywaggon Pike and then down to the col to the north. **Warning** Descending the steep slopes into the cove requires care.

Ruthwaite Cove and Nethermost Cove can also be easily approached from the United Utilities car park (NY 325 135) at the small church on the east side of Thirlmere. The well-constructed path offers the shortest approach to Helvellyn summit and Nethermost Pike. For Nethermost Cove follow the path to the col to the north of Nethermost Pike and descend down into the combe. For Ruthwaite Cove either head south from this col to High Crag or leave the path earlier where it starts to level out after the zigzags and head east to the rim of cove.

Ruthwaite Cove, *Striding Edge* and particularly Nethermost Cove are also easily accessible from Patterdale by following the road into Grisedale and continuing up to the respective cove.

Ruthwaite Cove is home to **rare alpine plants** – please climb here only in truly frozen conditions.

Nethermost Pike South Face

NY 346 139   ALTITUDE *750M*   SOUTH FACING

(Also known as Nethermost Crag). This contains one of the best gully lines on Helvellyn; due to its aspect is prone to sun-rot in clear conditions, but is well worth getting up early to catch it frozen.

Jogebar Gully   100m III ** 🌿 1955

The most prominent gully splitting the crags on the south-east side of Nethermost Pike. Start below the line of the gully.

1   30m. Steepening snow slopes lead to where the gully becomes better defined. Follow the gully to a large snow terrace.
2   35m. Continue up steepening snow, then an icy chimney above, to a snow ledge on the right.
3   35m. The iced slab above leads to a sometimes corniced finish. Beware of potential windslab on the exit slopes above.

Below and left of *Jogebar Gully* there are several areas of rock split by terraces. Many good icefalls form here and various lines (up to Grade IV) have been climbed. Once again it is worth remembering that the south-easterly aspect of the face means an early start can pay dividends.

Terrace Ice   60m III ** 🛇 1970s
The following line takes in the best of the ice mentioned above, starting left of *Jogebar Gully*.
1   15m. From the lowest rocks, follow a shallow gully.
2   25m. A steeper ice pitch on the left leads to a terrace.
3   20m. The final splendid icefall to the next terrace.

High Crag

NY 345 137   ALTITUDE 750M   EAST AND NORTH FACING

Immediately below the summit cairn of the subsidiary summit south of Nethermost Pike, two short gullies are situated in the north side of the crag facing *Jogebar Gully*. Around the arete to the left the east face of the crag contains a grass corner line and a narrow grassy groove line left again. The routes are described from left to right, starting with those on east face.

Grooving High   110m VI (6) 🛇 2011
The narrow grassy groove line running up the centre of the east face of the crag. This offers hard body-pumping climbing in its main central pitch.
1   15m. Climb the easy grassy start of the groove to where it becomes rocky and belay.
2   45m (6). Climb the steep grassy groove with some bold committing moves and a hard move to easy ground near the top. Finish up easy ledges to belay at an overhanging headwall.
3   50m (4). Climb up and left around the headwall with an awkward balancy step into a grassy corner. Follow this to the crest of the ridge and a block belay. Above a further 50m of Grade I/II climbing is required to reach the top of the buttress and the summit cairn.

Second Chance   110m VI (6) 🛇 2012
The corner line between *Grooving High* and the arete in the middle of the crag finishing up the obvious ridge. If the turf is not frozen don't think of going near this one.

1   15m. Climb the open grassy groove below the corner about 20m left of the arete of the crag. Belay to the left where the climbing starts to steepen.
2   50 (6). Continue up the corner line. Where the corner steepens make a hard move into a narrow groove followed by poorly-protected moves up the groove on turf. Easier climbing leads to an overlap with a blank wall below. Committing moves gain turf and eventually the belay shared with *Grooving High*.
3   45m (5). A short technical move up the headwall above and right of the belay leads to the crest and a large flake belay. Continue up the crest of the ridge at Grade I/II for a further 50m to reach the summit.

High Crag Grooves   105m V (6) 🌿 2010

This climbs the right (north) side of the ridge just to the left of wide *Gully A*. At about half-height a narrow chimney can be seen just right of the ridge but facing away from *Gully A*: aim for it.
1   20m (4). Start about 8m up from the left-hand end of the buttress. Climb a short wall via turf up and then left to gain a turfy groove. Follow this up and right to a large ledge and belay at the right-hand end.
2   40m (6). The rocky groove directly above the belay is poorly protected and difficult to start. Follow a second turfy groove above around a bulge and up to the chimney. (The chimney cannot be seen until the finish of the second groove). Climb the chimney and broad arete above until stopped by a rocky tower on the crest of the narrowed ridge.
3   45m (2/3). Drop down to the right into the left side of the top portion of *Gully A* to avoid the tower, then climb a turf groove to the broader buttress above. Climb this for 30m.
A further 50m of Grade I/II climbing leads to the summit.

Gully A   110m II 🌿

The obvious left-hand groove in the north side of the buttress leads to a diagonal traverse right over ice-covered slabs; then go directly to the top.

AB Buttress   105m III ** 🌿 1980

The buttress between the two gullies.
1   40m. Climb *Gully A* for 10m and then follow a steep turfy ramp going to the right for 15m (crux). Keep towards the left side of the buttress to reach a rocky step and a belay crack.
2   45m. Move up 25m and make a step left towards the gully. A spike belay is reached in a further 20m.
3   20m. Continue to the top of the buttress.

DOLLYWAGGON NORTH CRAG

Gully B   120mm I ❄
The right-hand and larger of the two grooves leads over bulges to a right-hand finish.

Left Branch   35m II ❄
Where *Gully B* branches, take the left fork directly up to an icy chimney which leads to an easy snow finish.

A subsidiary buttress stands to the left, south of *High Crag*. The gully running up between the two buttresses is Grade I.

Dollywaggon North Crag

NY 344 132   ALTITUDE 780M   NORTH FACING

This elevated crag is situated just north of a saddle between the true summit of Dollywaggon Pike (NY 346 131) and the northern subsidiary summit (NY 344 132) and is often in condition: if you have them take 60m ropes. The distinctive ramp-line of *Ramp It Up* is a good landmark. The routes are described from right to left.

Dolly Daydream   50m III (4) * ❄ 2005
Right of *Ramp It Up,* the crag turns around a prow with a steep clean wall on the right. Immediately right of this wall there is a groove which becomes larger higher up the crag. At its base there is normally a small ice weep. Start up this and follow the ramp above rightwards to a steep corner. Climb this with difficulty to a ledge, move left and climb the icy corner. Follow the obvious line above trending left to finish above the steep wall.

Acceleration due to Gravity   50m IV (5) ❄ 2003
Takes turfy grooves in the face right of *Thrash Corner*. Start just left of the toe of the buttress.
1   35m (5). Climb a shallow corner with a wide crack in the back to easy turf. Go up another short corner to emerge at the narrow section on *Ramp It Up*. Pull left onto the face and up the left-hand of two short corners, before stepping back right to pull though the bulge and belay on the crest.
2   15m. Easy ground the top.

LAKE DISTRICT WINTER CLIMBS

Dollywaggon North Crag

1 South Gully — II
2 Solo Symphony — III
3 Dolly Mixture — IV
4 Rescue Groove — IV
5 Mono Culture — III
6 Terminal Velocity — III
7 Thrash Corner — IV
8 Ramp It Up — II
9 Acceleration due to Gravity — IV
10 Dolly Daydream — III

Ramp It Up   50m II ❦ 2003
This follows the left-to-right ramp-line slanting through the main buttress, just right of centre to emerge on the crest of the buttress from where the top is soon reached.

Thrash Corner   50m IV (5) ** ❦ 2003
Start in the centre of the crag a few metres left of the ramp-line of *Ramp It Up*.
1   25m (3). Climb the open groove line leading to a block belay.
2   25m (5). Climb the corner above with difficulty and then more easily to the top.

Beat Variation   25m III (3) ❦ 2003
2   25m (3). The crux corner (described above) can be avoided in lean conditions by moves on the right.

Terminal Velocity   50m III (3) ❦ 2003
Start from a block at the top left of the snow bay, also used by *Mono Culture*. Climb a ramp diagonally up right to below a large roof – this is just left of the block belay on *Thrash Corner*. Traverse left onto the arete and finish directly as for *Mono Culture*.

Mono Culture   50m III (4) ❦ 2003
Step into your monos and start from the block at the top left of the snow bay and climb the first few metres of *Rescue Groove* before moving onto the arete on the right. An awkward section with a balancy crux leads to turf and the top.

Rescue Groove   50m IV (4) ** ❦ 2003
This climbs the obvious large groove line. From the block mentioned in *Mono Culture* climb the groove to where it steepens. A nut placement low on the left wall offers protection before hard moves round the bulge lead to a ledge. Further awkward moves lead past a poised flake and the top.

The next routes start in the left side of a bay to the right of *South Gully*.

Dolly Mixture   50m IV (4) * ❦ 2003
At the bottom left of the bay, below and left of the block start of *Rescue Groove*, is a blocky arete. Climb this to a turf ramp, cross the ramp and climb through the overlap to a groove which is followed to the top.

Solo Symphony 50m III 🍁 2006
Start 10m right of *South Gully* and climb the rightwards-trending ramp for 10m. After passing a prominent fault, climb the wall on the left to gain a ledge then make an awkward step left (crux) onto another ramp. Follow this briefly then step left again over a block (possible belay). Contour round to the right and up to gain a short icy corner then follow easy ground to the top, bearing right (away from *South Gully*).

South Gully 50m II 🍁 2003
The left end of the crag is defined by a shallow runnel which gets more difficult with height.

Southside 50m III 🍁 2008
This climbs the grooved ridge immediately left of *South Gully*. Start at the toe of the ridge and climb the right-facing groove which is technical in places. Emerge onto a snowfield and a choice of exits – continue up a turfy groove overlooking the gully or (easier) finish left.

The Tongue is the long ridge running north-east from Dollywaggon Pike. Midway along its north side the flank of the ridge is split by **Tongue Gully** (100m, I * 🍁).

COCK COVE 🍁

NY 349 131 NORTH-EAST FACING

The compact Cock Cove nestles between Dollywaggon Pike and Falcon Crag and contains two crags of interest, Dollywaggon South Crag and Cock Cove Crag. Both are easily accessible from Dunmail Raise and the path leading to Dollywaggon Pike. For Cock Cove Crag leave the path at the top of the zigzags and head to a small col between Dollywaggon Pike and Falcon Crag, where an easy gully just north of the crag gives access to the bottom of the cove. For Dollywaggon South Crag, continue until nearly at the summit before heading into the cove.

Cock Cove is home to **rare alpine plants** – please climb here only in truly frozen conditions.

Dollywaggon South Crag ✽ (NY 346 130)

NY 346 130   ALTITUDE 820M   SOUTH-EAST FACING

This small crag on the north side of Cock Cove is situated south of the summit of Dollywaggon Pike. The central groove is the line of *Turf-tastic*.

Dollymixture   40m III ✽ 2003
This climb, not to be confused with its similarly named neighbour on the North Crag (although it probably will be), follows an obvious line a few metres left of *Turf-tastic*. Start below two large flakes.

Climb up to the flakes and continue to a ledge, using turf and cracks. Traverse a few metres left then climb a mossy block and small rock steps to the top.

Turf-tastic   60m III ✽ 2003
The prominent cleft in the centre of the crag.
1   30m. Climb the obvious steep pitch passing a bulging chimney section on ice and turf.
2   30m. Continue more easily up the gully-line to the top.

Dolly Parton   50m III ✽ 2010
The gangway leading rightwards from the base of *Turf-tastic*.

Start at the base of *Turf-tastic* and after a few metres a steep pull gains the gangway running up rightwards. At its top a pull over bulges leads to easier ground.

Cock Cove Crag ✽

NY 349 129   ALTITUDE 750M   NORTH FACING

This crag lies up and right of Falcon Crag and is ideal for a short day, or when its bigger neighbours of Falcon and Tarn Crags are not in condition. Various people have climbed in this area over the years and it seems likely that many of the climbs on this crag have been done in the past but were not recorded due to their brevity. The routes are described from left to right.

Easy Gully   70m I ✽
The gully on the left of the crag separates Cock Cove Crag from the upper portion of Falcon Crag and finishes near the top of *Chock Gully*.

Cock Cove Crag

1 Bobbins Groove — V
2 Ramp Route — V
3 Central Route — III
4 Thanks for the Tip — II
5 Coco-Tara Direct — IV
6 Tip Off — III
7 Turf Corner — II

Cock Cove Crag

Bobbins Groove
30m V (7) * 🌳 2002

Climb the steep groove just right of *Easy Gully*. After a few metres turf on the right eventually leads steeply to an overhanging wide crack/chimney. Climb this with a chockstone for comfort.

For the next 20m the crag presents a steep bulging wall.

Ramp Route
40m V (6) ** 🌳 2002

The ramp to the right of the bulging wall. Climb the corner awkwardly for a few metres before making insecure moves to cross the ramp to turf on the arete. Follow the turf right before stepping back left into a shallow gully. Follow this to the top.

Direct Start
40m V (6) 🌳 2006

Climb the first turfy groove to the right of the start of *Ramp Route* to join *Ramp Route* at the upper groove.

Central Route
50m III (3) * 🌳 1994

About 20m right of *Ramp Route*, in the centre of the crag, is a shallow chimney. The steep section at mid-height provides the crux.

Coco-Tara Direct
50m IV (4) 🌳 2003

1   20m. Start about 5m right of *Central Route* at easy snow below a short chimney. Climb easily to the short chimney at 10m. Climb this to easy ground and belay at the base of a corner with an overhanging start.
2   30m. Climb the corner (crux) then easy ground to the top.

Thanks for the Tip
50m II 🌳 2002

Start as for *Coco-Tara Direct*. At the base of the chimney, traverse 20m right into the corner of *Turf Corner* and follow this to the top.

Always Leave a Tip
50m II 🌳 2009

An inferior variation, start up *Thanks for the Tip* but step right onto lower snowy ledges and traverse along these to gain *Turf Corner* which is followed to the top.

To the right of *Thanks for the Tip*, the base of the crag overhangs for the next 15m. *Turf Corner* climbs the corner bounding this area on the right.

Helvellyn

Lake District Winter Climbs

Tip Off   45m III (5) 🌿 2010

Midway between *Thanks for the Tip* and the overhang of *Equinox* is a shallow right-facing corner with an undercut start. Climb this direct to join *Thanks for the Tip* at its traverse and continue up a broken edge and the wall above to easier ground.

Equinox   45m V (7) 🌿 2006

Start under the big roof 5m left of *Turf Corner*. Climb the corner in the back of the recess under the roof and traverse right from the back using overhead torques in the roof crack. Pull out around the roof on hooks and using turf (care is required with a dangerous flake on the left as you exit the roof). Continue up right on a turfy ledge to join *Turf Corner* and follow this to the top.

Turf Corner   40m II 🌿 2003

Climb the corner to the right of the overhanging section with the difficulties in the lower half.

DOLLYWAGGON

Tarn Crag and Falcon Crag 🌿

NY 352 127   *ALTITUDE 620M*   *EAST FACING*

The southern end of the Helvellyn ridge is marked by the east-facing buttresses of Tarn and Falcon Crags. They can be quickly reached from Dunmail Raise by traversing the north side of Grisedale Tarn and continuing round first to Tarn Crag, then Falcon Crag. These often give excellent winter climbing but the harder routes can be disappointing in all but the best of years, the 'Cold Climbs' classic of *Chock Gully* being a case in point.

Tarn and Falcon Crags are home to **rare alpine plants**, mostly in the obvious and well-climbed gully-lines, but also at the bases of most climbs and on the buttresses too. This area has recently been surveyed and the results are described as 'impressive' – please help keep it that way by climbing here only in truly frozen conditions.

The crag becomes bigger towards the right-hand end. The routes are described from left to right, the first three gullies starting from a small amphitheatre on the left side of the crag.

Tarn Crag and Falcon Crag

1. Tarn Crag Gully I — I/II
2. Tarn Crag Gully II — I
3. Tarn Crag Gully III — I
4. Dollywaggon Gully — III
5. Dollywaggon Ridge — IV
6. Dollywaggon Chimney — III
7. Falcon Crag Gully — II
8. Chock Gully — IV
9. Dollywaggon Great Chimney — V

Photo: Nick Wharton

Tarn Crag Gully I   120m I/II * ❄

The first gully on the left of the amphitheatre. This narrow gully curves gently to the right, with one small pitch after about 80m.

Tarn Crag Buttress I   120m II * ❄ 1995

This takes the buttress to the right of *Tarn Crag Gully I*. Start up the initial short wall of *Tarn Crag Gully I* and, before the gully proper starts, move right and climb the buttress, keeping to the left side, overlooking the gully.

Tarn Crag Gullies II and III   100m I ❄

Both of these short gullies start from the top of the amphitheatre and give straightforward snow slopes either side of the dividing buttress.

Tarn Crag Buttress II   100m II ❄ 1995

The buttress between Gullies II and III. A steep start easier on the right leads to easier ground.

Peachey's Grand Day Out   100m III ❄ 2010

A variation finish to *Tarn Crag Gully III*. Follow the main gully for about 50m until a shallower gully up the left wall can be taken to a steep rock step turned on the left to reach easier ground.

Dollywaggon Buttress   140m II ❄ 2009

The buttress immediately left of *Dollywaggon Gully* offers exposed climbing.

Dollywaggon Gully   130m III ** ❄ 1936/7

The larger gully to the right of the amphitheatre.
1   15m. The chockstone is passed by a crack on its left side to gain a snow slope.
2   40m. Continue up the snow slope to a steep groove.
3   30m. In 10m the groove leads to another snow slope which is followed to the final pitch.
4   45m. The ice wall on the right leads to further snow and the top.

Dollywaggon Ridge   130m IV (4) ❄ 2010

Climb the ridge between *Dollywaggon Gully* and *Dollywaggon Chimney* starting at a corner on the lower right side and moving up and right until behind a pinnacle at about 15m. The climbing becomes easier above and the ridge broadens out. The saddle behind the pinnacle can also be reached from a corner-groove line about 10m up *Dollywaggon Gully*. Beware loose rock.

TARN CRAG AND FALCON CRAG

Dollywaggon Chimney 130m III

This is the narrow chimney immediately right of the start of *Dollywaggon Gully*.
1   50m. Follow snow to a narrowing chimney pitch.
2   50m. Follow the broader chimney to a headwall.
3   30m. Follow a narrow chimney through the headwall and onto mixed ground to finish.

Right-Hand Finish 80m IV (4) 1991

Start 50m up the chimney where it narrows to a crack.
1   30m. Climb the steepening groove on the right on frozen turf.
2   50m. Finish up mixed ground.

The crag is split by an indefinite gully line round towards the right of the bigger section.

Falcon Crag Gully 220m III *

1+2 80m. Several short ice bulges lead to a snow bay.
3   40m. From the bay follow the gully to another smaller snow bay.
4+5 100m. Climb the gully to finish.

Tic Tac Man 140m IV (4) 1987

A meandering route up the steep buttress left of *Chock Gully* passing through some impressive situations. Start on the left at the base of *Chock Gully*.
1   40m. Trend left to a steep wall past a small sapling to easier ground. Move left along an easy gangway, then up and back right to the base of a steep corner.
2   30m. A traverse right leads into *Chock Gully*. Climb diagonally left up the wall of the gully to gain a ledge above the steep corner. Traverse left to a detached pinnacle. With sufficient snow build-up, it is possible to reach the pinnacle directly from the steep corner.
3   50m. Climb the pinnacle and gain a gangway leading rightwards. Follow this for a few metres to a shallow corner and continue steeply to a second rightward-slanting gangway. This ends in a steep wall above *Chock Gully* and an escape up a shallow weakness to easier ground.
4   20m. More easy ground leads to the top.

Chock Gully 135m IV (4) ** 1936/7

The deeply cut gully blocked higher up by a large chockstone at the right side of the crag overlooking Grisedale. In the right conditions a classic, or with a lean ice coating a difficult challenge. It is usually lean!

1   25m (3). A choice of cracks to the left or the right of the chockstone leads to easy snow.
2   20m (3). A steep but short ice bulge leads to a belay on left.
3   25m (4). Climb to the capstone, arrange gear and pull out leftwards (crux) into the upper part of the gully.
4   55m (3). Awkward steps of ice, unconsolidated snow (worse) or banked out neve (best) leads to the top.

Dollywaggon Great Chimney 100m V (4) ** 🌳 1986

Round the corner to right of *Chock Gully*, the buttress is split by a shallow chimney-line.
1   30m (4). Climb the vegetated narrow gully, just above a ledge. Belay beneath a steep corner-crack on the left.
2   20m (3). Follow the crack, using a jammed flake, to the Birdcage. Move right below the roof and climb through the Skylight. Continue up the easy gully above through a second archway to belay.
3   50m (2). Continue up the gully and buttress above to finish just right of the top of *Chock Gully*.

Pinnacle Climb 80m IV (4) 🌳 2004

Start halfway between *Dollywaggon Great Chimney* on Falcon Crag and *Easy Gully* on Cock Cove Crag.
1   40m (4). Follow turfy ledges and grooves up rightwards until nearly looking over *Easy Gully*, next to a rock pinnacle/spike. Climb the wall behind the pinnacle and ledges above, to a belay.
2   40m (2). Finish easily up the wall.

PATTERDALE AND ADJACENT VALLEYS

Patterdale itself is a poor winter venue, but many of its subsidiary valleys give excellent climbing. Sleet Cove and Link Cove in Deepdale come into condition relatively frequently and offer several fine climbs on a number of crags. As well as more traditional routes such as *Inaccessible Gully* and *Black Crag Icefall* in Dovedale, there are many modern mixed climbs to be found, particularly on the crags of Scrubby and Hutaple.

PATTERDALE – EAST

The routes on the east side of the main valley of Patterdale are described first. Starting in the north, there are two low-lying watercourses which offer good ice climbing in a sustained freeze.

Swarthbeck Gill   120m II
On the east side of Ullswater, this west-facing gill on the western slopes of Arthur's Pike overlooks the lake (NY 453 208). Starting at the low altitude of about 250m, it needs a prolonged frost, so it's worth checking it out with binoculars from across the lake before making the drive round.

To the east of Ullswater, the secluded valley of Bannerdale is accessible from Pooley Bridge. The western slopes of the head of the valley contain a line of crags marked on the map as Heck Crag and Buck Crag (NY 420 151). North-east-facing Buck Crag is split by the obvious **Bannerdale Gully** (130m, II), which gives a pleasant climb passing a couple of chockstones.

Rampsgill Head Crag

NY 443 129   Altitude 670m   North-west facing

Rampsgill Head, on the old Roman road of High Street, has a broken crag below its north-west face, overlooking the valley of Ramps Gill. Isolated buttresses are scattered across the hillside just north of the main summit. The most significant of these is visible from the approach path as it rounds The Knott. From this point the

Lake District Winter Climbs

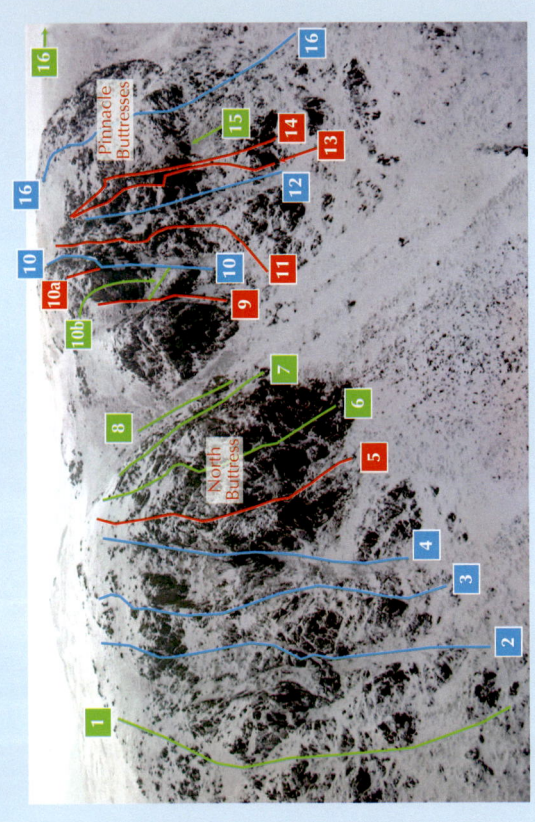

Rampsgill Head Crag

1	Easy Buttress	I/II
2	Umbrella Gully	II/III
3	Gendarmerie	III
4	Left Gully	III
5	Blow Out (approx. line)	IV
6	Buttress Groove	II
7	Right Gully	II
8	Wind Up	I/II
9	North Gully	IV
10	Central Gully	III
10a	Central Gully North Pinnacle Exit	IV
10b	Escape Exit	II
11	Central Ridge	IV
12	South Gully	III
13	Friends Above	V
14	South Pinnacle Ridge	IV
15	South South Gully	II
16	Windy Buttress	III
17	Original Route	II

buttress looks like an isolated top connected to the main mass of the mountain by a col; this is 200m past the summit of the mountain. Closer inspection reveals that it is in fact made up of three pinnacles with impressive gullies between them that provide some excellent traditional mountaineering routes about 100m long. Beware of loose blocks and flakes.

From the car park in the village of Hartsop, follow the bridleway to Hayeswater and continue along it, up the hillside to the north of the reservoir, to where the path curves south round The Knott. At this point the buttresses can be clearly seen. Strike east to the summit of Rampsgill Head. The main Pinnacle Buttress is 200m to the north and is reached after a scramble down to the col between it and the main mountain (1hr 30mins). Take care on the final **descent** by keeping on the right side (facing out) to avoid steep rocks to the left.

The first route is separate from the others on the most southerly buttress immediately below the summit. The top of the buttress is marked by a large cairn located about 20m north of the smaller summit cairn and at a slightly lower elevation on the Ramps Gill side of the hill.

Southern Buttress

The most southerly buttress has a steep wall at its base and is split by a large rambling ledge system, above which are easy turfy rocks that can be climbed anywhere at Grade II.

Original Route   90m II 2005
You've guessed it – the first route on the crag.
1   50m. Climb an easy turfy groove to the right of the steep lower section of buttress. Belay at the back of the rambling ledge.
2   40m. Continue up the middle of the back wall in the same line.

Windy Buttress   95m III (3) 2005
The narrow buttress some 200m left of *Original Route* and immediately right of *South South Gully*.
1   45m. Climb a shallow left-trending groove to a rock wall.
2   25m (3). Climb the wall by a groove (the right-hand of two), then another short wall.
3   25m. Finish easily.

Pinnacle Buttresses

The three pinnacles are named South, Central and North. The col behind Central Pinnacle is a convenient place to leave sacks, as many routes end back at this point. The best **descent** from here is to the north, past North Pinnacle and a gully to its north and past another smaller buttress to a broad gully of snow/very loose scree. Descend this and contour back under the crag.

South South Gully   90m II 2005
The gully at the right-hand side of South Pinnacle contains a couple of small steps which may bank out. With care it makes a descent from the col behind the pinnacles.

South Pinnacle Ridge   90m IV (6) ** 2005
A climb up South Pinnacle via its right side, passing a large conspicuous rock – the Diving Board.
1   40m (3). Climb a prominent groove in the middle of the base of the pinnacle and follow easy ground to belay where the buttress steepens.
2   50m (6). Climb a groove on the right of the buttress, formed by the right wall and the Diving Board. At the top of the groove climb up the right wall of the pinnacle on cracks and turf with some awkward bridging moves to gain the crest of the ridge. The obvious shorter deep groove just to the left may look inviting but isn't. Once on the ridge follow it to the top of the Pinnacle.

It's not all over yet: a short abseil into the gully between the two pinnacles will allow the *Central Pinnacle* to be traversed and downclimbed back to the col. If you're careful you can flick off your abseil sling!

Friends Above   100m V (7) * 2005
This takes the prominent corner-line on the left side of the buttress, halfway up South Pinnacle.
1   30m (2). From the foot of *South Gully*, climb up onto the turfy crest of the lower portion of the pinnacle and continue to belay at the base of the groove formed by the Diving Board.
2   20m (7). Climb up and traverse left along the quartz ledge at the base of the steep buttress. Hard committing moves gain the base of the corner on the left side of the buttress. Move further left to a sheltered belay ledge.
3   50m (7). Move back right into the corner and follow it with difficult climbing and awkward protection to good turf at the top, if you can reach it. Continue up the pinnacle, keeping to its left side, to a short 5m corner near the top which provides an avoidable sting in the tail.

RAMPSGILL HEAD CRAG

South Gully 100m III (3) 2005
The obvious gully to the left of South Pinnacle. A tree at half-height makes a good belay at the start of the difficulties.
1   40m (2). Follow the obvious gully easily to where it steepens just below the tree.
2   50m (3). Surmount the steep wall, passing the tree, into a narrower cleft. Climb out across the left wall on turf to where the gully widens. There are two possible exits from here. The steeper right-hand one is the one you want. Climb a vague open corner to the narrow gap between South and Central Pinnacles. Either climb through the chockstones at the top and down the other side into the top of *South South Gully* or, more aesthetically, climb onto Central Pinnacle on the left and belay.
3   10m (3). Climb over the top of the Central Pinnacle and down the back to the col.

South Gully Left-Hand 60m III (4) 2005
Follow the first pitch of *South Gully* to the tree belay.
2   30m (3). Climb past the tree, then either to the back of the narrow gully and up past jammed blocks or up the turfy left wall of the gully just beyond the tree. Where the gully widens above climb the left exit to a wall/buttress about 10m below the narrow chimney on *Central Ridge*.
3   30m (4). From the belay several exits are possible (mentioned in the *Central Pinnacle Gully* description). On the first ascent the centre of the buttress to the right of the belay was climbed to the top of the pinnacle.

Central Pinnacle Gully 90m III (4) 2005
From the base of *South Gully*, a shallow gully line runs leftwards up the side of Central Pinnacle. Follow this without difficulty until it ends at a ledge which is the junction with *Central Ridge*. Traverse awkwardly 2m right below a rock wall and continue up the side of the wall to join the upper portion of *South Gully Left-Hand*, about 10m below the narrow chimney on *Central Ridge*. From here a variety of finishes are possible. Either finish up the chimney as for *Central Ridge* (climb the centre of the buttress above) or climb up chockstones to the right of the buttress and then continue up to the summit.

Central Ridge 90m IV (5) ** 2005
An entertaining route. The upper section overlooks *Central Gully*.
1   20m (2). From the foot of *Central Gully/North Gully*, climb diagonally rightwards onto the turfy ridge and up to a small rocky wall.

2   40m (5). Climb up a groove to the top of a flake (5m), then make moves over a sloping rock ledge to turf. Climb a wide groove to another ledge with a spike runner and make delicate moves up a shallow corner to a substantial ledge with a large block on its right-hand side and a spike protruding out from the face at right angles. Chimney up behind the block and move up onto a ridge that is followed to the base of a narrow chimney on the left side of the pinnacle.

3   30m (4). Climb the chimney and a turfy groove overlooking *Central Gully*. Easy ground then leads to the top of the pinnacle.

Central Gully   90m III (4) * 2005

The obvious gully to the left of Central Pinnacle finishes at the col.

1   50m (3). Start up a shallow turfy groove/depression on the left of Central Pinnacle. After about 30m, a steeper step gains access to the well-defined gully which has some impressive walls. Pass another steep step and belay about 10m above this below the prominent large chockstone blocking the gully.

2   40m (4). Climb up a groove on the left of the chockstone and step across rightwards back into the base of the gully below some more jammed chockstones. Continue up the main gully-line which curves to the right to finish on the col.

Escape Exit   20m II ** 2005

Just below the second steep step (10m below the chockstone), climb the turfy left wall of the gully to easy ground and traverse left into the easy top section of *North Gully*.

Central Gully North Pinnacle Exit   40m IV (5) 2005

From the top of pitch one of *Central Gully*, pass the chockstone and, where the main gully goes up the right exit, take the corner-line on the left to finish on North Pinnacle. There are some loose flakes on the walls and the lower half is poorly protected.

North Gully   90m IV (5) *** 2005

The obvious gully to the left of North Pinnacle. The top pitch is an impressive narrow leaning cleft.

1   60m (2). Climb the easy turfy gully to the left of North Pinnacle, passing one steeper section, to belay at the base of the slanting cleft at the top.

2   30m (5). Thrutch up the cleft with an excursion onto the left wall at an obvious ledge where it narrows (several chockstones for protection – take at least five large slings). Belay at the buttress on the right at the top of the gully.

North Buttress

To the left of the wide **descent** gully (facing in) is a vegetated buttress. From the bottom of the descent, a gully containing a chockstone near its top is clearly visible on the right-hand side of the buttress (*Right Gully*). A traverse around the base of the buttress reveals another gully (*Left Gully*) with a short pitch up a series of chockstones about 40m up the easy lower gully.

Wind Up   60m I/II 2005
The shallow right-trending gully to the right of *Right Gully* and just left of the descent gully.

Right Gully   50m II 2005
From the base of the descent gully, climb the obvious gully on the right of the buttress to a chockstone. Surmount this and continue easily to the top.

Buttress Groove   50m II 2005
To the left of *Right Gully* is a faint vegetated groove running up the front of the buttress. Climb this to easy ground and pass a series of small walls to belay just left of the finish of *Right Gully*.

Blow Out   90m IV (3) 2005
On the North Buttress between *Buttress Groove* and *Left Gully* is a large vegetated depression.
1   45m. Climb the depression to a big shattered spike (hard to see from below), then slant leftwards to belays.
2   45m. Continue in the same line passing left of a protruding buttress and finish up a vague ridge.

Left Gully   80m III (4) * 2005
The most prominent gully on the left side of the buttress.
1   30m. Climb the easy turfy lower gully to belay at the base of the steep rock pitch where the gully walls narrow.
2   50m (4). Climb the chockstones on the right side of the gully (crux), then continue easily, passing two short steeper sections and belay at the top, just after a narrowing of the gully walls.

Gendarmerie   90m III 2005
Between *Left Gully* and *Umbrella Gully* is a shallow buttress with a prominent gendarme near its top.

Lake District Winter Climbs

1   35m. Climb the buttress just right of its crest to a spike belay.
2   45m. Continue just left of the crest. Pass immediately left of the gendarme and belay at the col.
3   10m. Finish leftwards.

Umbrella Gully   95m II/III 2005
The next shallow gully left of *Left Gully*.
1   35m. Follow the left-trending gully to a chockstone.
2   45m. Pass the chockstone on its left and follow the gully as it bends rightwards. Shortly before it peters out, climb straight up to a belay.
3   15m. Finish by a slim groove 7m left of the gendarme of the last route.

Easy Buttress   125m I/II 2005
Left of *Umbrella Gully*, start at a lower level and climb the easy grassy buttress in three pitches taking the easiest line.

Col Gully lies immediately left of *Easy Buttress* and gives a very easy **descent** from the col between Rampsgill Head and High Raise.

Threshthwaite Cove

NY 424 102   *Altitude 770m*   *North facing*

This cove on the east side of the valley is more famous for its rock climbing, but its pleasant isolated gully gives an enjoyable mountain day if combined with a return along the ridge over Hartsop Dodd.

Threshthwaite Gully   170m III * 1995
From the village of Hartsop, make the long trek to the head of the cove. The buttress to the west of the col can be clearly seen on the approach and is split by a deep gully. A chockstone guards the entrance, after which easier climbing leads to a steep 15m ice pitch about halfway up. Above this, 30m of easier-angled ice and then scrambling, lead to the ridge and Stony Cove Pike.

Patterdale – West

In the north is *Aira Force,* just above the western shore of the lake. The one solitary climb on the west side of the main valley, but that is more than made up for by what can be found in the side valleys.

Aira Force   25m III pre-1962
On the west shore of the lake, Aira Beck flows into Ullswater just north of the junction of the A592 Penrith road and the A5091 Keswick road. About 500m upstream from the lake is the famous waterfall at (NY 399 205). There is parking at the road's closest point to the fall. When frozen, the fall is approached by a narrow short gorge. However, being south-facing and at an altitude of only 200m, the force seldom freezes. When it does the main difficulty is usually staying out of the water still coming down.

Glencoyne

NY 359 187   Altitude 620m   East facing

This idyllic little valley runs west from the shores of Ullswater to Stybarrow Dodd. The headwall of the valley contains three short buttresses offering easy grade climbs in a tranquil setting. The headwall has been known to avalanche so **beware**.

From the car park at NY 386 188 take the track past the farm and up past a row of miners cottages on the south side of the valley. Once into the upper valley leave the path, which is heading over to Greenside and head directly for the back of the valley. A spoil heap on the north side is located below the North Buttress.

South Buttress

The most southerly of the buttresses doesn't get the sun in winter so retains snow well. It offers a Grade I snow gully on its right side and a narrower Grade II gully on its left.

Southern Buttress   40m II 2010
The front of the buttress rises to a small pinnacle, which can also be gained from snowy chimneys rising from the gullies at either side, or started from the lowest point of the buttress passing the pinnacle before heading up the buttress by the easiest line.

Lake District Winter Climbs

Headwall Groove 40m III 2010

Above and right of the pinnacle a prominent groove cuts through the small but steep headwall on the right side of the buttress. Start up easy snow slopes from the right-hand gully to a thrutch up the groove leading to the crest of the buttress.

Al Hinkes explores the Patterdale Pillar (photo: Mike Parsons)

Central Buttress

The central buttress midway between the North and South Buttress. The buttress has a Grade I snow gully on its right and a wider easier angled gully on its left. The left side of the buttress contains a distinctive V-groove. Towards the top of the left-hand snow gully is a 30m wall which can become thinly iced.

A faint fault on its left side offers Grade III while 5m further right is a thinner Grade III (4). The snow ramp under the wall furnishes the final pitch (II).

Central Groove   50m IV 2010
The prominent V-groove on the left side of the buttress. Access it from 10m up the left-hand gully. Easy turfy walls lead into the groove and a hard exit.

Central Buttress   50m II 2010
From the lowest point of the buttress take a faint depression up the left side to weave through heathery ledges to the top.

Right Ridge   50m II 2010
From the lowest point climb the ridge overlooking the right-hand snow gully.

North Buttress

Located about 50m above the spoil heap at the north side of the headwall lies a small heathery buttress.

Climb a faint heathery groove to the right of a vague arete in the centre of the buttress (20m II)

Trough Head

NY 386 146   ALTITUDE 480M   *EAST FACING*

Patterdale Pillar   40m IV (5) 2010
An impressive free-standing ice pillar forms at the head of Trough Head to the south of Glenamara Park and can be seen from the road.

The easiest approach is to follow the wall round from the Patterdale Hotel to the back of Trough Head, about 30mins. The fall is visible to the south east of Black Crag. Follow continuous steep ice with a free-standing cigar in its lower section. This leads into a groove-ramp and the top.

GRISEDALE

The valley of Grisedale, leading off Patterdale to its west, gives access to the crags and coves on Dollywaggon Pike and Nethermost Pike, though they are more easily and more regularly accessed from Dunmail Raise or The Swirls car park on the Thirlmere side to the west: these are covered in the Helvellyn section. However, St Sunday Crag (found on the southern flank of Grisedale) is best approached from Patterdale.

St Sunday Crag

NY 368 139   ALTITUDE 600M   *NORTH-WEST FACING*

This crag high up on the southern side of Grisedale offers panoramic views into the Helvellyn coves. The crag has four main gullies and several minor ones not worth detailed descriptions. Many of these routes were done during snowy winters in the 1960s and the gullies particularly do not usually receive the build-up of snow necessary to give them complete cover. This has lead to a decline in the crag's winter popularity although the ridges can still offer interesting sport.

Just north of Patterdale village a side road, becoming a private road and then a farm track, leads into Grisedale. NB There is no parking available on this road. Follow the track up the Grisedale valley until a wooden bridge is reached. A good view of the crag and its gullies is available from here. Slog up the hillside from here to the crag. Alternatively, if you know the lay-out of the crag, follow the zigzag path up from the end of the Elmhow plantation and traverse right to the crag.

Directly above the bridge is *West Chockstone Gully*, with *Y Gully* 100m to the left, in the centre of the crag. The left branch of *Y Gully* joins *Pillar Gully* at half-height. A further 50m left of *Y Gully* is *Pillar Gully*, separated from the former by the almost detached pillar. About 170m left again is *East Chockstone Gully*, the most interesting of the gullies.

West Chockstone Gully   70m I/II
When in condition this is a steep snow gully with a small rock step at half-height. Near the top of the gully it is possible to move left over the rib into *Y Gully*. The ridge to the left can give an interesting winter climb in its own right.

Y Gully (Right Fork)   65m I
When containing enough snow this is useful as a means of **descent**, providing the cornice at the top can be passed. The left fork of the gully leads into *Pillar Gully*.

St Sunday Crag

Boneyard Wall   42m III (4) * 1963
A good climb. About 35m up the right branch of *Y Gully* is a big right-angled corner above a triangle of ribs and snow-covered grass. Follow the grassy snow ledge down left for 10m and belay where the ledge ends beneath an exposed wall.
1   20m (4). Climb diagonally left across the wall to reach a flat ledge at the base of a clean-cut corner. Climb the iced slab on the right and belay at the top of the corner.
2   22m (3). Move back right and climb the overhang. Turn a second overhang on the left and move up over a nose to easier ground.

Pillar Buttress   50m II/III 2012
A pleasant ramble following a series of easy vegetated grooves up the centre of the pillar. Choose a line to the left of centre that suits your standard. Finish along the crest of the pillar into *Pillar Gully* and follow this or the vegetated rocks above.

Pillar Gully   75m I
The straightforward snow gully to the left of the pillar.

Flaky Rib   140m III (5) 2012
Follows the line of the summer climb *Dimanche* and then takes the continuation rib to the top. Start at the extreme right end of the Tiger Banded Rocks just left of a miniature gully.
1   25m (3/4). The initial steepening contains a turfy groove, which was unfrozen, so the rib at the extreme right end of the Tiger Banded Rocks was followed to a ledge.
2   55m (5). Cross the shallow gully on the right to the skyline rib and climb it through a short well-protected steep grooved section (crux) to a good platform.
3   30m (3). Continue up the groove above over a short steep wall to a ledge below a 3m steep wall; loose blocks on the ledge.
4   30m (3). Climb the short wall and continue up the knife-edged arete above. Only scrambling remains.

East Chockstone Gully   70m I/II
The most interesting of the gullies. There are often two rock steps low down; their difficulty varies with the snow build-up.

Slab Route Buttress   160m IV (6) ** 2010
This route climbs the summer routes, *Slab Route* and *Slab Route Continuation*. Start at the lowest point of the buttress to the left of *East Chockstone Gully*.

Looking down Pinnacle Ridge St Sunday Crag (photo: Paddy Cave)

1   55m (6). Climb turfy ledges to a rock slab split by two cracks. Climb the right-hand of the two cracks to the top of the slab. Move leftwards and climb a groove and continuation chimney with a jammed flake in it. Belay on ledges above this. Care is required with a little loose rock at the top of the chimney.
2   45m (3). Climb up rightwards over turfy ledges to a left-trending groove. Follow this to easier ground above. Belay below the rocky buttress.
3   30m (6). Climb a crack on the left of the buttress through a bulge to a ledge. Climb the short slab on the right into a short groove. Follow this to easier ground above. Belay at a large boulder below the final rock buttress.
4   30m (4). Climb the nose of the buttress above. From here 60 metres of easy ground leads to the top of the crag.

Pinnacle Ridge   180m II * 1977
About 180m left of *East Chockstone Gully*. Follow the line of the serrated arete to the summit. An interesting and enjoyable climb, though all difficulties can be turned. If you have taken them all direct award yourself a Grade III.

Girdle Traverse   700m III 1978
The Lake District's answer to Scotland's Creag Meagaidh Crab Crawl?! A right-to-left girdle of the complete crag. Starting up *West Chockstone Gully*, and at approximately half-height, it follows an obvious line until past *East Chockstone Gully*. Here mixed ground is followed to the area of the summer routes *Chockstone Gully Rib* and *Slab Route*. Under suitable conditions it is possible to climb almost anywhere on the crag at Grade III.

DEEPDALE

Many of the routes in Deepdale come into condition quickly after the onset of a cold spell and this makes it an excellent centre for winter climbing. The grassy truncated spur of Greenhow End divides the head of the valley, with the high hanging valley of Link Cove on its left. Link Cove contains the broken Hart Crag on its left and the more impressive Scrubby Crag on its right. The major branch of Deepdale, to the right of Greenhow End, is Sleet Cove and this contains the extensive Hutaple Crag and the smaller Black Buttress.

There is parking by the telephone box at Bridgend (NY 399 144) on the main Ullswater road, A592. If this is full, a larger car park lies 1km to the south near a sharp bend in the road. A good path leads initially past farms, then over the valley bottom, to below Greenhow End. For Hutaple Crag (about 750m

Deepdale

1 Step Gully   II/III   **2** Greenhow Gully   III   **3** Link Cove Gills   II and III

Hart Crag

further up on the right), cross the stream and, keeping it on your right, climb the hillside, past the slabs of Mart Crag. Link Cove and the climbs on Greenhow End, can be approached by a choice of frozen gills that give good climbs in their own right.

Sleet Cove and Link Cove (including Scrubby and Hutaple Crags) are home to **rare alpine plants**. The bits away from the crags provide even better homes, some of the crumbly easier gullies being rich with rare plants – please climb here only in truly frozen conditions.

The first climbs are two gills on the left (NY 374 122, Alt 400m), just before Greenhow End, which make a more interesting way of reaching Link Cove or the climbs on Greenhow End.

Link Cove Gill (Left Branch) 70m III
Less often in climbable condition than its neighbour due to its enclosed position, this popular scramble is nevertheless worthwhile when ice does form.

Link Cove Gill (Right Branch) 60m II
The more open of the two streams. An initial short steep ice pitch is followed by further easy-angled ice that peters out almost level with the start of the climbs on Greenhow End. There is another fall of a similar standard further up the stream. Often in condition.

Link Cove

Altitude 700m   *East facing*

The following climbs and crags are all in Link Cove, the prominent hanging valley to the left of Greenhow End when approaching up Deepdale. On entering the cove, a series of short but interesting icefalls form over a rock band on the right. Scrubby Crag is the obvious crag high up on the right of the cove, to the right of Link Hause, while to the left are the broken and scattered buttresses of Hart Crag.

Hart Crag

NY 370 114   Altitude 700m   *North facing*

This is the rambling collection of broken buttresses to the left of the col of Link Hause below the summit of Hart Crag. High elevation and a northerly aspect make for the most reliable and quick-forming ice on the Fairfield massif. Several good ice pitches form which may be linked together as you please – the routes described make the best of them.

Left Runnel   80m III (3) 🌱
The first shallow gully-line on the left is usually water ice with two steep sections.

Hart Crag Ice Falls   110m III (4) * 🌱
The series of icefalls to the right is linked by mixed turf climbing.
1   30m. Climb a short icefall to easier ground and continue to a steep wall.
2   30m. More ice leads to mixed ground. Belay left of the next icefall (pegs useful).
3   30m. Climb the icefall trending right.
4   20m. Step left and climb a groove and another steep icefall to the top.

Cold Lazarus   170m III (3) ** 🌱
Located on the central and highest buttresses, a series of stepped ice pitches form with good ledges and belays between each pitch. The difficulties increase with height. Start below a broad ice groove 100m to the right of the previous routes.
1   60m. Climb the groove to a broad ledge.
2   30m. Traverse right and climb a shallow chimney to ledges then go up right to belay below an ice runnel.
3   30m. Climb the runnel to belay on a block on the right.
4   50m. Easier climbing to the top.

Variation   IV (4)
A steep icefall often forms to the left of pitch 2 and is reach by traversing left from the top of the shallow chimney.

Short Chute   50m III (3) *
Right again is a prominent steep buttress. An excellent icefall often forms on the right of this. Climb the fall which narrows into a chimney at the top.

Six metres to the right again, an ice smear forms (IV 5).

Scrubby Crag

NY 367 115 *Altitude 710m* *South-east facing*

A good concentration of interesting technical routes are found on this crag, plus the more traditional *Pendulum Gully* on its right edge. Its elevated position means the latter is often 'in' and the mixed climbs are soon do-able in a cold snap. A more prolonged freeze allows ice smears to form on the main crag which, when complete, give some fine hard routes.

The routes are described from left to right. The prominent corner-line at the left end of the crag is *Juniper Crack*. The first climb takes the buttress to the left of this but starts from the base of the corner. The safest **descent** is from Link Hause (to the left of the crag when facing it).

Wall Climb   75m IV (4) 1987

A steep route up the buttress to the left of the prominent corner of *Juniper Crack*.
1   25m (4). From the base of the corner climb grooves on the left to a ledge and climb the wall above to a juniper-covered ledge and large flake runner. Follow the leftwards-rising crack awkwardly to a small stance where the crack straightens.
2   20m (4). Ascend the wall above for 3m until it is possible to traverse right and round a corner into a bay. From the back of the bay climb the corner to a stance beneath a corner-crack.
3   30m (3). Follow the obvious right-trending ramp-line at first then go straight up.

Juniper Crack   70m V (6) ** 2003

The obvious corner at the left end of the crag is a mossy and damp Hard Severe in summer: it makes a far better winter route.
1   25m (6). Climb the obvious corner to a stance below where the upper wall steepens.
2   45m (5). Move up the corner a few metres until it steepens then move left onto the wall and traverse left over blocks to a pinnacle on the arete and a ledge. It is possible to split the pitch here; otherwise continue up a crack then move to a ledge round the rib and finish up the corner-crack.

Long Ledge Entry and Exit   80m V (6) ** 1972

The earliest of the mixed routes on the crag offers superb climbing in its upper corner. Start as for *Juniper Crack*.
1   20m. Climb most of the first pitch of *Juniper Crack*, up the corner to a block belay.

Scrubby Crag

1 Wall Climb — IV
2 Juniper Crack — V
3 Long Ledge
  Entry and Exit — V
4 Heorot — VI
5 Midnight Special — V
6 Ringway Finish — V
7 Grendel — VI
8 Firedragon Finish — IV
9 Ginny Clegg — V
10 Pendulum Ridge — III
11 Pendulum Gully — II/III

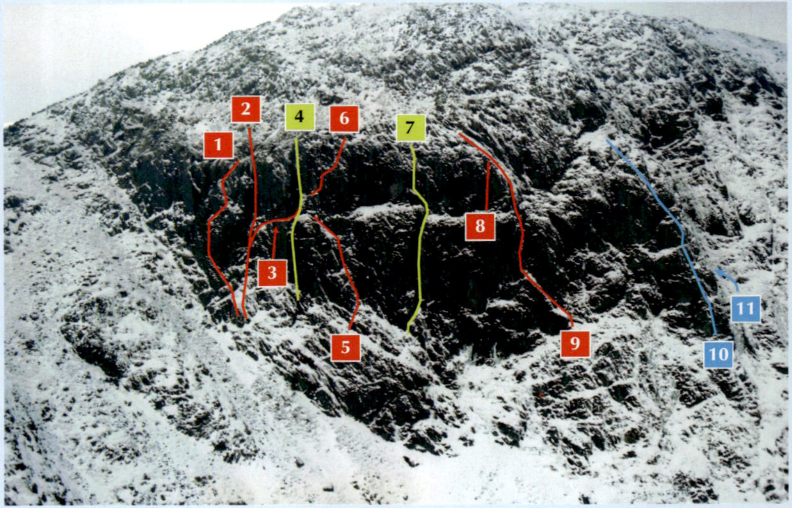

2   30m. From the belay, traverse the wall on the right and move up to an overhang and peg runner. Move back down, teeter right to an icicle and continue moving right to the welcoming *Long Ledge*.
3   30m. Finish up the steep dirty corner above, the top pitch of *Heorot*. This corner pitch can be thickly-iced and offer easy climbing protected by ice screws, or can be a thin smear of ice on one wall which is hard and poorly protected in its lower half. Either way the climbing is brilliant.

Heorot   70m VI (7) *** ❦ 1987

This connects to the prominent right-facing corner-line high on the crag, above and right of *Juniper Crack*, originally climbed as the exit pitch of *Long Ledge*. The first pitch is thin and sustained; the second is brilliant. One of the best routes in the cove.
1   40m. This pitch follows a very shallow groove line, which is not obvious, but is directly below the corner-line of the top pitch. From the left end of the ledge below the corner, below a flake, climb the right-hand of the two grooves to the obvious top corner.
2   30m. The obvious iced corner above. Exquisite!

Between the prominent corner of *Heorot* and the deep groove line of *Grendel* to its right, the wall is crossed by a leftward-slanting ramp-line leading to the top pitch of *Heorot*. This is *Midnight Special*.

Midnight Special   70m V (5) * ❦ 1986

A good mixed route that is often in condition. Start about 20m right of *Heorot*.
1   40m. The left-slanting ramp-line is gained from well to the right. Climb the ramp-line to a ledge and traverse this leftwards to the corner of *Heorot*.
2   30m. If you haven't done it yet, finish up the top corner of *Heorot*.

Ringway Finish   40m V (5) 1995

For those who've already climbed the top corner of *Heorot*: from the ledge move right for 8m to follow a steep arete to the top.

Grendel   90m VI (7) *** ❦ 1991

The fine groove right of the centre of the crag ices up in winter to give a superb route. The winter route climbs the main groove to *Long Ledge* before traversing left to exit up the top groove of the summer route *Sennapod*, which ices up more readily than the summer finish.

1   45m (7). Gain the pedestal at the foot of the corner-groove. Move left to easier ground to enter the main groove. Follow this until it is blocked by an overhang at the top that forces moves right to the arete. Follow this to *Long Ledge*.
2   45m (5). Move leftwards up a step to the upper ledge. Climb the wall for a few metres to a ramp-line running left to an iced corner and follow this to the top. A poorly-protected pitch. The *Firedragon Finish*, the last corner on *Long Ledge* approximately 10m to the right, has been used and comes into condition readily.

Ginny Clegg   105m VI (5) ❦ 1987

About 20m right of *Grendel* is a vegetated bay leading to a steep wall below the *Long Ledge*. This climb takes a meandering but central line up the large bay starting just left of the crag's lowest point and winds its way up to the higher rock buttress – really a winter version of the summer route *Firedragon* which goes up the back of the bay.

1   30m (3). Take as direct a line as possible up icefalls and turf ledges.
2   15m (4). Head leftwards to an ice pillar with runners in a bay on the right. Climb the pillar and belay to the right.
3   30m (5). A poorly-protected pitch, made more serious by its traverse. Traverse left for 15m and move precariously around a corner onto a ramp. Follow the ramp to belay on the obvious large flake above.
4   30m (3). Move left and up with a difficult move onto *Long Ledge*. Follow this to easy ground.

Firedragon Finish   20m IV (4) 1995

From *Long Ledge*, follow a line of turf to the right of the last corner at the right end of the *Ledge*. The summer line goes up the corner.

Pendulum Ridge   120m III (4) *** 1985

This takes the right-hand turfy arete of the main crag overlooking *Pendulum Gully* to its right. Start to the left of a prominent overhang low down. The initial moves up the short wall are difficult after which things tend to get easier as progress is made up the ridge.

Pendulum Gully   180m II/III *

The obvious gully defining the right end of the crag. A short ice pitch near the start of the gully leads to easy snow. The gully gradually steepens and splits. Follow the right fork to another ice pitch which leads to the top.

GREENHOW END

Halcyon   80m III 1991

Where the gully forks take the left branch, running back behind the main crag.

Above and right of *Pendulum Gully*, set back at a higher level than the main crag, is a series of broken buttresses mainly separated from each other by easy-angled snow gullies. Generally the buttresses do not give many continuous lines and they can be climbed just about anywhere at Grade III. The following route has been recorded as a sample.

Tongue and Groove   170m II/III ♣ 2003

About 20m right of *Pendulum Gully* is a buttress with an easy open gully to its right. This takes the shallow gully-line up the buttress.

1   20m. Climb the buttress easily for about 20m and then veer left towards *Pendulum Gully* into another shallow gully line.
2   50m. Follow this gully which takes a straight line running parallel with *Pendulum Gully* but about 10m to the right. Run the rope out of the gully across some easy ground, keeping left to maintain a parallel course with *Pendulum Gully*, to a spike belay in a small ampitheatre.
3   50m. Continue straight up the gully to a poor belay in a second small ampitheatre. From here it is possible to traverse right for 10m back onto the buttress.
4   50m. Either climb straight up the corner or a make a small zigzag back into the gully (crux), where it is blocked by several large flat rocks. Pass these (may bank over in heavy snow) to finish.

The rocky mass of Greenhow End separates Link Cove from Sleet Cove.

Greenhow End ♣

NY 370 120   ALTITUDE 600M   NORTH-EAST FACING

This large vegetated cliff is rather broken but does possess two interesting gullies. *Step Gully* is a line slanting left from broken ground below the centre of the buttress and provides a pleasant way into Link Cove and the crags there, whilst *Greenhow Gully* takes a rake-line running diagonally rightwards. The routes are described from left to right.

Step Gully   65m II/III *

Follow a leftward-slanting gully from the centre of the crag. Climb to the gully and follow it over several short ice pitches until easier snow is reached. Belay as required.

LAKE DISTRICT WINTER CLIMBS

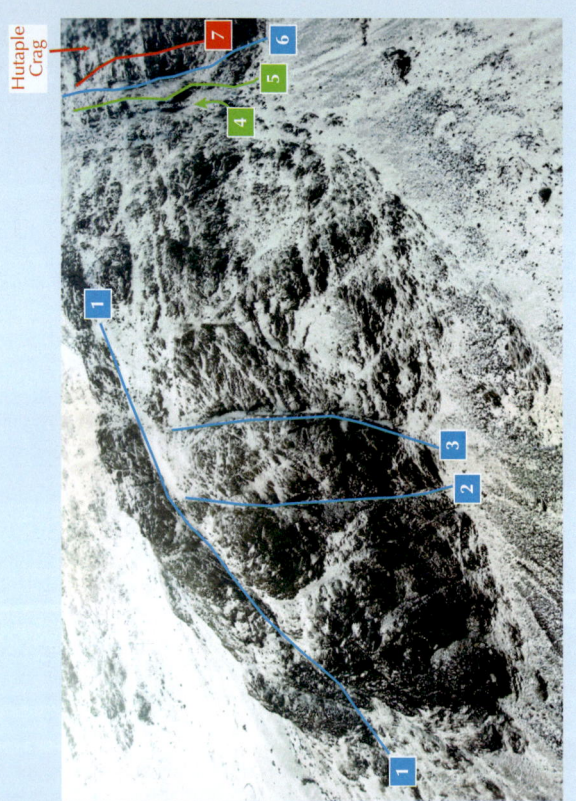

Greenhow End

1 Greenhow Gully	III
2 Deepdale Gully	III
3 Central Gully	III
4 East Hutaple Gully	II
5 The Memo	II
6 East Hutaple Groove	II/III
7 Scorpion	IV

GREENHOW END

Right Wall   35m IV
From about halfway up the gully, icefalls form on the right wall in a good season. Follow these to broken easier ground above or traverse off left when the angle eases.

Greenhow Gully   100m III (4) * 1960
Starting right of centre this follows a rightward-slanting diagonal line.
1   30m (4). Gain and follow the narrow chimney/gully, passing a small ice bulge.
2   25m. Easier ground leads to a chockstone.
3   15m (2). Pass the chockstone by bridging moves to an awkward landing above.
4   30m. Either pass the next small chockstone on the left or take the slab on the right and continue to the top.

Variation Finish   III 2003
4   40m (4). Avoid the easy finish by entertaining mixed climbing up the tiered left wall of the upper gully.

SLEET COVE

Sleet Cove lies to the right of Greenhow End. About 100m right from the lowest point of Greenhow End is the first of two gullies.

Deepdale Gully   100m III
This contains several ice pitches.
1   20m. Follow the gully up to a chockstone which is passed on the right.
2   30m. Easy ground leads to a steepening in the gully.
3   25m. The steep chimney leads to a belay ledge.
4   25m. Easier snow leads to the top.

Central Gully   80m III ❄
Another worthwhile gully: it lies 30m right of *Deepdale Gully*.
1   25m. A small ice pitch leads to steep snow and turf which is followed to a fork in the gully.
2   20m. Follow the left branch passing slabby ground to belay below a large chockstone.
3   35m. Take the chockstone on the left and follow the gully bed passing further small chockstone and chimney pitches to the top.

The buttresses to either side of *Central Gully* can be climbed at Grade II/III and provide a useful escape if the gully is not in condition.

Hutaple Crag 🌿

NY 367 120   Altitude 640m   *North-west facing*

This large rambling crag is over 150m high and sits in a prime position in the cove. The crag is bounded by *East Hutaple Gully* on its left and *West Gully* to its right and is split by the prominent line of *Curving Gully*. To the left of *Curving Gully*, *The Amphitheatre* is a steep open corner above vegetated slabs. A series of ledges run across the top of the crag and must be climbed/scrambled over before making a descent. The best **descent** is on the right of the crag.

The routes are described from left to right.

East Hutaple Gully   100m II

This is really two parallel gullies very close together giving only small ice pitches; climb where it looks best. The turfy buttress dividing the two gullies also gives good climbing (II).

Devious Exit   25m IV 2003

From the bay below the twin ice pitches in *East Hutaple Gully*, climb out left on a snow and turf ramp-line to a horizontal traverse which leads to a belay on the edge of another gully (the right branch of *Central Gully*). Finish easily up this.

The Memo   100m II 🌿 2006

A line up the turfy easy-angled wall on the right-hand side of *East Hutaple Gully*, between the *Gully* and the *Groove*.

Follow the wall on the right-hand side of *East Hutaple Gully*. The route steepens at mid-height and can be easily joined there from the gully. From this point, 60m of steep heather and turf lead to a short rock corner. Interest is maintained and warthogs are recommended. Easier ground above leads to the top.

East Hutaple Groove   140m II/III ** 1986

A good climb when in condition. Start just right of *East Hutaple Gully* at a clean steep buttress.
1   50m. Take the easiest line up the iced slabs to a steep terrace below the left-hand side of the buttress proper.
2   50m. Wide iced slabs to the left of the steep buttress gradually steepen towards the headwall. Traverse right to a block belay on the terrace.

Hutaple Crag

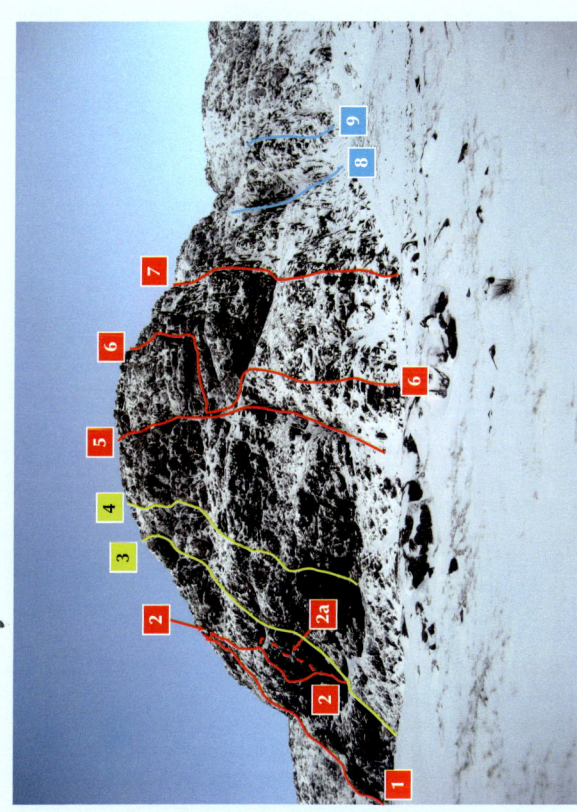

#	Route	Grade
1	East Wall Route	IV
2	Sleet Wall	V
2a	Sleet Wall – Variation Start	V
3	The Amphitheatre	VIII
4	Full Frontal Activity	VII
5	Curving Gully	IV
6	West Hutaple Variations	III/IV
7	West Hutaple Edge	IV
8	West Hutaple Gully	II/III
9	Far West Rib	III

Photo: Nick Wharton

3   40m. Either return back left into the gully and finish up this or climb steep mixed ground on the right of the belay.

Scorpion   120m IV (5) ** 1997
The left-facing corner-cleft high on the left side of the buttress.
1   40m (3). Climb the iced slabs of *East Hutaple Groove* pitch 1 to belay where *East Hutaple Groove* goes up the left side of the crag.
2   40m (3). Traverse rightwards 10m to the end of the large ledge and climb the obvious chimney, passing several ledges, to belay below a steep headwall.
3   40m (5). The crux, where it should be gives powerful but well-protected climbing in an impressive position. Climb the steep wall, past the chockstone, to a thread belay and easier ground. Belay well back on the right.
Easier ground leads to the top of the cliff.

East Wall Route   120m IV (5) * 1966
A good route venturing up the left edge of the main face.
1   50m (3). Follow *Scorpion* to the base of the chimney on pitch 2.
2   20m (5). Climb a corner/groove above for 5m until it is possible to step right round the arete and move up to a ledge and belay.
3   20m (4). Move diagonally right over slabby ground to belay at a large bollard.
4   30m (3). Climb a small corner near the belay and continue up over broken ground and steep short steps to a rightwards-sloping ledge system at the top.

Migraine   94m III/IV Early 1960s
This climb is not known to have been repeated and this description is from the FRCC Eastern Crags guidebook. Very much a variant on *East Wall* and stances are frequently shared. Start midway between *East Wall* and *Sleet Wall*.
1   40m. Climb slightly rightwards up steep turfy snowed-up rock to the lowest point of a narrow grass/snow ledge. Follow the ledge leftwards and then climb up grooves to the terrace. Walk up right to a scarred area and climb up to the belay at the foot of the wall (as for *East Wall*).
2   15m. Step right and climb a groove to a ledge. Move up to a higher ledge beneath a slanting groove.
3   21m. Climb the groove, ledge, move right and climb slabs to a recess and bollards.
4   18m. Climb the rib on the right of the recess and traverse to the right to a block at the foot of a rib. Climb the rib and ascend the overhang. Scramble up to the traverse ledges.

HUTAPLE CRAG

Sleet Wall   110m V (6) * Early 1960s

A demanding climb with difficult route finding. Start about 10m to the left of the open corner of *The Amphitheatre* in a steep shallow corner above broken ground.

1   20m (5). Follow the shallow corner for 7m before moving left across the wall to a ledge, then back right along a terrace to belay on a perched block below an overhang.
2   50m (6). Move right along the terrace to a leftward-slanting weakness through the overhang. Follow this to a snow bay. Use a wide steep crack at the top right of the bay to climb out (it may be easier and better to move right to a large block and go up from there). Follow the crack for about 7m, then make a difficult and precarious mantelshelf onto a ledge on the right. Follow vegetated slabs for about 20m to a ledge and continue to a spike belay (can be done on a 50m rope).
3   40m (5). Move up and left to a short groove. Follow this to a small grassy ledge, then a large snow bay.

Easy snow plodding leads to the top.

Variation Start   VI (7) 1989

The leftmost groove in the wall between *Sleet Wall* and *The Amphitheatre* offers a hard alternative start. Begin to the right below the open-book corner of *The Amphitheatre*.

1   25m (7). Climb up to a narrow ledge cross the wall leftwards to the corner-groove right of the normal start. Follow this up and left to join *Sleet Wall* below pitch 2.

The Amphitheatre   150m VIII (8) 2007

A brilliant icy mixed line based around the summer line. But for a short section of steep and technical mixed climbing in the iced crux groove this would be a fantastic VI (6) ice climb. Requires a good build up of water ice.

1   50m (3). Climb the broad ice line to the base of the corner and belay on a large ledge.
2   40m (8). Climb the obvious ice formation on the left-hand side of the slabby wall into the corner. The summer line climbs out right on the slab but instead continue up the corner into the undercut overhanging groove (crux). Pull right out of the groove to an icicle and warthog belay on a turfy ledge.
3   40m (6). Step back left off the belay and climb the icy groove. Continue up easy mixed ground to good belays.
4   20m (3). Pick a line to the top of the crag.

Accidental Discharge   175m IV (4) * 1986

Start below and right of *The Amphitheatre*.

1   35m. Climb easily up trending slightly left to belay at a ledge in a snow bay.

2   35m. At the left end of the ledge is an obvious ramp. Make some awkward moves to gain this and follow it to another large snow bay and block belay.
3   40m. A zigzagging pitch. From the back of the bay, follow a series of vague grooves and ledges, first leftwards, then back rightwards, to belay at the foot of a snowy corner.
4   65m. Follow the corner on the right of the belay for 10m until a step left onto the arete is possible. Continue, trending left, to easy ground and the top. The pitch may be split at several places.

Full Frontal Activity 150m VII (8) 2012

Midway beween *The Amphitheatre* and *Curving Gully* is a prominent right-facing corner at the bottom of the crag. The route takes this and an icy chimney directly above it at the top of the crag.
1   40m (8). From the base of the corner follow it to where it steepens near the top. A flake on the right offers protection before making awkward and committing moves leftwards to escape the corner and gain easier ground. Continue over short steep grooves and vegetation to a good ledge in a shallow cave. The rock near the top of the corner is loose and blocky.
2   40m (4). Passing an overlap to the right of the belay proves tricky and leads to easy-angled scrambling to below an icy chimney.
3   40m (5). Follow the prominent icy chimney moving left into a groove at the top and follow this to belay above.
4   30m. Easy ground leads to the top of the crag.

Curving Gully 160m IV (5) * 1960s

The prominent gully in the centre of the crag. A snow ramp rises from the right to cut through the route. Unfortunately the lower pitches below the ramp are rarely iced.
1   25m. Follow a snowy gully to a narrower chimney section.
2   30m. Climb the steep series of chimneys to the snow ramp and a belay.
3   45m. Follow a second chimney system above to a stance beneath chockstones.
4   25m. Climb past two chockstones to a ledge and follow the line of the gully into a groove.
5   35m. Easier snow leads to the top of the crag.

West Hutaple Variations 180m III/IV 2001

An unsatisfactory meandering line starting at the summer route *Terrace Wall Variant*. Start about 20m left of *West Hutaple Gully*.
1   60m. Follow a corner and easier ground to a spacious ledge below a steep blank wall.

2   40m. From the left end of the ledge, follow *Curving Gully* for 3m to a tree and traverse under this to a long delicate traverse right to a second large ledge above the blank wall and below a right-facing corner. It is possible to escape right and up to easier ground from here, or continue up pitch 3.
3   20m. Climb a turfy right-facing corner in the middle of the wall (possibly the summer route *Interrupted Grooves*) to another spacious ledge.
4   60m. Move left and climb a series of turf-ridden corners and grooves.

West Hutaple Edge   150m IV (4) 2000

From the foot of *West Hutaple Gully*, climb the turfy buttress on the left. This route is probably based on the summer route of *Broken Ridge* in its lower parts.
1   30m. Climb past a small tree to a large block belay.
2   40m. Follow the turfy ramp for 20m until a short groove can be climbed steeply to the foot of an overhang. Break out left and belay above in a shallow cave.
3   40m. Move left and wind up through steep sections to a bay.
4   40m. Up and then left on a horizontal ledge to below the final steep wall, which is climbed via some cracks to the top.

West Hutaple Gully   75m II/II ✽

The next prominent gully to the right. In summer this is a dangerously loose rock climb. Make sure it's well frozen and iced up before trying it in winter.

Far West Rib   70m III ✽ 1995

The rib to the right of *West Hutaple Gully*.
1   20m. Start 10m right of the gully and climb the rib to a ledge.
2   50m. Move left and continue up the rib to the top.

Western Avenue   50m III ✽ 1995

This climb takes the buttress starting from a ledge above and right of *Far West Rib* and makes a good continuation to that route. Follow the buttress and rib on frozen turf.

West Gully   85m I

This prominent gully gives straightforward snow climbing and can be useful as a means of **descent**.

The broken ground either side of Hutaple Crag offers several other gullies and much for those of an exploratory bent.

Black Buttress

NY 365 118   Altitude 650m   *North facing*

To the right of Hutaple Crag is a wide open gully of scree and snow and to its right is a prominent pillar of rock, Black Buttress. The summer rock climb of *Portcullis Ridge* (VD) takes the right-hand edge of this triangular shaped buttress. It also makes an enjoyable winter outing. The left side of the ridge is bounded by a pleasant snow gully, *Black Gully,* containing a few short steps.

Black Gully   100m II * 2006
The obvious gully bounding the left side of the steep left walls of *Portcullis Ridge*. The gully may have a short step at its start which can bank out. Above there are another couple of steep steps before the gully narrows where the walls close in. Above this, the gully widens and eventually joins the top of the ridge.

Black Groove   100m IV (5) * 2006
Approximately 50m right of *Black Gully* a shallow wide fault/groove runs up the steepest part of the buttress. Climb easy turfy ledges to the start of the fault and continue up this 20m to easier ground. From here it is possible to move right over easy ground to *Black Chimney* or take a traverse line leftwards at a higher level to join the top of *Black Gully*.

Black Chimney   100m V (5) ** 2006
Approximately 30m right of the groove of *Black Groove* is a deeper cleft about 30m up the crag. Climb to its base and struggle up to easier ground. Follow this to join *Portcullis Ridge* just below the top.

Portcullis Ridge   100m IV (4) ** 1963
A mountaineering route with the crux in the lower section of the buttress.
1   20m (4). From the lowest point of the ridge either climb a corner on the left-hand side of the buttress/ridge or, more usually, start up the chimney on the right-hand side of the ridge: either way lands you on a ledge on top of the buttress.
2   30m (4). From the ledge, climb the steep wall, with a difficult but well-protected section near the top. This leads to the easier ground on the ridge proper.
3   50m (2). The ridge is followed more easily.

Cofa Wall   100m IV (5) * 1988
This vague line on the right side of the ridge starts about 10m right of the chimney at the start of *Portcullis Ridge*.

BLACK CRAG

1   30m. About 20m right of *Portcullis Ridge* follow an ill-defined groove on steep turf for 25m until about 5m below a roof then traverse 5m right to a stance.
2   30m. Continue up the more obvious groove above.
3   40m. Easier climbing leads to the top.

Ramparts Chimney   **60m II (3) 2004**
About 30m right of the start to *Portcullis Ridge* is an obvious gully/chimney bounding the right side of the crag. The crux is a chockstone at half-height.

DOVEDALE

Dovedale contains fewer climbs than its neighbouring valley but *Inaccessible Gully* and *Black Crag Icefall* are two of the best routes in the Eastern Fells.

All the crags share the same approach. Start from the Brotherswater Inn on the northern side of Kirkstone Pass. From the car park behind the inn, take the path which keeps to the north side of Dovedale. Black Crag is passed on the right after about 30 minutes, whilst Dove Crag is the obvious crag at the head of the valley, a further 20 minutes away. For Heirloom Crag follow the path as for Dove Crag until nearly below Black Crag but keep on the south side of the beck and follow its southern branch from the confluence. At the head of the stream turn right (westwards) and head steeply uphill to the crag easily recognised by a shapely V-groove line up its centre. South Heirloom Crag is the lower crag to the left.

Black Crag

NY 378 116   ALTITUDE *550M*   SOUTH-EAST FACING

Its south-easterly aspect ensures the crag soon catches any sun, so an early start or nocturnal visit is necessary, particularly in clear conditions. The icefall down the centre of the crag is obvious when approaching the crag from the path directly below.

Black Crag Icefall   **60m IV (4) *** Early 1960s**
Frozen solid the waterfall makes a fantastic route. Start from trees at the bottom of the fall.
1   30m (4). Follow the fall direct, passing the first steep bulge at 10m and others to the sanctuary of a small belay corner.

Lake District Winter Climbs

Dovedale

Dove Crag

2 30m (3). Continue up the iced slab on the right to overhanging ice at the top. Either pass this by the chimney on the left or via the **Right-Hand Finish** (4), gained by an exposed traverse.

To the left of the main fall, a line of iced slabs and short walls finishing up a rightward-slanting ramp has been known to form occasionally (**Left-Hand Climb** 50m, III, 1986).

Between Black Crag and Dove Crag, the path crosses **Houndshope Cove Gill** (II) (NY 379 114, Alt 410m) which can be use to approach Hart Crag in Link Cove. Follow the stream up and take the right fork which gets quite interesting after 100m (II).

Some 300m due west of *Houndshope Cove Gill* the un-named crag between Black and Dove Crags offers a short 15m vertical icefall (**November Sunshine** III,4 2010) topped by a further 10m of easier ice.

Dove Crag

NY 376 109   Altitude 600m   *North-east facing*

Leave the A592 at the Brotherswater Inn and follow the main path up Dovedale which almost passes by the right edge of this, the major crag of the valley. A broad open gully, generally filled with snow (if you are lucky), leads to steep slopes reaching to the base of the crag. The routes are described from left to right.

South Gully   100m I/II

This gully (surprisingly enough) bounds the south (left) side of the crag and leads to the summit. It is home to **rare alpine plants** and should be climbed only in truly frozen conditions. From where the path reaches the base of the crag, traverse left below the lowest point of the crag and into the start of the gully.
1 70m. A snow slope leads to below a small chimney pitch.
2 30m. Climb the chimney sometimes on ice, to easy snow, then a final icy steepening. A further steep snow slope leads to the summit.

Inaccessible Gully   110m IV (5) *** c1940

The initial ice pitch that provides access into this hanging gully makes this one of the best climbs in the Lakes. It takes time to form and can't be seen until you are below. Take the obvious gully splitting the south-east face of the crag, starting 40m up *South Gully*.

1   55m (5). From the base of a small ramp, go up right and over an ice bulge. Pass another bulge to reach a narrow ledge (peg runner and uncomfortable belay). Better to continue; 15m of very steep ice on the left leads into the gully. A further small ice step gives access to a peg belay on the right.
2   45m (5). Some think this is the crux – they could be right! Steepening snow leads to a chockstone. Bridge up until it is possible to pull out right onto steep snow – this can be very thin. A second chockstone above is turned on the right to gain a belay in cave.
3   10m. Congratulate yourself and escape left onto easy snow to finish.

Westmorland's Route   160m IV (5) *** 1970/1

Based on the summer classic rock route but with turfy winter variations. The route is not often in good condition as it doesn't readily hold snow. It takes the ridge at the left-hand side of the crag just right of the entrance to *South Gully*. Start to the right of the rock ridge in a turfy bay.
1   40m (3). Follow steepening turf to a rock belay.
2   40m (4). Continue leftwards to two left-slanting vegetated grooves which lead to the ridge. Climb the lower of these over bulges to a corner. Bridge up until a pull over right gains a small platform.
3   40m (5). Above, step right at the top of a short steep section of rock to the base of a broad left-slanting slab in 10m. Ascend the slab for 10m to a short wall on the right which gives access to a narrow left-slanting ramp. Precariously shuffle along this to an exposed position at its end and a rounded spike (crux). Delicately step leftwards onto what ice is available and follow this to good turf if your luck holds. This zigzags left, then right, up to a large ledge.
4   40m (2). A rightwards traverse with some exposed moves leads to a turfy gully. Follow this over a few bulges to easier broken ground and the top.

Hangover   85m VII (7) 2010

The prominent corner and rightward-sloping ledge system just right of centre of the crag. Start to the right of the chimney line of the summer route *Extol*.
1   20m (5). Climb the wall and traverse right to a ledge at the base of the corner.
2   30m (7). Climb the corner with the crux at the top where a bulge forces you left onto the slab. Belay at the top of the slab.
3   35m (6). Move right along a large flake ledge to a pinnacle. Climb up and right into the right-hand of two V-grooves which leads to an easy snow gully and a belay higher up.

Right-Hand Gully   80m IV
The gully high up on the right side of the crag, right of the cave. Generally easy climbing with one 20m ice pitch.

Heirloom Crag

NY 377 107   ALTITUDE 700M   NORTH-EAST FACING

The crag is found about 500m to the south (left) of Dove Crag. The crag has a terrace running along its base; the rocks below this are generally loose. The terrace may be reached from the right or up a groove directly below *Heirloom*, the prominent groove in the centre of the crag. This lower tier contains much loose debris and should be treated with care. Routes are described from left to right starting with the diagonal running groove of *Grooving High*, high on the left of the crag.

Grooving High   50m II/III 2010
The highest prominent groove on the left of the crag.
   Climb easy turfy walls to the groove which can be walked up to its back wall which steepens and offers a choice of finishes; on the right (II) or left up the steeper corner (III).

Gravity and Grace   55m IV (4) * 2008
Start in a turfy shallow groove 15m right from the lowest point of the buttress, below and left of the hanging arete of the summer route *Genetic Edge*.
1   20m (3). Climb the groove to a good ledge and corner (this is the belay for the start of *Genetic Edge*).
2   35m (4). Climb the corner to the left of the corner of *Genetic Edge* for about 15m, then move right and finish direct to the top of the crag and boulder belays.

Silent Torquing   55m IV (5) ** 2008
1   25m (3). Start 10m right of *Gravity and Grace* and climb a turfy/snowy ramp. After 10m, step left into a deep chimney, climb this over the top and downclimb on jammed blocks the other side to the same belay as for the top of the first pitch of *Gravity and Grace*.
2   30m (5). Climb the corner left of *Gravity and Grace* up onto a ledge and recess below an overhanging chimney. Climb this steeply on torques and hooks to a resting spike above. Move right and up turfy cracks to a large dagger of rock. Climb above this and pull out left to a slab. Climb the slab back right to the top of the buttress.

Sunset Boulevard   55m IV (4) 2008
1   20m (3). Follow pitch 1 of *Gravity And Grace*.
2   35m (4). Climb the right-hand corner/groove as for the start of the summer route *Genetic Edge*, on turfy hooks, heading for the parallel crack in the head wall above. Climb up and over this to the top of the crag.

Heiress   50m VI (6) *** (2010)
This follows *Heirloom* until just below the belay ledge on its final pitch where the groove on the left is taken.
1   20m (2). Climb the groove through the lower tier of the crag to the large ledge system and a belay below the prominent V-groove cutting the height of the buttress.
2   30m (6) Climb the narrow groove of *Heirloom* until it steepens before the easy snow ledge. Move left into a groove and up a few metres until it is possible to step left across the top of a flake into a blank groove running up the left wall of *Heirloom*. Thin climbing gains the top of this groove.

Heirloom   56m VI (6) *** 2004
The attractive central groove line on this obscure crag is one of the best winter routes in the Lakes.
1   20m (2). As for *Heiress* up the groove through the left-hand side of the lower tier.
2   18m (6). Climb up the obvious central groove which gives good technical mixed climbing, stepping right onto a good ledge to belay.
3   18m (5). Continue to the top more easily, via a turfy corner with an awkward bulge near its top. These two pitches can be combined.

Heir Apparent   60m V (6) ** 2010
From the terrace this climbs the start of the next prominent groove right of *Heirloom* before stepping across the slab on turf after about 10m to join the summer route of *Reunion* at a prominent flake on the arete and finishing up a chimney in the left wall of *Heirloom*'s top pitch.
1   25m (2). Climb the lower groove as for *Heirloom* to the ledge system and a belay below the groove to the right of *Heirloom*.
2   35m (6). Unprotected turfy climbing at the start of the groove leads to easy snow. Unless you're bold – arrange a high runner in the corner above then make a thin traverse left across the slab on turf knobbles to the prominent flake on the arete of *Reunion*. Step round into the easy snow on *Heirloom* and go diagonally up to a chimney cutting through the left wall of the top groove. Climb this to exit by the pinnacle at the top.

Sidewalk   120m II 2008
A traverse across the crag using the large ledge system. Follow *Heirloom* to the large ledge and continue right until turning an arete overlooking the north side of the buttress. From this point climb directly up and left on steeper turf to the top of the buttress.

South Heirloom Crag

NY 377 105   Altitude 730m   North facing

Located to the south of Heirloom Crag and separated from it by a wide snow or scree-filled slope and a rocky island. This crag slopes diagonally downhill and is really the north side of an easy heathery ridge, which is followed after completing a route, or a **descent** can be made down one of the easy snow gullies.

Approach as for Heirloom Crag. If approaching from the Fairfield Horseshoe ridge at the 792m summit head due north-east for about 200m to a broad snowy gully. Downclimb the gully, keeping the buttress on your south-east side. As you descend look out for the prominent corner of *False Alarm* which is above several easy gullies. These in turn are above a small yew tree about 10m up the wall. *Shift Switching* follows the turfy corner 10m below this. The routes are described from right to left or top to bottom descending the wall.

False Alarm   40m V (7) 2010
Across the snowy/scree covered slope and level with the base of Heirloom Crag and 20m up from the *Forked Gullies* is a prominent turfy corner with a steep finish – a Grade III climb with a Grade 7 finish!

Climb the obvious corner to protection behind a flake. Take a tempting line of turf diagonally rightwards to a ledge on the arete. This avoids the steep-looking finishing corner but offers instead a steep undercut poorly protected move up the arete.

Forked Gully Left, Centre and Right   50m I 2008
About 20m below *False Alarm* are a group of 3 gullies, *Right Gully*, *Centre Gully* and *Left Gully*. All are about 50m in length and Grade I. These share the same initial slopes and are really three alternative exits.

Left of the three gullies is another easy snow gully, **Far Left Gully** (I, 50m, 2010). The next route starts at a yew tree 10m lower down the slope and part way up the wall.

*Heiress, Heirloom Crag
(photo: Stephen Venables;
climber: Brian Davison)*

Come Out Swinging   80m III 2008
Start under the yew tree and pass it on the left side via a big patch of mossy turf into the back of a snowy bay. Exit this by a steep short groove direct to the top.

Silent Prayer   80m III 2008
Start 10m down from the yew tree in a turfy corner. Pull up on turf into a gully then take the groove immediately right. At its top, step right and follow the shallow turfy groove to the top.

Little Big Corner   80m IV (4) 2008
1   20m. As for *Silent Prayer* pull up on turf into a gully. Follow this into a snowy bay.
2   60m (4). Take the first steep groove in the headwall on the right then corners above to the top. Quite technical climbing.

Happiness Happening   80m I 2008
Follow the previous route to the snowy bay. Step right and follow a small gully up to a jammed block. Step right above and follow short corners to the summit of the buttress.

Shift Switching   80m I 2008
Pull up on turf into a gully and onto a snowy bay. Turn left and take the ramp up and left to the summit of the buttress.

RED SCREES EAST COVE

Lower down the wall turns a corner to face east and is split by a large heathery ledge. The shorter lower tier can be breached in several places while the upper wall offers several short grooves and corners. The one route here **Central Ramp** (II, 50m 2010), climbs a right to left diagonal in the centre of the upper wall.

KIRKSTONE PASS

Red Screes East Cove

NY 396 084   ALTITUDE 600M   *EAST FACING*

Just to the north-west of the Kirkstone Pass Inn, on the west side of the road, is the eastern cove of Red Screes containing Raven Crag. This area is very accessible from the road and provides a good practice area that forms ice quite often. There is a large parking area near the summit of the pass opposite the Inn. The climbing is reached by a short walk to the end of the car park, before heading up the Red Screes path and into the cove.

Raven Crag Left-Hand Gully   **100m II 1983**
This is the obvious gully high up on the left side of Red Screes East Cove (NY 395 083). An ice pillar is avoided on the right via a ramp.

Direct Variation   IV
Climb the ice pillar direct.

Raven Crag itself (towards the left-hand side of the cove) produces quite a good icefall (III).

The back of the cove contains several easy gullies (I).

Directly above the road, the right-hand side of the cove forms a buttress split by the distinctive **Kilnshaw Chimney** (I/II) (NY 398 085). The difficulties extend for 80m but are no more than I/II. It can be reached in 15 minutes.

Just north of the pass, on the west side of the road and immediately above a small car park, **Kirkstone Curtain** (IV (4), 1983) a 20m pitch of steep ice, occasionally forms on the tiny Kirkstone Crag (NY 401 086, where it says 'Kirk Stone' on the 1:25,000 SE map). Beware of loose rocks at the top.

Red Screes North Cove

NY 398 089   Altitude 600m   *North-east facing*

On the north by north-east side of Red Screes, above and north of Kirkstone Pass, is a small cove with a crag just below a spur to the east of the summit.

The crag is split by a wide easy gully, a useful **descent**. Facing the crag to the right of the descent gully are four obvious icefalls about 70m long and other easy snow runnels. The left-hand one, **Rob's Icefall** (II/III, 1995), is the best of the routes: a slightly more pronounced gully with two possible starts at III on the left and II on the right. The other three falls are all about II, with steep starts and give excellent introductory water ice only 30 minutes from the road. To the left of the descent the buttress is higher, with the obvious gully **Buttress Gully** (II, 70m, 2005) on the right side, just 5m left of the descent gully. **Gully Arete** (II/III, 40m, 2006), the arete between this and the descent gully, has also been climbed; it has some pleasant steep moves in its lower section, though there is some loose rock. The centre of the buttress has been climbed from its lowest point, **Buttress Route** (II, 70m, 2006), though it is possible to climb this heathery buttress at any point and a detailed description is not necessary.

Several hundred metres lower down in the centre of the cove a short 15m section of steep water ice often forms (**Lower Icefall** III/IV, 1995) and can be combined with other numerous shorter icefalls that form around the combe and in the main stream.

Kirkstone Quarry

NY 391 072   Altitude 490m   *South facing*

Located on the south side of Snarker Pike on the north side of 'The Struggle', (the Kirkstone Pass to Ambleside road) below the steep hairpin bends, the back wall of this working quarry holds three stepped vertical pillars of ice about 20m in height; **Left Pillar** (IV, 2006), **Middle Pillar** (V, 2010) and the harder slightly steeper **Right Pillar** (V, 2010). Remember this is a working quarry, so you will be trespassing!

FAR EASTERN FELLS

The Far Eastern Fells lie to the east of the main mass of the hills around Patterdale and Ullswater and are generally approached via Shap or Kendal depending on which valley one is aiming for.

MARDALE

Although isolated from the rest of the Lake District, easy access from the M6 through the village of Shap to the head of Haweswater (NY 268 108) makes this valley an attractive proposition, particularly for a short day. During periods of dry easterly winds, ice often forms quickly in Mardale and the fells round about may collect snow while the rest of the Lake District is bare.

From the north end of Shap village, take the minor road to Bampton. In the centre of the village, turn left and follow the road along the east shore of Haweswater to a car park at the southern end of the reservoir.

The crags are described from south to north.

Harter Fell Crag

NY 468 098   *ALTITUDE 550M*   NORTH-EAST FACING

From the car park Harter Fell (NY 460 093) can be clearly seen to the south-west and its gullies reached in about 30 minutes.

As viewed from car park, the fellside is split by a Y-shaped gully. *Arrowhead Buttress* rises up from the confluence of the two branches. *Little Harter Gully* can be seen about 100m to the left of the main *Y-Gully*. *Harter Fell Gully*, which is marked on the 1:25,000 map, can be found by following the Gatescarth Pass path south for about 1km then striking up the hillside to the obvious deep cleft. Approximately 300m to the left of *Harter Fell Gully*, ice forms down the easy-angled terraced face. Connecting the ice together with traverses along ledges gives approximately 150m of Grade II/III climbing. Further left along the face is a gully (I) which makes a useful **descent** when snow filled. The ridge to its left-hand side is pleasant (II) with a tricky 10m start.

Lake District Winter Climbs

FAR EASTERN FELLS

Harter Fell Gully
200m II

This gully splits the north-east face of the mountain at an altitude of 500m (NY 467 098). Sadly it only gives about 30m of climbing.

Right-Hand Finish
40m III

A 40m pitch can be found on the upper right wall of the gully.

Little Harter Gully
90m II 2003

About 100m left of *Y Gully* is a parallel-sided gully, clearly seen when walking up to *Harter Fell Gully*. This gully ends on a turfy ridge overlooking *Y Gully*. Once on the ridge, either climb the ridge itself or descend into *Y Gully* and finish up that.

Y Gully, Left and Right Branches
200m II 1997/2003

The Y-shaped gully clearly seen from the car park. There are few difficulties in either branch other than finding them frozen.

Arrowhead Buttress
120m II 2003

Between the two branches of *Y Gully* is a turfy buttress shaped like an arrowhead when viewed from below. Start from the confluence of the Y and keep in the middle. A couple of small rock steps provide some interest but can be outflanked on either side.

Small Water Crag

NY 455 097   Altitude 530m   NORTH FACING

The tarn of Small Water is reached by following the path for Nan Bield Pass westward for about 30 minutes (1.5km). The crag is clearly seen on the south side of the tarn. The crags in the area are home to **rare flora** so climb with care only in frozen conditions. The right side of the crag holds several short easy-angled ice slabs to play on, which need no further description and which can be linked to weave a way to the top of the crag. The left side of the crag contains a more defined Grade I/II gully, **Small Water Crag Gully** (I/II, 2010) near its left side. In lean conditions this may offer a couple of short icy steps. The leftmost buttress of the crag offers a ridge, **Small Water Crag Left Ridge** (I/II, 2010), just to the left of the gully at an interesting Grade II if you avoid the one steep wall, or III if the centre of the ridge and wall are kept to. The original route climbs the ridge on the right side of the gully starting at a chimney 10m above a large tree.

BLEA WATER CRAG

Cavers on the Crag   110m III (3) * 2007

Mixed turfy climbing between large ledges. Start at the left side of the crag about 20m right of the gully and above a tree.

1   35m (3). Climb an open icy chimney with some bridging to exit right at the top onto a rock step.
2   25m (3). Climb the groove immediately left of the belay (crux). Continue up the turfy groove to the next rock step and belay below an obvious left-slanting turfy groove.
3   25m (3). Continue up more turfy ledges to the groove and hook your way to the next rock step and a small spike belay.
4   25m (2). Ascend the left-slanting turfy groove to gain the arete overlooking the gully and continue over the blocky arete to the top.

BLEA WATER

Situated below the summits of High Street and Mardale Ill Bell, the combe containing Blea Water (NY 448 107) is often referred to by climbers as Mardale.

Blea Water is due west of the car park at the head of the valley and is reached by taking the path round the head of the lake before branching off to the left and ascending into the combe (1hr).

Blea Water Crag

NY 445 106   ALTITUDE 570M   *EAST FACING*

This broken crag, situated at the back of the combe above Blea Water, contains some of the fastest-forming ice in the Lake District.

Blea Water Crag is important for **rare alpine plants** (particularly *Birkett's Gully* and the buttresses to its right) – please climb here only in truly frozen conditions.

The most significant icefalls have been described but there are many more icy steps to play on. The back of the combe particularly around *Blea Water Gill* offers numerous ice bosses at various altitudes. Linking several together can offer a variety of options to gain the top of the combe.

There are a series of short icefalls at Grade III on the right-hand side of the combe which catch the early sun. High up is the very obvious cleft of *Birkett's Gully*. Above, and about 300m right of *Birkett's Gully*, is a small hanging valley (NY 443 111) with a short gully on its left side (**Racecourse Gully** II, 2005).

Lake District Winter Climbs

Blea Water Crag

1 Blea Water Cleft — IV
2 Far Left Fall — II/III
3 Blea Water Icefall — III
4 Blea Water Gill — III
5 Blea Water Buttress — III
6 Birkett's Gully — II/III
7 Racecourse Gully — II/III
8 Racecourse Hill Recourse — IV
9 Grade III Icefalls — III

BLEA WATER CRAG

Racecourse Hill Recourse   50m IV 2005
The steep grassy headwall at the back of the small hanging valley leads directly to the summit plateau.

Birkett's Gully   130m II/III ** 1973
This well-defined gully is seen as a deep cleft high on the crag, above and right of *Blea Water Gill*. Below the cleft is an icefall, a good long cascade with an initial pitch and then steps. The deeply cut upper cleft can give three short pitches of increasing difficulty, although it may be banked out.

The next routes start down and left of *Birkett's Gully* and not far above Blea Water.

Blea Water Buttress   130m III * 1991
In good winter conditions a narrow but substantial cascade of snow ice forms to the right of *Blea Water Gill*, roughly in the middle of the buttress down from, and left of, the well-defined cleft of the upper section of *Birkett's Gully*. It gives an enjoyable outing comprising 40–50m of snow ice followed by mixed ground.

Blea Water Gill   130m III ** 1985
An excellent route. Start at a narrow chimney just left of the lowest point of the crag and down and left of *Birkett's Gully*. The chimney leads to a short but steep ice wall, then a shallow gully which is followed to easy ice and the top.

Blea Water Icefall   30m III ** 1985
Follow *Blea Water Gill* to the shallow gully and then move left to climb the fine icefall pitch. Sometimes more short falls above (II and then III/IV) can be linked to make a good outing; or traverse back right and finish up the *Gill*.

Far Left Fall   50m II/III
The most obvious fall left of *Blea Water Gill* peters out halfway up the crag, but a traverse can be made rightwards into the *Gill*.

There are many other short icefalls on the crag, but nothing warranting description.

Blea Water Cleft   130m IV (4) 1996
Well to the left of the other climbs on the crag, on a separate rocky section of the combe and 400m left (south-east) of *Birkett's Gully*, are gullies leading up from right to left and an obvious chimney/cleft. Climb to and then up the chimney, exiting after 15m with difficulty. Continue up easier ground following ice and snow gullies above to finish below a cairn on Mardale Ill Bell.

Lake District Winter Climbs

The next two valleys, Riggindale and Whelter Bottom to the north of Haweswater, are home to a variety of upland birds, including England's only resident golden eagle. **The area is an RSPB reserve. Golden eagles are easily disturbed. To allow these magnificent birds to flourish in this area it is imperative that no climbing should take place at any time.**

Routes have been climbed here but no details are given as eagles are resident all year and are sensitive to disturbance. The crags with recorded routes have been identified to ensure that climbers are fully aware of the crags and restrictions and do not drive along the lake looking north at the impressive ice on Bason Crag thinking they have just discovered a major ice climbing venue. Respecting these restrictions fosters good relations with the RSPB, Lake District National Park Authority and Natural England facilitating access agreements in the spring nesting season. Please observe this restriction.

Riggindale

This is the next valley to the north of Upper Mardale.

Twopenny Crag

NY 441 123 *Altitude 650m* *South-east facing*

Whelter Bottom

Whelter Crag

NY 462 137 *Altitude 490m* *East-north-east facing*

Bason Crag

NY 463 143 *Altitude 570m* *South facing*

SWINDALE

Better known for its rock climbing, Swindale holds little of interest for the winter climber. However, following a prolonged cold spell with temperatures in the minus teens, **Hobgrumble Gill** (IV 4, ❄❄ 1996), which faces north at the head of the valley (NY 501 112), has been known to freeze. It then gives several pitches up a narrow slot with occasional rock protection.

LONGSLEDDALE

The valley is approached from the A6 at Garnet Bridge 7km north of Kendal. Travelling this road can feel a rather long and trying expedition, particularly in the kind of frozen icy conditions required to bring these low-lying climbs into condition. *Underhill Gill* is on the left of the valley about 2km before the end of the metalled road. The other climbing is found about 2km further up a drove road. Galeforth Gill and Buckbarrow Crag are clearly visible on the right while, opposite these, snow/scree slopes lead to Goat Crag and the gully to its north.

Underhill Gill   200m II 2010

From High Swinklebank Farm on the road along Longsleddale cross the river to Underhill Wood and the gill at NY 489 043. The gill to the left of Hill Cottage runs up the right side of the woods starting from an obvious slabby area and continuing up a series of steps to peter out in pasture above.

Galeforth Gill Fall   45m III (3) 1982

From the end of the metalled road, Galeforth Gill is visible on the eastern slopes to the right, about 1km up the continuation track (NY 486 066). The gill forms a fall where it goes over a rock band. A series of short pitches (I/II) lead to the main pitch. After 20m this is split by a small bay that leads to steeper ice and a choice of finishes, the left-hand one being the steepest.

Buckbarrow Crag

NY 483 073   ALTITUDE *380M*   SOUTH-WEST FACING

About 2km up the track, at the head of the valley, Buckbarrow Crag is the broken crag on the right. The vegetated central buttress is known as The Dandle. The chimney-line high on the left side of the face defines the route of *Dandle Face Direct,* starting at a rib at the bottom left corner. The best and safest **descent** is to the right of the buttress.

Dandle Face Direct   100m IV (5) 1996

The obvious groove and chimney at the left side of the face.
1   50m (3). Climb turf to the right of a rock rib to belay at the tree at the base of the short chimney.
2   30m (5). Ascend the chimney and grass ramp above to the edge of the buttress. Move diagonally right along a narrow ramp to a large ledge and belay overlooking the gully.
3   20m (3). Continue up and right along ledges to finish up a chimney-groove.

Dandle Buttress   50m III 1969

This route follows the left edge of *Dandle Buttress* overlooking the Cleft.
1   30m. About 5m below a large chockstone is a corner on the right wall of *Cleft Gill*. Climb the corner to gain the edge of the buttress and follow this up a chimney.
2   20m. Keep to the left edge and continue to the top.

Cleft Gill   80m II 1982

The deep cleft bounding the left end of the buttress. The chockstone may prove tricky and is best taken on its left.

Goat Scar is clearly visible on the left of the track at (NY 477 070). The obvious **Goat Scar Gully** (100m, I, 1986) is the snow gully on its right side and provides a good route to the summit of Kentmere Pike.

KENTMERE

This valley, easily accessible from the south of the district, has a pleasant horseshoe walk round its ridges but not much for the winter climber.

On the west side of the valley the east facing Rainsbarrow Crag (NY 444 067, Alt 500m) has a climb following obvious weaknesses and rakes to zigzag up the face of the cliff (II). North-east-facing Rainsbarrow Cove, to the north of the crag, contains several obvious short gullies (I/II). Across the valley on the east side, facing west is the narrow cleft of **Ullstone Gill Quarry** (40m, IV, 2010) (NY 456 080, Alt 450m) clearly visible from the path to Nan Bield Pass. The back of the quarry offers a good 40m icefall climbable in one or two pitches. Take care with ropes on sharp edges.

OUTLYING AREAS

Enjoying a great day at Cautley Spout (photo: Nick Wharton)

THE HOWGILLS

These rounded fells to the east of the Lake District and the M6 lie between Tebay and Sedbergh. The scenic waterfall of *Cautley Spout* has long been a winter classic, while the summits provide secluded winter walking.

Cautley Spout   250m III *** 1967

Visible from the Cross Keys Inn on the A683 Sedbergh to Kirkby Stephen road at (SD 683 975) this accessible low-lying east-facing fall on Calf Fell requires a sustained period of cold temperatures.

From the inn follow the track to the point where it steepens, contour leftwards into the gorge and climb easily to the main pitch. This can be 30m high and is usually best taken starting on the left and moving to the centre. Above are several shorter but easier pitches.

Brussels Spout Variation   IV * 1995

When the main fall is not fully formed or is full of climbers, a variation following turf and ice on the left wall may be climbed before returning to the main watercourse. It is actually quite good, being steeper and more strenuous than the main fall, but purists will no doubt feel it rather misses the point!

Walking into Cautley Spout (photo: Nick Wharton)

Black Force   60m II

The impressive little gorge starting at about 400m on the north side of Fell Head at (SD 644 992). Follow the ice.

Jeffrey's Mount Escarpment (Tebay)

NY 609 024   A*LTITUDE 250M*   E*AST FACING*

Just south of Junction 38 on the M6, the cutting at the side of the A685 forms a 100m-wide continuous icefall. This is visible from the motorway and gives numerous Grade III/IV pitches of 15–30m height. Truly roadside cragging!

NORTHERN PENNINES

South of Kirkby Stephen can be found **Upper** and **Lower Ais Gill** (SD 771 975) and **Hell Gill** (SD 786968), located to the west and east respectively of the B6259 Kirkby Stephen to Garsdale Head road in the Mallerstang valley. These unusual narrow roofless cave passages offer a unique combination of Grade II ice and potholing: use of a wet suit is optional. After a prolonged freeze **Hell Gill Force** (III (4), 2010), visible from the road (SD 778 965) can form offering 12m of more conventional steep ice climbing.

High Cup Nick

NY 745 262   A*LTITUDE 370M*   W*EST FACING*

High Cup Nick and its waterfall have been viewed by many happy Pennine Way walkers but few ever venture there to climb: be warned, the area is known for its poor rock quality. The watercourse cuts an impressive cleft through a horseshoe of crags on the hillside above the village of Dufton, just off the A66.

Two routes have been recorded on the south side of the Nick and so face north. Approach from the back of High Cup, from where the stream runs down into the scree slope. Traverse under the crags to the first obvious deep twin gullies, separated by a prow.

Unsullied Gully   35m I 2006
A mixed climb up the left-hand gully to fan-shaped exit slopes (and possible cornice). A perched block at about half-height needs treating with care.

Grotty Gully   35m III 2006
The right-hand gully is easily identified, as it is bounded on the right by a striking three-tiered rock pillar. The gully is a natural drainage line that ices up readily if conditions are cold enough. Climb the ice trickle (or patches of scree and a beck) to carefully pass a huge Damoclean block wedged right across the gully. Beyond a steeper section of ice there is a choice of finishes, either straight up the main gully via another ice step (II, but may be unclimbed) or up a short icy groove on the left wall leading to the prow separating the two gullies, which is followed to the top.

Hope Head Icefall   35m IV * 1986
At an altitude of about 400m, the scenic waterfall of High Ashgill near Alston (NY 758 404) can form a short free-standing pillar of ice in a severe winter.

Pasta Pasture   6m II 2010
This is a rather short water ice climb on Crammel Linn Waterfall itself. This rarely comes into condition. The description will probably be longer than the climb! Leave the A69 Carlisle to Hexham road at Greenhead and head north on the B6183 for Gilsland. On leaving Gilsland turn right (north) onto a small road for the Gilsland Hotel and Spa. If you're tempted past this then follow the road through the woods and out the other side. The waterfall is to the right near two buildings about 600m away to the west. The climb is on the smaller left-hand side of the waterfall (looking upstream).

DRY TOOLING ROUTES

Paddy Cave hanging tough on First Blood, The Paddy Cave (photo: Steve Ashworth)

LAKE DISTRICT WINTER CLIMBS

First Blood, (The) Paddy Cave (photo: Steve Ashworth)

As this guide was being prepared for publication the first dedicated dry tooling venues in the Lake District were being developed near Tilberthwaite, just north of Coniston in the South Lakes. Routes now established in two disused slate quarries are described below. These quarries were not previously climbing venues and contained no previous recorded rock routes. These routes are bolt protected, usually with ring bolt lower-offs. As they are on slate offering little in the way of protection or axe placements, they have been engineered.

They offer a useful training venue for those snowless days. **Dry tooling should be practised only in these areas and not on established rock climbing venues.**

Warning While the two quarries offering climbing have not been worked for several years spoil extraction is still being carried out in a nearby quarry so care should be taken. Slate can cleave leaving very sharp edges which may slice through ropes so care is needed when climbing and abseiling. The quarried slate can also be notoriously loose and unstable. A serious accident occurred here in 2012 as the guide was being finalised.

Individuals are responsible for assessing the safety of the area and the route they choose to climb. Climbers enter the quarries at their own risk and those participating in these activities do so at their own risk. Climbers are reminded of the BMC Participation Statement and the Warning at the front of this guide.

The Works

NY 313 017   ALTITUDE 165M   SOUTH AND NORTH-WEST FACING

This scenic hole in the ground offers several routes on a slightly inclined wall and a large cave roof. This small quarry is close to a larger hole from which material is still being periodically excavated though no blasting is now undertaken. Please do not enter the working quarry or do anything to prejudice relations with the quarry owners.

From the entrance to Hodge Close car park follow a track behind a locked gate on the west side of the road passing some shipping containers in 200m used by the quarry workers. The large working quarry is visible in front of you and the track bends round to the right. Follow this until it starts to go downhill and in about 100m a path cuts off left under a fence to a quarry. An old electrical cable (of unknown provenance) has been tied around a tree to help access into the quarry at this point. From here the slightly overhanging wall on the left has five short routes on it. The right-hand of the two large caves has three routes going through the roof from the back of the cave.

Industrial Sector

The slightly impending wall by the descent into the quarry offers five routes with undercut starts. The routes are described from left to right increasing in difficulty. The wall under the start of the routes offers a low-level traverse for those wanting a warm up.

1 Time and a Half   9m M4 5B 2012
Get cracking at the left side of the undercut wall.

2 Double Time   9m M5 4B 2012
Eases once you get your feet up.

3 Overtime   9m M6 4B 2012
Hard work pulling past a downward spike leads to spaced pick placements.

4 Stein Pull   9m M6 5B 2012
Where the wall finally touches to the ground – this doesn't make it any easier! The initial fierce pull to a slot has been climbed with and without a figure of four and leads to the Stein manoeuvre.

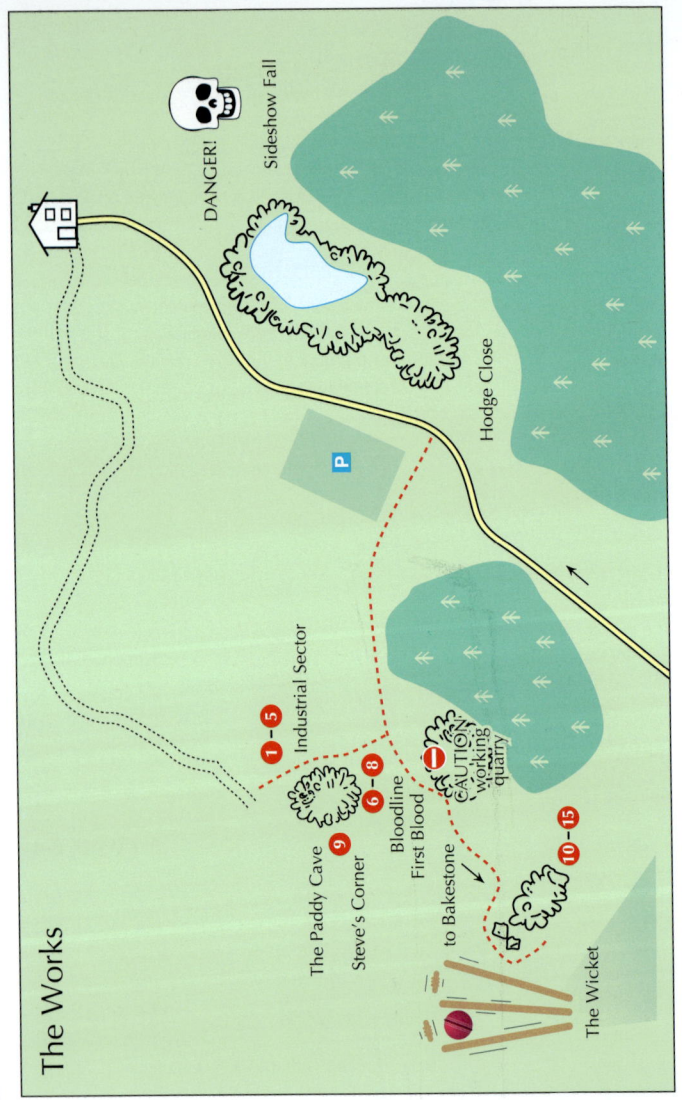

Ian Duham traversing in the dry (photo: Andy Rutherford)

A variation start from the back of the cave following an inverted V in the roof reaches the slot.

5 Grand Design   9m M7 4B 2012
This route may not have an undercut start, but things are getting harder. Dynamic moves on spaced pockets require strength and lots of axe swapping; leave your leashes at home.

The right-hand of the two caves has a left to right route running from the back wall of the cave diagonally through the roof.

The Paddy Cave

The rightmost of the two caves offers a good wet weather venue if you have the arm strength.

6 Bloodline   20m M10 8B 2012
The crack-line running parallel to the roof starting from the left side of the cave. More overhanging madness with a long powerful reach near the end.

7 Blood Donor 15m M9 8B 2012
Start up *First Blood* and then cut left across the roof with one powerful move to the groove and lower off of *Bloodline*.

8 First Blood 20m M9+ 10B 2012
From the middle of the back of the cave follow the bolts in the pillar up and right to break through a series of smaller roofs onto steep small walls. Traversing ever rightwards to the lower-off at the right side of the cave.

Project 15B
The steep rib from the back of the cave to the lower-off for *First Blood*.

Project 5B
The arete to the left of *Steve's Corner*.

9 Steve's Corner 15m M6 7B 2012
Right of the cave entrance in a corner starting from slightly lower down the slope. A short slabby wall leads into the corner. Move past a shallow roof on the right into a corner with difficult moves leading to its top. Hang left and you're at the lower-off.

Bakestone Quarry

NY 32015   ALTITUDE *190M*   NORTH-WEST FACING

This small quarry has a large cave at its back sporting a pleasant fang at the entrance and a smaller hole to the left capped by a flat overhang and a smooth overhanging left wall.

Follow the track to the shipping containers then follow a path to the right of the active quarry to a flat mossy area at the top of the quarry. Pass this and take a higher grassy incline passing an old tunnel then traverse across scree to two old ruined buildings. Go up the steps and the quarry is on the left approached along an old grassed-over quarry path now looking like a cricketing seam; that and a cricket bat found at the site have resulted in the names.

Another approach can be made via a path from the houses passed just prior to reaching the Hodge Close parking area. Please do not park at the houses as there is limited parking here reserved for the residents. Walking back to the houses from the car park will be good exercise and help maintain good relationships.

Playing on the Wicket (photo: Andy Rutherford)

The Wicket

The grassy quarry path leads to a large cave with a fang in its entrance and a slabby corner to its right side and a wall above the cave on its left side. Routes are described from right to left.

10 Right Slip 15m M5 4B 2012
The slabby corner to the right of the cave. Step left from a pinnacle to a sloping ledge below an overlap and into the corner. Awkward moves lead through the overlap onto the easier slab. Follow this to a natural finishing crack.

11 The Fang 15m M8 8B 2012
With a name like that need I say more. The fang in the entrance to the cave. Steep strenuous pulls lead to powerful moves leftwards across the blank overhanging wall of the fang and into a bottomless groove if you're lucky. Entering and passing the lower groove offers the crux. Thankfully the angle of the higher groove eases, as does the climbing, but it's still a long way to the top.

The next routes are on the small wall above left of the cave entrance.

### 12 Left Slip	10m M5 4B 2012
The line of bolts in the buttress left of the cave. Follows a groove up the right side of the wall. Some thin moves lead to good ledges before a final steep headwall and the lower-off.

### 13 Silly Mid On	10m M4 4B 2012
The line of bolts in the middle of the wall, just right of the tree. Pass several small ledges using torques behind flakes to gain a thin crack and the lower-off.

On the left of The Wicket is a rubble-filled hole with a long flat roof and a smooth left wall. A low-level traverse has been manufactured along the base of the smooth wall left from the back of the hole.

### 14 Outfield	20m M6 7B 2012
From near the back of the hole climb a shallow groove to the roof then follow the junction between the vertical wall and roof out of the hole to respite on the flake of *Outside Leg* before tackling its crux and final moves to the lower-off.

### 15 Outside Leg	12m M5 6B 2012
The left edge of the hole. The route comes with a left or right start, take your pick. Climb up to stand on a large flake then make an awkward move to stand on a sloping ledge on the arete. It's not over yet, move right and over the roof to the lower-off of *Outfield*.

FIRST ASCENTS

*Skew Gill: Early days in Wasdale
(FRCC Collection © Abraham Family)*

LAKE DISTRICT WINTER CLIMBS

1870 Jan 10 South Gully, Bowfell J Stogdon, GH Wollaston, AR Stogdon

The Lake District's first recorded winter route. The group set off from Elterwater on a clear morning with a sharp frost to climb Bowfell by 'the great couloir' and then continued on to Wasdale Head. John Stogdon takes up the story:

'The slope got steeper and steeper, steps were always necessary, and at last having come up 350 feet or more, we found ourselves within a few feet of the top on a slope of 63°, with an overhanging cornice of ice above us, and snow nearly up to our waists for a few feet below the top, which I could just reach with my axe. The next few minutes must have been pleasant to my friends below me, as the cornice was gradually tumbling upon their ears in a shower of icy fragments. Then I pulled myself up by my hands on to the level snowfield above, and a short run up easy slopes soon bought us to the top.'

John Stogdon, 'The English Lakes in Winter',
Alpine Journal (1870)

1873 Mar Sharp Edge, Blencathra G Seatree and party

'In March 1873 a party of us ascended when the first part of the steep slope from the edge to the summit was snow and ice covered. In those days there were no ice axes or ropes used, and in fact we came very close to a serious accident by reason of the conditions.'

George Seatree, 'Reminiscences of Early Lakeland Mountaineering', *FRCC Journal* (1910)

1880 Apr 4 Cust's Gully, Great End Cust and party

Arthur Cust and over twenty members of the Alpine Club (who said crowds on Great End were anything new?). Almost certainly ascended prior to this by Cust.

'On Sunday the party…leaving the carriages at the farmhouse above Seatoller, climbed Scafell Pike by a very interesting chimney or couloir, which, being filled with snow and ice, gave unexpected satisfaction. There is a very remarkable natural arch in the couloir, which Mr Cust claims to have been the first to discover, and he was therefore entrusted with the guidance of the party.'

DW Freshfield, 'Alpine Meeting at the Lakes',
Alpine Journal (1882)

AL Mumm and JE King glissaded down Cust's Gully in 1882.

1882 Deep Ghyll, Scafell C Pilkington, L Pilkington, E Hulton

FRCC Journal Number 2 1908, p199. Messrs Charles and Lawrence Pilkington, with Mr E Hulton, climbed the ghyll in 1882. Wintery conditions prevailed, and an hour and a half was taken over the second pitch.

First ascents

1886 Mar 29 Branch Gully, Great End H Hastings, J Mason, WC Slingsby

First recorded winter ascent, but may have been climbed earlier.

'The same party made a variation on Mr Cust's Gully on Great End. They made first for the great or central gullies up which one of this party and a friend had climbed on Easter Monday 1884, but as during the previous night about four inches of snow had fallen on the old hard snow, it was deemed to be unwise to attempt such a steep and awkward gill so they turned to the smaller gully. A grand glissade could have been made from the mouth of the gill down almost to the footpath below. The party cut their way with axes steadily forward and instead of going up through the natural arch of rock, which looked most weird through the mist, they turned up the right-hand branch, and after one short awkward climb over a fallen block of rock, and a fairly steep snow slope they found themselves on the top in a furious snow storm. A few good glissades and a scramble down the side of Grain's Gill ended a most enjoyable morning's adventure.'

WC Slingsby, Wasdale Hotel Visitors' Book, 1885–1891

1887 Jan 4 Great Doup Gully, Pillar JW Robinson, TG Creak

First recorded winter ascent, but probably climbed earlier (see Slingsby on Pillar, March 1885 above).

'Mountains covered with ice and snow. Ascent of Pillar via Great Doupe, very tough near the top owing to frozen snow and the cornice.'

Wasdale Hotel Visitors' Book, 1885–1891

'We now decided to try our luck up the Great Doupe, for the moon was beginning to show and the light increasing. Formidable indeed, as we looked up, was the steep snow slope at the head of the hollow, surmounted by an immense cornice. "Shall we want the rope?" I asked. "Oh no, it's in the sack and it won't help us!" I did not feel at all sure about this, as, unable for the moment to get any further, I crouched under the great protruding lip of the cornice, and looked into the black and uncertain depth below. "Can we get out," I said. "We must, so here goes, hold my feet on this big step whilst I try to cut down the overhanging edge." Ten minutes more, a struggle, a gasp, and breathless we emerged into the moonlight of the Pillar – 6.30pm. We scurried away to Wasdale, and never were climbers more thankful for their suppers.'

JW Robinson, 'A Novice in Snow', *FRCC Journal* (1907)

1887 Feb 5 Central Gully, Great End (via the Left Branch) G Hastings and party (including some or all of the following **C Hastings, J Mason, JA Slingsby, CH Slingsby, AE Preston, HA Beeching**)

First recorded winter ascent, but may have been climbed earlier (an entry in the Visitors' Book in 1886 March 29th, for example, mentions that Central Gully had been climbed at Easter 1884 by Slingsby or Hastings – however, without a record of the conditions we have no way of knowing if this was a winter ascent).

'Climbed up Great End by the Central Chimney which starts at the head of the long scree close to Grains Gill. The snow came well down onto the scree, and was in good order; we took the left-hand branch and had to take to the rocks to overcome the "block". We then crossed over the Pikes to Mickledore, the rocks of which were very wet. The early part of day was very wet, snowed hard while we were in the "Central Chimney" and did not cease until we got on to Scafell, when it cleared up, and we had a glorious view of the mists rolling up out of the valleys, and disappearing leaving all the hills quite distinct.'

Wasdale Hotel Visitors' Book, 1885–1891

Second recorded winter ascent, probably by the Right Branch, JW Robinson, E Carr, G Hastings, E Peile, WA Wilson, 1890 Dec 26 or 27

'The central gully in Great End took about 2 hours with the help of the steps cut by Mr Robinson's party a day or two before in the magnificent upper ice-fall. Without their assistance it would perhaps have been barely possible within the limits of a winter day.'

RC Gilson, Dec 28 1890, Wasdale Hotel Climbing Book, 1890–1919

Chimney Finish, R Bennett, R Lavender, 1972. The Arete Direct was added by S Ashworth and P Rowlands, Jan 20 2001, and Grande Finale by S Ashworth and J Kelly, Feb 20 2006. Left Branch Middle Way was the work of B Davison and S Ashworth, March 18 2006. It was their fourth new route of the day and the third valley visited.

1887 Mar 7 Skew Gill, Great End G Hastings and party (including some or all of the following ELW Haskett Smith, C Hopkinson, WC Slingsby)

First recorded winter ascent, but may have been climbed earlier.

'Ascended by Skew Gill, a very interesting and neat cut to the north face of Great End. We climbed, duly roped together the western gully on the north face by the snow, and turned up the left of the two forks (Cust's Gully) and after many hundred steps had been cut in the hard snow by our axes, we went through the well known arch of rock and, after one hour forty minutes step cutting we stood in the sunshine on the top of Great End. After a short walk along the top we looked down the fine Central Gully, and Hastings pointed out to us the steps he had cut on the ascent of this gully on February 5th. After a capital glissade, we made our way over the moors to Stickle Tarn to attempt the ascent of Pavey Ark by the Central Gully.'

Wasdale Hotel Visitors' Book, 1885–1891

First ascents

'To go by Grainy Gill and this one [Skew Gill], and so up Cust's Gully, has for many years been the regulation expedition for the first day of a winter sojourn at Wastdale Head.'

WP Haskett Smith, *Climbing in the British Isles* (Longmans, 1894)

The Direct Finish was added by M Green and J Bradley in 1987, and the Left-hand Branch by P Kennet and party in February 1996, while the Grade III Variation appeared in January 1997.

1890 Jan 3 South-East Gully, Great End RC Gilson and party

First recorded winter ascent.

'At the point where the gully forks, less than half way up, we chose the steeper left-hand branch, but finding it very full of hard ice took to the arete between the two branches and crossing this with some trouble followed up the right-hand side to the point where the branches reunite, hence over easy rocks to the top. Time 3 hours 20 mins: every ledge being choked with ice or glazed snow.'

Wasdale Hotel Climbing Book, 1890–1919

The entry in the climbing book kept at the Wasdale Hotel (today the Wasdale Head Inn) is signed 'A.G.', which is confusing as it was certainly written by Cary Gilson, the man who donated the climbing book to the hotel.

1890 Dec 29 Eagle's Nest Gully, The Napes RC Gilson and party

'Ascended the gully to the left (as you face the mountain) of the gully coming down to the left of the Needle. This gully does not seem to have been described before and I have no idea how it goes in summer. On this occasion it presented no particular difficulty except, just above a large boulder about one third of the way up, where a smooth slab was thinly glazed. Near the top we passed to the left onto the arete, and then rushed down Hell Gate screes to escape the blizzard on the ridge.'

Wasdale Hotel Climbing Book, 1890–1919)

1890 Dec 30 Shamrock Gully, Pillar JW Robinson, C Hopkinson, G Hastings, RC Ritson and party

'"This has only once been ascended previous to the ascent recorded below and on the first occasion 5 feet of snow gave a good start in surmounting the vertical wall on the right side of the stone… Yesterday Geoffrey Hastings followed by Charles Hopkinson and John W. Robinson succeeded in passing successfully up the gully and taking the right-hand side of the boulder completed the first ascent without the aid of a snowdrift. They afterwards went onto the Pillar Rock which was unusually tedious owing to the iced state of the rocks. JW Robinson." Mr Robinson's note above shows what may be done in the depth of even the severest winter. It is hard to imagine rocks in worse condition for climbing than during the past ten days, though the enormous accumulations of ice have probably rendered some waterfalls possible which are very rarely so.'

RC Gilson, Wasdale Hotel Climbing Book, 1890–1919

Previously climbed in semi-winter conditions, 5 March 1887, by ELW Haskett Smith and G Hastings with the aid of snowdrift (Wasdale Hotel Visitors' Book, 1885–1891).

1890 Dec 30 Slab and Notch Climb, Pillar C Hopkinson, JW Robinson, G Hastings

'Ice and snow…up over Notch and down Ledge and Chimney Route (this is the Easy Way – a variation on Slab and Notch). The Slab one mass of ice, Hopkinson led during the ascent and I was last man in coming down, time 1hr 40mins in ascent, 20mins coming down. Took one hour to cross the Slab.'

JW Robinson's Climbing Diary, FRCC Archive

However an earlier ascent on Feb 6 1887, by G Hastings and party, may also have been in winter conditions.

'Bright sunny day with hard frost. Ascended Pillar Fell by gully direct from Mosedale. Climbed Pillar Rock by easy way and then descended down the gully to the west side and ascended the rock again, descending again by the easy way. The slab on the rock was coated with ice which had to be cut away.'

Wasdale Hotel Visitors' Book, 1885–1891

1890/1 New Year Grainy Gill, Lingmell A Marshall and party

In the Wasdale Hotel Climbing Book 1890–1919 is a somewhat confusing account which clearly describes the narrow ridge between the two branches of the gill, and an ascent of the right branch of Grainy Gill, but has wrongly been ascribed as Greta Gill Right Branch.

'What is marked Grainy Gill in the Ordnance Map (situated between Skew Gill and Greta Gill, the left-hand branch of Piers Gill) is, in reality two water courses, distinct though separated in parts by a very narrow ridge. The right-hand branch (facing the mountain) which it has been proposed to call Corney Gill, contains two very fine falls, ascended so far as is known for the first time by Prof. Marshall's party this winter.'

Wasdale Hotel Climbing Book, 1890–1919

The exact date of Professor Marshall's ascent is unknown but it was, almost certainly, the first ascent of the gill in winter conditions.

1891 Easter Needle Ridge, The Napes GA Solly, WC Slingsby, M Schintz

In descent.

First ascents

'It was not till Easter, 1891, that I had a chance of attempting any of the serious courses. I was staying at Seatoller with WC Slingsby and M Schintz, and on our way down from Great Gable, we descended the Needle Ridge. It had then, I think, been only once ascended, and this was the first descent under winter condidtions… Slingsby led and I came last.'

GA Solly, 'Some Early Recollections', *FRCC Journal* (1909)

1891 Apr 1 Central Gully, Gable Crag A Marshall, WI Beaumont, HB Dixon.

'Up Central Gully on N. side of Gable. Snow in good order.'

Wasdale Hotel Climbing Book, 1890–1919

The Smart Exit was added in 1937 by S Cross, A Nelson, AT Hargreaves, R Hargreaves and A Cooper as a direct finish. The route involved delicate cutting up frozen moss on the crux wall and tenuous moves to reach the top. Albert Hargreaves was due to address the Pinnacle Club's annual dinner in the Sun Hotel at Coniston that evening, and Cross remembers him practising his speech all the way up the climb (Interviews with Sid and Jammy Cross (nee Nelson), 1996). L Kendall and R McHaffie (alt) added the Contrived Eliminate, 10 Dec 1960 and the Less than Smart Exit was soloed by B Davison, 31 March 1996.

1891 Apr 3 Old Professors' Chimney, Scafell AM Marshall, HB Dixon, WI Beaumont, AG (HA Gwynne?)

First recorded winter ascent, but may have been climbed earlier.

'After heavy snow storm of day before Deep Ghyll was nearly full of soft snow. Had to cut a channel 4 – 5 foot deep through the powdery snow. First obstacle quite easy. Second obstacle just impossible to do straight up. Had to return and go up chimney to left. This was very bad owing to the rocks being iced under loose snow. Up Professors Chimney which was comparatively easy. Took 7 hours from Hotel to top of Scawfell.'

Wasdale Hotel Climbing Book, 1890–1919

1891 Apr 19 Mickledore Chimney, Scafell OG Jones, WE Sumpner, CG Munro

'This proved to be very difficult the snow being 6 or 7 feet deep and very rotten. At the obstacle we were brought to a stop for the rocks on the left were ice covered and no handholds seemed available. O.G.J. managed to climb up after a struggle and returned by Broadstand, the others descended the chimney again.'

Wasdale Hotel Climbing Book, 1890–1919

There is also a detailed account of this ascent in OG Jones's Rock Climbing in the English Lake District (Longmans, 1897). AL Mumm descended the gully in snowy conditions dropping the last few feet into snow, Easter 1881 (FRCC Journal, 1922).

Variation **Icefall Start and Finish** added by JJS Allison and L Kendall, 14 Dec 1960.

1891 Apr 21 New Professors' Chimney, Scafell OG Jones, WE Sumpner, CG Monro

'Instead of continuing straight up Deep Ghyll, they turned up the gully to the left, from which springs Professors Chimney. (This gully apparently is as yet nameless). There appeared to be too much snow on the rocks in the Professors Chimney so they continued their ascent up the nameless gully and reached the top after cutting through a fine ice cornice.'

Wasdale Hotel Climbing Book, 1890–1919

1891 Dec 25 Steep Ghyll, Scafell JN Collie, WLW Brodie, EW Marshall

There are only brief references to this remarkable and futuristic climb, the first to be given Grade V. The history of the ascent remained hidden for many years due to Collie's reticence in recording it, probably because of its 'unjustifiable' severity.

'My recollection of the latter [Steep Ghyll] in snow and ice, is that it is one of the most dangerous climbs I have ever made.'

FRCC Journal (1926)

'Another party of three strangers – Dr Norman Collie, Messrs. Wilfred L.W. Brodie, and E.W. Marshall had arrived, and on Christmas Day made a desperate climb of Steep Ghyll under frozen conditions, while Robinson's party climbed on Great End.'

FW Jackson, 'Some Early Climbing at Wasdale and an Episode', *Rucksack Club Journal* (1925)

The Direct Start was added by JJS Allison and L Kendall in January 1963.

1891 Dec 25 South-East Buttress, Great End JW Robinson, G Hastings

'Up S. Gully then out onto right-hand face and straight up, built cairn at top with Hastings.'

JW Robinson's Climbing Diary, FRCC Archive

1892 Dec 27 B (Great) Gully, Wastwater Screes G Hastings, JW Robinson, JN Collie

The gullies of the Wasdale Screes were labelled from left to right by Haskett Smith in 1895, A, B and C; B Gully also being known as Great Gully. In the original 1979 winter guide to the Lakes only Great and C Gullies were recorded, but by the second edition of the guide in 1986, two minor gullies towards the right-hand (west) end of the crag had been climbed and were mistakenly named A and B. In this set-up Great Gully was assumed to be D, and gullies climbed to its left (east) were then labelled E and F (E actually already being A Gully, and F being another gully further left which was actually Seven Pitch Gully, although this may have been wrongly assigned in the 1924 FRCC guide)! Hopefully the situation is now resolved.

'It was on a perfect winters morning, many years ago now, that we started for the great gully in the screes. Not a breath of air stirred; hoar frost covered the ground: the trees were a mass of silver, glittering in the morning sun… Perpendicular walls rose on both sides for several hundred feet; above us stretched cascade after cascade of solid ice, always at a very steep angle and sometimes perpendicular. Up these we cut our way with our axes, sometimes being helped by making steps close to the walls and using any small inequalities on the rock face to steady us in our steps.'

JN Collie, *Climbing on the Himalaya and other Mountain Ranges* (David Douglas, 1902)

'Great help was afforded by the waterfall being almost completely ice and the turf also being frozen hard' (Wasdale Hotel Climbing Book, 1890–1919). It is interesting to note that this ascent was made the day after the first ascent of Moss Ghyll, during which no mention is made of ice or winter conditions. This must have been a sustained period of high pressure with hard frosts overnight and little or no snow.

The Right-Hand Branch was climbed in 1978 by J Loxham and R Wilson, and also around this time, or possibly earlier, by W Pattison and A Dunn. Chimney Finish added by W Pattison and J Arthy, 1984/5.

1893 Jan 9 Moss Ghyll, Scafell OG Jones

An amazing tour de force by Jones, arguably his finest hour. Climbed solo despite the encumbrance of a clinometer and broken ribs sustained by a fall from the Collie Step (luckily he was saved from worse thanks to the backrope he had fixed through a chockstone). OG Jones, *Rock Climbing in the English Lake District* (Longmans, 1897). It should be noted that the first ascent of the Moss Gill occurred only a few days prior. If Jones encountered ice on his ascent it is likely that Collie and his party encountered similar conditions but these were understated in their account.

The Direct Finish up Collier's Chimney was climbed by T Furness and J Fotheringham on 18 Feb 1984, but had probably been done earlier – the FRCC Journal (1917) notes that in 1917 GS Bower and Masson made an ascent of the Chimney. 'This was iced but was not rendered appreciably more difficult thereby, since we took the outside route up to the Sentry Box.' The Mechanical Orange variation finish was added by B Davison and RAL Jones on 14 Feb 1987, 'Named after a youth club in Puno, Peru. So poorly protected that the second unclipped from the belay and stood on the great chockstone ready to jump in order to prevent a groundfall should the leader come off!'

LAKE DISTRICT WINTER CLIMBS

1894 Striding Edge, Helvellyn WP Haskett-Smith

Climbed around this time, and probably before. This was a regular venue during the 1860s and 1870s for the Alpine Club who used it for alpine practice.

1896 Dec 25 Napes Needle, The Napes OG Jones and party

The Needle was covered in snow and the fells were very wintery. A photograph of the ascent, taken by the Abraham brothers, was published in the second edition of Jones's Rock Climbing in the English Lake District (Abraham, 1900); the date of the ascent and a note identifying Jones as one of the climbers in the picture appeared a few years later in a magazine article written by one of the Abrahams. It is doubtful if the Needle is ever anything more than a snow-covered rock climb, but ascents have been made when full winter conditions embraced the fells; Jones's may have been the first. George Sansom led three others up the Needle on 3 Jan 1911, finding it 'fairly stiff with snow on it', and the meet report in the FRCC Journal for Easter 1913 records ascents of the Needle and Needle Ridge when 'the fells were covered in snow and ice [and] nearly all rock work impossible'.

Prior to 1899 Needle Gully, The Napes OG Jones and party

The ascent was photographed by the Abrahams. Jones was killed in the Alps later that year

1899 Jan The Curtain and the Arete, Pillar OG Jones, G Abraham

'Though ice and snow masked the rocks insidiously, there seemed a chance of success'.

G Abraham, *Mountain Adventures at Home and Abroad* (Methuen, 1910)

1899 Apr 8 North Climb, Scafell G Barton, C Barton, Cowley, Davey

'The wind had gone due N. & with the snow as well things were moderately alpine...this was our first encounter with snow and ice... North Climb proved moderately hard under the present conditions.'

Barton Climbing Book, FRCC Archive

1901 Dec 26 Great Gully, Pavey Ark Two unknown Climbers' Club members.

'The cave and the small climb immediately above were successfully passed: then came a steep snow slope of 40 to 50 feet, and a short vertical climb, beyond which lay another slope terminating in what was considered the Mauvais Pas of the ascent, an almost "A.P." wall of 20 to 30 feet securely encased in ice... The leader...had got up some twenty feet...when hearing a rush of snow below he turned his head and was astonished and dismayed to behold his companion disappearing down the gully on his back. A bundle of Harris Tweed, enveloped in a cloud of snow, shot over the pitch immediately beneath, and the leader waited for the jerk, which he knew he would be powerless of withstand. But the jerk never came, for the second man, during his enforced idleness, noticing a large rock tooth on the left side of the gully, had swung the rope round it in a loop. When the platform of snow…gave way… the rope so jammed that it never even tightened between the leader and the tooth.'

'Christmas at Langdale Head', *Climbers Club Journal* (1902)

1903 New Year New West Climb, Pillar WF Wright, L Meryon, WG Clay, TL Winterbottom

An epic to say the least!

'They started about midday but found the conditions very icy… Eventually they arrived at the (final) slabs and found them glazed with ice. The leader attempted in vain to make progress further than a ledge 15 feet above the shattered rocks. Prolonged effort led to a sudden and unexpected descent. The second climber apparently possessed no belay, but when the fall occurred he instantly hitched the rope around a slight excrescence and braced himself for the strain. The leader went flying out over the ledge; the rope held and he hung suspended in the darkness over the abyss. The last man on the rope, anchored by his companion in front, was just traversing around the sensational corner from the chimney at the time. The sight of the flying leader so startled him that he also lost his balance and swung pendulum-like into a crack in the cliff where fortunately he became wedged, in a more or less dazed condition… The second climber, with commendable courage, undertook to lead them up the disastrous slabs; and after many attempts he was at last successful'.

Amalgam of quotes from George Abraham writing in *British Mountain Climbs* (Routledge, 1908), *Mountain Adventures at Home and Abroad* (Methuen, 1910) and *Adventures in Climbing* (Pelham 1964, p36).

Three of the party were killed in the Alps a year later.

1905 Feb 1 Mare's Nest Gully, Pike Crag Scafell Pike GH Almond, CT Oulton, CT Beecroft, WI Cumberlidge, PR Parkinson

Sometimes known as E Gully. Although not the first ascent, the details of the previous party are unknown.

'Climbed this gully completely in ice and snow. It afforded interesting climbing and has one difficult pitch which was turned by a previous party. The pitch was ascended by backing up the left wall with the aid of shoulders and ice axe from below and jamming the left knee in between this wall and the chockstone. Probably the gully is uninteresting in summer but in winter it is worth a visit.'

Wasdale Hotel Climbing Book, 1890–1919

Lake District Winter Climbs

1906/7 West Wall Traverse, Scafell A large party of Climbers' Club members

Over twenty climbers – including George Seatree, Geoffrey Hastings, the Abraham brothers, Lehmann Oppenheimer and AE Field – were staying at the Wastwater Hotel; the majority as part of a Climbers' Club meet. Heavy snow had fallen recently and large teams struggled up Skew Ghyll, Deep Ghyll, Lord's Rake and the West Wall Traverse. This is the first recorded winter passage of the last of these routes, but it had certainly been done earlier, possibly in the 1880s.

1907 Easy Terrace, Dow Crag SH Gordon, H Goodier

'Easy Terrace. Finish up Intermediate in ice and snow.'

Coniston Parkgate Climbing Book, FRCC Archive

1907 Dec 31 North Climb, Pillar Rock

On page 156 of the *FRCC Journal* Number 2 (1908)

1908 Rake's Progress, Scafell, and AB Buttress, Pike Crag Scafell Pike FRCC parties

'There was an unusually large quantity of snow on the fells, particularly on the North face of Scafell Pike. Ice and frozen snow abounded… Rakes Progress…presented genuine difficulties, being so choked with ice and ice covered snow that a party of three took over two hours to traverse it, cutting steps nearly the whole way from the foot of Lord's Rake to Mickledore Ridge. At the same time another party were experiencing a good deal of trouble with the buttress between A and B gullies on Pikes Crag.'

FRCC Journal (1908)

Pre-1909 Angle Tarn Gully, Hanging Knott G Abraham

'In wintertime…Hanging Knott is well worth a visit'.

G Abraham, *British Mountain Climbs* (Routledge, 1909)

Although the gully is not mentioned by name, it seems a very likely target.

1910 Easter Engineer's Chimney, Gable Crag CS Worthington and JD Gemmel

While a winter ascent is credited the exact level of winter cover and style of the ascent is unknown. 'During this Easter holiday the two (Worthington and Gemmel) did nearly all the severe and very difficult climbs in the Pillar, Gable and Scafell crags. A notable climb was Engineer's Chimney with a considerable amount of ice in it.'

TC Ormiston-Chant, 'In Memoriam: Claude Swanwick Worthington', *FRCC Journal* (1919)

First Ascents

1910 Easter North Gully, Bowfell SF Jeffcoat, TW Oliver, J Wilding

Actually a descent of the gully after ascending the continuation at the other side of the buttress. Probably climbed before. The party

'set out with the intention of climbing Bowfell Buttress by Oppenheimer's route, but returned with an account of a traverse of the buttress on snow. On arriving at the climb, they were unable to distinguish the route owing to mist. They therefore took to the snow in the gully to the left of the buttress, and by this reached the top… It was therefore, decided to descend the gully on the right side of the buttress which contained steep snow, in which good steps could be kicked all the way down.'

'Easter Meet 1910 Langdale', *Rucksack Club Journal* (1911)

1911 Jan 5 Arrowhead Ridge Direct, The Napes GS Sansom, JC Brunskill, A Woodsend

'There was a great deal of snow on the ridge and we had a very fine climb. At my "mauvais pas" below the Arrowhead I used my knee on the little holds and found them distinctly safer under icy conditions.'

George Sansom, *Climbing at Wasdale Head before the First World War* (Castle Cary Press, 1982)

1911 Great Gully, Dow Crag TC Ormiston-Chant, Balfour, Smith, Parker, Huntley, Pidcock, Lyon

'Fells snowbound, rocks about Great Gully badly glazed with ice… Two thermos flasks were smashed during the climb.' [The start of a great Lakeland tradition.]

Coniston Parkgate Climbing Book, FRCC Archive and *FRCC Journal* (1913)

Traverse and Slab Variation was added by J Ashcroft and C Bett, 9 Feb 1986.

1912 Black Chimney, Dow Crag L Hardy, G Milligan, HC Diss

'Black chimney (snow).'

Coniston Parkgate Climbing Book, FRCC Archive

1912 Woodhouse's Route, Dow Crag D Murray, Miss Eckland, L Hardy

'Woodhouse's Route of B Buttress (ice)' (Coniston Parkgate Climbing Book, FRCC Archive). Climbed on the same day that Rosalind Murray climbed North Gully, so the route was almost certainly in winter condition.

Rosalind Murray, 'A Blizzard on Doe Crags', *FRCC Journal* (1913)

1912 North Gully, Dow Crag Miss R Murray and party

'It was only my fourth attempt at climbing, and I had never climbed in snow… It was I was assured a very easy climb under ordinary conditions… This time, however, the "under ordinary conditions" was a saving clause, for our conditions were not ordinary. The rocks were covered with two inches of solid ice; genuine ice that had to be cut through with an ice axe before any hand or foot holds could be found.'

Rosalind Murray, 'A Blizzard on Doe Crags', *FRCC Journal* (1913)

1913 Mar 24 Central Jordan Climb, Pillar FRCC party

'A large gathering of climbers, the fells covered with snow and ice, a heavy fall taking place on Easter Saturday night and Sunday…plenty of step cutting…'

FRCC Journal (1913)

West Jordan Climb was descended the same day.

1913 Mar 24 The Old West Route, Pillar FRCC party

Almost certainly done earlier, but this is the earliest definite recorded ascent discovered to date. However, there is a reference to climbing Pillar Rock from the west side on Feb 6 1887, by G Hastings and party, when it seems to have been in winter conditions. Realistically this is likely to have been by the Old West.

'Bright sunny day with hard frost. Ascended Pillar Fell by gully direct from Mosedale. Climbed Pillar Rock by easy way and then descended down the gully to the west side and ascended the rock again, descending again by the easy way. The slab on the rock was coated with ice which had to be cut away.'

Wasdale Hotel Visitors' Book, 1885–1891

'Fells covered in snow and ice…nearly all rock work was impossible… North on Pillar was ascended by a party of two, a very fine performance under the conditions.'

'Easter at Wasdale Head', *FRCC Journal* (1913)

1913 Mar 25 Kern Knotts Chimney, Kern Knotts FRCC party

1913 Easter Overbeck Chimneys, Overbeck S Herford, G Sansom

'North on Pillar was ascended by a party of two, a very fine performance under the conditions, the same two also visited Overbeck Chimneys.'

'Easter at Wasdale Head', *FRCC Journal* (1913)

1914 New Year Walker's Gully, Pillar SW Herford, GS Sansom, CF Holland

'The gully was reached about noon and promised to be difficult as the lower reaches were draped with ice… For the next three quarters of an hour threading operations ensued, but at last an object appeared. It proved to be Herford's head: soon the rest of his body joined it from the bowels of the earth and he commenced a devastating assault on the upper icefall… The leader, after much toil, succeeded in attaining a somewhat doubtful position on a slope of ice below the top boulder. Here he found further progress impossible without imbedding the axe in frozen scree and using it as a handhold. The first attempt failed, as the scree went on strike and the leader's quiet remark, "I am coming off now," was immediately justified. The thread did its work and a second shot was successful. The writer now joined Sansom in a horrible ice well which exuded much moisture. Sansom had been immured here for about an hour and a half, and was a "demned damp moist unpleasant body." The next two pitches were speedily routed, though the writer has stirring memories of backing up with his right ear on one wall and his left toe on the other, with a ruck-sack possessed of at least seven devils on his back. This rucksack turned out to be really an octopus disguised as a rucksack, and by way of retarding prowess apparently attached suckers to the rocks when its bearer was not looking. When viewed from below the top pitch had appeared tolerably free from ice, but a closer inspection revealed the unpleasant fact that all the rock was covered with what the writer believes the Germans call 'Verglas.' (He hopes it isn't swearing.) For the next hour or so important threading operations ensued. Finally Herford performed marvellously on the right wall, assumed a backing up position and disappeared. Now it was Sansom's turn to do surprising things on the wall, apparently preserving his statu quo by sticking his head into ante-chambers in the rock while he unthreaded. Meantime, he who tells the tale had retired into the recesses of the cave and kept the octopus quiet by sitting on it. Subsequently this went aloft guarded by the ice-axe, which throughout displayed great strength of character.'

CF Holland, 'Walker's Gully', *FRCC Journal* (1914)

OG Jones, GD Abrahams and AE Field made the first ascent of this route in semi-winter conditions in 1899. There is a fine account of his epic ascent in his book *Rock Climbing in the English Lake District* (2nd ed, Abraham, 1900).

1914 Feb 21 South Chimney, Jones's Route and Blizzard Chimney, Dow Crag
CS Worthington, SW Herford, GS Sansom, AR Thompson, WB Gourden

This large party climbed these and Black Chimney. Although the record is not sufficiently detailed to prove that these climbs were in true winter condition, the fact that 'six inches of snow lay on the fells' that day suggests that there was a good chance that they were (Coniston Parkgate Climbing Book, FRCC Archive).

Pre-1915 Tarn Crag Gully, Thirlmere GD Abraham

'Worth a visit, especially in snow time' GD Abraham, *FRCC Journal* (1915)

1918 Easter Gully and Scoop Route, Dow Crag Mr and Mrs Murray, Mr and Mrs Ormiston-Chant, WA, JPR and one other

'Easter 1st pitch, traverse west… S. Chimney… good scramble in hard snow.'

Coniston Parkgate Climbing Book, FRCC Archive

1919 Jan North Gully, Low Water Crag JJ Bower, RP Vickers

'Snow gully from Low Water to Old Man Ridge (gully slopes up to L just to right of crags). Much step cutting… Time c4 hrs.'

Coniston Parkgate Climbing Book, FRCC Archive

1919 Feb 'C' Ordinary Route, Dow Crag TC Ormiston-Chant, G Wilson, D Pilley and party

'Dorothy Pilley and I will never forget Ormiston-Chant's astonishing lead of 'C' Buttress on Dow when it was a solid mass of ice, about half the climb being made in pitch darkness owing to the time spent in lowering various members of the party who had succumbed to the cold.'

Graham Wilson, 'In Memoriam: TC Ormiston-Chant', *FRCC Journal* (1957)

Graham Wilson's obituary, published a few years later, mentions that he attended his first FRCC meet at Coniston in Feb 1919, and the meet report says 'the weather was delightful, beautiful fine and cold, while the mountains glittered under a vesture of snow, frozen so hard as to support the boot, but not so hard as to prevent the delightful crunch which only the nails of a climbing boot can make on hard snow.' This strongly suggests it may have been the same meet during which the 'C' Buttress ascent took place, especially as the February Coniston meets in the following two years recorded mild weather.

1919 Intermediate Gully, Dow Crag PR Masson, C Alexander, G Bower

'Very badly iced' (Coniston Parkgate Climbing Book, FRCC Archive). Bower and Borrowman also record that they climbed Intermediate Gully in 1918 'in snow'. Unfortunately, the entry in the Parkgate Book is rather too vague to ascertain whether the gully was in true winter condition, or simply that snow was falling.

1925 Jan 4 Mitre Ridge, Grey Crag RST Chorley, KC Hopkinson, M Barber, GS Adair and 'another'

Ascended 'under snow'. However it seems likely this meant sweeping aside the powder to uncover rock, as the log records the snow's arrival occurring shortly before this, on the 3 January, after three days of gales (FRCC Buttermere Climbing Book).

First Ascents

1926 Hiatus, Gimmer Crag

'Hiatus – the whole course has been traversed under ice and snow…'. George Basterfield, *FRCC Journal* (1926) – though it may only have been top-roped.

1928 Jan Fleetwith Gully Chorley, KC Chorley, Pilkington, G Adair

'Climbed under alpine condition' (FRCC Buttermere Climbing Book). 'Chorley' was Lord Theo Chorley, husband of Katherine (nee Hopkinson). Early 1928 seems to have been one of the few periods of the decade when good conditions obtained, allowing skating to take place on Bleaberry Tarn.

1933 Pisgah from Jordan Gap, Pillar Rock J Carswell, F Carruthers

'Completely iced up' (Interview with Jack Carswell, 2006).

1935 The Barn Door, Birkness Combe J Carswell, B Beck

The ascent was filmed by Austin Barton, and the film survives: a copy is held in the FRCC Archives.

1936/7 Dollywaggon Gully and Chock Gully, Helvellyn S Cross, A Nelson

1937 Pisgah Buttress Direct, Scafell AT Hargreaves, S Cross, A Nelson

Hargreaves led the hardest pitches, after they had tossed a coin for the privilege (Interviews with Sid and Jammy Cross (née Nelson), 1996).

1937/8 Bowfell Buttress, Bowfell S Cross, A Nelson

Cross recalled tackling the crux crack pitch using Nelson's axe as a foothold while torqueing his own axe (an ancient implement given to him by the famous Lakes pioneer George Bower) higher up the crack. Later on in the climb (on which the pair led through) he displayed even more prescient technical skills when he used a Scout knife, which he carried on climbs for splicing hemp rope, as an ice-dagger. (Interviews with Sid and Jammy Cross (née Nelson), 1996).

1930s Little Gully, Pavey Ark S Cross A Nelson

1930s Pier's Gill, Lingmell S Cross, A Nelson

1930s Angle Tarn Icefalls, Langdale S Cross, A Nelson

c1940 Inaccessible Gully, Dove Crag J Birkett

An ascent which went unnoticed for many years thanks to Jim Birkett's famously reticent habit when discussing his activities, and his opinion that Lakes' winter climbing was 'cold and nasty'. Hence, the exact dating is still vague. An impressive achievement, especially as Birkett climbed this steep, technical route 'wearing tricounis and sporting a single long ice-axe'.

Bill Birkett, *Lakeland's Greatest Pioneers* (Hale, 1983)

1941 Apr Birkness Chimney, Eagle Crag W Peascod, B Beck

Famously climbed using rocks as ice daggers.

'I had asked Bert to bring up with him a suitable stone for hacking purposes and when he saw my belay he went back down the snow slope to find a larger one. Just above me was a small chockstone completely iced into the parent rock. With our primitive tools I attacked the ice, hoping to break a hole through behind the chock to form a thread belay. Hacking at ice, frozen pebbles and clay is painful work, particularly without gloves. Soon the gore from cut fingers mingled with the ice and clay to form an unpleasant melange.'

Bill Peascod, *Journey after Dawn* (Cicerone Press, 1985)

1947 Pinnacle Ridge, Gable Crag CR Wilson, B Williamson

'A severe winter with many roads blocked but with few routes climbed due to the scarcity of petrol and austerity of rationing after the war'.

Memories passed on to Les Kendall from Charlie Wilson, notes from Les Kendall (2006)

1940s Low Water Beck, Coniston

1954 Goat Gill, Buttermere Raffles Alpine Club

The Raffles Alpine Club was a small group of Carlisle Climbers led by the indefatigable Ray McHaffie; and at one time the only other member was Les Kendall.

1955 Feb 7 Jogebar Gully, Nethermost Pike South Face F Fitzgerald, GA Leaver, Miss SE Evans

1959 Central Gully, Raven Tor Barrow MCC

1950s Trough Gully and Carrock Fell Icefall, Carrock Fell Raffles Alpine Club

Notes from Les Kendall (2006). Trough Gully Icicle Start was probably added in 1986.

1960 Jan 8 Harrow Buttress, Grey Crag T Greenbank, Diggery, J Quinn

1960 Jan 21 Sergeant Crag Gully, Sergeant Crag L Kendall, J Curry

'Heavy snow' (Notes from Les Kendall, 2006).

First ascents

1960 Feb 20 Great Gable Traverse, Gable Crag R McHaffie, L Kendall (both solo)

'Also known as Traverse of the Gods as a result of Mac's wild antics. He had high hopes for the line and had pre-christened it. He did his best to make that grand name appropriate by taking some hair-raising variations while I plodded along the obvious easy way'.

Notes from Les Kendall (2006)

1960 Feb 22 Tophet Bastion, Tophet Wall L Kendall, H Sumner

'Very exceptionally deep consolidated snow gathers on the Napes ridges to give alpine style climbing of some quality. Good signs are the formation of a bergschrund along the foot of Tophet Wall and distinct cornices on the wall tops. Tophet Bastion was done in just such conditions.'

Notes from Les Kendall (2006)

1960 Mar Greenhow Gully, Deepdale N Hewett, C Hewett

Variation Finish CA Usher, M Humphries, 28 Jan 2003

1960 Dec 10 Moses's Back Door, Gable Crag L Kendall, R McHaffie (alt)

1960 Dec 11 North-West Climb, Pillar L Kendall, R McHaffie (alt)

The pair soloed up the initial slabs of North-by-North-West, kicking steps in the deep snow, until they got to a ledge just below the top of the Bounding Buttress, where they stopped to rope up and McHaffie took a photo of Kendall.

'Above the rock seemed free of all but a sprinkling of ice, a sad deception as we were soon to discover. Mac set off on the initial groove which was Very Severe. Now followed the first of the main pitches, Le Coin, which went nicely though I had to clear every hold of snow and chop one hold in the ice. As we made height, it became readily apparent that things were becoming increasingly severe. Where we had been able to avoid or clear ice below, it now became impossible to advance without painstakingly chipping away verglas. At Lamb's Chimney we found the crux. Half an hour's chopping holds from an ice bulge, combined tactics, and a piton for direct aid, finally saw us up with stick-like fingers to a safe stance near the final chimney.'

Les Kendall's Climbing Diary

It was repeated in January 1961. 'This was in difficult conditions with a foot of ice in the chimney, where a piton had to be used for aid (6 hours)'

JJS Allison, 'Winter Climbing in the English Lake District', *Nottingham University Climbing Club Journal* (1962/3)

1960 Dec 12 Columba's Gully, Borrowdale JJS Allison, D Moya

1960 Dec 12 Great Eastern Route, Scafell East Buttress L Kendall, J Douglas

Climbed in nailed boots with an axe and slater's hammer. When the going got too hard, the latter was used to knock the ice off so the rock could be used.

Direct Start, January 12 1999, B Davison, N Hewitt.

1960 Dec Chapel Crag Gully, Chapel Crags L Kendall

Also climbed by D Greenop and party about this time in conditions when the gully was completely banked out. Almost certainly climbed previously, as Greenop had been told about it by Bill Peascod. Direct Start: SJH Reid, S Prior, 5 Feb 2003 (but may well have been climbed before in banked out conditions); Pitch 2 Variation and Right-Hand Variation on Second Chockstone, B Davison, 1 March 1998.

1960 Dec Bleaberry Chimney, Chapel Crags L Kendall

1960 Dec Gillercombe Buttress, Gillercombe L Kendal, R McHaffie, J Douglas

1960 Dec Clark Gable, Gable Crag J Douglas, J Currie

1960 Dec 18 Gable End, Gable Crag R McHaffie, L Kendall (both solo)

1961 Dec 8 Little Chamonix, Shepherd's Crag AH Greenbank and party

Pre-1962 Aira Force, Ullswater JJS Allison

JJS Allison, 'Winter Climbing in the English Lake District', *Nottingham University Climbing Club Journal* (1962/3)

Pre-1962 Scale Force, Buttermere JJS Allison

Although not claimed as the first ascent, this is the earliest record so far found

JJS Allison, 'Winter Climbing in the English Lake District', *Nottingham University Climbing Club Journal* (1962/3)

Pre-1962 Taylor Gill Force, Borrowdale JJS Allison

Although not claimed as the first ascent this is the earliest record so far found

JJS Allison, 'Winter Climbing in the English Lake District', *Nottingham University Climbing Club Journal* (1962/3)

Pre-1962 Sour Milk Gill, Borrowdale JJS Allison

Although not claimed as the first ascent this is the earliest record so far found

First Ascents

JJS Allison, 'Winter Climbing in the English Lake District', *Nottingham University Climbing Club Journal* (1962/3)

1962 Summit Route, Low Water Crag JF Hool

Climbed previously by Barrow MCC.

1962 South Gully, Low Water Crag JF Hool

Climbed previously by Barrow MCC.

1962/3 Doctor's Chimney, Gable Crag J Douglas, J Currie

1963 Jan Kirk Fell Gill, Kirkfell L Kendall, A Todd

1963 Jan Ignition Buttress, Kirkfell L Kendall, A Todd

1963 Jan Pigott's Route, Birkness Combe L Kendall, A Todd

1963 Dec High Scawdell Gill and Scaleclose Gill, Borrowdale L Kendall

1963 Feb 27 C Gully, Wasdale Screes R Blain, R Heatherington.

'Ice all the way. Hampered in upper section by large flows of spin drift powder snow down the ice' (FRCC Brackenclose Hut Book). However a note in the Wasdale Hotel Climbing Book (1895) states: 'This gully is said to have been climbed throughout in winter. As there is no account in the book we shall be glad if our description elicits further information.'

1963 Feb 28 Cascade, Scafell Shamrock R Byfleet, R Blain, C Whalley

'Scafell Shamrock Tower by right-hand flank. 3 ice pitches – rest snow and rock. Previous parties steps had filled in. Enjoyable route of no great difficulty.'

FRCC Brackenclose Hut Book

It is not known who the previous party were, but JR Lees and a group from Ullswater Outward Bound were also at the hut and did several routes.

1963 Apr 14 Boneyard Wall, St Sunday Crag N Allinson, B Bullivant

'Plastered in snow.'

1963 Y Gully, Haystacks R McHaffie, A Liddell, M Burbage, A Todd

1963 Ill Gill, Kirkfell Raffles Alpine Club

1963 Lorton Gully, Buttermere L Kendall

LAKE DISTRICT WINTER CLIMBS

1963 Buttermere Gully, Grasmoor L Kendall

1963 Stack Gill, Haystacks L Kendall, J Douglas

'500 feet of gleaming blue water ice' (from a conversation with Les Kendall).

1963 Eagle Front, Birkness Combe R McHaffie, S Bradshaw

'Mac had persuaded a large Carlisle party up to Birkness Combe. Eagle Crag was completely plastered in snow and ice and Mac was very enthusiastic, but, by the time they got to the foot of the climb, most of the rest of the team were so intimidated that they had drifted off to Grey Crags to go rock-climbing instead. Only Stan, who was a bit slower on the uptake, remained.'

From a conversation with Les Kendall

'I was one of the team that opted out – we went and did West Gully and then waited for Mac and Stan. The entire buttress was encased in ice and verglas, and how Mac got up it I just don't know. He was wearing so little clothing that he was absolutely frozen and when he finally got to the top his arms were numb to the elbows!'

From a conversation with Alan Ferguson

1963 Central Chimney, Birkness Combe R McHaffie, J Holliwell, A Quey

Probably its only other ascent occurred when Brian Davison soloed it in 1988 having mistaken it for Birkness Chimney.

1963 Warnscale Beck, Buttermere L Kendall

1963 Combe Gill, Combe Head L Kendall

1963 Hind Gill, Borrowdale L Kendall

1963 Grains Gill, Borrowdale L Kendall

1963 Ruddy Gill, Borrowdale L Kendall

1963 Goat Crag Icefall, Goat Crag L Kendall

1963 Portcullis Ridge, Black Buttress N Allinson, B Bullivant

1964 Grey Crag Icefall, Grey Crag, Coniston Barrow MCC

First Ascents

Early 1960s Black Crag Icefall, Dovedale N Allinson, J McReady

A step-cutting tour de force – one axe, no ice screws, and l-o-o-o-ng run outs! Dachstein Mitts had just appeared in the UK that winter, and Jim bought Neil Allinson a pair as a reward for getting him up the route in one piece.

Early 1960s Sleet Wall, Hutaple Crag N Allinson and party

Variation Start added by B Davison, B Attwood, 26 Feb 1989.

1966 Feb Dove Crag Gully, Buttermere W Freeland, JJS Allison

Chicken Out P Dowthwaite, S MaCallum 1990s

Cluck It P Waiteshores, O Jones 1 Mar 2010

Fdge On P Cave, M Thomas 3 Mar 2010

c1966 Dec East Wall Route, Hutaple Crag N Allinson, J Soper

The original line of ascent may have been closer to East Wall as described in the current FRCC Eastern Crags guidebook.

1966/67 Force Crag Waterfall, Coledale WA Barnes, S Clark, A Jackman

'Barney' had been watching the fall through binoculars for several winters waiting for it to come into condition.

1967 Feb Percy's Passage, Low Water Crag J F Hool, C McGreath

1967 Feb Cautley Spout, Howgills W Pattison, A Robson

'May have been done before, but no-one I knew then knew of anyone who had climbed it earlier. My gear consisted of one axe, a Commando knife, one corkscrew ice-screw, and ex-army crampons with all the rigidity of lead sheet – you had to stop every few moves to knock them back into shape!'

Conversation with Bill Pattison (2006)

The Brussels Spout Variation was added by C Wells and M Hill, 29 Dec 1995.

1969 The Tilberthwaite Boys, Glassy Crag M Myers and party.

Climbed by local lads who used the area as a playground.

1969 Jan 30 The Direct Route, Scafell Shamrock R Bennett, R Lavender

Lost Arrow Traverse added by R Bennett and R Lavender in 1972

Pillar added by W Pattison and A Dunn, early 1970s

LAKE DISTRICT WINTER CLIMBS

1969 Feb Honister Crag Gully, Honister Crag E Cleasby, N Bulmer

1969 Mar 1 Dandle Buttress, Buckbarrow Crag M Lynch, D Jewell

1969 March West Waterfall Gully, Pillar BJ Clarke, J Stanger

A banked out grade II at the time – and in fact they followed someone else's footprints up it. The big ice pitch was first know to have been climbed by R Wilson, J Loxham and C Downer in March 1978, though the entry below is from JW Robinson and T Creak, January 1887!

'The deeply drifted snow gave us easy passage over the first fall, and in a few minutes the upper fall was before us, a solid column of hard ice. This was so vertical, and as no opportunity presented itself of gaining support from the wall of the ghyll, progress was no easy matter. Steadily cutting step over step with a deep notch for hand holds, we were able to get within six feet of the top – when down came darkness, and we quickly realised that we must make tracks at once or spend the night in that uncanny place.'

JW Robinson, 'A Novice in Snow', *FRCC Journal* (1907)
(NB The date in this article is incorrect, but it is right in his diary.)

1960s Curving Gully, Hutaple Crag N Allinson, K Harrison

1960s Curving Gully, Chapel Crags D Greenop and party

Originally known as Central Chimney. Probably climbed previously, as Greenop had been told of the crag by Bill Peascod.

Direct Variation added by J Martin and D Wilkinson, 20 Jan 2001.

1960s Troutdale Pinnacle, Black Crag AH Greenbank and party, also R McHaffie and party

1960s Corvus, Raven Crag R McHaffie and party

1960s Western Gully, Steeple and Variation Finishes **D Greenop**

1970 Jan Spiral Gully, Dove Crag D Roberts, A Austin

'Austin forgot his crampons and followed cutting steps'

FRCC Journal (1970)

1970 Feb 16 Eliminate A, Dow Crag WF Hurford, M Wragg

'Fells covered in snow down to the valley floor. A sunny day. The first two pitches were mainly rock with ice in the cracks, the upper pitches well iced. A peg was used for aid higher up.'

From a conversation with Wil Hurford

First Ascents

The route awaits a true winter ascent.

1970 Dec 20 Grooved Arete, Scafell Pike C Read, J Adams

1970 Hen Crag Buttress, Hen Crag, Wetherlam C Brown

The Left-hand Finish was added in 1980 by G Cock and D Andrews, and the Direct Start by A Hyslop and AH Greenbank, 26 Dec 1993. The Direct Finish was added by D Birkett (solo) in 2000.

1970/1971 Westmorland's Route, Dove Crag N Allinson, D Shakeshaft

1972 Mar 12 Stoat's Crack, Pavey Ark AH Greenbank, C Bacon

1972 Great Doup Buttress, Pillar R Bennet, R Lavender

1972 Long Ledge Entry and Exit, Scrubby Crag J Loxham, D Noels

1973 Grossbuttock, Great End A Rutherford, P Denny

Exceptional conditions during the early 1960s allowed many gully and ice lines to be climbed.

'In the exceptional conditions of 1960–1963 much then new ground was climbed on Great End by Geoff Oliver, Jeff Allison, Ray McHaffie, Les Kendall and others. Little was left untouched. In general it was found possible to climb anywhere, the standard rarely exceeding III to IV+.'

Notes from Les Kendall (2006)

1973 Feb Birkett's Gully, Mardale TW Birkett, M Myres

Rumoured to have been climbed previously.

1974 Window Gully Icefall, Great End R Bennett and party

Early 1970s Greathall Gill, Wasdale Screes W Pattison, A Dunn, D Barras, K Thompson

Early 1970s A Gully, D Gully, E Gully, Wasdale Screes W Pattison (solo)

Early 1970s Greathall Gill, Wasdale Screes W Pattison, A Dunn, D Barras, K Thompson

Early 1970s The Ramp, The Ramp Left-Hand, Wasdale Screes W Pattison, A Dunn

Early 1970s Seven Pitch Gully, Wasdale Screes W Pattison (solo)

Variation Icefall added by W Pattison and A Dunn around the same time

Early 1970s Juniper Ridge, Wasdale Screes **W Pattison (solo)**

Early 1970s Lost World Gully, Lingmell **W Pattison, A Dunn**

Early 1970s Stanley Force, Eskdale **W Pattison, D Barras**

Early 1970s Birker Force, Eskdale **W Pattison, D Barras**

Early 1970s Harter Fell Gill, Eskdale **W Pattison, D Barras**

Early 1970s Scale Force Gill, Eskdale **W Pattison, D Barras**

1976 Shoulthwaite Gill, Thirlmere **C Downer, C Samuels**

1976 Bramcrag Quarry Fall, Thirlmere **C Downer, S Kysow**

1977 Feb 24 Pinnacle Ridge, St Sunday Crag **I Wall, S Parr**

1978 Girdle Traverse, St Sunday Crag **N Kekus, R Cox**

1978 Gully of the Plods, Green Gable Crag **C Read**

> However, when considering this and other Green Gable Crag ascents it is worth noting,
>
> 'In the early '60s New Year parties were held at Dubbs Hut high on Fleetwith Pike. The proximity of Green Gable Crag ensured its popularity with those who were less hungover. Members of the Keswick, Carlisle and Raffles Alpine Clubs did everything imaginable. Notably some of the easier slopes were done by a dog which would bark for a top-rope if things became too difficult.'
>
> Notes from Les Kendall (2006)

1978 Robinson's Gully, Dove Crag **CM Wornham, G Bradshaw**

1978 Left and Right-Hand Grooves, Great End **B Jenkins and party**

> The direct version of Left-Hand Groove was added later by persons unknown.

1978 Girdle Traverse, Great End **R Bennett and party**

1978 Walla Crag Gully, Walla Crag **N Kekus, R Cox**

1979 Jan 21 Cambridge Crag Climb, Cambridge Crag **R Bennett, D Mounsey**

1979 Dec Southern Corner, Pikes Crag **E Cleasby, A Phizacklea**

FIRST ASCENTS

1979 Dec Gwynne's Chimney, Pavey Ark A Phizacklea, B McKinley, P Fleming

Direct Finish added by M Thomas, 14 March 2006.

1970s Cable Gully, Left-Hand Gantry Curtain, Right-Hand Gantry Curtain and Right Gantry Icefall, Honister Crag R McHaffie, P Hirst

1970s Western Gully and Left Gully, Haskett Buttress D Greenop

However Greenop is certain that they had been climber earlier. The Variation Finishes were soloed by B Davison, 29 Dec 2003.

1970s Terrace Ice, Ruthwaite Cove N Allinson, J Loxham

The pair climbed several other lines in this area.

1980 Stanger Gill, Borrowdale C Downer and party

1980 Nexus, Raven Crag I Conway, C Bacon

1980s AB Buttress, Ruthwaite Cove N Allinson, J Loxham

1981 Dec 13 Crinkle Cut, Crinkle Gill A Phizacklea, B McKinley, P Fleming

1981 Dec 28 Cook's Tour, Pavey Ark A Phizacklea, D Geere

1981 Module, Grey Crag, Coniston A Phizacklea, B McKinley

1982 Jan 16 Pudding Beck, Coledale M Lynch R Wightman

1982 Jan 16 Tranearth Quarry Icefall A Phizacklea, Ed Cleasby

1982 Jan 16 Parrock Quarry Icefalls A Phizacklea , Ed Cleasby (solo)

The same team top-roped Sasquatch (8) in Hodge Close Quarry – it has still to be led.

1982 Dec 23 White Ghyll Chimney, White Ghyll A Hyslop, S Hubbard

1982 Dec 26 Tilberthwaite Trundle, Tilberthwaite Gill A Phizacklea

1982 Dec 26 Side Show Icefall, Hodge Close Quarry A Phizacklea

Top-roped the day before, after Christmas Dinner, by R Graham and A Hyslop.

1982 Dec Mere Gill, Thirlmere L Kendall

1982 Dec Galeforth Gill Fall, Longsleddale L Kendall

LAKE DISTRICT WINTER CLIMBS

1982 Dec Cleft Gill, Buckbarrow Crag L Kendall, P Kendall

1983 Jan Born Free, Great End P Hirst, R McHaffie

1983 Feb 9 Photon Corner, Pillar D Kay, R Andrews

**1983 Feb 14 Raven Crag Left-Hand Gully and Kirkstone Curtain, Kirkstone Pass
P Dowthwaite, J Dowthwaite**

1983 Feb 18 Cave Route, Hobcarton Crag M Armitage

1983 Horse and Man Rock, Pikes Crag

1983 Crenation Ridge, Pikes Crag

1983 Steeplechase Groove, Pikes Crag

1984 Jan 20 Birkness Gully Wall, Eagle Crag J Fotheringham, C Bonnington

1984 Jan 21 Jones's Route Direct, Scafell A Phizacklea, E Cleasby

1984 Jan 29 Border Buttress, Eagle Crag M Armitage, T Daly

1984 Feb 15 Botterill's Slab, Scafell A Phizacklea, D Kay

Although unlikely, it is perhaps worth noting the following mention of a possible much earlier ascent by Geoffrey Winthrop Young:

'A little later another lesson was driven home, when we came upon Fred Botterill, upon whose eponymous slab on Scafell H.V. Reade and I had just made the first winter ascent cautiously and admiringly, much adrift upon the iced holds of the Professor's Chimney, which gave our Alpine technique no pause.'

GW Young, *Mountains with a Difference* (Eyre & Spottiswood, 1951)

The reference to this alleged first winter ascent is, however, a little puzzling. The mention of the 'Professor's Chimney' which lies at the head of Deep Ghyll, for example, is confusing, but it is possible that he meant the chimney up which Botterill's Slab finishes. In addition, the tone suggests that they first met Botterill shortly after their ascent. It is known that Young met Botterill at Wasdale Christmas 1907 ('The Club Meets', FRCC Journal, 1908), and he may have met him still earlier, yet the records credit Herford and Sansom with the second ascent of the route in 1913. Young wrote this brief account many years later, so we may never know what really happened, but the reference remains intriguing and misleading.

1984 Feb 18 May Day Direct, Scafell A Phizacklea, E Cleasby, S Swindells

First Ascents

1984 Feb 18 White Slab, Scafell E Cleasby, A Phizacklea

1984 Mar 1 Minotaur, Scafell A Phizacklea, D Geere

1984 Mar 24 Slime Chimney, Scafell J Fotheringham, S Howe

1984 Dec 21 Sod's Law, Scafell A Phizacklea, G Smith

1984 Central Groove, Kirkfell

1984 Urchin's Groove, Pikes Crag J Fotheringham and party

1984 Sinister Ridge, Black Crag W Pattison

1984 Dexter Slab, Black Crag W Pattison

1984 Black Crag Gully, Black Crag W Pattison

1984 Straight Gill – Right-Hand Arete, Lingmell W Pattison

1984 Castor, Scafell

1984 The Wrinkled Crinkle, Crinkle Gill J White

1985 Jan 19 Moss Ghyll Grooves, Scafell B Davison, R Jones, A Perkins

Several parties were vying for the first winter ascent. On the successful ascent the slab pitches were covered in unconsolidated snow with thin ribbons of ice in the corners. The route finally received its second ascent in 2010 by S Ashworth and P Cave.

1985 Jan 20 Mosedale Gully, East Gully B Davison, R Jones

1985 Jan 27 The Eagle's Claw, Eagle Crag S Clark, J Rigg, A Wardropper

1985 Jan 27 Central Icefall, Spout Head FRCC party

1985 Jan 27 Shamrock Chimneys, Pillar D Kay, M Lynch

1985 Jan Sledate Ridge, Gable Crag B Davison, P Herrold

1985 Feb 16 Engineer's Slabs, Gable Crag B Davison, R Durran, M Phillips

The Arete Finish was added by D Hetherington and D Donovan, 8 Jan 1997.

1985 Nov 27 Pendulum Ridge, Scrubby Crag S Miller, D Kay (alt)

Lake District Winter Climbs

1985 Nov 28 Overhanging Wall, Scafell J Fotheringham, G Bonington

1985 Intermittent Chimneys, Scafell Shamrock

1985 Sandbed Gill Crag, Thirlmere E Cleasby, M Lynch

1985 Bleawater Gill and Icefall, Bleawater Crag M Duxbury, C Clarkson, JD Kitchig

1985/86 Dungeon Ghyll, Langdale J White, I Williamson

Although portions had been climbed numerous times before, this is the earliest recorded ascent of the entire gill.

1986 Jan 3 Great Chimney, Scafell J Fotheringham, G Bonington

1986 Jan 4 Tricouni Slab, Scafell A Phizacklea, G Smith

On this ascent the team continued up the obvious continuation groove rather than moving right into the exit chimneys of Botterill's Slab

Also climbed about the same time by J Fotheringham and V Saunders.

1986 Jan 5 Left-Hand Route, Cambridge Crag A Hyslop, R Graham

1986 Jan 5 Right-Hand Route, Cambridge Crag R Wightman, D Seddon

One nut was used for aid on the crux pitch due to soggy turf.

The Direct Start was added by R Graham and L Steer, 13 Jan 1991.

1986 Jan 7 Deception, Pavey Ark A Hyslop, R Graham

1986 Jan 7 Gomorrah, Pillar D Kay, J Grinbergs

1986 Jan 25 Duncan's Groove, Great End D Richards, TW Birkett

1986 Jan 27 Left-Hand Climb, Black Crag, Dovedale M Cocker, R Andrews

1986 Jan 31 Middling Buttress, Pavey Ark T Walkington, B Rogers

1986 Jan Plaque Route, Bowfell Buttress D Sanderson, M Halsey

1986 Feb 9 Age Concern, Scafell S Howe, J Grinbergs, D Kay, M Lynch

1986 Feb 9 Steep Ghyll Grooves, Scafell T Stephenson, K Murphy, L Rutland

1986 Feb 13 Sinister Slabs, Bowfell Buttress R Graham, SJH Reid

First Ascents

1986 Early Feb Whiteout, Crinkle Gill J White, SJH Reid

A bold lead on rotting ice by John White.

1986 Feb 16 Hopkinson's Gully, Scafell R Wightman, M Lynch

1986 Feb 16 West Wall Climb, Scafell D Kay, S Lowe

1986 Feb 18 Ray of Sunshine, Crinkle Gill J White, J Thorpe

1986 Feb 19 Restless Natives, Scafell D Kay, J Grinbergs.

1986 Feb 19 Bridge of Sighs, Scafell S Howe, T Stephenson, P Andrews

1986 Feb 20 Siamese Chimneys, North Buttress R Wightman, R Graham

1986 Feb 20 Wight-Out, Crinkle Gill R Graham, R Wightman

1986 Feb 22 Moonbathing, Scafell A Phizacklea, D Richards

1986 Feb 26 Midnight Special, Scrubby Crag A Phizacklea, M Halsey

The Ringway Finish was added by A Phizacklea and A Rowell, 2 Jan 1995.

1986 Feb 26 Accidental Discharge, Hutaple Crag D Kay, J Grinbergs

1986 Feb West Buttress, Steeple J Loxham, M Mills

1986 Feb Steeple East Buttress, Steeple J Loxham, J Coradice

1986 Feb Border Buttress Gully, Eagle Crag P Dowthwaite, G Phillips, D Liddy

1986 Feb Oxford and Cambridge Ordinary Route, Grey Crag P Dowthwaite, G Phillips, D Liddy

1986 Feb Viking Buttress, Red Tarn Cove, Helvellyn W Freeland, A James

The Thor's Corner variation was added by S Ashworth, 1 March 2002. Arete Finish added P Cave 15 Jan 2007

1986 Mar 1&2 Central Buttress, Scafell A Moore, T Brindle

An imperfect ascent of the classic summer line which took place over two separate days. The Flake Crack was climbed without crampons as Moore had insisted he did not want to damage such an historical pitch. For the same reason he refused to carry pitons – much to the annoyance of Brindle who felt the climb would have been a lot safer with them. The party had gone with the intention of bivying out in duvet jackets on Jeffcoat's Ledge, but as the temperature plummeted they realised that hypothermia was highly likely if they stayed put, and they beat a hasty retreat to the valley, whereupon they were whisked round to a party at the Old Dungeon Ghyll. The next morning the pair walked in from Langdale, abseiled in and completed the route – an epic two days that immediately aroused a storm of controversy.

1986 Mar 2 Impunity Slabs, Scafell A Phizacklea

1986 Mar 2 Sod All, Scafell M Lynch, A Phizacklea

However a similar line was climbed c1972 by R Bennett and R Lavender.

1986 Mar 16 Upper Deep Ghyll Route, Scafell A Phizacklea

1986 Dec 20 Dollywaggon Great Chimney, Falcon Crag J Grinbergs, R Kenyon, S Ely

1986 Dec 22 Huckleberry Grooves, Nethermost Cove M Halsey, S Coxon

1986 Dec 27 Goat Scar Gully, Longsleddale I Waller, O Turnbull, SJH Reid

It was Ivan Waller's 80th birthday.

1986 Hope Head Icefall, High Ashgill – Alston J Fotheringham

1986 Birkside Gill, Thirlmere

1986 East Hutaple Groove, Hutaple Crag

1987 Jan 9 Wall Climb, Scrubby Crag J Grinbergs, D Kay

1987 Jan 10 Tic Tac Man, Falcon Crag S Miller (solo)

1987 Jan 11 Harvest Crunch, Scafell B Davison, R Mulvaney

1987 Jan 11 Ginny Clegg, Scrubby Crag J Grinbergs, D Kay

The Firedragon Finish was added by R Graham and I Weetman on 3 Jan 1995 during an early repeat of Grendel.

1987 Jan 17 Left of Centre, Pikes Crag A Phizacklea, D Kirby

1987 Jan 18 Heorot, Scrubby Crag A Phizacklea, B McKinley

1987 Jan 18 Slate Cap, Honister Crag C Downer, M Armitage

First Ascents

1987 Feb 21 V-Corner, Red Tarn Cove B Davison (solo)

    Extended Finish added prior to 1995 by persons unknown.

1987 Feb 21 Aspirant, Great End B Davison, A Wells

1987 Mar 21 Slanting Groove, Pikes Crag B Davison, A Atkinson

1987 Pollux, Scafell A Phizacklea, A Rowell, P Plowright

1987 Scabbard, North Buttress P Cornforth

    An impressive solo of which not much is known. Even the first ascentionist can't remember anything about it!

1988 Nov 22 Cofa Wall, Black Buttress N Kekus, S Kekus, J Fotheringham

1989 Feb 25 Horizon Climb, Boat Howe Crag A Phizacklea, D. Kirby

1989 Feb 25 Right of Centre, Pikes Crag B Davison, B Attwood

1980s Mjölnir, Red Tarn Helvellyn B Davison

1990 Jan 28 Deep Ghyll Integrale, Scafell A Phizacklea, J Holden

1990 Feb Starboard Chimney, Boat Howe Crag N Kekus, J Fotheringham

1990 Nov 28 Sodom, Scafell A Phizacklea, A Rowell, P Plowright

1991 Jan 6 Grendel, Scrubby Crag B Davison, B Attwood

1991 Jan 10 Dollywaggon Chimney Right-Hand Finish, Tarn Crag J Bumby, M Curtis

1991 Jan 10 Ledge and Groove, Bowfell Buttress R Graham, L Steer

1991 Jan 10 Halcyon, Scrubby Crag J Rigg, N Hewitt, B Davison

1991 Jan 12 Kirkby's Folly, Lonscale Fell M Kirkby, A Archer, M Robinson

1991 Feb 1 Central Route, Bowfell Buttress R Graham, L Steer

1991 Feb 12 Diagonal Gully, Dead Crag J Coyle, C Moyle

1991 Feb 13 Central Ice Fall, Dead Crag C Moyle, J Coyle

1991 Feb 16 Broad Crag Gully – Left Wall, Broad Crag J Daly, K Phizacklea, J Hudson

LAKE DISTRICT WINTER CLIMBS

1991 Feb 16 Left Branch Greta Gill J Daly, K Phizacklea, J Hudson

1991 Feb Blea Water Buttress, Blea Water J Loxham, A Loxham, J Morgan

1991 Feb Arlecdon Aquarian, Great End G Wilks, J Loxham

1991 Fisherplace Gill, Thirlmere P Yardley and party

1991 Rigghead Quarry Icefalls, Borrowdale R McHaffie, J Pierson, K Woolsoncroft

c1991 The Enforcer, Coledale P Wright, T Bryden, G Lee, D Nichol, A Hall

1991/92 Dob Gill, Thirlmere S Fletcher, J Metcalfe

Almost certainly done before.

1993 Nov 24 Evening Buttress, Angle Tarn D Wright, J Bean

1993 Isaac Gill, Langdale J White

1994 Jan 2 Overhanging Wall – Original Finish, Scafell A Phizacklea, D Donnini

Dom Donnini was heard to utter 'He's mad! He's going to kill himself! There's no ice!' In fact, according to Al, there was plenty of ice, just not as thick as Dom liked it.

1994 Jan 8 Right Wall Eliminate, Bowfell Buttress B Attwood, B Davison

1994 Jan 16 Right Buttress Crack, Brown Cove Crag B Davison (solo)

1994 Jan16 Central Route, Cock Cove Crag B Davison (solo)

1994 Eel Crag Gully and Eel Crag Main Ridge, Eel Crag S Miller

1994 Scott Gully, Scott Crag S Miller

1995 Jan 25 Vegiburger, Foule Crag O Ross

However, Bill Freeland and the FRCC had been climbing on Foule Crag since the 1960s without putting pen to paper.

1995 Jan 30 Traverse of the Sods, Foule Crag O Ross

1995 Jan 30 Wowzers, Foule Crag O Ross

1995 Jan East Gully, Scoat Fell Crag N Kekus, T Mather

1995 Feb 25 Corner and Rib, Bowfell Buttress B Davison, B Attwood

1995 Feb 26 Tarn Crag Buttress I & II, Tarn Crag B Davison (solo)

1995 Feb Oblique Reference, Gable Crag J Fotheringham

1995 Feb Jeffrey's Mount Escarpment P Dowthwaite, M Taylor

1995 Mar 4 North-West Gully, Pike of Stickle B Davison, C Ottley, C Wells (solo)

1995 Mar 5 Base Brown – Left Fork, Base Brown B Davison, C Wells (solo)

1995 Mar 9 Calculator, Parallel G, Garden of Eden, Arjuna, Green Gable Crag B Davison, C Wells

1995 Mar 9 Beta Hammer Belter, Epsilon Chimney, Ride the Wild Turf, Green Gable Crag C Wells, B Davison

1995 Mar 9 Sod-U-Like, North Gully, Green Gable Crag B Davison, C Wells (solo)

1995 Mar 12 Low Man by the Right Wall of Steep Ghyll, Scafell B Davison, C Wells

> The start was climbed by the Barton brothers and friends as a start to Slingsby's Chimney Route on April 11 1899.

1995 Mar 16 Chockstone Gully, Traverse Crag M Cocker, P Cocker

1995 Mar 18 Slingsby's Chimney Route, Scafell B Davison, C Wells

> A historic ascent using the combined practices of the time was achieved in Apr 1899 by G Barton, C Barton, Cowley, Davey. They were three and a half hours on the climb, which they describe as an 'encounter with snow and ice on difficult rocks with an "entirely incompetent climber"', and came to the conclusion that the route 'is nowhere really difficult barring the 60 ft in the middle of the climb which includes the Slingsby Chimney'! Nevertheless the Bartons admitted that, 'Our position on the Pinnacle wall was chilling in the extreme.... it was quite by chance we did not get frost bitten'
>
> Barton Climbing Book, FRCC Archive
>
> The exact line they took is not entirely certain.

1995 Mar 19 Buttress Right of Right-Hand Groove, Buttress Left of Left-Hand Groove, Great End R Graham

1995 Mar 19 Green Gable End, Green Gable Crag C Wells, B Davison

LAKE DISTRICT WINTER CLIMBS

1995 Mar 19 East of Eden, Green Gable Crag **B Davison, C Wells**

1995 Mar 19 North Face, Green Gable Crag **B Davison**

1995 Mar 21 Great Western, Scafell **B Davison, C Wells**

1995 Mar 27 Summer Time Blues, Gable Crag **B Davison, C Wells**

1995 Mar Turf At The Top, Honister Crag **C Downer, C Bacon**

1995 Mar Captain Patience, Honister Crag **C Downer, D Sanderson, A Stockford**

1995 Dec 21 Pulse, Foule Crag **O Ross**

Pulse Direct, O Ross Dec 21 1996

1995 Dec 24 Bottlescrue, Gable Crag **D Bodecott, P Bunting**

1995 Dec 24 Secondhand, Foule Crag **O Ross**

1995 Dec 24 Blunt Gully, Sharp Edge **O Ross**

1995 Dec 28 Crowdless Raven, Raven Crag **B Poll, F Dooley**

1995 Dec 28 Raven Crag Grooves, Raven Crag **N Clement, D White**

1995 Dec 28 Hopkinson's Crack, Dow Crag **B Davison, P Clay**

> However, although open to interpretation, John Jackson's description of his and his brother Ron's solo ascents of a frosty and verglassed Hopkinson's Crack sounds very much like the condition in which the route might be tackled using crampons and axes in the modern era, though they were climbing in nailed boots and without axes (J Jackson, 'The Iron Lung', FRCC Journal (2002)). Ron was known to have soloed Eliminates A, B and C on Dow in a morning wearing nails, and John notched up over fifty Himalayan expeditions during his lifetime. There is also an intriguing reference to George Basterfield:

> 'In his very early days, he found himself in the arena of Eastern Gully. Hopkinson's Crack, snow filled, seemed to him the easiest way out, and knowing or caring nothing of its reputation, he forced a way up it.'

> 'In Memoriam: George Bower', *FRCC Journal* (1950)

> Basterfield lived from 1877 to 1949. His first new route on Dow was in 1917, so presumably this ascent would date from about that time.

1995 Dec 29 Threshwaite Gully, Threshwaite Cove **B Davison, P Clay**

FIRST ASCENTS

1995 Dec 29 Far West Rib, Western Avenue, Hutaple Crag R Graham

1995 Dec Mill Gill, St Johns in the Vale P Ramsden, S Barker

1995 Rob's Icefall and Lower Icefall, Red Screes Northern Cove R Lee, R Lee

1996 Jan Oblique Chimney, Gable Crag N Kekus, A Park

OG Jones, L Amery and party made an early ascent in the style of the day. Climbed in conditions of heavy snow with Great Gable 'a picture of alpine solitude' and Styhead Tarn frozen over.

'There was much ice and fresh snow plastering the rocks…though the gully overhangs too much to prevent any drift snow to settle in it, the smooth walls of the gully were black and shiny with ice… I had started with my back resting against the left wall, bracing my feet as firmly as the ice would permit…'

OG Jones, *Rock Climbing in the English Lake District* (Longmans, 1897)

1996 Jan 13 Blake Rigg Ice Fall, Langdale TW Birkett, J White

1996 Jan 27 Hell Gill, Langdale N Green, B Davison, C Spark, N Lewis (solo)

1996 Jan 27 Hole in One, Bowfell Links B Davison, N Green, N Lewis, C Spark

1996 Jan 28 Hidden Gully, Bowfell Links B Davison (solo)

1996 Jan 28 Chimney Crack, Bowfell Links B Davison (solo)

1996 Jan 28 Pitch and Putt, Bowfell Links N Lewis, N Green, B Davison

1996 Jan 28 The Caddy, Bowfell Link C Spark, N Lewis

1996 Jan 28 Half Way Up, Bowfell Links B Davison, N Green, N Lewis

1996 Jan 28 Sunday Special, Bowfell Links N Green, B Davison

1996 Jan 28 Green Buttress, Bowfell Links B Davison, N Green

1996 Jan 28 Two Under Par, Bowfell Links N Lewis, C Spark (solo)

Direct Finish added by B Davison (solo), 21 Feb 1996

1996 Jan Hobgrumble Gill, Swindale J Lowther, J Fotheringham

1996 Jan Silver Screen, Greta Gill P Kennet and party

Lake District Winter Climbs

1996 Feb 3 Beckthorns Gill, St Johns in the Vale P Dowthwaite, R Pearson, S Umpleby, A Plimmer

1996 Feb 20 Dandle Face Direct, Buckbarrow Crag B Davison, C Wells

1996 Feb 21 No. 1 Gully, Tower Buttress, Twisting Turf, Great Gully, Great Gully Wall, Vulcan Buttress, Bowfell Links B Davison (solo)

1996 Feb 21 Shelter Corner, Shelter Icefall, Central Chimney, A Gully, B Gully, Gully Icefall, Shelter Crag, Langdale B Davison (solo)

1996 Feb 24 Tia Maria, Scafell K Phizacklea, S Merry

1996 Feb 25 Combe Head B Davison, P Clay

> However, the crag was climbed on extensively by the Raffles Alpine Club in the early 1960s.

1996 Feb 27 Arete, Chimney and Crack, Dow Crag D Sanderson, J Coe

1996 Feb 27 Broadrick's Crack, Dow Crag B Davison, C Wells

> C Read and B Robinson climbed Broadrick's Crack to the Bandstand and finished via Hopkinson's Crack, 9 March 1974.

1996 Feb 28 Smoken, Foule Crag O Ross

1996 Feb 28 Centre Route, Scafell B Davison, N Green

1996 Feb South-East Gully Left-Hand Buttress, Great End P Kennet and party

1996 Mar 2 Zero Gully, Gladstone Knott B Davison, P Clay

1996 Mar 2 Left Corner, Y Route One, First Chimney, Second Chimney, Fifth Chimney, Gladstone Knott B Davison (solo)

1996 Mar 2 Y Route Two, Third Chimney, Gladstone Knott P Clay (solo)

1996 Mar Arctic Spring, Scott Crag S Miller, J Lowther

1996 Mar Ema Ho, Chamber's Crag J Fotheringham, D Hayward

1996 Mar Big Question, Ill Crag J Fotheringham, D Hayward

1996 Mar Pier Review, Piers Gill J Fotheringham, D Hayward

1996 Nov 24 Twisting Gully, Scafell P Dowthwaite, S Edmondson

FIRST ASCENTS

1996 Nov 28 Fourth Chimney, Gladstone Knott **B Davison**

1996 Dec 29 Blea Water Cleft, Blea Water **D Scott, P Braithwaite**

1996 Dec 31 Black Crag Grooves, Black Crag **C Wells, M Hill**

1996 Quarryman's Falls, Honister Crag **C Downer, G Lee**

1996 Left Wall of Greta Gill Left-Hand Branch, Lingmell **P Kennet and party**

1997 Jan 1 Scorpion, Hutaple Crag **B Davison, N Hewitt**

1997 Jan 1 The Main Ridge Climb by the Lower Slabs Ordinary Route, Black Crag **C Wells, M Hill**

> Variation Gully Finish added by A Clifford 15 Feb 2003

1997 Jan 2 Gone with the Wind, Gable Crag **P Kennet and party**

1997 Jan 2 Eye Spy, Scafell **B Davison, N Hewitt**

1997 Jan 2 Dharma Armour, Scafell **N Hewitt, B Davison**

1997 Jan 2 Chimney Stack, Scafell **B Davison, N Hewitt**

1997 Jan 4 Mallory's Corner, Gable Crag **D Bodecott, R Johnson**

> Direct Start added by S Ashworth and P Ashworth, 27 Dec 1999.

1997 Jan 4 Lesser Fall, Honister Crag **B Davison (solo)**

1997 Jan 5 Tunnel Vision, Honister Crag **B Davison (solo)**

1997 Jan 5 Y-Gully Left Branch, Harter Fell Crag **D Scott, P Braithwaite**

Right Branch, **B Davison, 1 Feb 2003**

1997 Jan 11 High Beck, Ennerdale **N Kekus, B Davison**

1997 Jan 11 Savage Gully, Pillar **B Davison, N Kekus**

> An epic ascent that finished in a thunderstorm in the dark as all true epic ascents should – the struggle down through the forest was equally gruelling:
>
> 'We had one poor head-torch between the two of us which only worked for 3 or 4 seconds at a time, and wasn't good enough for us to find our way off the crag so we resorted to abseiling down the route by feel. Pulling down the ropes dislodged a block and we could hear it in the dark, rattling down the groove towards

us – fortunately it missed. We got separated in the woods and I walked into a tree and got a foot long piece of branch stuck in my eye. I managed to pull it out, but couldn't see anything, fortunately I wasn't blinded , it was just so dark. We finally reached the car at 3am'.

Interview with Brian Davison

The Direct Finish was added by SJH Reid and S Prior, 30 Jan 2004 during the second ascent.

1997 Jan 22 Bottleneck Blues, Gable Crag C Bonington, D Bodecott

1997 Greta Garbo, Greta Gill P Kennet and party

1998 Feb 28 Left-hand Buttress, Great Carrs S Parson

1998 Feb 28 Central Buttress, Great Carrs R Jarvis

1998 Dec 6 Slab and Groove, Right-Hand Gully, Left-Hand Gully, Middle Gully, Hobcarton Crag B Davison (solo)

1998 Dec 7 Black Shiver, Black Crag A Hyslop, J Burrell

1998/1999 Vestry Wall, Scafell Pike P Kennet and party

1999 Jan 16 Straight Gully, Chapel Crags B Davison (solo)

1999 Jan 17 Sunday Chimney, Chapel Crags B Davison, D Wilkinson

1999 Jan 17 Narrow Gully, Curving Gully Variation Finish Chapel Crags B Davison, D Wilkinson (solo)

1999 Jan 17 Straight Buttress, Chapel Crags B Davison (solo)

Climbed via its right-hand side. Climbed via its left-hand side by N Kekus, S Kekus, 19 Dec 2004.

1999 Jan 17 Bootlegger's Groove, Gable Crag M Armitage, D Bodecott

1999 Feb 19 Flying Buttress, Chapel Crags B Davison, P Bartlett, D Wilkinson

Right-Hand Start added by B Davison (solo), 27 Dec 1999.

1999 Mar 6 Big Answer, Ill Crag D Hayward, I Armstrong

1999 Mar Crack Magic, Flat Crag A Nelhams, D Mounsey

1999 Dec 11 Jacob's Ladder, Scafell P Dowthwaite, P Smalley

FIRST ASCENTS

1999 Dec 26 Hind Cove Gully and Rib and Gully Climb, Hind Cove B Davison (solo)

However, RC Gilson left a short note of his ascent of Hind Cove Gully on 1 January 1897 in the Wasdale Climbing Book. He makes no mention of snow or ice.

1999 Dec 27 Monday Chimney, Chapel Crags B Davison (solo)

1999 Dec 29 Mary Ann, Flat Crag B Davison, N Turton

Variation Summer Finish P Cave, C Sterling, 13 Mar 2006

2000 Mar 4 Hooch, Gable Crag D Bodecott, R Kenyon

2000 Dec 20 Pinnacle Crack, Gable Crag S Ashworth, D Noddings

2000 Dec 26 West Hutaple Edge, Hutaple Crag A Hyslop, S Wood

2000 Dec 30 The Neckband, Neckband Crag A Hyslop, J Hughes

2000 Dec 30 Groove and Ramp, Neckband Crag D Birkett, M Jenner

2001 Jan 18 A Carton of Hobnobs, Sheep Buttress, Hobcarton Crag D Wilkinson, J Martin

2001 Jan 19 Sodomy, Turf Accountant, Chapel Crags D Wilkinson, J Martin

2001 Jan 20 West Hutaple Variations, Hutaple Crag B Davison

An unsatisfactory day soloing.

2001 Jan 20 Little Sod, Chapel Crags J Martin, D Wilkinson

2001 Jan 20 Raven Crag Buttress, Raven Crag A Blackburn, I Grimshaw, T Hawkins

2001 Dec 29 Rape and Pillage, Red Tarn Cove S Ashworth, D Davies

Pitch 1 was originally named Prince of Darkness and was climbed by S Ashworth and B Malcolm at night after work.

Variation Finish added by M Thomas and C Badcock, 2 Jan 2002.

2001 Dec 30 Warn Gill, Haystacks B Davison, D Wilkinson

In lean conditions – best left until the next ice age.

2001 Dec 31 Right-Hand Gully, Parallel Gully Right and Left, Brant Bield Crags B Davison, D Wilkinson

Lake District Winter Climbs

2002 Jan 1 Grass Corner, Gully Arete, Chapel Crags B Davison (solo)

2002 Jan 1 Bear Left, Right Frog, Chapel Crags B Davison, D Wilkinson

2002 Jan 2 Mutley's Icy Wait, Green Gable Crag A Clifford (solo)

2002 Jan 3 Skint and Single, North Buttress M Thomas, D Almond

2002 Feb 2 Close to the Edge, Steel Edge S Harvey

2002 Feb 2 South South Gully and South South Groove, South Hen Crag S Harvey, P Bardsley

2002 Feb 2 Hen's Teeth, Hen Crag S Harvey, P Bradsley

2002 Feb 2 North Buttress, Hen Crag S Harvey

2002 Feb 28 Torquers are no Good Doers, Gable Crag S Ashworth, M Fryer

2002 Feb Hollyway, Penny Lane, Twopenny Crag C Dandridge

2002 Mar 2 Windy Ridge, Gable Crag H Davies, I Vermeulen

First claimed ascent, however climbed numerous times in the past.

Variation Finish B Davison (solo), Dec 30 2003 – also probably climbed before.

2002 Dec 8 Blade Runner, Red Tarn Cove S Wood, J Corrie

2002 Dec 20 Bobbins Route, Ramp Route, Cock Cove Crag S Wood, A Hyslop

Direct Start added by M Thomas and C Ensoll, 20 March 2006.

2002 Dec 21 Thanks for the Tip, Cock Cove Crag A Clifford

Variation Always Leave a Tip D Bell, R McGibbon, 8 Feb 2009

2003 Jan 3 Snicker Snack, Gable Crag S Ashworth, S Wood

The winter ascent of this classic summer E3 aroused considerable controversy at the time, mainly revolving around whether it was in winter condition or not, whether aid had been used, and whether it would seriously damage a fine summer climb. The first was refuted by photographic evidence, the second vehemently denied, and only time will tell regarding the third. It certainly was a fine achievement, despite an abseil inspection immediately prior to the ascent, and it inspired a wave of development of modern winter routes on the crag.

'A lot of people must have been quite relieved when I finally climbed Snicker Snack as I had been obsessed by it for at least a year. Captured by the photo in the summer guide and knowing that the crag offers great winter conditions, this 40m, pick-width crack seemed like a dream line for the winter climber. My first attempt ended in failure, it was after work and the crag was in the best condition I have ever seen it in, I got carried away and decided to set off up it, with hindsight this was pretty foolish, even with 4 headtorches (1 on each ankle, one pointing up and one pointing down) I still couldn't see enough to begin unlocking the sequency climbing. All too soon the climbing became too hard and to add insult to injury I snapped the head unit off my axe. Route 1: Climber 0. With an air of healthy competition permeating the Lakes' winter scene I headed up to Gable yet again, aware that conditions were building and that a strong team knew about my route and were heading up to do it the next day. I rapped the line on the day to try and persuade myself that it was possible and that my previous struggles were merely due to darkness, this didn't really help and I just had to get on with it. The climbing was fantastic, very thin and sequency for your feet but near perfect hooks all the way. The top pitch was surprisingly good with excellent positions. Snicker Snack was climbed with leashes, I think a more modern leashless approach will take at least a grade off the difficulty and make the whole experience more enjoyable. The route received a very impressive on sight ascent the following day at the hands of Nick Bullock and Dave Hunter.' Steve Ashworth 2006

2003 Jan 3 Ramp It Up, South Gully, Ruthwaite Cove A Hyslop

2003 Jan 4 Troll, Gable Crag D Birkett, M Jenner

2003 Jan 4 Turf Wars, Turfs Up, New Turf, Deep Cut Chimney, Turf Walls, Pinnacle Groove, Turf Time, Black Chimney, No 2 Buttress Traverse, Chapel Crags B Davison (solo)

2003 Jan 4 Coco-Tara Direct, Cock Cove Crag A Clifford, P Newton

2003 Jan 4 East Hutaple Gully Devious Exit, Hutaple Crag W Walker, M Blackburn

2003 Jan 5 Sheltered Accommodation, Shelter Crag B Davison (solo)

2003 Jan 5 Thrash Corner, Rescue Groove, Dolly Mixture, Ruthwaite Cove A Hyslop, J Lagoe

2003 Jan 5 Swallow Gully, Nethermost Cove P Jackson and party

However this area was extensively climbed on by N Allinson and friends in the 1960s and 1970s.

LAKE DISTRICT WINTER CLIMBS

2003 Jan 6 Jabberwock, Gable Crag D Birkett, P Deady

J Cartwright and M Dickinson repeated the route and added the Left-Hand Finish the following day, not without excitement as Dickinson had left his crampons behind but managed without!

2003 Jan 7 Back Off, Trundle Ridge, Gable Crag S Wood, S Ashworth

'Woody and myself were convinced that an elaborate conspiracy was taking place against us with various collaborators trying to send us to crags that weren't in condition. Gable was clearly the place to go. We were disappointed to hear that Dave Birkett had beaten us to the brilliant winter line of Jabberwock the previous day, so we had to pick another objective. With an early start we were already half way up Trundle Ridge when one of the teams who had been trying to throw us off the scent arrived at the crag. We finished the day with a second new route, Back Off, so called because both me and Woody failed to lead our respective pitches, I led Woody's pitch and he led mine.'

Steve Ashworth 2006

2003 Jan 7 That 'ard, Bason Crag J Fotheringham, D Hayward

2003 Jan 7 White Russian, First Cut, Whelter Crag J Fotheringham, D Hayward

2003 Jan 8 Mono Culture, Ruthwaite Cove J Lagoe, A Hyslop

2003 Jan 8 Die Another Day, North Buttress S Ashworth, M Panton

2003 Jan 8 Gimps to the Left of Them, The Flying Gimp Trick, North Buttress Bowfell S Wood, D Kells

2003 Jan 10 Browney Gill, Great Knott Langdale and Variations B Davison (solo)

2003 Jan 11 Bus Shelter, Shelter Ridge, Thirty Nine Steps, Central Chimney Left Finish, Shelter Crag B Davison, N Hewitt

2003 Jan 11 Anderson, Morrison, Shelter Crag S Muir, D Wilkinson

2003 Jan 11 Turf Corner, Cock Cove Crag A Clifford

2003 Jan 11 Swallow Rake, Nethermost Cove P Jackson, M Would, R Rushworth

However this area was extensively climbed on by N Allinson and friends in the 1960s and 1970s.

2003 Jan 11 Turf-tastic, Ruthwaite Cove P Sanday, C Pope

First ascents

2003 Jan 12 Big Issue, Shelter Crag B Davison, N Hewitt

2003 Jan 12 In Her Mouth, Gable Crag K Williams, R Horton

2003 Jan 17 West Gully Tunnel Route, Black Crag A Clifford

2003 Jan Juniper Crack, Scrubby Crag A Hyslop, H Davies, D Hunter

2003 Feb 1 Little Harter Gully, Arrowhead Buttress, Harter Fell B Davison (solo)

2003 Feb 4 Fibre Tube, Wimp's Route, Flypaper, Bason Crag J Fotheringham, D Hayward

2003 Feb 5 Further from the Edge, Steel Edge, Wetherlam R Jones, R Jones

2003 Feb 22 Easy Gully and West Gully Cave Route, Black Crag A Clifford, C Thistlethwaite

2003 Mar Acceleration due to Gravity, Terminal Velocity, Dollywaggon North Crag S Ashworth, A Hyslop

2003 Dec 22 Wild World, Low Water Crag S Harvey, R Jones

2003 Dec 28 Tongue and Groove, Scrubby Crag T Marshall, G Marshall

2003 Dec 31 Dollymixture, Ruthwaite Cove A Clifford (back rope solo)

2004 Jan 2 Haskett Gully, Haskett Buttress B Davison (solo)

2004 Jan 2 West Chimney Route, North Gully, Steeple West Buttress B Davison (solo)

2004 Jan 4 Hen Pecked, Hen Crag S Harvey, P Bardsley

2004 Jan 17 Threepenny Bit, Twopenny Crag B Davison

2004 Jan 18 Loki, Red Tarn Cove K Telfer, P Morgan

2004 Jan 18 Scoating for Boys, Scoat Fell Crag C Wells, M Twomey

2004 Jan 29 Soul Vacation, North Buttress D Almond, M Thomas

2004 Jan 29 Gimpsuit Fall, Bowfell S Keenor, I Almond

2004 Feb 29 Green Ledge Icefall, Pillar SJH Reid, D Bodecott (solo)

2004 Feb 29 Incline Fall, Honister Crag A Cannon, N Smith

Lake District Winter Climbs

2004 Mar 12 First Cut is the Deepest, Great End S Ashworth, M Fryer, G Howarth

2004 Mar 13 Pinnacle Climb, Falcon Crag H Davies, I Vermeulen, R Bilton

2004 Dec 19 Icy Chimney, Ramp Line, North Buttress B Davison (solo)

2004 Dec 19 Left Gully, Buttress Gully, Traverse Buttress B Davison (solo)

2004 Dec 19 Ramparts Chimney, Black Crag S Harvey, P Bardsley

2004 Dec 19 Heirloom, Heirloom Crag A Nelhams, T Lofthouse

2004 Dec 27 Mulled Wine, Low Water Crag S Harvey

2004 Dec 28 Serendipity Ridge, Scoat Fell Crag SJH Reid, C Wells

2004 Dec 28 Scoathanger, Scoat Fell Crag C Wells, SJH Reid

Finished via Scoating for Boys. The Direct Finish was added by SJH Reid and C Wells 16 Feb 2005.

2004 Dec 29 Professor, Cambridge Crag A Nelhams, P Yardley

2005 Feb 2 Racecourse Hill Recourse, Blea Tarn A Phizacklea

2005 Feb 2 Racecourse Gully, Blea Tarn A Phizacklea, K Phizacklea

2005 Feb 16 Turf Wars, Scoat Fell Crag SJH Reid, C Wells

2005 Feb 16 Sod this for a Lark, Scoat Fell Crag C Wells, SJH Reid

2005 Feb 26 Original Route, Rampsgill Head Crag B Davison, D Wilkinson

2005 Feb 26 South South Gully, Rampsgill Head Crag B Davison, D Wilkinson (solo)

2005 Feb 26 South Pinnacle Ridge, Rampsgill Head Crag D Wilkinson, B Davison

2005 Feb 26 South Gully, Rampsgill Head Crag B Davison, D Wilkinson

Left-Hand Variation added by B Davison and D Wilkinson, 6 March 2005.

2005 Feb 26 Butterfingers, Westmorland Crag A J Huddart, JA Stevenson

2005 Feb 26 Drop Out, Dropping Crag A Phizacklea, K Phizacklea

2005 Feb 26 Middleboot Gill A Phizacklea, K Phizacklea (probably done before)

2005 Feb 27 Follow Your Nose, Westmorland Crag AJ Huddart, JA Stevenson

First Ascents

2005 Feb 27 Central Gully, Rampsgill Head Crag B Davison (solo)

Escape Exit B Davison (solo)

North Pinnacle Exit B Davison and D Wilkinson, the same day.

2005 Feb 27 North Gully, Rampsgill Head Crag B Davison, D Wilkinson

2005 Mar 5 Central Ridge, Rampsgill Head Crag B Davison, D Wilkinson

2005 Mar 5 Left Gully, Rampsgill Head Crag B Davison, D Wilkinson

2005 Mar 5 Right Gully, Rampsgill Head Crag B Davison (solo)

2005 Mar 6 Buttress Groove, Rampsgill Head Crag B Davison, D Wilkinson

2005 Mar 6 Friends Above, Rampsgill Head Crag B Davison, D Wilkinson

So called because the first ascentionists were buzzed by friends in a helicopter during the climb – taking aerial crag photographs.

2005 Mar 6 Central Pinnacle Gully, Rampsgill Head Crag B Davison (solo)

2005 Mar 6 Evolution, Great End S Ashworth (unseconded)

'After a hard spell of training in the previous autumn, and fired up by two weeks of climbing in Scotland, it was time to climb something at home. Having stood underneath it on a number of occasions, I knew that this route wouldn't suit my style of climbing (hence a concentration on more explosive moves in my training), so it was going to be a challenge, and I wanted to climb it ground up and on sight. I took one impressive clattering whipper onto a Friend 5 which I had placed before committing to the crux, dropping an axe in the process. I descended, pulled the ropes and set off again. The route was very pumpy, pulling on quite tenuous hooks. Even with both axes in the turf over the top I still felt that I might fall off'. Steve Ashworth 2006

2005 Mar 6 Central Buttress Variation Start, Chapel Crags N Kekus, S Kekus

Direct Start B Davison, D McGimpsey 31 Jan 2010

2005 Mar 6 No Way Out, Cambridge Crag A van Lopik, T Fish

2005 Mar 8 The Girdle Traverse, Scafell S Ashworth, B Davison

'A route that had been in the back of my mind for some time, I just needed someone to climb it with. Brian had been in touch with me over the production of the new guidebook, saying that he felt a crag had matured once it had a girdle traverse. He agreed to come along. I felt like some young pretender with my leashless axes and monopoints standing next to Brian in with his slightly more dated gear. It was a great route, one of the best I have done, the conditions were so good that it all seemed to pass in quite a relaxed manner. Neither of us had a camera that worked with us, so you'll just have to picture the temperature inversion, alpenglow picking out Gable in the early evening and glistening neve on the crest of the pinnacle.'

Steve Ashworth 2006

2005 Mar 12 Blow Out, Rampsgill Head Crag D Wilkinson, D Williams (alt), R Gray

2005 Mar 12 Windy Buttress, Wind Up Rampsgill Head Crag D Wilkinson, D Williams, R Gray

2005 Mar 13 Gendarmerie, Umbrella Gully, Easy Buttress Rampsgill Head Crag D Wilkinson, R Gray

2005 Mar 13 Long Walk, Crinkle Gill Area B Davison, D Donnini, N Wharton

2005 Nov 26 Band on the Run, Traverse Crag S Ashworth

Soloed during his lunch hour from work!

2005 Nov 26 Misty Mountain Hop, Cambridge Crags S Ashworth

Also soloed during his extended lunch hour from work.

2005 Nov 27 B.B. Corner, Flat Crags S Ashworth, J Kelly

2005 Nov 27 Dolly Daydream, Dollywaggon North Crag J Rigg, W Tapsfield

2005 Nov 29 Into the Groove, Traverse Crag S Ashworth B Davison

2005 Nov 29 Big Groove, Traverse Crag B Davison, S Ashworth

During this cold snap Ashworth climbed five new routes during four days at work!

2005 Nov 30 First of Many, Black Crag W Sim, E Booth

2005 Dec 29 Buttress Gully, Red Screes Northern Cove B Davison (solo)

2006 Left Pillar, Kirkstone Pass Quarry P Cave and party

2006 Feb 25 Solo Symphony, Dollywaggon North Crag H Worsnop

2006 Mar 3 Cambridge Girdle, Cambridge Crag S Ashworth, B Davison

2006 Mar 3 Bowfell Girdle, Bowfell Buttress B Davison, S Ashworth

First ascents

The second traverse of a snowy day.

2006 Mar 4 Southern Cross, Scafell Pike N Kekus, S Kekus

2006 Mar 4 Buttress Route and Gully Arete, Red Screes North Cove B Davison (solo)

2006 Mar 5 The Memo, Hutaple Crag R McGibbon, D Bell

2006 Mar 5 Riboletto Groove, Cambridge Crag A van Lopik, S Normington

2006 Mar 5 Two Grooves, Brown Crag Cove B Davison, N Wharton, D Donnini

Variation Finish 2010 Jan 1 H Davies, J Bumby, M Holt

2006 Mar 13 The Crack Direct, Gimmer Crag D Birkett, M Edwards

The Crack was recorded as having been climbed in winter prior to 1962 but it is not known exactly what the conditions were or what route was taken

JJS Allison, 'Winter Climbing in the English Lake District', *Nottingham University Climbing Club Journal* (1962/3)

It was also climbed on 9 March 1969 by WF Hurford and S Town. The pair avoided the first pitch by starting up Hiatus. Conditions were described as 'Lots of snow, but not full-blown iced up' (Interview with Wil Hurford).

2006 Mar 14 Inferno, White Ghyll D Birkett, M Edwards

2006 Mar 15 Turfed Out, Green Gable Crag BJ Clarke (solo)

2006 Mar 16 The Gnomon, North Buttress M Thomas, D Almond

2006 Mar 17 Salvation, Neckband Crag M Thomas

A nerve-wracking rope solo.

2006 Mar 17 Antarctic Monkeys, Lingmell H Worsnop, M Balmer

2006 Mar 18 Ill Gully, Ill Crag B Davison, S Ashworth (solo)

2006 Mar 18 Chambers Ramp, Chambers Crag B Davison, S Ashworth (solo)

2006 Mar 18 Chambers Pinnacle, Chambers Crag B Davison, S Ashworth

2006 Mar 19 Rib and Groove, Cambridge Crag M Thomas, D Drown

2006 Mar 19 Late Season Flurry, Gable Crag BJ Clarke (solo)

Lake District Winter Climbs

2006 Mar 20 Equinox, Cock Cove Crag M Thomas, C Ensoll

2006 Mar 22 Unsullied Gully, High Cup Nick C Harrison (solo)

However F Stevenson has done many unrecorded routes here in winter.

2006 Mar 22 Grotty Gully, High Cup Nick D Bailey (solo)

2006 Mar 22 Black Gully, Black Groove, Black Chimney, Black Buttress B Davison (solo)

2007 Jan 21 Crinkle Picker, Curving Ridge, Great Cove, Crinkle Gill S Ashworth (solo)

2007 Jan 24 Mid-winter Madness, Great Gable S Ashworth, B Davison

2007 Jan 24 Seasonal Affected Disorder, Great Gable B Davison, S Ashworth

2007 Jan 25 SOS, East Buttress Scafell D Birkett, M Edwards

The first pitch was climbed by the same pair on 20 Mar 2006 who returned to make a complete ascent of the line to the top of the buttress

2007 Jan 26 The Amphitheatre, Hutaple Crag S Ashworth, S Wood

2007 Feb 10 Cavers on the Crag, Small Water Crag A Dye, R Middleton

2007 Mar 20 Snow Patrol, Pike Crag M Thomas, D Almond

2007 Mar 21 Sunny Days, Boat Howe, Kirk Fell B Davison, S Ashworth (solo)

2008 Jan 04 Little Corner and Bennison's Chimney, Pavey Ark B Davison, S Ashworth

2008 Jan 21 Groove Girdle, Brown Cove Crags M Walker (solo)

2008 Feb 2 Roundabout Direct and Gibson's Chimney B Davison, N Wharton

2008 Nov 30 Coldplay, Pike Crag M Thomas, D Almond

2008 Dec 2 Winterceptor, Great Gable R Cross, A Turner, S Ashworth

2008 Dec 3 Forked Gully, Come Out Swinging, Silent Prayer, Little Big Corner, Happiness Happening, Shift Switching, South Heirloom Crag M Thomas (solo)

2008 Dec 3 Xerxes, Scafell R Cross, A Turner, S Ashworth

2008 Dec 6 Gravity and Grace, Sidewalk, Silent Torquing, Sunset Boulevard, Heirloom Crag M Thomas (solo)

First Ascents

2008 Dec 6 Mindbender, North Buttress P Cave, K Hort

2008 Dec 7 Southside, Dollywagon North D Sarkar C Wright

2009 Jan 20 Conditionalist, Flat Crag P Cave, T Hodgkin

2009 Feb 4 Harlequin Chimneys, Pillar C Wells, SJH Reid

2009 Feb 6 Broad Gully, South Hen Crag J Daly

2009 Feb 7 Twin Ribs Climb Direct, Scoat Fell Crag A Brown, D Fitzsimons

2009 Feb 8 Dollywaggon Buttress, Tarn and Falcon Crag D Bell

2009 Feb 8 Gimmer Chimney, Gimmer Crag S Ashworth, J Kelly

'Taking advantage of the snowfall yesterday afternoon and knowing that the turf would be solid I thought Gimmer Chimney would be worth a look at yesterday evening. It was in brilliant condition and gave a really good mixed climb with technical balancey climbing. Gimmer is rarely in condition. Gimmer Chimney is probably in condition more often than you would think and has a healthy covering of turf, being able to see it from the house probably helps in catching it just right.' Steve Ashworth 2009

2009 Feb 9 Zitternd, Great End D Willey, T Booth

2009 Feb 10 Diclofenac, Thirlmere C Downer, C Fowler

2009 Feb 12 Cry Wolf, Great End P Graham, B Bathgate, R Graham

2009 Mar 10 The White Cross, Bowfell P Cave

2009 Dec Route 1, Upper Scout Crag S Ashworth, J Kelly, R Armatige

2009 Dec 1 Fight or Flight, Cambridge Crag P Cave, P Bedford

2009 Dec 18 Crazy Torque, Ladd Crag F Cookson, D Warburton

Variation Finish B Davison (solo) 28 Nov 2010

2009 Dec 19 Obvious Gully, Esk Pike West Face B Davison

2009 Dec 19 Slanting Gully, Esk Pike West Face B Davison, S Ashworth, P Ashworth

2009 Dec 19 Turfy Corner, Ribs and Ridge, Esk Pike West Face S Ashworth, B Davison

2009 Dec 20 Samaritan Corner, Gimmer Crag S Ashworth, B Davison

2009 Dec 21 Tarn Crag Gully, Tarn Crag Langdale M Walker, B Robinson

2009 Dec 21 Forked Tongue, Neckband Crag A Nelhams, T Lofthouse

    Climbed as far as the roof 2000 Dec 30 by D Birkett, A Hyslop

2009 Dec 23 Blunt Gully Buttress, Foule Crag W Smith, S Caldwell

2009 Dec 28 Steel Edge Crag, Left, Right & Central Gullies B Davison (solo)

2010 Jan 1 F Buttress, Dow Crag R McGibbon, D Bell

2010 Jan 1 Gimme Shelter, Shelter Crag B Davison, N Wharton

2010 Jan 2 Hangover, Dove Crag B Davison, S Ashworth

2010 Jan 3 Against All Odds, Gillercombe A Dye, M Griffin S Gillespie

2010 Jan 5 D Route, Gimmer Crag S Ashworth, M Rudge

    The pair were intending to do Gimmer Crack but seeing the exceptional conditions on the Alphabet face changed their objective. Living in the valley has its advantages when good conditions appear yet still Steve Ashworth had to visit the crag at least a dozen times before he finally caught Gimmer Crack in condition. Another one chalked up to the local lad on this fickle crag.

2010 Jan 6 Trespasser Groove, Esk Buttress D Birkett, A Mitchell

2010 Jan 7 North Wall, Bowfell P Cave, A Marcinowicz

2010 Jan 8 West Cove Buttress, West Cove Ennerdale P Cave, A Marcinowicz

2010 Jan 8 South Chimney, Dove's Nest M Walker, B Robinson

2010 Jan 9 Quick Draw McGraw, Brim Fell J Daly, S Laheney, M Vogler

2010 Jan 9 Gatesgarth Chimney, High Crag J Kettle, S Ozanne

2010 Jan 9 Lower Incline Fall, Honister S Ringrose, J Hodgson, A Cannon

2010 Jan 10 Long Bendy Straight Thing, Honister Icefalls D Birkett, M Jenner

2010 Jan 11 Underhill Gill, Longsleddale M Walker, S Forbes

2010 Jan 11 One Armed Bandit, Buckstone How D Birkett, M Edwards

2010 Jan 14 Zipsor, Thirlmere S Scott, D Donnini

First Ascents

2010 Jan 17 Henry's Rake, Easedale M Whiteley, A Charlton, H Bean (solo)

2010 Jan 23 Skeleton Bob, Hen Crag J Daly (solo)

2010 Jan 25 White Spider, Hen Crag J Daly (solo)

2010 Jan 30 Shelter Stone, Air Raid Shelter, Shelter Crag B Davison, D McGimpsey

2010 Jan 30 & 31 Never Ever Say Never, Scafell East Buttress D Birkett, M Jenner, A Mitchell

> 1st day, M Jenner. 2nd day, D Birkett, A Mitchell with an abseil into the high point. The line still awaits a complete ground up ascent in a single push.

2010 Jan 31 Dolly Parton, Dollywagon South S Miller, P Andrews

2010 Jan 31 Number Three Buttress and Bleaberry Buttress, Chapel Crag B Davison, D McGimpsey

2010 Feb 20 North-East Climb, Pillar A Smith, C Fisher

2010 Feb 8 Edge your Bets, Steel Edge J Daly, N Harvey, R Purdy

2010 Feb 12 Into the Wild, Scafell P Cave, E Luke

2010 Feb 13 South Buttress, Headwall Groove, Central Groove, Central Buttress, Right Ridge all other routes in Glencoyne B Davison (solo)

2010 Feb 13 Cold Steel, Steel Edge Crag J Daly

2010 Feb 14 Grooving High, Heirloom Crag B Davison, D McGimpsey

2010 Feb 14 False Alarm, Far Left Gully, South Heirloom Crag B Davison, D McGimpsey

2010 Feb 27 The Tower Buttress, Winter Variation, Scafell Shamrock I Armstrong, J Graham

2010 Feb 27 Heir Apparent, Heiress, Heirloom Crag B Davison, S Venables

2010 Mar 6 Collier's Groove and Shamrock Icefall, Scafell B Davison, D MacGimpsey

2010 Mar 7 Grey Doctor, Scafell B Davison, D McGimpsey

2010 Mar 13 Collier's Left Hand Variant and Upper West Wall Climb, Scafell B Davison, D McGimpsey

Lake District Winter Climbs

2010 Mar 14 Impunity Slab Corner, Scafell B Davison, D McGimpsey

2010 April 2 Central Ramp, South Heirloom Crag B Davison (solo)

2010 Nov 28 Comb Crag Gully and Corner, Comb Crag B Davison (solo)

2010 Nov 28 Tip Off, Cock Cove Crag B Davison (solo)

2010 Nov 28 Dollywaggon Ridge, Tarn and Falcon Crag B Davison (solo)

2010 Nov 28 High Crag Grooves, High Crag Ruthwaite Cove H Davies, J Bumby

2010 Nov 28 Fragile Existence, North Crag First C Sterling, T Greenwood, P Cave

2010 Dec Stand Out, Standing Crag A Nelhams, T Lofthouse

2010 Dec Middle Pillar, Right Pillar, Kirkstone Quarry A Nelhams, T Lofthouse

2010 Dec Aurora and North Star, Honister Crag A Nelhams, D Mounsey

2010 Dec 1 Crypt and Fingers Climb, Pointing the Finger, Nab Crag S Ashworth, J Kelly

2010 Dec 3 Peachy's Grand Day Out, Tarn and Falcon Crag H Goodall, I Peachey

2010 Dec 3 November Sunshine, Dovedale M Seaman, S Wooley

2010 Dec 4 Asterisk, Gimmer Crag S Ashworth, S Wood

2010 Dec 4 Moondance, Scafell East Buttress D Birkett, M Jenner

2010 Dec 4 Grace and Favour, Brown Cove Crag J Bursnall, T Woodhead

2010 Dec 5 Pasta Pasture, Outlying Areas A Weeks, E Bray

2010 Dec 5 Ullstone Gill Quarry Icefall, Kentmere A Dickinson, A Turner

2010 Dec 5 Brim Fell Icefall, Brim Fell J Daly, N Harvey, R Purdy

2010 Dec 12 Small Water Crag Gully, Small Water Crag Left Ridge, Small Water Crag B Davison (solo)

2010 Dec 19 Slab Route Buttress, St Sunday Crag H Davies, C Thorpe

2010 Dec 19 E Buttress, Dow Crag R McGibbon, D Bell

First Ascents

2010 Dec 20 Woolly Juniper, Gimmer Crag M Bagness, J Kelly

2010 Dec 22 Line 2 and Line 4, Ashness Bridge N Smith (solo)

2010 Dec 22 Line 1, Ashness Bridge A Cannon (solo)

2010 Dec 22 Line 3, Ashness Bridge N Smith, A Canon

2010 Dec 22 Patterdale Pillar, Patterdale A Hinkes, M Parsons

2010 Dec 26 Electron-Positron, Pillar W Sim, C Fisher

2010 Dec 28 Hell Gill Force, Mallerstang I Conway, I Tod, A Dougherty

2010 Dec 29 Short Cut Icefall, Black Crag Wasdale D Gainor, K Gainor

2011 Jan 8 Bryns Edge, Harrison Stickle B Wakeley, A Charlton

2011 Jan 8 Tower Postern, Pillar C Fisher, A Smith

2011 Jan 9 Grooving High, High Crag Ruthwaite Cove B Davison, N Wharton

2011 Jan 9 Optimists' Corner, Pike of Stickle A Dye, M Griffin, A McCulloch

2011 Jan 9 Lost in the Wild, Low Water Crag B Wakeley, A Charlton

2011 Dec 16 The Angel of Mercy, Great Gable P Cave, S Ashworth

2011 Dec 17 Juniper Buttress Scafell Pike Crag R Cross, N Williams

2011 Dec 18 Bowstring, Bowfell Buttress B Davison, S Ashworth

2011 Dec 18 Moon Shadow, Flat Crag P Cave, T Greenwood

2011 Dec 18 Rubicon Groove, Bowfell R Cross, N Wallis, N Williams

2011 Dec 18 Chimney and Crack, Brown Cove Crags K Telford, G Telford, P Morgan
Variation finishes added Feb 2012 B Davison

2012 Jan 28 Flaky Rib, St Sunday Crag A Dye, M Griffin

2012 Feb 2 The Gibli, North Buttress Bowfell B Davison, P Cave

2012 Feb 2 Crack and Chimney, Bowfell P Cave, B Davison

2012 Feb 4 Full Frontal Activity, Hutaple Crag B Davison, N Wharton

Originally named after the warm front that passed through during the climb, the name became more apt when the pair suffered a head on collision with a bus travelling up Patterdale in the snow storm.

2012 Feb 8 Ambroise's Amble, Catstye Cam R Kenyon

2012 Feb 11 Second Chance, High Crag Ruthwaite Cove S Ashworth, B Davison

The previous year Davison and Wharton had rescued friends from the line who had become crag fast after failing to find any protection on the main pitch.

2012 Feb 19 Pillar Buttress, St Sunday Crag B Davison

2012 Apr 12 Stein Pull, Industrial Sector P Cave, B Davison

2012 Apr 12 Overtime, Industrial Sector P Cave, B Davison

2012 Apr 14 Double Time, Industrial Sector P Cave, B Davison

2012 Apr 14 Grand Design, Industrial Sector P Cave, B Davison

2012 Apr 22 Left Slip, The Wicket P Cave, B Davison

2012 Apr 22 Silly Mid On, The Wicket B Davison, P Cave

2012 May 5 Right Slip, The Wicket B Davison, P Cave

2012 May 5 Outside Leg, The Wicket P Cave, B Davison

2012 May 5 Steve's Corner, Industrial Sector P Cave, B Davison, S Ashworth

2012 May 6 Time and a Half, Industrial Sector B Davison, I Durham, P Powell

2012 May 7 Outfield, The Wicket B Davison, T Greenwood, A Rutherford

2012 May 9 The Fang, The Wicket P Cave, M Scales, B Davison

2012 May 11 First Blood, The Paddy Cave P Cave, S Ashworth, B Davison

2012 July 12 Bloodline, The Paddy Cave A Turner, T Broadbent, P Cave

2012 Aug 14 Blood Donor, The Paddy Cave A Turner, T Broadbent, P Cave

APPENDIX A

Winter climbing and nature conservation

by Simon Webb of Natural England (www.naturalengland.org.uk)

The Lake District mountains and fells provide opportunities for climbing, walking and quiet enjoyment of landscape, wildlife and geology. The crags, buttresses and gullies are a rich and sensitive environment full of heathers, rare arctic-alpines, colourful flowering herbs and dwarf trees. If future generations are to continue enjoying the Lake District, it is essential that we all contribute towards its long-term conservation.

Climbers can play an important role in protecting the mountain environment. The first step is to be aware that the best places for winter climbing are also the most important locations for upland vegetation and the home to rare plants and ferns. These places are sensitive and vulnerable and climbers must take extra care to minimise their impact.

WHAT SORT OF VEGETATION IS FOUND IN THE UPLAND CRAGS AND GULLIES?

The most impressive examples of upland vegetation are found amongst the cliffs and gullies of the Lake District high fells. Here, the steep ground provides refuge from grazing sheep and in many cases offers the specialised soils and climatic conditions favoured by upland plants.

Although the fells and mountains are often thought of as natural or wild, the vegetation has been greatly modified by man. For example, the impact of increasing sheep numbers over the past 50 years has led to a huge reduction of heathland vegetation in the area.

The heathery vegetation seen on crags and steeper slopes is simply surviving there away from the hungry mouths of grazing sheep. These areas are important as they are reservoirs of heathers and flowers that can re-colonise the uplands now that conservation organisations are negotiating lower sheep numbers. The best examples of heathland have many different types of heather – ling, bell heather, bilberry, crowberry, cowberry and bearberry can all be found in a mixture of colours and textures.

Similarly, there are more trees on the crags than on the open fellside. Young trees are nibbled away by sheep and only on the steeper slopes (or where grazing pressure is very low) can they get beyond the seedling stage. Some of the Lake District upland trees are rare and specialised. Juniper is probably the most well known. A native conifer, it is evergreen

Mixed heathers found on crags and steep ground (photo: Jean Johnston)

Juniper clings to crags and steep slopes (photo: Simon Webb)

and prickly, with its berries smelling strongly of gin when they are purple and ripe. A specialist dwarf type of juniper inhabits the crags above 500m. Even rarer is the downy willow. This bushy tree, with leaves that are downy white underneath, is restricted to 10 individual plants growing in the Helvellyn Coves.

The Lake District is the English stronghold for arctic-alpine plants. These plants thrive in the cold and harsh conditions of high latitudes and high altitudes. When the last ice age came to an end (some 10,000 years ago) they dominated the Lake District vegetation, but now they are restricted to the highest ground, especially north and east-facing coves and gullies. This is also where the most consistent winter climbing is found.

The arctic-alpines include purple saxifrage, moss campion, alpine cinquefoil, mountain avens, alpine catchfly and alpine mouse-ear. These species often flourish where the soils are rich in basic minerals. In the high fells this generally equates to the gullies or flushes (water seepages/ice smears), so again winter climbing locations coincide with the botanically richest areas.

The gully sides and areas with richer and deeper soil are also home to a type of plant assemblage called tall herb ledge vegetation. This looks remarkably like a Pennine hay meadow growing high in the mountains. Tall colourful herbs such as wood crane's-bill, globeflower, water avens, wild angelica and roseroot cover ledges and gully bottoms in a

Appendix A – Winter climbing and nature conservation

Purple saxifrage – a widespread arctic alpine in the Lakes (photo: Simon Webb)

luxuriant and spectacular show of mountain colour.

The preferred location for winter climbers and vulnerable vegetation is therefore the same place – the steepest ground, north and east-facing coves, gully lines and damp upland turfs and ledges.

Upland vegetation and rare plants are vulnerable to the impact of winter climbing because their area of growth is restricted (and therefore even a small amount of damage can be significant) and because they are easily damaged – especially in marginal winter climbing conditions. For some of the winter, the plants will be safe beneath a snow cover or frozen deep in a crack. But in a changing climate winter conditions are fickle and plants will more often be exposed to the impact of axes and crampons.

HOW CAN CLIMBERS HELP PROTECT UPLAND VEGETATION AND RARE PLANTS?

Climbers and other recreational upland users are not generally responsible for the decline in the extent and quality of wildlife habitats in the UK. However the nature of the sport is such that it takes climbers to the most sensitive parts of the landscape, to areas unaffected by grazing pressure and to the places best suited to rare plants. Climbers need to be aware that they are going to these special places, that there is legal protection in place for Sites of Special Scientific Interest (SSSIs) and beyond (see below) and that climbers must take extra care not to damage or disturb them.

The following best practice gives some pointers on how climbers can minimise their impact on the environment:

- If weather conditions are marginal and the snow or ice is thin and melting, then rare plants will be vulnerable. For climbers who have trudged up the mountain with a full sack, it will be tempting to go for it anyway, but this will certainly lead to loss of mountain plants.
- Climbing turf routes is not a trend that will ever be good for upland vegetation. In marginal conditions it could be a disaster, as it often causes loose lumps of turf to slide off. Some rare plants in the Lake District (alpine saxifrage, mountain avens and scrubby cinquefoil for example) are limited in numbers

to a few individual plants, so even localised impact is significant.

- Placing protection can also have an impact. Resist the temptation to clean out the cracks with your axe just to see whether you can slot a nut home. Many of these plants die back in winter and grow up again in spring. Cleaning their rootstock from cracks will quite simply kill them.
- Route preparation (or gardening) is more of a feature of summer climbing, but does occur for winter new routes too. Cleaning that crack to get a peg placement or kicking off that loose block may have an unacceptable impact. As detailed below, this vegetation is protected by law and if route preparation will damage mountain vegetation it should not go ahead.
- Any trees growing above 600m are likely to be really important ecologically, or a rare species, or both. These are not good places for runners, belays, lower-offs or a quick hook and heave with the ice tool. Give the mountain trees the respect they deserve.
- Dry tooling, hooking or torquing are best reserved for steep and non-vegetated crags. There are aesthetic arguments against this type of climbing on traditional climbing lines (crampon scratches, etc) but there are strong ecological arguments about damage to vegetated crags too.

WHAT DOES THE LAW SAY?

Natural vegetation and birds are an important part of our heritage and government has enacted strong laws to protect them. These laws apply to both landowners and those enjoying outdoor recreation. This legal framework is part of the UK's national and international obligations towards conservation.

Much of the upland landscape of the Lake District is within SSSIs. Although there is much of interest to conserve outside these sites, SSSIs do form the central core of the statutory conservation system in the UK. This wildlife law doesn't just give powers to designate and protect special sites, it also provides for many positive initiatives to conserve wildlife, including mechanisms for grants, management agreements and action plans, as well as open access provision.

In general terms all wild birds and their nests and eggs are protected by law, with heavy penalties for disturbance. While this is unlikely to be an issue for winter climbers – most birds nest in the spring and summer – ravens do nest as early as the end of February. The voluntary raven bans which are widely advertised should steer climbers clear of the most likely locations for conflict.

Natural vegetation is also protected by legislation both within SSSIs and beyond. Reckless damage to an SSSI carries severe penalties with a £20,000 maximum fine. In addition to general protection there is a suite

APPENDIX A – WINTER CLIMBING AND NATURE CONSERVATION

of the rarer plants and animals that receive additional protection.

These laws are strong, but if you take time to find out about the birds and natural vegetation in the mountain environment you are visiting it is unlikely that there will be conflicts. Following the codes of conduct and best practice is always a better alternative to court cases or permanent climbing bans.

WHERE ARE THE MOST VULNERABLE AND IMPORTANT AREAS?

The vegetation described is so rare and vulnerable that any example of it that is left is important to conserve. The following section describes the most extensive and richest areas.

Without question the **Helvellyn and Fairfield** range is the most important and vulnerable area. This extended north–south ridge has the geology, altitude and aspect that is perfect for rich upland vegetation. The east-facing coves, their back walls and their gullies contain the most important English populations of the plants described above. Here in Red Tarn Cove, Nethermost Cove, Ruthwaite and Cock Coves, in the gullies at Tarn and Falcon Crags and (on the Fairfield side) Sleet Cove to Link Cove (including Scrubby Crag and Hutaple Crag), there are extensive stands of tall herb ledge vegetation together with locations for the rare arctic-alpines and mountain willows. The real rarities grow here – alpine saxifrage, scrubby cinquefoil, holly fern and downy willow.

The top of **Honister** pass – the icefall, old mine workings and the crag itself are of considerable interest. The tall herb vegetation is so luxuriant that it has been described as the 'hanging gardens of Honister'. The area around Buckbarrow Crag and Yew Crags is also good, but it does not match the colourful splendour of the main Honister Crag.

On the **Scafell range** areas of upland or rare vegetation are much more patchy. The gullies are the most interesting, especially Piers Gill, Skew Gill, Greta Gill and Ruddy Gill. A few of the crags are good – Cam Spout Crags, Horn Crag and Lingmell Crags – and it is quite likely that there are good areas that have not yet been found. **Great End** seems to be less interesting apart from South-East Gully, where the only Cumbrian location for a plant called dwarf cornel is found.

The **Wasdale Screes** are important too – the loose and mineral-rich rock favours arctic-alpine plants. Both the gullies and buttresses are vulnerable to summer or winter visits. Their looseness means that climbing could bring down blocks – amongst which some of the rarities grow.

The crags below **High Street** (including Blea Water Crag and the areas above Small Water) are also strongholds for tall herb ledge vegetation and arctic-alpines. If the icefall is in condition then the plants here will be well buried, but the gullies

LAKE DISTRICT WINTER CLIMBS

Lychnis at Hobcarton Crag (photo: Simon Webb)

and crags elsewhere are much more vulnerable.

The areas around **Pillar and Ennerdale** are very variable – some being ecologically poor others extremely rich. Pillar Rock itself is made of quite acidic rock and as many plants like a base-rich environment, the main climbs are of lower ecological value. Much of Pillar rock is covered with junipers and great care and respect needs to be shown here. *West Waterfall* is probably the richest area on the rock itself and is best avoided in poor conditions. Without doubt the main area to avoid is Hind Cove. Here is the healthiest Cumbrian population of scrubby cinquefoil. This plant's only UK locations are in the Lake District and Teesdale. This would be really vulnerable to turf climbing or climbing in poor conditions as cinquefoil favours the wetter areas (these will be where the ice is).

Another area to avoid is the gully lines and loose buttresses of **Hobcarton Crag** high above Whinlatter Forest. This is the only English locality for alpine catchfly (and one of only two UK places where this grows). Again this rare and beautiful plant is vulnerable to winter climbing, although as it grows on loose and short buttresses you would have to be fairly desperate to climb there.

SUMMARY

Winter climbers in the Lake District can play an important role in safeguarding the colourful and vulnerable natural vegetation of the mountains. It is difficult to picture when everything is covered with snow or ice, but you can make a positive difference. Understand that winter climbers and upland vegetation often need the same places, but the two can co-exist if the best practice above is followed.

APPENDIX B

Procedure for mountain accidents

by Dr John Ellerton (an LDSAMRA team doctor)

Mountain rescue in the Lake District is well served by 13 voluntary teams backed up by special search and cave/mine rescue units. They are equipped to a high standard and work closely with the RAF helicopters and Air Ambulance services. Consequently, only minor casualties should come within the scope of treatment and evacuation by the climber's companions. The rule for all other cases is to make the casualty safe, start first aid and send for a Mountain Rescue Team.

Sending for help

A reliable member of the party, with full information about the nature of the injuries and the position of the incident (including, if possible, the map reference), should use a mobile phone (which can save a considerable amount of time) or be sent to find the nearest telephone.

The emergency number is 122 from a mobile or 999 from a landline, ask for the Police, who will notify the appropriate mountain rescue team. The sender of the message should keep their mobile phone on and keep within reception range (reception is often better on the tops or ridges of the mountains), or stay by the landline phone, as the rescue team leader will call back to give instructions.

Lack of help

You have a difficult decision to make when the casualty is severely injured, possibly unconscious and you are alone. You should try to summon help from nearby climbers or walkers by shouting, giving the distress call on a whistle (6 blasts spread over one minute and repeated regularly), flashing a torch (6 flashes spread over one minute repeated regularly) or sending up a red flare. If there is no response then assess the relative dangers of leaving the casualty and of failing to get help and then act decisively in the interest of the casualty.

EMERGENCY PRECAUTIONS AND FIRST AID

While waiting for the rescue team, you should check for further danger and then carry out basic first-aid treatment.

Safety first

Are you and the casualty safe from further danger? If not try and make yourselves safe: either by moving, or

Is the casualty's AIRWAY open?
If necessary, open it by a simple jaw thrust or lift. If possible, avoid moving the neck after trauma. An open airway is essential if the casualty is unconscious or semi-conscious as reduced consciousness can cause death from asphyxia as the tongue falls back blocking the airway. The position of the casualty, in particular his head and tongue, should be adjusted to open the airway and be continually reassessed.

Is the casualty BREATHING?
Look, feel and listen for breathing. Basic life support should be started, if you are trained, when the casualty is unconscious and shows no signs of breathing, and it can be continued until help arrives and where there is a chance of recovery (lightning, drowning, heart attack). It is usually futile in casualties with internal injuries, and it is probably best to defer in cases of severe exposure/hypothermia until expert help is available. An unconscious and breathing casualty should be put in the recovery position if possible. Check the airway is still open.

Is the casualty's CIRCULATION adequate?
Stop any bleeding from wounds by elevation and direct pressure with dressings or clothing. The pressure needs to be applied continuously for at least 10 minutes. Raising the legs and/or lowering the head may be appropriate. Internal haemorrhage should be suspected if the casualty has sustained blows to the chest or abdomen or broken the femur (thigh bone). The condition often deteriorates and all steps should be taken to facilitate the rapid arrival of the mountain rescue team and, if possible, a helicopter. A record of the pulse rate and consciousness level is very helpful.

Is the casualty DISABLED due to damage to their head or spine?
Record the casualty's consciousness level – alert, responsive to voice, responsive to pain or unresponsive? Has the spine been damaged? If so, do not move the casualty unless essential for safety reasons. Maintain the head in the normal straight position using your hands.

Appendix B – Procedure for Mountain Accidents

Wasdale Mountain Rescue team

anchoring yourselves, or both. Check whether the casualty is responsive (see ABCD in box opposite).

Hypothermia (exposure)

Hypothermia occurs when a person's heat loss exceeds their heat generation. To avoid hypothermia yourself, use a two-pronged approach by dressing appropriately and avoiding exhaustion. Modern mountain clothing is very effective at conserving heat in a wide range of climates; wind resistance and keeping the surface of the body dry are important factors when choosing clothing.

The best way of generating heat is muscular exercise. Bear in mind that to maintain this you should eat carbohydrate snacks and drink regularly during the day. Alcohol, even the previous night, can significantly reduce your exercise endurance.

The symptoms of hypothermia start with feeling cold, apathy, clumsiness and stumbling, followed by shivering. More severe hypothermia is recognised by confusion, lack of shivering, an inability to walk and finally coma. In the early stages, increased insulation, warm drinks and 'carbs' should allow a retreat to safety by walking.

Established, more severe hypothermia, is more difficult to manage as sudden movements of the casualty can precipitate a cardiac arrest.

- Insulate the casualty as best as you can without disturbing the casualty's position too much.
- Shelter the casualty from wind and rain.
- Wrap them in as many layers of clothing as possible and encase them in a 'poly bag' or other impermeable barrier.
- Do not forget to insulate the head and the area underneath the casualty.
- Then call for a mountain rescue team.

Even people with severe hypothermia showing 'no signs of life' have been resuscitated successfully, but when to start basic life support is complex and best discussed with the mountain rescue team before you start.

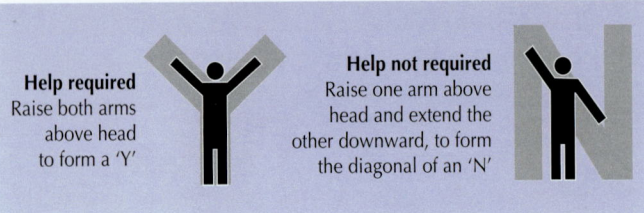

Help required
Raise both arms above head to form a 'Y'

Help not required
Raise one arm above head and extend the other downward, to form the diagonal of an 'N'

Check the limbs for fractures

In cases of fracture, immobilise the limb by the simplest method available. For a fracture of the arm, pad it and bandage it to the chest; and in the case of the leg, pad it and bandage it to the other leg.

Helicopter rescue

A helicopter may arrive before the mountain rescue team. Extinguish all flames and secure all equipment. The downdraught can knock you over, so get in a safe position. Do not approach the helicopter until clearly signalled to do so by the pilot. (See box for the correct way to signal to a helicopter.)

FURTHER POINTS TO CONSIDER

Large, **organised groups** should bear in mind that mountain rescue teams are a finite resource and it is wrong to assume their availability.

The majority of climbers killed in the Lake District as a result of a climbing accident die from a head injury. A **helmet**, whilst not being 100% effective, can make the difference between living and dying. This would seem particularly pertinent in winter where falling ice and long tumbling falls add to the hazards.

While **mobile phones** can be very useful in emergencies, any temptation to use them in the hills to call the emergency services in non-emergency circumstances should be resisted. If you are not sure whether it is an emergency or not, please investigate a little yourself first before reaching for your phone.

GPS systems, while useful, are no substitute for carrying a **map** and **compass** and knowing how to use them.

The routine carrying of a suitable **head-torch** would save many needless call-outs.

Lake District mountain rescue teams are made up of unpaid volunteers and rely on charitable contributions. Your consideration and a 'Thank you' go a long way to ensure the service continues.

The Lake District Search and Mountain Rescue Association (LDSAMRA) acts as an umbrella body for the Lakeland mountain rescue teams. It has a website at: www.ldsamra.org.uk which gives contact details for the individual teams.

APPENDIX C
Useful contacts

The telephone numbers and websites listed below were correct at time of going to press.

Climbing
British Mountaineering Council
Tel: 0870 0104878   www.thebmc.co.uk

Fell & Rock Climbing Club
www.frcc.co.uk

National Mountaineering Exhibition, Rheged, Penrith
Tel 01768 868000   www.rheged.com

Lake District weather
Fell Top Weather Forecast
Tel 0870 0550575   www.lake-district.gov.uk/weatherline/home/index.php

Lake District National Park Authority
Head Office
Tel: 01539 724555   www.lake-district.gov.uk

Bird Restrictions
Tel 017687 79633   www.frcc.co.uk/rock/birds.htm

Tourist information
Cumbria Tourist Board
www.golakes.co.uk

Ambleside	015394 32582	Egremont	01946 820693
Bowness	015394 42895	Keswick	017687 72645
Broughton in Furness	01229 716115	Kendal	01539 725758
Coniston	015394 41533	Penrith	01768 867466
Glenridding	017684 82414		

Camping barns
Lakeland Camping Barns
01946 758198   www.lakelandcampingbarns.co.uk

Public transport
Cumbria County Council Journey Planner
Tel 01228 606705   www.cumbria.gov.uk

APPENDIX D
Campsites and camping barns

The campsites and camping barns in the Lake District listed below are only those known to be open during the winter months. Fuller details will be available from the Tourist Information Offices. This information is current in 2012 but will almost certainly alter and it is probably best to make telephone contact before going to a particular site or barn.

Southern Lake District

Campsites	Grid Ref	Telephone	Website
Coniston, Coniston Hall	SD 304 962	015394 41223	
Coniston, Hoathwaite	SD 297 949	015394 41349	
Coniston, Park Coppice	SD 297 957	015394 41555	www.caravanclub.co.uk
Hawkshead, Croft	SD 353 982	015394 36374	www.hawkshead-croft.co.uk
Skelwith, Tarn Foot	NY 343 038	015394 32596	
Langdale, National Trust	NY 287 059	015394 37668	www.ntlakescampsites.org.uk
Windermere, Troubeck, Limefitt Park	NY 414 032	015394 32300	www.southlakeland-caravans.co.uk
Camping Barns	**Grid Ref**	**Telephone**	**Website**
Broughton-in-Furness, Fell End Farm	SD 239 881	01946 758198	www.lakelandcampingbarns.co.uk

Appendix D – Campsites and camping barns

Langdale, Sticklebarn	NY 295 064	015394 37356
Grasmere, Broadrayne Farm	NY 337 094	015394 35055
Grasmere, The Hollens	NY 344 073	015394 63831	www.ntlakescampsites.org.uk

Western Lake District

Campsites	Grid Ref	Telephone	Website
Buttermere, Sykes Farm	NY 173 171	017687 70222	
Buttermere, Dalegarth	NY 186 159	017687 70233	
Lorton, Wheatsheaf Inn	NY 155 259	01900 85199	
Lorton, Whinfell Hall	NY 150 254	01900 85260	
St Bees, Seacote Park	NX 962 120	01946 822777	www.seacote.co.uk
Holmrook, Seven Acres	NY 073 018	01946 822227	
Wasdale, Santon Bridge	NY 111 017	019467 26286	
Nether Wasdale, Church Stile	NY 126 042	019467 26252	www.churchstile.com
Wasdale Head	NY 185 088	019467 26384	www.ntlakescampsites.org.uk
Wasdale Head – National Trust	NY 185 073	019467 26220	
Eskdale, Hollins Farm	NY 178 010	019467 23253	
Camping Barn	**Grid Ref**	**Telephone**	**Website**
Buttermere, Cragg	NY 174 172	01946 758198	

Loweswater, Waterend Farm, Swallow Barn	NY 116 226	01946 758198	www.lakelandcampingbarns.co.uk
Loweswater, Holme Wood Bothy	NY 123 216	01946 816940	www.holmewoodbothy.org.uk
St Bees, Tarn Flatts Hall Farm	NX 947 146	01946 692162	www.lakelandcampingbarns.co.uk
Ennerdale, High Gillerthwaite	NY 142 141	01946 758198	www.lakelandcampingbarns.co.uk
Gosforth, Mill House Barn	NY 100 044	01946 758198	www.lakelandcampingbarns.co.uk
Wasdale, Murt Barn	NY 131 040	01946 758198	www.lakelandcampingbarns.co.uk

Northern Lake District

Campsites	Grid Ref	Telephone	Website
Braithwaite, Scotgate	NY 235 236	017687 78343	www.scotgateholidaypark.co.uk
Keswick, Castlerigg Hall	NY 280 225	017687 74499	www.castlerigg.co.uk
Keswick, Castlerigg	NY 283 223	017687 72479	www.castleriggfarm.co.uk
Keswick, Derwentwater	NY 260 232	017687 72392	www.campingandcaravaningclub.co.uk
Borrowdale, Stonethwaite, Langstrath	NY 268 133	017687 77234	
Borrowdale, Stonethwaite, Chapel Farm	NY 257 140	017687 77602	
Borrowdale, Seathwaite Farm	NY 232 122	017687 77394	

Camping Barns	Grid Ref	Telephone	Website
Caldbeck, Hudscales	NY 332 375	017687 72645	www.lakelandcampingbarns.co.uk
St Johns in the Vale, Low Bridge End	NY 316 205	01946 758198	www.campingbarn.com

Appendix D – Campsites and camping barns

Thirlmere, Causeway Foot	NY 294 218	017687 72290	
Newlands, Catbells Barn	NY 243 208	01946 758198	www.lakelandcampingbarns.co.uk
Rosthwaite, Dinah Hoggas Barn	NY 259 151	01946 758198	www.lakelandcampingbarns.co.uk

Eastern Lake District

Campsites	Grid Ref	Telephone	Website
Hartsop, Sykeside	NY 401 120	017684 82239	www.sykeside.co.uk
Watermillock, Ullswater	NY 435 229	017684 86666	www.uccmp.co.uk
Pooley Bridge, Waterside	NY 463 231	017684 86332	www.watersidefarm-campsite.co.uk
Pooley Bridge, Roe Head	NY 475 242	017684 86363	
Penrith, Lowther	NY 526 263	01768 863631	
Penruddock, Beckes	NY 417 277	017684 83224	
Berrier, Hopkinson Park	NY 405 288	017684 83456	

Bunkhouses			
Glenridding, Gillside	NY 382 168	017684 82346	www.gillsidecaravanandcampingsite.co.uk
Hartsop, Sykeside	NY 401 120	017684 82239	www.sykeside.co.uk

Camping barns			
Greenside, Swirral Barn	NY 364 174	01946 758198	www.lakelandcampingbarns.co.uk

APPENDIX E
Climbing walls

There is a good range of climbing walls available to those living in or visiting the Lake District, of which the best, or most readily accessible, are described here for use on those occasional rainy days and dank evenings.

Ambleside: St Martin's College (formerly Charlotte Mason's College)
The wall is due to be demolished and a new one built. In the meantime the access to the wall is restricted to students of the college.
Tel: 015394 30300, www.ucsm.ac.uk

Barrow: Park Leisure Centre
Good access, low-cost but limited climbing – rather compact with a tall narrow wall and a bouldering area. Excellent other facilities. Open all day until 21:45 weekdays; 10:00 to 18:00 weekends.
Access check – tel: 01229 871146, www.barrowbc.gov.uk

Carlisle:
Eden Rock
A huge new >10,000sq m bouldering wall. Easy access M6. Café, shop and function rooms. Open 10am–10pm weekdays and 09:00–20:00 weekends.
facebook.com/edenrockclimbing, twitter: @edenrockclimbing
Access check – tel 01228 522127, www.edenrockclimbing.co.uk

The Sands Centre
Reasonable, low-cost climbing facility in a large sports centre. Good bouldering and leading. Very good access and excellent general facilities. Open 09:30 to 22:30 seven days a week.
Access check – tel: 01228 625222, www.thesandscentre.co.uk

Cockermouth: Sports Centre
Varied bouldering with natural stonework and Bendcrete. Low-cost and good access. Other sports facilities available. Open 08:00 to 22:00 Monday to Thursday; 08:00 to 21:30 Friday; 09:00 to 17:00 weekends.
Access check – tel: 01900 823596, www.allerdale.gov.uk

Egremont: Wyndham Sports Centre
A good facility located in the centre of Egremont on the west coast, only half an hour from Wasdale Head. There are practice areas, bouldering, leading walls and a huge roof. Unfortunately no longer open to the public except on a club booking basis.
Access check – tel: 01946 820356

Appendix E – Climbing walls

Ingleton: Inglesport Climbing Barn
Best of the small walls. In Yorkshire, but only just. Very good use of space with leading and bouldering. Regular innovations. Relaxed friendly atmosphere. Café and shop nearby. Open 09:00 to 22:00 Monday to Thursday; 09:00 to 17:30 Friday; 08:30 to 18:00 weekends.
Access check – tel: 015242 41146, www.inglesport.co.uk/wall.html

Kendal: The Lakeland Climbing Centre
A magnificent indoor climbing facility with excellent bouldering and leading. Includes a very impressive 24m main wall (with fixed gear) and a huge roof. Located on the Lake District Business Park, across the A6 from Morrison's supermarket. Changing and shower facilities. Open Winter (September to April): 10:00 to 22:00 Monday to Friday; 10:00 to 19:00 weekends and Bank Holidays. Summer (May to August): 10:00 to 22:00 Monday to Friday; 10:00 to 17:00 weekends and Bank Holidays.
Access check – tel: 01539 721766, www.kendalwall.co.uk

Keswick: Keswick Climbing Wall and Activity Centre
Located to the east of town at Goosewell Farm. Follow signs for the Castlerigg Stone Circle. There is quite extensive bouldering, with some leading and top-roping walls. Friendly atmosphere. Open 9:00 to 17:00 Friday to Monday and 9:00 to 21:00 Tuesday to Thursday.
Access check – tel: 017687 72000, www.keswickclimbingwall.co.uk

Penrith: Penrith Leisure Centre – Eden Climbing Wall
An excellent wall adjoining the town's swimming pool. Good bouldering and excellent leading walls. Cheap entry. Open 10:00 to 21:30 weekdays; 10:00 to 21:00 weekends.
Access check – tel: 01768 863450, www.leisure-centre.com

Botterill's Slab Scafell Crag (photo: Nick Wharton)

APPENDIX F
Taking better climbing photographs

by Nick Wharton

Digital cameras have made it much easier to capture exciting climbing images and we are all trying to do it. There are no really hard and fast rules about what makes a good photo, but people regularly send their inspiring photographs in to the FRCC which sadly cannot be used in the guidebooks for technical reasons. Here are a few pointers to help you take photos that may be suitable for publication in the future.

- Set the camera to the highest resolution possible – this reduces the number of shots available so make sure you've got a high capacity memory card.
- Think about what the final photo will show, for example the tension and effort in the climber's face or more of the route. (We all want more information about routes, which could be captured in the right photograph.)
- Position your subject. We can all recognize a posed photograph, but that doesn't mean we shouldn't wait for the best body position. Don't be afraid to shout across and direct the climber to look up or get the second to look that their leader. It's great if we can see people's eyes.
- Think about where the light is coming from. What exposure is the camera set to? Try to expose and focus for the climber. They are generally your main subject.
- Watch out for scruffy clutter in the background. Gear and rucksacks left lying around are very distracting and can ruin a great photo.
- It is rare that seconds make good subjects. The rope above is often distracting and also removes any drama or tension from the shot – we can see that they are safe!

Composition is a massive subject and impossible to cover in a few lines. For further inspiration, try looking at all those books and magazines and find the photos that make you stop and look. These are the ones to emulate... Cicerone also publish *Outdoor Photography* (2011) which has a useful chapter on 'Roped sports – climbing, abseiling and mountaineering'.

And, of course, when you go out always have in the back of your mind photographs for the next FRCC guidebook! Photos should be submitted via the FRCC website at www.frcc.co.uk.

INDEX OF ROUTES

A

AB Buttress	300
A Carton of Hobnobs	242
Acceleration due to Gravity	301
Accidental Discharge	341
Against All Odds	265
Age Concern	136
A Gully, Pikes Crag	152
A Gully, Shelter Crags	47
A Gully, Wasdale Screes	119
Aira Force	321
Air Raid Shelter	47
Amphitheatre, The	341
Anderson	47
Angel of Mercy, The	194
Angle Tarn Gully	75
Angle Tarn Icefalls	75
Antarctic Monkeys	160
Arctic Spring	240
Arete, Chimney and Crack	90
Arjuna	203
Arlecdon Aquarian	262
Arrowhead Buttress	358
Ashness Gill	245
Aspirant	261
Aurora	214

B

Back Off	198
Band on the Run	53
Base Brown	264
BB Corner	54
Bear Left	226
Beckthorns Gill	275
Bennison's Chimney	84
Beta Hammer Belter	200
B Gully, Pikes Crag	152
B Gully, Shelter Crags	47
Big Answer	113
Big Groove	53
Big Issue, The	45
Big Question	112
Birker Force	109
Birkett's Gully	361
Birkness Chimney	220
Birkness Gully	220
Birkness Gully Wall	220
Birkside Gill	276
Black Chimney, Black Buttress	344
Black Chimney, Chapel Crags	227
Black Crag Grooves	123
Black Crag Gully	124
Black Crag Icefall	345
Black Force	367
Black Groove	344
Black Gully	344
Black Sail Gully	205
Black Shiver	123
Blade Runner	293
Blake Rigg Icefall	37
Bleaberry Buttress	230
Bleaberry Chimney	230
Blea Water Buttress	361
Blea Water Cleft	361
Blea Water Gill	361
Blea Water Icefall	361
Blood Donor	374
Bloodline	373
Blow Out	319
Blunt Gully	269
Blunt Gully Buttress	269
Bobbins Groove	307
Boneyard Wall	325
Bootlegger's Groove	197
Border Buttress	220
Border Buttress Gully	218
Botterill's Slab	127
Bottleneck Blues	191
Bottlescrue	192
Bowfell Buttress	70
Bowfell Girdle	73
Bowstring	70
Bramcrag Quarry Fall	275
Branch Gully	254
Bridge of Sighs	132
Brim Fell Icefall	96
Broad Crag Gully	157
Broad Crag Gully Left Wall	158

Index of Routes

Broad Gully 102
Broadrick's Crack 93
Browney Gill 38
Bryns Edge 78
Bus Shelter 45
Butterfingers 187
Buttermere Gully 237
Buttress Groove 319
Buttress Gully 53
Buttress Left of Left-Hand Groove 262
Buttress Right of Right-Hand Groove ... 261
Buttress Route 150

C
Cable Gully 210
Caddy, The 52
Calculator 200
Cambridge Crag Climb 59
Cambridge Girdle 67
Cam Spout 109
Captain Patience 210
Carrock Fell Icefall 272
Cascade 143
Castor 142
Cautley Spout 366
Cave Route 242
Cavers on the Crag 359
Central Buttress, Glencoyne 323
Central Buttress, Chapel Crags 228
Central Chimney, Shelter Crags 46
Central Chimney, Eagle Crag 221
Central Groove, Clencoyne 323
Central Groove, Black Sail Buttress 205
Central Gully, Greenhow End 337
Central Gully, Rampsgill Head Crag 318
Central Gully, Brown Cove Crags 285
Central Gully, Raven Tor 100
Central Gully, Gable Crag 197
Central Gully, Great End 258
Central Gully Right Arete 258
Central Gully Right Branch 258
Central Icefall 267
Central Pinnacle Gully 317
Central Ridge 317
Central Route, Cock Cove Crag 307
Central Route, Bowfell Buttress 70
Centre Route 136
C Gully, Pikes Crag 152
C Gully, Wasdale Screes 117

Chambers Pinnacle 112
Chambers Ramp 112
Chapel Crag Gully 230
Chicken Variation, The 234
Chimney and Crack 285
Chimney Crack 51
Chimney Stack 142
Chock Gully 311
Chockstone Gully 53
Clark Gable 191
Cleft Gill 364
Close to the Edge 102
Coco-Tara Direct 307
Cofa Wall 344
Cold Lazarus 330
Coldplay 155
Cold Steel 101
Collier's Groove 127
Collier's Left-Hand Variant 127
Columba's Gully 250
Comb Crag Gully and Corner 276
Come Out Swinging 352
Conditionalist 54
Cook's Tour 82
'C' Ordinary Route 92
Corner and Rib 72
Corvus 249
Crack and Chimney 68
Crack Magic 54
Crazy Torque 296
Crenation Ridge 156
Crescent Climb 81
Crinkle Cut 41
Crinkle Picker 42
Crowdless Raven 248
Crypt and Fingers Climb 277
Cry Wolf 256
Curving Gully, Chapel Crags 228
Curving Gully, Hutaple Crag 342
Curving Ridge 42
Cust's Gully 255

D
Dandle Buttress 364
Dandle Face Direct 364
Deception 81
Deep Cut Chimney 225
Deepdale Gully 337
Deep Ghyll 135

Deep Ghyll Integrale 142
Descent Gully 156
Dexter Slab 123
D Gully, Pikes Crag 153
D Gully, Wasdale Screes 117
Dharma Armour 142
Diagonal Gully 268
Diclofenac 278
Die Another Day 65
Direct Route, The 143
Doctor Grey 140
Doctor's Chimney 199
Dolly Daydream 301
Dollymixture 305
Dolly Mixture 303
Dolly Parton 305
Dollywaggon Buttress 310
Dollywaggon Chimney 311
Dollywaggon Great Chimney 312
Dollywaggon Gully 310
Dollywaggon Ridge 310
Double Time 371
Dove Crag Gully 234
Drop Out 157
Duncan's Groove 256
Dungeon Ghyll 78

E

Eagle's Claw, The 220
Eagle Front 221
East Chockstone Gully 325
Easter Gully – Scoop Route 93
East Gully 170
East Hutaple Groove 338
East Hutaple Gully 338
East of Eden 203
East Wall Route 340
Easy Buttress 320
Easy Gully, Black Crag 173
Easy Gully, Cock Crove Crag 305
Easy Gully, Dow Crag 90
Easy Gully, Scafell Shamrock 144
Easy Gully Left Branch 90
Easy Gully Right Branch 90
Easy Terrace 91
E Buttress 95
Edge your Bets 102
Eel Crag Gully 240
Eel Crag Main Ridge 240

E Gully 117
Electron-Positron 180
Ema Ho 112
Enforcer, The 239
Engineer's Chimney 193
Engineer's Slabs 195
Epsilon Chimney 203
Equinox 308
Evening Buttress 75
Evolution 255
Eye Spy 142

F

Falcon Crag Gully 311
False Alarm 351
Fang, The 375
Far Left Fall 361
Far West Rib 343
F Buttress 95
Fifth Chimney 41
Fight or Flight 60
First Blood 374
First Chimney 40
First Cut is the Deepest, The 255
First of Many 123
Fisherplace Gill 276
Flaky Rib 325
Fleetwith Gully 215
Flying Buttress 231
Flying Gimp Trick, The 65
Follow Your Nose 187
Force Crag Waterfall 239
Forked Gully Left, Centre and Right 351
Forked Tongue 49
Foule Crag Gully 271
Fourth Chimney 41
Fragile Existence 63
Friends Above 316
Full Frontal Activity 342
Further from the Edge 102

G

Gable End 196
Galeforth Gill Fall 363
Garden of Eden 203
Gatesgarth Chimney 217
Gendarmerie 319
Gibson's Chimney 85
Gibli, The 63

Index of Routes

Gillercombe Buttress 265
Gillercombe Gully 264
Gimme Shelter 45
Gimps to the Left of Them 65
Gimpsuit Fall 73
Ginny Clegg 334
Girdle Traverse, Great End 263
Girdle Traverse, St Sunday Crag 327
Girdle Traverse, The 137
Gnomon, The 62
Goat Gill 237
Gomorrah 184
Gone with the Wind 198
Grace and Favour 283
Grainy Gill 163
Grand Design 373
Grass Corner 226
Gravity and Grace 349
Great (B) Gully 118
Great Chimney 139
Great Doup Buttress 185
Great Eastern Route 149
Great Gable Traverse 199
Great Gully, Bowfell Links 51
Great Gully, Dow Crag 90
Great Gully, Pavey Ark 81
Great Gully Wall 51
Greathall Gill 117
Great Western 140
Green Buttress 52
Green Crag Gully 215
Green Gable End 203
Greenhow Gully 337
Green Ledge Icefall 181
Grendel 333
Grey Crag Icefall 100
Groove and Ramp 50
Grooved Arete 155
Groove Girdle 286
Grooving High, Heirloom Crag 349
Grooving High, High Crag 299
Grossbuttock 263
Grotty Gully 368
Gully 1 291
Gully 1 Buttress 293
Gully 2 293
Gully 3 295
Gully A 300
Gully B 301
Gully of the Plods 200
Gwynne's Chimney 82

H
Half Way Up 52
Hallsfell Ridge 268
Hangover 348
Happiness Happening 352
Harlequin Chimneys 179
Harrow Buttress 222
Hart Crag Ice Falls 330
Harter Fell Gully 358
Harvest Crunch 129
Haskett Gully 166
Headwall Groove 322
Heir Apparent 350
Heiress 350
Heirloom 350
Hell Gill 39
Hen Crag Buttress 104
Hen Pecked 104
Henry's Rake 86
Hen's Teeth 104
Heorot 333
Hidden Gully 50
High Crag Grooves 300
Hind Cove Gully 185
Hole and Corner Gully 124
Hole and Corner Gully Icefall 124
Hole in One 51
Honister Crag Gully 214
Hooch 192
Hope Head Icefall 368
Hopkinson's Crack 94
Hopkinson's Gully 135
Horizon Climb 205
Horse and Man Rock 152
Huckleberry Grooves 297

I
Ill Gill 204
Ill Gully 113
Impunity Slab Corner 137
Impunity Slabs 137
Inaccessible Gully 347
Incline Fall 209
In Her Mouth 199
Intermediate Gully 92

Intermittent Chimneys 145
Into the Groove 53
Into the Wild 139
Isaac Gill 39

J
Jabberwock, The 195
Jack's Rake 82
Jacob's Ladder 139
Jogebar Gully 298
Jones's Route Direct 135
Juniper Buttress 153
Juniper Crack 331
Juniper Ridge 119

K
Kirkby's Folly 268
Kirk Fell Gill 205

L
Late Season Flurry 188
Launchy Gill 278
Ledge and Groove 71
Left Branch 285
Left Branch of Greta Gill 162
Left Buttress 286
Left Corner 40
Left Gully 319
Left-Hand Gantry Curtain 213
Left-Hand Groove 262
Left-Hand Route 57
Left of Centre 154
Left Ramp 157
Left Runnel 330
Left Slip 376
Lesser Fall 210
Line 1, Ashness Bridge 246
Line 2, Ashness Bridge 246
Line 3, Ashness Bridge 246
Line 4, Ashness Bridge 246
Link Cove Gill (Left Branch) 329
Link Cove Gill (Right Branch) 329
Little Big Corner 352
Little Corner 84
Little Gully 79
Little Harter Gully 358
Little Sod 225
Loki 291
Long Bendy Straight Thing 213
Long Gully, Haystacks 216
Long Gully, Pikes Crag 150
Long Ledge Entry and Exit 331
Long Walk 42
Lorton Gully 237
Lost in the Wild 99
Lost World Gully 158
Lower Incline Fall 209
Low Man by the Right Wall of
    Steep Ghyll 133
Low Water Beck 96

M
Main Ridge Climb by the Lower Slabs
    Ordinary Route, The 173
Mallory's Corner 189
Mare's Nest Gully 153
Mary Ann 56
Memo, The 338
Mickledore Chimney 145
Middleboot Gill 162
Middling Buttress 81
Midnight Special 333
Mid-winter Madness 192
Migraine 340
Mill Gill 276
Mindbender 62
Misty Mountain Hop 59
Mjölnir 290
Module 100
Monday Chimney 231
Mono Culture 303
Moonbathing 135
Moondance 148
Moon Shadow 56
Morrison 47
Moses's Back Door 198
Moss Ghyll 130
Moss Ghyll Grooves 129
Mulled Wine 97
Mutley's Icy Wait 200

N
Narrow Gully 232
Neckband, The 50
Nethermost Gully 295
Never Ever Say Never 149
Newlands Hause Waterfall 237
New Professor's Chimney 137

Index of Routes

New Turf.. 225
New West Climb 184
Nexus... 249
No 1 Gully 50
North Buttress.................................... 104
North Climb, Pillar Rock 182
North Climb, Scafell Crag................... 126
North-East Climb 181
North-East Gully 88
North Face 203
North Gully, Bowfell Buttress............... 71
North Gully, Dow Crag....................... 95
North Gully, Green Gable Crag 203
North Gully, Hen Crag....................... 104
North Gully, Low Water Crag 99
North Gully, Rampsgill Head Crag..... 318
North Gully, Steeple West Buttress...... 168
North Star... 214
North Wall 71
North-West Climb 183
North-West Gully 75
No Way Out 60
Number Three Buttress 228

O
Oblique Chimney.............................. 192
Oblique Reference 191
Old Professor's Chimney.................... 137
Old West Route, The......................... 184
One Armed Bandit............................ 207
One Pitch Gully 256
Optimists' Corner 76
Original Route................................... 315
Outfield... 376
Outside Leg 376
Overhanging Wall 148
Overtime... 371
Oxford and Cambridge
   Ordinary Route 222

P
Parallel G... 200
Pasta Pasture 368
Patterdale Pillar 323
Peachey's Grand Day Out.................. 310
Pendulum Gully 334
Pendulum Ridge 334
Percy's Passage................................... 99
Peregrine Gully 109
Photon Corner 180
Pier Review 161
Piers Gill 160
Pigott's Route 221
Pike Gully 297
Pillar Buttress.................................... 325
Pillar Gully 325
Pinnacle Climb.................................. 312
Pinnacle Crack 189
Pinnacle Groove................................ 226
Pinnacle Ridge, Gable Crag................ 191
Pinnacle Ridge, St Sunday Crag 327
Pisgah Buttress Direct 131
Pitch and Putt 51
Plaque Route 68
Pointing the Finger............................ 277
Pollux 142
Portcullis Ridge................................. 344
Professor... 57
Pudding Beck 239
Pulse 271

Q
Quarry Fall 208
Quarryman's Falls 213
Quick Draw McGraw 96

R
Racecourse Hill Recourse................... 361
Ramp, The 117
Ramparts Chimney 345
Ramp It Up 303
Ramp Route...................................... 307
Rape and Pillage................................ 291
Raven Crag Buttress 249
Raven Crag Grooves 249
Raven Crag Gully 248
Raven Crag Left-Hand Gully 353
Ray of Sunshine 42
Rescue Groove 303
Restless Natives 131
Rib and Groove 57
Rib and Gully Climb.......................... 185
Rib and Ridge 113
Riboletto Groove 59
Ride the Wild Turf............................. 203
Right Branch of Greta Gill 162
Right Buttress Crack.......................... 285
Right Frog 227

Right Gantry Icefall (Left and
  Right-Hand).................................. 213
Right Gully 319
Right-Hand Gantry Curtain............... 213
Right-Hand Groove 261
Right-Hand Gully 349
Right-Hand Route 59
Right of Centre 154
Right Ridge 323
Right Slip 375
Right Wall Eliminate 72
Robinson's Gully 234
Roundabout Direct 82
Rubicon Groove 68

S

Salvation 49
Sandbed Gill 275
Sandbed Gill Crag 275
Savage Gully 182
Scabbard 65
Scale Force 232
Scoathanger 172
Scoating for Boys 172
Scorpion 340
Scott Gully 240
Seasonal Affected Disorder (SAD) 193
Second Chance 299
Second Chimney 40
Secondhand 272
Serendipity Ridge 172
Sergeant Crag Gully 247
Seven Pitch Gully 119
Shamrock Chimneys 180
Shamrock Gully 179
Shamrock Icefall 145
Sharp Edge 269
Shelter Corner 43
Sheltered Accommodation................... 43
Shelter Icefall 45
Shelter Ridge 46
Shelter Stone 43
Shift Switching 352
Short Chute 330
Short Cut Icefall 124
Shoulthwaite Gill 278
Siamese Chimneys 62
Side Show Icefall 105
Sidewalk... 351

Silent Prayer 352
Silent Torquing.................................. 349
Silly Mid On...................................... 376
Sinister Ridge.................................... 122
Sinister Slabs....................................... 68
Skeleton Bob 103
Skew Gill... 252
Skint and Single.................................. 65
Slab and Groove 242
Slab and Notch Climb 178
Slab Route Buttress 325
Slanting Groove................................ 155
Slate Cap 210
Sledgate Ridge.................................. 193
Sleet Wall 341
Slime Chimney 149
Slingsby's Chimney Route................ 133
Smoken 272
Snicker Snack 194
Sod All 141
Sodom... 141
Sodomy 231
Sod's Law 141
Sod this for a Lark............................ 172
Sod-U-Like 200
Solo Symphony 304
SOS 146
Soul Vacation 63
Sourmilk Gill, Bleaberry Combe 222
Sourmilk Gill, Borrowdale 264
South-East Buttress........................... 260
South-East Gully 260
Southern Buttress............................. 321
Southern Corner 156
Southern Cross 156
South Gully, Bowfell Buttress............ 67
South Gully, Dollywaggon North 304
South Gully, Dove Crag 347
South Gully, Hen Crag 103
South Gully, Low Water Crag 97
South Gully, Rampsgill Head 317
South Pinnacle Ridge....................... 316
Southside.. 304
South South Groove 103
South South Gully, Rampsgill Head .. 316
South South Gully, South Hen Crag .. 102
Spiral Gully 233
Stack Gill.. 216

Stand Out	278
Stanger Gills	247
Stanley Force	108
Starboard Chimney	204
Steep Ghyll	132
Steep Ghyll Grooves	132
Steeplechase Groove	153
Steeple East Buttress	169
Stein Pull	371
Step Gully	335
Stepped Ridge	286
Steve's Corner	374
Stickle Ghyll	79
Stoat's Crack	84
Stony Buttress	81
Straight Buttress	227
Straight Gill	160
Straight Gill Right-Hand Arete	160
Straight Gully	227
Striding Edge and Swirral Edge	289
Summer Step	285
Summer Time Blues	192
Summit Route	97
Sunday Chimney	232
Sunday Special	52
Sunset Boulevard	350
Swallow Gully	297
Swallow's Rake	296
Swarthbeck Gill	313

T

Tarn Crag Buttress I	310
Tarn Crag Buttress II	310
Tarn Crag Gullies II and III	310
Tarn Crag Gully I	310
Taylor Gill Force	263
Terminal Velocity	303
Terrace Ice	299
Thanks for the Tip	307
Third Chimney	41
Thompson's Chimney	242
Thrash Corner	303
Threshthwaite Gully	320
Tia Maria	146
Tic Tac Man	311
Tilberthwaite Boys, The	105
Tilberthwaite Trundle	105
Time and a Half	371

Tip Off	308
Tongue and Groove	335
Toreador Gully	215
Torquers Are No Good Doers	189
Tower Buttress	51
Tower Buttress, Winter Variation, The	144
Tower Postern	181
Tranearth Quarry Icefall	106
Traverse of the Sods	271
Trespasser Groove	110
Tricouni Slab	127
Troll	194
Trough Gully	272
Troutdale Gully	246
Trundle Ridge	196
Tunnel Vision	209
Turf Accountant	232
Turf at the Top	210
Turf Corner	308
Turfed Out	199
Turf's Up	225
Turf-tastic	305
Turf Time	226
Turf Walls	225
Turf Wars, Chapel Crags	224
Turf Wars, Scoat Fell Crag	169
Twin Ribs Climb Direct	170
Twisting Gully	144
Twisting Turf	51
Two Grooves	283
Two Under Par	51
Tyro's Gully	249

U

Umbrella Gully	320
Underhill Gill	363
Unsullied Gully	368
Upper Deep Ghyll Route	138
Upper West Wall Climb	138
Urchin's Groove	154

V

V-Corner	293
Vegiburger	271
Vestry Wall	157
Viking Buttress	290
Vulcan Buttress	52

W

Walker's Gully	181
Walla Crag Gully	245
Wall and Ramp	293
Wall Climb	331
Warn Gill	216
West Buttress	168
West Chimney Route	168
West Chockstone Gully	324
West Cove Buttress	176
West Cove Gullies	176
Western Avenue	343
Western Gully	166
West Gully	343
West Gully Cave Route	175
West Gully Tunnel Route	175
West Hutaple Edge	343
West Hutaple Gully	343
West Hutaple Variations	342
Westmorland's Route	348
West Wall Climb	140
West Waterfall Gully	183
White Ghyll Chimney	85
Whiteout	42
White Cross, The	72
White Spider	103
Whitewater Dash Waterfall	267
Whorneyside Force	39
Wide Gully	231
Wight-Out	42
Wild World	97
Window Gully	256
Wind Up	319
Windy Buttress	315
Windy Ridge	188
Winterceptor	194
Woodhouse's Route	91
Wooly Juniper	77
Wowzers	271
Wrinkled Crinkle, The	41

X

Xerxes	141
Yew Crag Gully	207

Y

Y Gully	216
Y Gully, Left and Right Branches	358
Y Gully (Right Fork)	324
Y Route One	40
Y Route Two	40

Z

Zero Gully	40
Zipsor	278
Zitternd	254

LISTING OF CICERONE GUIDES

BRITISH ISLES CHALLENGES, COLLECTIONS AND ACTIVITIES

The End to End Trail
The Mountains of England and Wales
  1 Wales & 2 England
The National Trails
The Relative Hills of Britain
The Ridges of England, Wales and Ireland
The UK Trailwalker's Handbook
The UK's County Tops
Three Peaks, Ten Tors

MOUNTAIN LITERATURE

Unjustifiable Risk?

UK CYCLING

Border Country Cycle Routes
Cycling in the Hebrides
Cycling in the Peak District
Cycling the Pennine Bridleway
Mountain Biking in the Lake District
Mountain Biking in the Yorkshire Dales
Mountain Biking on the South Downs
The C2C Cycle Route
The End to End Cycle Route
The Lancashire Cycleway

SCOTLAND

Backpacker's Britain
  Central and Southern Scottish Highlands
  Northern Scotland
Ben Nevis and Glen Coe
Great Mountain Days in Scotland
North to the Cape
Not the West Highland Way
Scotland's Best Small Mountains
Scotland's Far West
Scotland's Mountain Ridges
Scrambles in Lochaber
The Ayrshire and Arran Coastal Paths
The Border Country
The Great Glen Way
The Isle of Mull
The Isle of Skye
The Pentland Hills
The Southern Upland Way
The Speyside Way
The West Highland Way
Scotland's Far North
Walking in the Cairngorms
Walking in the Ochils, Campsie Fells and Lomond Hills
Walking in Torridon
Walking Loch Lomond and the Trossachs
Walking on Harris and Lewis
Walking on Jura, Islay and Colonsay
Walking on Rum and the Small Isles
Walking on the Isle of Arran
Walking on the Orkney and Shetland Isles
Walking on Uist and Barra
Walking the Corbetts
  1 South of the Great Glen
Walking the Galloway Hills
Walking the Lowther Hills
Walking the Munros
  1 Southern, Central and Western Highlands
  2 Northern Highlands and the Cairngorms
Winter Climbs Ben Nevis and Glen Coe
Winter Climbs in the Cairngorms
World Mountain Ranges: Scotland

NORTHERN ENGLAND TRAILS

A Northern Coast to Coast Walk
Backpacker's Britain
  Northern England
Hadrian's Wall Path
The Dales Way
The Pennine Way
The Spirit of Hadrian's Wall

NORTH EAST ENGLAND, YORKSHIRE DALES AND PENNINES

Historic Walks in North Yorkshire
South Pennine Walks
St Oswald's Way and St Cuthbert's Way
The Cleveland Way and the Yorkshire Wolds Way
The North York Moors
The Reivers Way
The Teesdale Way
The Yorkshire Dales
  North and East
  South and West
Walking in County Durham
Walking in Northumberland
Walking in the North Pennines
Walks in Dales Country
Walks in the Yorkshire Dales
Walks on the North York Moors – Books 1 & 2

NORTH WEST ENGLAND AND THE ISLE OF MAN

Historic Walks in Cheshire
Isle of Man Coastal Path
The Isle of Man
The Lune Valley and Howgills
The Ribble Way
Walking in Cumbria's Eden Valley
Walking in Lancashire
Walking in the Forest of Bowland and Pendle
Walking on the West Pennine Moors
Walks in Lancashire Witch Country
Walks in Ribble Country
Walks in Silverdale and Arnside
Walks in the Forest of Bowland

LAKE DISTRICT

Coniston Copper Mines
Great Mountain Days in the Lake District
Lake District Winter Climbs
Lakeland Fellranger
  The Central Fells
  The Mid-Western Fells
  The Near Eastern Fells
  The Northern Fells
  The North-Western Wells
  The Southern Fells
  The Western Fells

Roads and Tracks of the Lake District
Rocky Rambler's Wild Walks
Scrambles in the Lake District North & South
Short Walks in Lakeland
  1 South Lakeland
  2 North Lakeland
  3 West Lakeland
The Cumbria Coastal Way
The Cumbria Way and the Allerdale Ramble
Tour of the Lake District

DERBYSHIRE, PEAK DISTRICT AND MIDLANDS

High Peak Walks
Scrambles in the Dark Peak
The Star Family Walks
Walking in Derbyshire
White Peak Walks
  The Northern Dales
  The Southern Dales

SOUTHERN ENGLAND

A Walker's Guide to the Isle of Wight
Suffolk Coast & Heaths Walks
The Cotswold Way
The North Downs Way
The South Downs Way
The South West Coast Path
The Thames Path
Walking in Berkshire
Walking in Kent
Walking in Sussex
Walking in the Isles of Scilly
Walking in the New Forest
Walking in the Thames Valley
Walking on Dartmoor
Walking on Guernsey
Walking on Jersey
Walks in the South Downs National Park

WALES AND WELSH BORDERS

Backpacker's Britain – Wales
Glyndwr's Way
Great Mountain Days in Snowdonia
Hillwalking in Snowdonia
Hillwalking in Wales Vols 1 & 2
Offa's Dyke Path
Ridges of Snowdonia
Scrambles in Snowdonia
The Ascent of Snowdon
Lleyn Peninsula Coastal Path
Pembrokeshire Coastal Path
The Shropshire Hills
The Wye Valley Walk
Walking in Pembrokeshire
Walking in the South Wales Valleys
Walking on Gower
Walking on the Brecon Beacons
Welsh Winter Climbs

INTERNATIONAL CHALLENGES, COLLECTIONS AND ACTIVITIES

Canyoning
Europe's High Points
The Via Francigena (Canterbury to Rome): Part 1

EUROPEAN CYCLING

Cycle Touring in France
Cycle Touring in Ireland
Cycle Touring in Spain
Cycle Touring in Switzerland
Cycling in the French Alps
Cycling the Canal du Midi
Cycling the River Loire
The Danube Cycleway
The Grand Traverse of the Massif Central
The Rhine Cycle Route
The Way of St James

AFRICA

Climbing in the Moroccan Anti-Atlas
Kilimanjaro
Mountaineering in the Moroccan High Atlas
The High Atlas
Trekking in the Atlas Mountains
Walking in the Drakensberg

ALPS – CROSS-BORDER ROUTES

100 Hut Walks in the Alps
Across the Eastern Alps: E5
Alpine Points of View
Alpine Ski Mountaineering
  1 Western Alps
  2 Central and Eastern Alps
Chamonix to Zermatt
Snowshoeing
Tour of Mont Blanc
Tour of Monte Rosa
Tour of the Matterhorn
Trekking in the Alps
Walking in the Alps
Walks and Treks in the Maritime Alps

PYRENEES AND FRANCE/SPAIN CROSS-BORDER ROUTES

Rock Climbs in The Pyrenees
The GR10 Trail
The Mountains of Andorra
The Pyrenean Haute Route
The Pyrenees
The Way of St James France & Spain
Through the Spanish Pyrenees: GR11
Walks and Climbs in the Pyrenees

AUSTRIA

The Adlerweg
Trekking in Austria's Hohe Tauern
Trekking in the Stubai Alps
Trekking in the Zillertal Alps
Walking in Austria

EASTERN EUROPE

The High Tatras
The Mountains of Romania
Walking in Bulgaria's National Parks
Walking in Hungary

FRANCE

Chamonix Mountain Adventures
Ecrins National Park
GR20: Corsica
Mont Blanc Walks
Mountain Adventures in the Maurienne
The Cathar Way
The GR5 Trail
The Robert Louis Stevenson Trail

Tour of the Oisans: The GR54
Tour of the Queyras
Tour of the Vanoise
Trekking in the Vosges and Jura
Vanoise Ski Touring
Walking in Provence
Walking in the Cathar Region
Walking in the Cevennes
Walking in the Dordogne
Walking in the Haute Savoie North & South
Walking in the Languedoc
Walking in the Tarentaise and Beaufortain Alps
Walking on Corsica

GERMANY

Germany's Romantic Road
Walking in the Bavarian Alps
Walking in the Harz Mountains
Walking the River Rhine Trail

HIMALAYA

Annapurna
Bhutan
Everest: A Trekker's Guide
Garhwal and Kumaon: A Trekker's and Visitor's Guide
Kangchenjunga: A Trekker's Guide
Langtang with Gosainkund and Helambu: A Trekker's Guide
Manaslu: A Trekker's Guide
The Mount Kailash Trek
Trekking in Ladakh

IRELAND

Irish Coastal Walks
The Irish Coast to Coast Walk
The Mountains of Ireland

ITALY

Gran Paradiso
Italy's Sibillini National Park
Shorter Walks in the Dolomites
Through the Italian Alps
Trekking in the Apennines
Trekking in the Dolomites
Via Ferratas of the Italian Dolomites: Vols 1 & 2
Walking in Abruzzo
Walking in Sardinia
Walking in Sicily
Walking in the Central Italian Alps
Walking in the Dolomites
Walking in Tuscany
Walking on the Amalfi Coast
Walking the Italian Lakes

MEDITERRANEAN

Jordan – Walks, Treks, Caves, Climbs and Canyons
The Ala Dag
The High Mountains of Crete
The Mountains of Greece
Treks and Climbs in Wadi Rum, Jordan
Walking in Malta
Western Crete

NORTH AMERICA

British Columbia
The Grand Canyon
The John Muir Trail
The Pacific Crest Trail

SOUTH AMERICA

Aconcagua and the Southern Andes
Torres del Paine

SCANDINAVIA & ICELAND

Trekking in Greenland
Walking in Norway

SLOVENIA, CROATIA AND MONTENEGRO

The Julian Alps of Slovenia
The Mountains of Montenegro
Trekking in Slovenia
Walking in Croatia

SPAIN AND PORTUGAL

Costa Blanca: West
Mountain Walking in Southern Catalunya
The Mountains of Central Spain
The Northern Caminos
Trekking through Mallorca
Walking in Madeira
Walking in Mallorca
Walking in the Algarve
Walking in the Canary Islands: East
Walking in the Cordillera Cantabrica
Walking in the Sierra Nevada
Walking on La Gomera and El Hierro
Walking on La Palma
Walking on Tenerife
Walks and Climbs in the Picos de Europa

SWITZERLAND

Alpine Pass Route
Canyoning in the Alps
Central Switzerland
The Bernese Alps
The Swiss Alps
Tour of the Jungfrau Region
Walking in the Valais
Walking in Ticino
Walks in the Engadine

ICELAND

Walking and Trekking in Iceland

TECHNIQUES

Geocaching in the UK
Indoor Climbing
Lightweight Camping
Map and Compass
Mountain Weather
Moveable Feasts
Outdoor Photography
Polar Exploration
Rock Climbing
Sport Climbing
The Book of the Bivvy
The Hillwalker's Guide to Mountaineering
The Hillwalker's Manual

MINI GUIDES

Avalanche!
Navigating with a GPS
Navigation
Pocket First Aid and Wilderness Medicine
Snow

For full information on all our guides, and to order books and eBooks, visit our website:
www.cicerone.co.uk.

Walking – Trekking – Mountaineering – Climbing – Cycling

Over 40 years, Cicerone have built up an outstanding collection of 300 guides, inspiring all sorts of amazing adventures.

Every guide comes from extensive exploration and research by our expert authors, all with a passion for their subjects. They are frequently praised, endorsed and used by clubs, instructors and outdoor organisations.

All our titles can now be bought as **e-books** and many as iPad and Kindle files and we will continue to make all our guides available for these and many other devices.

Our website shows any **new information** we've received since a book was published. Please do let us know if you find anything has changed, so that we can pass on the latest details. On our **website** you'll also find some great ideas and lots of information, including sample chapters, contents lists, reviews, articles and a photo gallery.

It's easy to keep in touch with what's going on at Cicerone, by getting our monthly **free e-newsletter**, which is full of offers, competitions, up-to-date information and topical articles. You can subscribe on our home page and also follow us on **Facebook** and **Twitter**, as well as our **blog**.

Cicerone – the very best guides for exploring the world.

CICERONE

2 Police Square Milnthorpe Cumbria LA7 7PY
Tel: 015395 62069 info@cicerone.co.uk
www.cicerone.co.uk